THE ESSENTIAL LEWIS AND CLARK

THE ESSENTIAL
LEWIS &
CLARK

EDITED *by* ANTHONY BRANDT

MERIWETHER LEWIS
& WILLIAM CLARK

NATIONAL
GEOGRAPHIC

WASHINGTON, D.C.

Published by National Geographic Partners, LLC
1145 17th Street NW Washington, DC 20036

ISBN 978-1-4262-1717-3

Previously published as The Journals of Lewis and Clark

The Library of Congress has cataloged the 2002 edition as follows:
Lewis, Meriwether, 1774-1809
[Original journals of the Lewis and Clark Expedition, Selection]
The journals Lewis and Clark/by Meriwether Lewis and William Clark; edited and abridged by Anthony Brandt.
    p. cm.
Includes bibliographical references (p.) and index.
ISBN 0-7922-6921-7
1. Lewis and Clark Expedition (1804-1806) 2. Lewis, Meriwether, 1774-1809–Diaries. 3. Clark, William 1770-1838–Diaries. 4. Explorers–West (U.S.)–Diaries. 5. West (U.S.)–Description and travel. 6. West (U.S.)–Discovery and exploration. I. Clark, William, 1770-1838. II. Brandt, Anthony. III. Title.
F592.4 2002b
917.804'2–dc21
                    2010014720

Since 1888, the National Geographic Society has funded more than 12,000 research, exploration, and preservation projects around the world. National Geographic Partners distributes a portion of the funds it receives from your purchase to National Geographic Society to support programs including the conservation of animals and their habitats.

National Geographic Partners
1145 17th Street NW
Washington, DC 20036-4688 USA

Get closer to National Geographic explorers and photographers, and connect with our global community. Join us today at nationalgeographic.com/join

For information about special discounts for bulk purchases, please contact National Geographic Books Special Sales: specialsales@natgeo.com

For rights or permissions inquiries, please contact National Geographic Books Subsidiary Rights: bookrights@natgeo.com

Interior design: Callie Strobel

Printed in the United States of America

17/QGF-LSCML/1

CONTENTS

A NOTE ON THE AUTHORS

—◦◦◦—

MERIWETHER LEWIS, born August 18, 1774, in Virginia, served in the U.S. Infantry during Gen. Anthony Wayne's Northwest Territory campaigns and in 1801 became President Thomas Jefferson's private secretary. He had blond hair and was bowlegged. A serious man, he was known to be subject to periods of melancholy. After the expedition he was appointed governor of the Louisiana Territory. He died on October 11, 1809, apparently by his own hand.

WILLIAM CLARK, born August 1, 1770, in Virginia, was the brother of George Rogers Clark, a hero of the American Revolution. He served in the U.S. Army as an artillery officer. Clark had red hair and was a popular leader; he was also popular among the Indians and served as Indian Agent in the Louisiana Territory. After Lewis's death, he was the governor of Missouri. He died September 1, 1838.

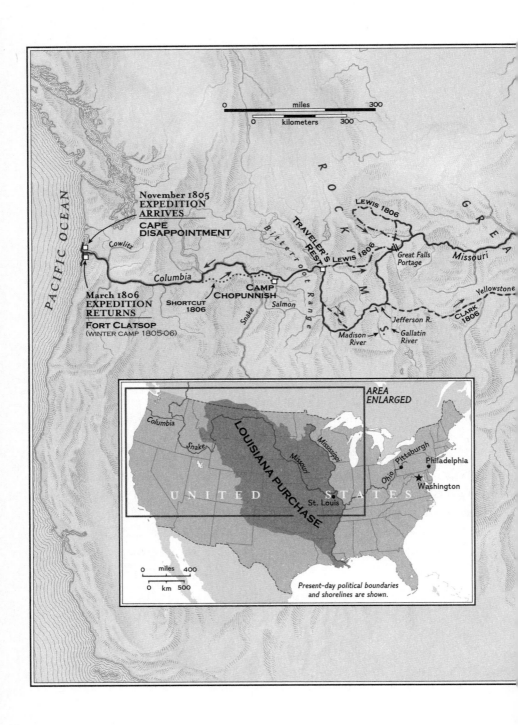

November 1805
**EXPEDITION
ARRIVES**
**CAPE
DISAPPOINTMENT**

March 1806
**EXPEDITION
RETURNS**
FORT CLATSOP
(WINTER CAMP 1805-06)

PACIFIC OCEAN

Cowlitz

Columbia

SHORTCUT
1806

CAMP
CHOPUNNISH

Snake

Salmon

Bitterroot Range

TRAVELER'S
REST

LEWIS 1806

LEWIS 1806

Great Falls
Portage

Missouri

Yellowstone

CLARK 1806

Jefferson R.

Madison
River

Gallatin
River

R O C K Y

M

G R E A

miles   300

kilometers   300

AREA
ENLARGED

Columbia

Snake

LOUISIANA PURCHASE

Missouri

Mississippi

Ohio

Pittsburgh

Philadelphia

Washington

U N I T E D   S T A T E S

St. Louis

miles   400

km   500

*Present-day political boundaries
and shorelines are shown.*

THE LEWIS AND CLARK EXPEDITION

MAY 1804 – SEPTEMBER 1806

Lake Superior

Lake Michigan

POINT OF REUNION
AUGUST 12, 1806
FORT MANDAN
(WINTER CAMP 1804-05)

Little Missouri

P L A I N S

Cheyenne

Missouri

Niobrara

Vermillion River

☐ **SERGEANT FLOYD'S GRAVESITE**

Platte

Kansas

Missouri

Osage

May 1804
EXPEDITION BEGINS
CAMP WOOD
(WINTER CAMP 1803-04)

○ St. Louis

September 1806
EXPEDITION ENDS
ST. LOUIS

Mississippi

Ohio

EXPEDITION MEMBERS

Captains:

MERIWETHER LEWIS

WILLIAM CLARK

Sergeants:

CHARLES FLOYD, born in Kentucky, was one of the first men to enlist in the expedition, on August 1, 1803, and was the only member to die during its course. On August 20, 1804, he died from what is generally thought to have been a ruptured appendix. He is buried at Floyd's Bluff near Sioux City, Iowa.

PATRICK GASS, born in Pennsylvania on July 12, 1771, was elected sergeant to replace Floyd after Floyd's death. He was an infantryman and a skilled carpenter and the first to publish his journal of the expedition. He fought in the War of 1812; at the age of 60 he married a woman of 20 and fathered six children. He died in April 1870, at the age of 98.

JOHN ORDWAY, born in 1775, went to Washington, D.C., with Meriwether Lewis after the expedition returned and later became an extensive landowner in Missouri. He was originally from New Hampshire. Ordway died in 1817. His journals were lost for over 100 years and were not published until 1916.

NATHANIEL PRYOR was born in 1772 in Virginia; he was Charles Floyd's cousin. After the expedition returned, he stayed in the Army until 1810, when he went into the fur trade on the upper Missouri. After being nearly killed by the Indians he reentered the Army. At some point he married an Osage woman and afterward lived among the Osage until he died in 1831. Pryor, Oklahoma, is named after him.

Privates:

WILLIAM BRATTON, born in Virginia on July 27, 1778, served as a gunsmith and blacksmith on the expedition and was also one of its better hunters. After serving in the War of 1812, he moved to Ohio, then to Indiana, where he died in 1841, having fathered ten children.

JOHN COLLINS was from Maryland. He was, like Bratton, a good hunter, but he was also in disciplinary trouble more than any other member of the expedition. He died on June 2, 1823, in a battle with the Arikara on the upper Missouri.

JOHN COLTER, a Virginian, left the expedition while it was coming home and returned to the upper Missouri to trap, becoming the first member of the expedition to enter that trade. In a famous encounter with the Blackfeet in 1809 he barely escaped with his life. He returned to Missouri and settled on a farm; he died in 1813.

PIERRE CRUZATTE, dates unknown, had only one eye, but he was an experienced riverman and fur trader. He owned a violin and often entertained the party at night with his playing. He is the man who accidentally shot Lewis in August 1806, on the return voyage. He was the son of a French father and an Omaha mother.

JOSEPH FIELDS AND REUBEN FIELDS, born in Virginia, were related by marriage to William Clark; they were both excellent woodsmen, and they were both with Lewis on the Marias River when he had his run-in with the Blackfoot hunting party.

ROBERT FRAZER, about whom little is known, settled in Missouri after the expedition returned and died there.

GEORGE GIBSON was from Pennsylvania. He died in St. Louis in 1809. Gibson served as an interpreter on the expedition, possibly becoming adept at Indian sign language.

SILAS GOODRICH, from Massachusetts, was known as the best fisherman of the party. He reenlisted in the Army after the expedition returned.

HUGH HALL was born in Pennsylvania and was something of a drinker. He and John Collins got themselves into trouble early on by tapping into the expedition's liquor supply without permission. Hall was still alive in 1828.

THOMAS PROCTOR HOWARD was born in 1779 in Massachusetts. One of his sons entered the fur trade in the 1820s.

FRANCOIS LABICHE, like Cruzatte, was half French, half Omaha. A valuable member of the expedition, he knew several Indian languages. He was an excellent tracker and one of the better hunters. He lived until at least 1828.

JEAN BAPTISTE LEPAGE joined the expedition on November 2, 1804, at the Mandan villages, to replace Pvt. John Newman, who had been discharged for insubordination. That he was French Canadian is obvious, but otherwise little or nothing is known about him. He had, however, been to the Black Hills. He went to the Pacific and back.

HUGH MCNEAL was a Pennsylvania man and an excellent hunter. Otherwise, little is known about him.

JOHN POTTS was a German immigrant, a miller by trade, who joined the expedition early on and became a fur trapper after returning to St. Louis in 1806. In 1810 he died in the same fight with the Blackfeet that John Colter escaped.

GEORGE SHANNON, a Pennsylvania man born in 1785, was the youngest member of the expedition. He lost a leg in 1807 in the same fight with the Arikara in which Nathaniel Pryor tried to return the Mandan chief Sheheke from Washington to his tribe. He helped Nicholas Biddle edit the first edition of the Lewis and Clark journals; later he became a senator from Missouri.

JOHN SHIELDS, a Virginian born in 1769, was the oldest member of the party and kin to Daniel Boone. He was extremely valuable to the expedition as a blacksmith and gunsmith, particularly at the Mandan villages, where his blacksmithing work kept the party in corn. He died in 1809.

JOHN B. THOMPSON. Little is known about this man.

PETER M. WEISER was born in Pennsylvania and became a fur trapper after the expedition returned. He gave his name to the town of Weiser and the Weiser River, both in Idaho.

WILLIAM WERNER may have been a Kentuckian. He helped Clark for a time in his capacity as Indian Agent after the expedition returned.

JOSEPH WHITEHOUSE was a Virginian, born in 1775. He kept a journal during the expedition and was known as a tailor and hide-curer and made some of the men's clothes.

ALEXANDER HAMILTON WILLARD was born in 1778 in New Hampshire and lived until 1865. He was a blacksmith in 1808, and a soldier in the War of 1812. He moved to Wisconsin in the 1820s and in 1852 moved to

California. He is the only member of the expedition known to have had his photograph taken.

RICHARD WINDSOR. Little is known of Windsor. He lived in the late 1820s in Illinois.

Non-Military Members:

TOUSSAINT CHARBONNEAU, a French Canadian born in the late 1750s, has not received much respect from historians; he was often a bungler and something of a coward. He could cook, however, and was the husband of Sacagawea. Charbonneau was important to the expedition as an interpreter during the winter at Fort Mandan.

SACAGAWEA was a Shoshone woman whom Charbonneau acquired from a Hidatsa warrior. She became invaluable as a guide in the region of her birth, near the Three Forks of the Missouri, and as an interpreter between the expedition and her tribe when the expedition reached that area. She also quieted the fears of other Indians, for no war party traveled with a woman and a small baby.

JEAN-BAPTISTE CHARBONNEAU was Sacagawea's son, whom Clark later raised and educated. He was known as Pompey or Pomp to the members of the expedition and later became a mountain man and a guide for, among others, John Charles Frémont.

GEORGE DROUILLARD, "Drewyer" to the captains, was the son of a French father and a Shawnee mother. After the captains, he was probably the most valuable member of the expedition. He was fluent in Indian sign language, a superb hunter, a highly skilled woodsman, and an excellent scout. He died at the hands of the Blackfeet near the Three Forks of the Missouri in 1810.

YORK was Clark's black slave, willed to him by his father. The two men had grown up together. York was tall, very strong, a valuable member of the expedition, and devoted to Clark, who freed him when they returned to St. Louis. Subsequently Clark set him up in the draying business.

Dog:

SEAMAN, the Newfoundland dog Lewis had bought for $20, went to the Pacific and back with the expedition. Indians were constantly offering to buy him but Lewis would not part with the animal. Nothing is known of his ultimate fate.

INTRODUCTION

BY ANTHONY BRANDT

In 1803 Thomas Jefferson, then president of the United States, negotiated the purchase from the government of France of the enormous territory drained by the Mississippi and Missouri Rivers known as Louisiana. The price was 60,000,000 francs, or $15,000,000. France had itself only obtained the territory from Spain in 1800 in a secret exchange for a Tuscan kingdom in Italy that would go to the Duke of Parma. That transfer was delayed, however, for two years. When Jefferson completed the purchase, the French flag had yet to be raised over its briefly owned empire in the American West. In a surreal ceremony in St. Louis in March 1804, the Spanish flag was lowered and the French flag raised while the guns of the fort fired a salute. Then the French flag came down in turn and American troops raised the Stars and Stripes. Thomas Jefferson had doubled the size of the United States and its territories.

Meriwether Lewis was present at this ceremony; he was one of the signers of the documents making the transfer of power official. Almost certainly his friend and fellow Army officer William Clark was present as well. They, along with the sergeants and privates under their joint command as well as a group of French *engagés,* would leave in a month and a half for the upper Missouri and the Pacific Ocean on an expedition that Jefferson and Lewis had been planning for more than a year, well before the Louisiana Purchase took place, and that Lewis had had in mind for 10 years and Jefferson nearly as long. They were to explore the entire length of the Missouri, find a route across the Rocky Mountains to the Pacific, contact Indian tribes, take latitudinal and longitudinal readings, gather specimens of flora and fauna, make maps, and keep journals. The list of instructions was quite detailed. Jefferson was an expansionist president with a vision for the American nation that included access to the Pacific and thereby to the markets of the Orient beyond. He foresaw a nation that stretched from coast to coast, and he wanted all the knowledge he could obtain about the intervening territory: the Indian tribes living within it; the possibilities for trade, especially in furs; the nature of climate; soils; the navigability of rivers—everything.

The expedition was unquestionably ambitious. No white man had ever gone farther up the Missouri than the Mandan villages, which were located in what is now western North Dakota. Alexander MacKenzie had crossed the Rocky Mountains in Canada to the Pacific 10 years before, but no white man knew anything at all about the Rockies south of the 49th parallel except that they were there. An entirely conjectural geography postulated that they were low lying, much like the mountains of the Appalachian chain, and that a portage between the headwaters of the Missouri and those of the Columbia River, which the American ship captain Robert Gray, master of the *Columbia*, had discovered in 1792, would take very little time—perhaps half a day. The entire trip, both ways, it was thought, ought to take no more than a year.

Lewis and Clark left their winter camp on Wood River in Illinois Territory on April 26, 1804, and returned to St. Louis on September 24, 1806, after most people had long since given them up for dead. Thomas Jefferson was one of the few still hopeful of their return. They did indeed reach the Pacific Ocean at the mouth of the Columbia. It took them a year and a half to get there, and they overcame great difficulties to do so. They faced suspicious Indian tribes; fought off grizzly bears; went hungry for periods of time; tore up their feet on prickly pear cactus; withstood hailstones the size of lemons; dragged their boats over rapids and across shoals; got sick on unfamiliar food; slept without shelter, sometimes under the wind and rain; endured winter temperatures in North Dakota that dropped to minus 40 degrees Fahrenheit; lost horses to Crow cattle thieves; ran out of trade goods to barter; and found that the supposedly low-lying Rocky Mountains rose against them for hundreds of miles and reached altitudes that left them permanently covered with snow in many places. The return trip only took half a year, since most of it was downstream, but it was harrowing in other ways. Nevertheless, in the end the team had lost only one man, to what appears to have been a burst appendix. The rest came back alive and healthy.

This in itself was an extraordinary achievement, but it is nothing compared with the discoveries they made. They filled in huge blank spaces on the map. They met and lived with Indian tribes all across the northern tier of what was becoming the continental United States, some of whom had never seen a white man before. They were the first to meet the Nez Percé and the tribes of eastern Washington. The Shoshone had never seen a white man either before Lewis and Clark appeared in the eastern Rockies one day in August 1805. Lewis recorded great descriptions of Indian dress and ways of life.

And the expedition came upon and described scores of new species, both floral and faunal. They were the first white Americans to cross paths with the grizzly bear, and Lewis's determination of its status as a single species, given its numerous color variations, was masterly. They were also the first to see coyotes, the vast gopher cities of the Great Plains, the pronghorn, the mountain beaver, mule deer and the black-tailed deer of the Columbia River Valley, the California condor, dozens of smaller birds (two of which are named after them: Clark's nutcracker and Lewis's woodpecker), snakes and reptiles, and insects of various kinds. Lewis was an expert naturalist, and his descriptions of trees, berries, grasses, shrubs, and animals are splendidly detailed and authoritative.

That Lewis and Clark wrote it all down is in a way the most astonishing fact of all. Huddling under makeshift shelters in the midst of storms, waiting out winters in the forts they built for themselves, on days when ocean swells were battering their campsite in Grays Harbor at the mouth of the Columbia or when the Teton Sioux were threatening to stop their progress up the Missouri—under the worst of circumstances, in the worst of weather, they wrote. They did not miss a single day. The result, from Lewis and Clark alone, not counting the journals kept by Patrick Gass and Joseph Whitehouse and John Ordway and Charles Floyd, is something like a million words of text. There are weather entries, maps and the notations on them, descriptions of new species and of tribal customs, measurements of latitude and longitude, the directional courses of rivers, tables and lists of various kinds, descriptions of the countryside, and, most important of all, accounts of what happened each day, every day.

Some of the daily entries, to be sure, are short. The final entry, for September 26, 1806, is just six words long. But many run to more than a thousand words, and the whole is massive. In the first scholarly edition of the journals, edited by Reuben G. Thwaites and appearing in 1901–1904, Lewis and Clark by themselves fill five thick volumes, plus a sixth devoted to the miscellaneous reports and other material they produced (the journals of other members of the expedition take up the seventh volume of the Thwaites edition). The edition edited by Gary E. Moulton and published from 1989 to 2001 by the University of Nebraska Press in a total of thirteen volumes devotes seven of them to the daily entries of Lewis and Clark. For good reason the journals have been called *the* American epic, and Lewis and Clark the writingest explorers who ever lived.

BUT WHO WERE THESE PRODIGIOUS EXPLORERS? Why were they chosen, who were the men under them, what experience, if any, did they bring to the business of exploration? Who was in charge, Lewis or Clark? The central fact is that the Corps of Discovery, as it came to be called, was a U.S. Army expedition, made up primarily of the two Army officers, Lewis and Clark, and of sergeants and privates recruited from frontier units east of the Mississippi. There were hired hands as well, mostly half-breed French/Indian *engagés* who knew the Missouri below the Mandan villages and had extensive experience navigating it and trading with the tribes who lived along its banks.

Lewis was Thomas Jefferson's secretary, a Virginian by birth who had served all over the Northwest Territories during his Army career and had lived in the wilderness and knew its ways. William Clark was a Virginian, too. The youngest son of the large Clark family, William had spent time serving in the Northwest Territories. His older brother, George Rogers Clark, had gained fame during the Revolution and in the subsequent wars with Indian tribes and their British supporters on the Northwest frontier. Lewis had served there with William, and he asked him to come with him on the expedition and share the command. To mask the fact that Clark held a lesser rank, Lewis proposed that they be co-captains, with equal authority, and so it was.

It is difficult to find in the journals any evidence of disagreement between them. They spoke as one, acted as one. Clark was the better waterman, and emotionally more settled than Lewis, who was subject to fits of depression. Lewis had received scientific training in Philadelphia from the country's leading naturalists before leaving for the West and was the better naturalist;

he had been taught to use instruments to determine latitude and longitude and was more literate than Clark. But both were top-notch commanders.

They had to be, given the crew they wound up with. Lewis had to take what the Army unit commanders offered him as he passed down the Ohio River, and they seldom gave him their best; rather it was the misfits and most troublesome men who joined the expedition. They were young, wild, independent, ornery, insubordinate—frontier types all, with the one advantage of being crack shots, and physically strong. They spent the winter of 1803–1804 at the camp they established on the Wood River in Illinois, across the Mississippi from St. Louis, and discipline problems were serious. It took the entire trip up the Missouri to the Mandan villages and the winter spent there to turn this motley crew into a unit that is today deemed exemplary for its discipline and its devotion to the expedition. People have been studying Lewis and Clark's leadership skills ever since.

The real standout among the men was George Drouillard, whose name everyone pronounced as Drewyer; he was the son of a French father and a Shawnee mother, a master of the universal Indian sign language, cool in a crisis, an expert hunter and marksman. Lewis had to pry him away from his commander at Fort Massac on the Ohio River, who did not want to let him go. Drouillard always seemed to be present when someone with exceptional skills was needed.

There were others of interest as well. A man named Privet could dance on his hands, to the amusement of both the Corps and the Indians. Pierre Cruzatte, an expert riverman with long experience on the Missouri, carried a fiddle with him and played around the campfires at night. George Shannon, the Corps's youngest member, stood out for the wrong reason, his inveterate tendency to become lost. John Shields used his blacksmithing skills to make war axes, and ordinary axes, too, for the Mandan, who traded corn for them and kept the Corps in corn during the long cold winter at Fort Mandan. That time solidified the Corps into a true unit.

It was also then that Sacagawea joined the Corps. Her husband, a half-breed Frenchman named Charbonneau who had bought her from Indians after she was kidnapped from her tribe, the Shoshone, was hired on as an interpreter. Sacagawea has been credited with a major role as a guide to the Corps all through the West. That decidedly overstates the case. She was indeed useful when the Corps reached her tribe, where she recognized her brother, and helped the captains negotiate the purchase of Shoshone horses, which they needed to cross the Rockies. And it helped to have her along when they encountered strange tribes. No Indian war party ever traveled with women and children. Sacagawea was a woman and she had a baby. This was a sure sign that the expedition came in peace. But she did not play the major role her legend imagines for her.

By the time the Corps left Fort Mandan, Lewis could describe his party as all acting "in unison, and with the most perfect harmony," and wholly devoted to the mission in hand. They would need this spirit to overcome the formidable obstacles they would soon encounter.

AMONG THESE CHALLENGES WAS THEIR own misunderstanding of the complex trade relationships among the Indian tribes of the Great Plains and the Far West. The standard procedure Lewis and Clark followed when they came to a new tribe was to sit down with the chiefs, smoke their ritual pipes, explain to them that they had a new great white father in Washington, try to awe them with the power and the vast numbers of white people, bestow medals on the chiefs, and then urge them to stop fighting with other tribes and promise trade advantages if they would do so. They did not seem to understand that warfare was indigenous to the Indian way of life. Bravery in warfare was a way to distinguish yourself in a given tribe, a way to acquire power and respect, a way to become a chief in the first place. Chiefdom was not hereditary, it was acquired, and the young warriors of a tribe were nothing if not ambitious.

Yet trading went on regardless. A tribe that routinely raided other tribes would also trade with the same tribes. The Sioux, who were nomadic, periodically raided the Arikara, who lived farther north on the Missouri and were agriculturalists, but they also traded with them, horses for corn, to the mutual advantage of both. Trade knitted the Plains together. When the Corps reached the Shoshone in August 1805, they found one of the war axes that John Shields had made for the Mandan the previous winter. Through Indian trade routes the axe had beaten them west. And despite the presence of Sacagawea, the Shoshone, who had a plentiful supply of horses, drove hard bargains with the captains for them, more or less using up their supply of trade goods.

In general the tribes were friendly to the expedition, and helpful as well. During the Mandan winter Lewis and Clark consulted often with the chiefs, trying to find out what faced them as they moved farther west. The information was accurate up to a point. The tribe members told them about the Great Falls of the Missouri, located in what is now eastern Montana, but said it would take only half a day to portage around them. In fact it took two weeks of struggle. They told Lewis and Clark about the Missouri's main tributaries—the Yellowstone, the Milk, and others—but failed to mention the Marias River (Lewis named it), which held up the explorers for three days while they tried to determine whether it was the actual Missouri or not.

When they did reach the source of the Missouri, the Shoshone made it clear to the explorers that the west-flowing stream over the next hill was wild and impassable. They would have to travel across the Bitterroots on horseback to reach navigable tributaries to the Columbia, thus scotching Jefferson's dream of an easy water route across the continent, a favorite myth of eastern geographers.

The expedition killed a number of myths. Jefferson had instructed the explorers to look for "Welsh" Indians, survivors of a legendary journey west supposedly made in medieval times by a Welsh prince named Madoc. Could they find Welsh words in the language of the Mandan? They could not. Jefferson believed in the "great chain of being," a theory that postulated a hierarchy of species in the animal kingdom that could not be broken—i.e., species could not disappear. He told the explorers, therefore, to look for mastodons, whose bones were turning up in places like a salt lick in Kentucky and in digs in upstate New York. Traversing a continent and seeing not a single mastodon sign but millions of buffalo—herds to the horizon— was enough to put an end to that.

But the positives famously outweighed the negatives. The hundreds of new species, the geographic realities, the minerals, the overall sublimity and magnificence of the landscape—the Corps of Discovery opened up the West as no other expedition. The expedition wiped out the imaginary geography of the West and replaced it with Captain Clark's superb map. It added birds and plants and animals of all sorts, buzzards to prickly pear to gophers, badgers to Douglas fir to cutthroat and steelhead trout, Sitka spruce to prairie rattlers to creeping juniper. Lewis remarked of the last that it would make an excellent ground cover for a Virginia garden. Lewis and Clark's mineral findings served as a guide to later geologists. Their names, separately and together, are written all over the map of the West, as state parks, counties, cities, rivers, mountain ranges. No wonder they have centennial celebrations. They did as much as anyone to define America.

HOW ODD, THEN, THAT IT WOULD take a hundred years to see the actual journals into print. What was printed, in 1814, was an edited two-volume narrative of the expedition that drew on the journals but rewrote them and omitted all the scientific material the two captains had collected. The editor was a young Philadelphia writer named Nicholas Biddle, followed, when he grew weary of the task, by a man named Paul Allen, who finished it. By that time, eight years after returning to St. Louis, one of the sergeants, Patrick Gass, had published his own version of the expedition and it had run through several editions. Gass was nearly illiterate and probably had a ghostwriter, but he did tell the story, and thereby exhausted the market.

The official Biddle edition was printed in 2,000 copies, 500 of which were defective and had to be destroyed, but it sold so poorly that it was not reprinted until 1842, in an abridged edition, and after that not at all. That first Biddle edition thus became one of America's great literary rarities. Copies in good condition, if you can find one, now run to more than $200,000 apiece.

The blame for the journals' delayed publication would have to fall on Lewis himself. He was much celebrated when he returned to Washington, and arranged with a Philadelphia firm to publish the journals. Jefferson appointed him governor of the northern half of the Louisiana Territory, and Clark, who was given the rank of general, to the post of Indian Agent (he handled all dealings with Indian tribes) for that territory. Lewis did not take up his appointment for a year, however. During that time he courted several women we know of, all of whom turned him down, and played the part of the young bachelor in Washington and Philadelphia. But he did not write. The journals languished, but he did not write.

When he finally took up his duties in St. Louis, Lewis walked into a nest of enemies he did not know he had, turned out to be a poor administrator, and got in trouble. In 1810 he set off on horseback to Washington to vindicate himself and rescue his honor, only to come to an ignominious end in a house in Tennessee, where he shot himself. Clark and Jefferson both knew the reason when they heard about it; Lewis was subject to long fits of depression. He was a brilliant leader but not a stable man.

Clark was left with the journals but did not feel up to the job of turning them into a book on his own. He had no illusions about his own abilities as a writer. Eventually Biddle was persuaded to write the book, but even then it was slow moving; the War of 1812 put everything on hold, and there were a million words with which to contend. And Meriwether Lewis was dead by his own hand.

Clark lived on, married a Virginia woman named Julia Hancock, had children, and ran his Indian agency. Four biographies of him have appeared within the past 15 years. The Indians liked him and called him "Red" for his hair. During his years as Indian Agent he was responsible for more treaties with Indian tribes transferring more of their land to the ownership of the United States than any other U.S. official before or since. He also added steadily to the map of the West that he kept in his St. Louis office, relying on the accounts of subsequent explorers and fur trappers.

The other members of the expedition scattered to their fates. John Colter went back upriver with fur trappers even before the expedition returned to St. Louis and was the first white man to penetrate into what is now Yellowstone National Park, which, from his descriptions, acquired the name Colter's Hell. Young George Shannon, who was always getting lost, lost a leg in a subsequent skirmish with the Arikara, then had a distinguished career in politics. Sacagawea died young, but Clark took her young son, who had gone with her all the way to the Pacific and back, under his wing and saw that he was educated, and he became a scout and guide in the West and eventually ran a hotel in San Francisco. George Drouillard lost his life in a skirmish with the Blackfeet while he was trapping beaver at the Three Forks of the Missouri. Many of the men went back to their military careers. All got double pay and a grant of land for their service with the expedition. The last survivor, Patrick Gass, died in 1870 at the age of 98.

EDITOR'S NOTE

A million words. It was obvious from the start that the journals would have to be abridged to fit them into one volume. This task was easier than it looked on the surface. On many occasions, and sometimes for long stretches, Clark simply copied what Lewis had written. The idea was to double the chances that an account would survive. For those sections, I simply eliminated Clark's entries, which were generally shorter and less detailed than Lewis's. But the journals were still too long for this edition. So I made the decision to give whole sections in full, but to abridge others that could be well summarized. Such were the winter camps, at Fort Mandan the first winter, Fort Clatsop in Oregon the next—and some periods in between. Nothing of significance has been left out of the narrative flow, and liberal quotes from the actual text are still used in these summarized sections.

Grammar, spelling, and to some extent punctuation also presented a serious problem. None of these aspects of the writing was something to which either captain gave a great deal of care. It is doubtful whether the captains ever intended to see the journals themselves published, but rather a written account of the trip such as was common in expedition literature. But it is the journals themselves, with all their immediacy and power, their smell of the campfire, their wonder, their struggle, that we want to read. And we want it in their words.

To make those words accessible to a modern reader, I have therefore updated their diction, cleaned up the grammar where sentence structure is confusing, corrected the spelling and often-faltering punctuation throughout. Scholars have amused themselves occasionally by tallying the variant spellings of some of the more difficult words in the text—23, or possibly 26, versions of the word "Sioux," for example. It serves no purpose to retain these original mistakes, which the captains would have been appalled to see in print, when the events themselves are vivid enough to hold anyone's interest. But I did not rewrite them. What the reader will find here, except in the summaries, is in the language of either Meriwether Lewis or William Clark. These are still their journals.

A NOTE ON THE TEXT

For reasons of copyright I have relied primarily upon the Thwaites edition, which is in the public domain, as the source of this edition. The Moulton edition includes more material, it is more up to date, and it has the advantage of being able to use the abundant modern scholarship on the expedition, some of which I have myself used. But the bodies of the main texts in the two editions are drawn from the same manuscript sources and are close enough to being identical where it counts, in the narrative, that using Thwaites does not constitute a serious loss. He is a reliable source for an abridgement.

Where there are differences between the texts—where, for example, Thwaites has "this" and Moulton "thus," either of which works in the context—I have generally used the Thwaites reading. Moulton has served as a useful guide to other scholarly material. Moulton's edition is indeed masterful, one of the great scholarly achievements of the last century. He deserves enormous credit for what has clearly been his life's work.

Thwaites does not print the fragment of a journal that Lewis kept on his trip down the Ohio in the fall of 1803, when he brought the keelboat to the Mississippi and the expedition's winter camp on Wood River in the Illinois territory. The manuscript of this journal, known as the Eastern Journal, was not discovered until a few years after Thwaites had published his edition. I have used the edition of this fragment edited by Milo M. Quaife and published in 1916 by the State Historical Society of Wisconsin. All the countless changes made to the text to bring it into line with modern standards of punctuation, grammar, and spelling are my own.

JEFFERSON'S INSTRUCTIONS TO

MERIWETHER LEWIS

To Meriwether Lewis, esquire, Captain of the 1st regiment of infantry of the United States of America:

Your situation as Secretary of the President of the United States has made you acquainted with the objects of my confidential message of Jan. 18, 1803, to the legislature. You have seen the act they passed, which, tho' expressed in general terms, was meant to sanction those objects, and you are appointed to carry them into execution.

Instruments for ascertaining by celestial observations the geography of the country thro' which you will pass, have been already provided. Light articles for barter, & presents among the Indians, arms for your attendants, say for from 10 to 12 men, boats, tents, & other travelling apparatus, with ammunition, medicine, surgical instruments & provision you will have prepared with such aids as the Secretary at War can yield in his department; & from him also you will receive authority to engage among our troops, by voluntary agreement, the number of attendants above mentioned, over whom you, as their commanding officer are invested with all the powers the laws give in such a case.

As your movements while within the limits of the U.S. will be better directed by occasional communications, adapted to circumstances as they arise, they will not be noticed here. What follows will respect your proceedings after your departure from the U.S.

Your mission has been communicated to the Ministers here from France, Spain, & Great Britain, and through them to their governments: and such assurances given them as to it's objects as we trust will satisfy them. The country of Louisiana having been ceded by Spain to France, the passport you have from the Minister of France, the representative of the present sovereign of the country, will be a protection with all its subjects: and that from the Minister of England will entitle you to the friendly aid of any traders of that allegiance with whom you may happen to meet.

The object of your mission is to explore the Missouri river, & such principal stream of it, as, by its course & communication with the water of the Pacific ocean may offer the most direct & practicable water communication across this continent, for the purposes of commerce.

Beginning at the mouth of the Missouri, you will take observations of latitude and longitude at all remarkable points on the river, & especially at the mouths of rivers, at rapids, at islands & other places & objects distinguished by such natural marks & characters of a durable kind, as that they may with certainty be recognized hereafter. The courses of the river between these points of observation may be supplied by the compass, the log-line & by time, corrected by the observations themselves. The variations of the compass too, in different places should be noticed.

The interesting points of the portage between the heads of the Missouri & the water offering the best communication with the Pacific ocean should be fixed by observation, & the course of that water to the ocean, in the same manner as that of the Missouri.

Your observations are to be taken with great pains & accuracy to be entered distinctly, & intelligibly for others as well as yourself, to comprehend all the elements necessary, with the aid of the usual tables to fix the latitude & longitude of the places at which they were taken, & are to be rendered to the war office, for the purpose of having the calculations made concurrently by proper persons within the U.S. Several copies of these as well as of your other notes, should be made at leisure times, & put into the care of the most trustworthy of your attendants, to guard by multiplying them against the accidental losses to which they will be exposed. A further guard would be that one of these copies be written on the paper of the birch, as less liable to injury from damp than common paper.

The commerce which may be carried on with the people inhabiting the line you will pursue, renders a knolege of these people important.

You will therefore endeavor to make yourself acquainted, as far as a diligent pursuit of your journey shall admit,

>with the names of the nations & their numbers;
>the extent & limits of their possessions;
>their relations with other tribes or nations;
>their language, traditions, monuments;
>their ordinary occupations in agriculture, fishing, hunting, war, arts, & the implements for these;
>their food, clothing, & domestic accommodations;
>the diseases prevalent among them, & the remedies they use;
>moral and physical circumstance which distinguish them from the tribes they know;
>peculiarities in their laws, customs & dispositions;
>and articles of commerce they may need or furnish, & to what extent.

And considering the interest which every nation has in extending & strengthening the authority of reason & justice among the people around them, it will be useful to acquire what knolege you can of the state of morality, religion & information among them, as it may better enable those who endeavor to civilize & instruct them, to adapt their measures to the existing notions & practises of those on whom they are to operate.

>Other objects worthy of notice will be
>the soil & face of the country, it's growth & vegetable productions, especially those not of the U.S.;
>the animals of the country generally, & especially those not known in the U.S.;
>the remains & accounts of any which may be deemed rare or extinct; the mineral productions of every kind; but more particularly metals, limestone, pit coal & saltpetre; salines & mineral waters, noting the temperature of the last & such circumstances as
>may indicate their character; Volcanic appearances;
>climate as characterized by the thermometer, by the proportion of rainy, cloudy & clear days, by lightening, hail, snow, ice,

by the access & recess of frost, by the winds, prevailing at
different seasons,

the dates at which particular plants put forth or lose their
flowers, or leaf, times of appearance of particular birds,
reptiles or insects.

Altho' your route will be along the channel of the Missouri, yet you
will endeavor to inform yourself, by inquiry, of the character and extent of
the country watered by its branches, & especially on it's Southern side. The
North river or Rio Bravo which runs into the gulph of Mexico, and the
North river, or Rio colorado which runs into the gulph of California, are
understood to be the principal streams heading opposite to the waters of
the Missouri, and running Southwardly. Whether the dividing grounds
between the Missouri & them are mountains or flatlands, what are their
distance from the Missouri, the character of the intermediate country, &
the people inhabiting it, are worthy of particular enquiry. The Northern
waters of the Missouri are less to be enquired after, because they have been
ascertained to a considerable degree, and are still in a course of ascertain-
ment by English traders & travellers. But if you can learn anything certain
of the most Northern source of the Mississippi, & of its position relative to
the lake of the woods, it will be interesting to us. Some account too of the
path of the Canadian traders from the Mississippi, at the mouth of the
Ouisconsin river, to where it strikes the Missouri, and of the soil and rivers
in its course, is desirable.

In all your intercourse with the natives treat them in the most friendly
& conciliatory manner which their own conduct will admit; allay all jeal-
ousies as to the object of your journey, satisfy them of it's innocence, make
them acquainted with the position, extent, character, peaceable & commercial dispositions of the U.S., of our wish to be neighborly, friendly &
useful to them, & of our dispositions to a commercial intercourse with
them; confer with them on the points most convenient as mutual empo-
riums, & the articles of most desirable interchange for them & us. If a few
of their influential chiefs, within practicable distance, wish to visit us,
arrange such a visit with them, and furnish them with authority to call on
our officers, on their entering the U.S. to have them conveyed to this place
at the public expense. If any of them should wish to have some of their
young people brought up with us, & taught such arts as may be useful to

them, we will receive, instruct, & take care of them. Such a mission, whether of influential chiefs or of young people, would give some security to your own party. Carry with you some matter of the kine pox, inform those of them with whom you may be, of it's efficacy as a preservative from the small pox; and instruct & encourage them in the use of it. This may be especially done wherever you may winter.

As it is impossible for us to foresee in what manner you will be received by those people, whether with hospitality or hostility, so is it impossible to prescribe the exact degree of perseverance with which you are to pursue your journey. We value too much the lives of citizens to offer them to probable destruction. Your numbers will be sufficient to secure you against the unauthorised opposition of individuals, or of small parties: but if a superior force, authorised or not authorised by a nation, should be arrayed against your further passage, & inflexibly determined to arrest it, you must decline it's further pursuit, and return. In the loss of yourselves, we should lose also the information you will have acquired. By returning safely with that, you may enable us to renew the essay with better calculated means. To your own discretion therefore must be left the degree of danger you may risk, & the point at which you should decline, only saying we wish you to err on the side of your safety, & to bring back your party safe, even if it be with less information.

As far up the Missouri as the white settlements extend, an intercourse will probably be found to exist between them and the Spanish posts at St. Louis, opposite Cahokia, or Ste. Genevieve opposite Kaskaskia. From still farther up the river, the traders may furnish a conveyance for letters. Beyond that you may perhaps be able to engage Indians to bring letters for the government to Cahokia or Kaskaskia, on promising that they shall there receive such special compensation as you shall have stipulated with them. Avail yourself of these means to communicate to us, at seasonable intervals, a copy of your journal, notes & observations of every kind, putting into cypher whatever might do injury if betrayed.

Should you reach the Pacific ocean, inform yourself of the circumstances which may decide whether the furs of those parts may not be collected as advantageously at the head of the Missouri (convenient as is supposed to the waters of the Colorado & Oregon or Columbia) as at Nootka sound or any other point of that coast; & that trade be consequently conducted through the Missouri & U.S. more beneficially than by the circumnavigation now practised.

On your arrival on that coast, endeavor to learn if there be any port within your reach frequented by the sea-vessels of any nation, and to send two of your trusty people back by sea, in such way as shall appear practicable, with a copy of your notes. And should you be of opinion that the return of your party by the way they went will be eminently dangerous, then ship the whole, & return by sea by way of Cape Horn or the Cape of Good Hope, as you shall be able. As you will be without money, clothes or provisions, you must endeavor to use the credit of the U.S. to obtain them; for which purpose open letters of credit shall be furnished you authorizing you to draw on the Executive of the U.S. or any of its officers in any part of the world, in which draughts can be disposed of, and to apply with our recommendations to the consuls, agents, merchants, or citizens of any nation with which we have intercourse, assuring them in our name that any aids they may furnish you shall be honorably repaid, and on demand. Our consuls Thomas Howes at Batavia in Java, William Buchanan of the Isles of France and Bourbon, & John Elmslie at the Cape of Good Hope will be able to supply your necessities by draughts on us.

Should you find it safe to return by the way you go, after sending two of your party round by sea, or with your whole party, if no conveyance by sea can be found, do so; making such observations on your return as may serve to supply, correct or confirm those made on your outward journey.

In re-entering the U.S. and reaching a place of safety, discharge any of your attendants who may desire & deserve it: procuring for them immediate paiment of all arrears of pay & cloathing which may have incurred since their departure and assure them that they shall be recommended to the liberality of the legislature for the grant of a souldier's portion of land each, as proposed in my message to Congress: & repair yourself with your papers to the seat of government.

To provide, on the accident of your death, against anarchy, dispersion & the consequent danger to your party, and total failure of the enterprise, you are hereby authorised, by any instrument signed & written in your own hand, to name the person among them who shall succeed to the command on your decease, & by like instruments to change the nomination from time to time, as further experience of the characters accompanying you shall point out superior fitness: and all the powers & authorities given to yourself are, in the event of your death, transferred to & vested in the successor so named, with further power to him, & his successors in like manner to name each his successor, who, on the death of his predecessor shall be invested with all the powers & authorities given to yourself.

Given under my hand at the city of Washington, this 20th. day of June 1803.

Th. Jefferson,

Pr. U.S. of America

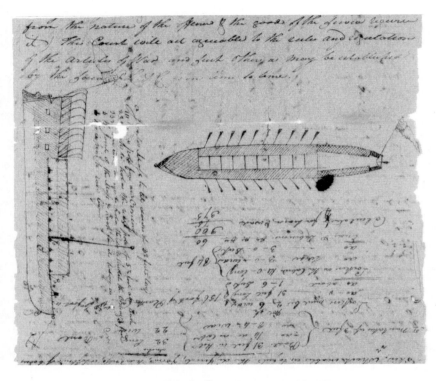

Two views of the keelboat, January 17-20, 1804

AUGUST 30 TO SEPTEMBER 18, 1803

PITTSBURGH TO WOOD RIVER

———————————⤖◈◈◈⤆———————————

August 30, 1803 [Lewis]

Left Pittsburgh this day at 11 o'clock with a party of 11 hands, 7 of which are soldiers, a pilot and three young men on trial, they having proposed to go with me throughout the voyage. Arrived at Bruno's Island three miles below, halted a few minutes. Went on shore and being invited by some of the gentlemen present to try my air gun which I had purchased brought it on shore, charged it, and fired myself seven times 55 yards with pretty good success. After which a Mr. Blaze Cenas, being unacquainted with the management of the gun, suffered her to discharge herself accidentally. The ball passed through the hat of a woman about 40 yards distant, cutting her temple about the fourth of the diameter of the ball. She fell instantly and the blood gushing from her temple, we were all in the greatest consternation and supposed she was dead. But in a minute she revived, to our inexpressible satisfaction, and by examination we found the wound by no means mortal or even dangerous.

Called the hands aboard and proceeded to a ripple of *McKee's Rock* where we were obliged to get out, all hands, and lift the boat over about 30 yards. The river is extremely low, said to be more so than it has been known for four years. About [blank] we passed another ripple near [word missing]. Passed another bar or ripple with more difficulty than either of the others. Halted for the night much fatigued after laboring with my men all day. The water being sufficiently temperate was much in our favor. Gave my men some whiskey and retired to rest at 8 o'clock.

Air guns work by compressed air and are not as powerful as guns fired with explosives. Lewis used this particular gun to impress Indians all through the journey. They were astonished by it. No one is entirely sure who the men were that Lewis had with him on this portion of the trip.

September 1, 1803 [Lewis]

The pilot informed me that we were not far from a ripple which was much worse than any we had yet passed, and as there was so thick a fog on the face of the water that no object was visible beyond 40 paces he advised remaining until the sun should acquire a greater altitude, when the fog would ascend and disappear. I consented. We remained until eight o'clock this morning, when we again set out. These fogs are very common on the Ohio at this season of the year, as also in the spring, but I do not think them as frequent or thick in the spring. Perhaps this may in some measure assist us to account for the heavy dews which are more remarkable for their frequency and quantity than in any country I was ever in. They are so heavy the drops falling from the trees from about midnight until sunrise give you the idea of a constant gentle rain. This continues until the sun has acquired sufficient altitude to dissipate the fog by its influence, and it then ceases. The dews are likewise more heavy during summer than elsewhere, but not so much so as at this season. The fog appears to owe its origin to the difference of temperature between the *air* and *water*, the latter at this season being much warmer than the former. The water being heated by the summer's sun does not undergo so rapid a change from the absence of the sun as the air does. Consequently when the air becomes most cool, which is about sunrise, the fog is thickest and appears to rise from the face of the water like the steam from boiling water.

We passed the *Little Horsetail* ripple or riffle with much difficulty, all hands labored in the water about two hours before we effected a passage. The next obstruction we met with was the *Big Horsetail* riffle. Here we were obliged to unload all our goods and lift the empty boat over. About five o'clock we reached the riffle called Woolery's Trap. Here, after unloading again and exerting all our force, we found it impracticable to get over. I therefore employed a man with a team of oxen, with the assistance of which we at length got off. We put in and remained all night, having made only ten miles this day.

September 2, 1803 [Lewis]

Set out at sunrise, two miles and a half to a riffle. Got out and pulled the boat over it with some difficulty. At nine o'clock reached Logtown Riffle, unloaded and with much difficulty got over. Detained four hours. The hills on either side of the Ohio are from 3 to 400 feet which, running parallel to each other, keep the general course of the river, at the distance of about two miles [*i.e., the valley is about two miles wide*], while the river pursuing a serpentine course between them alternately washes their bases, thus leaving fine bottomland between itself and the hills in large bodies, and frequently in the form of a semicircle or the larger segment of a circle or horseshoe form. The weather is extremely dry but there was some appearance of rain this morning which seems now to have blown over. I supposed I had gotten over Logtown Riffle but found ourselves stranded again. Supposed it best to send out two or three men to engage some oxen or horses to assist us. Obtained one horse and an ox, which enabled us very readily to get over. Paid the man his charge, which was one dollar. The inhabitants who live near these riffles live much by the distressed situation of travelers, are generally lazy, charge extravagantly when they are called on for assistance, and have no philanthropy or conscience. Passed the mouth of two little creeks to the north, called Allfour's and a riffle ahead. The boat rubbed for some distance but by getting out and pulling her on by the thwarts we got her over. On each side of the river there are three banks, or sudden rises, from the summits of which the land generally breaks off for a certain distance pretty level until it arrives at the high hills before mentioned which appear to give a direction to the river. The first bank, or that which the river washes, is generally from 20 to 25 feet, and the bottom lying on a level with this is only overflown in remarkable high floods. The consequence is that there is no drowned or marsh lands on this river. This bottom, which is certainly the richest land from its being liable sometimes to be overflowed, is not esteemed so valuable as the second bottom. The second bottom usually rises from 25 to 30 feet above the first and is always safe or secure from inundation. It is usually good when wide from the third bank and contrary when the bottom is narrow or the river breaks against the second near the third bank, which it sometimes does. What is called the third bottom is more properly the high benches of the large range of hills before noticed and is of a more varied description as well as it respects the fertility of its soil as shape and perpendicular height. The river sometimes but very seldom breaks against this bank. The second and third of these banks always run parallel with the high hills and that bordering on the river is of course shaped by it.

Passed Waller's Riffle with but little difficulty. Thermometer stood at seventy-six in the cabin; the temperature of the water in the river when immersed about the same. Observed today the leaves of the *buckeye*, gum, and sassafras begin to fade, or become red.

September 3, 1803 [Lewis]

Very foggy this morning. Thermometer 63° Fahrenheit, immersed the thermometer in the river, and the mercury rose immediately to 75° or summer heat. So there is a 12° difference, which is sufficient to show the vapor which arises from the water. The fog thus produced is impenetrably thick at this moment. We were in consequence obliged to lie by until nine this morning. Mr. Gus Bryan arrived with two boats loaded with furs. He informs me that if I can reach and get over the Georgetown bar 24 miles I can get on; this is some consolation. We set out at nine this morning and passed a riffle just below us called Atkins's. Got over with tolerable ease. Passed the mouth of Big Beaver Creek and came to anchor off McIntosh, being 2 and a half miles. Discharged one of my hands. Passed the riffle below McIntosh. About three miles from this we stuck on another riffle, the worst I think we have yet passed. Were obliged to unload and drag over with horses. Stayed all night, having made only six miles.

September 4, 1803 [Lewis]

Morning foggy, obliged to wait. Thermometer at 63°, temperature of the river water 73°, being a difference of ten degrees, but yesterday there was a difference of twelve degrees, so that the water must have changed its temperature two degrees in twenty-four hours, *colder*. At a quarter past eight the mercury rose in the open air to 68°, the fog disappeared, and we set out. The difference therefore of five degrees in temperature between the water and air is not sufficient to produce the appearance of fog. From the watermark we fixed last evening it appeared that the river during the night had fallen an inch perpendicularly. The pirogue was loaded, as has been my practice since I left Pittsburgh, in order as much as possible to lighten the boat [*i.e., the keelboat; Lewis was running the Ohio during the season when it is generally at its lowest, late summer and early fall*]; the [*men*] who conducted her called as in distress about an hour after we had got under way. We came to and waited her coming up, found she had sprung a leak and had nearly filled. This accident was truly distressing, as her load, consisting of articles of hardware intended as presents to the Indians, got wet and I fear are much damaged. Proceeded about three miles further, got fast on a bar below Georgetown, and with the assistance of some of the neighboring people got over it with much difficulty. At Georgetown purchased a canoe complete with two paddles and two poles, for which I gave $11, found that my new purchase leaked so much that she was unsafe without some repairs. Came to about a mile below the riffle on the eastern shore pretty early in the evening where we stayed all night, having made about 13 miles this day. Opened the articles which had gotten wet and exposed them to the sun. Set some of my hands to repairing the canoes, which I effected before night. Had the articles well oiled and put up in oilcloth bags and returned to the casks in which they previously were. Hired another hand to go with me as far as Wheeling. The articles were not as much injured as I had supposed.

About two miles above my camp passed the line which divides the States of Virginia and Pennsylvania on the east side of the river and on the west that of Pennsylvania from the State of Ohio. This line is made visible from the timber having been felled about 60 feet in width. The young timber has sprung up but has not yet attained the height of the other, so that it can with ease be traced with the eye a considerable distance. It passes the Ohio River at the mouth of Mill Creek. The water is so low and clear that we see a great number of fish of different kinds, the sturgeon, bass, catfish, pike, etc. We fixed some spears after the Indian method but have had too much to attend to of more importance than gigging fish.

It is difficult to determine exactly what Lewis meant by a pirogue, since he often called the same boat a pirogue and a canoe. The French word "pirogue" generally designates a dugout or open boat, usually large enough to carry up to ten men. Lewis and Clark took two of them up the Missouri, along with the keelboat. One, the larger, was known as the white pirogue or the "eight ton" pirogue, capable presumably of carrying eight tons of load, although that seems excessive. The other was known as the red pirogue. Whether either of these is among the boats that came down the Ohio with Lewis is not known. The "hardware" that got wet would have been such things as knives, kettles, and other trade goods.

September 5, 1803 [Lewis]
Again foggy, loaded both my canoes and waited till the fog disappeared. Set out at eight o'clock. Had some difficulty passing several riffles but surmounted it without having recourse to horses or oxen. Rained at six this evening and continued with some intervals through the night to rain pretty hard. Took up at the head of Brown's Island. It grew very dark and my canoes, which had on board the most valuable part of my stores, had not come up; ordered the trumpet to be sounded and they answered. They came up in a few minutes after. The stores in the canoes being well secured with oilcloth, I concluded to let them remain on board and directed that the water which they made should be bailed out of them occasionally through the night, which was done. They still leaked considerably, notwithstanding the repairs which I had made on them. We came 16 miles this day.

September 6, 1803 [Lewis]
The fog was as thick as usual this morning. Detained us until half past seven o'clock, when we set out. Observed the thermometer in the air to stand at 71°, water 73°. The fog continued even with that small difference between the temperature of the air and water. Struck on a riffle which we got over with some difficulty and in the distance of two miles and a half passed four others, three of which we were obliged to drag over with horses. The man charged me the exorbitant price of two dollars for his trouble. Got on pretty well to Steubenville, which we passed at two o'clock, being six miles from encampment. Hoisted our foresail, found great relief from it. We ran two miles in a few minutes when the wind becoming so strong we were obliged to haul it in lest it should carry away the mast; but the wind abating in some measure we again spread it. A sudden squall broke the sprit and had very nearly carried away the mast, after we furled and secured the sail, though the wind was so strong as to carry us at a pretty good speed by means of the awning and furled sails.

Struck on a riffle about two miles below the town. Hoisted our mainsail to assist in driving us over the riffle. The wind blew so hard as to break the sprit of it, and now having no assistance but by manual exertion and my men worn down by perpetual lifting, I was obliged again to have recourse to my usual resort and sent out in search of horses or oxen. Steubenville is a small town situated on the Ohio in the state of Ohio about six miles above Charlestown in Virginia and 24 above Wheeling. It is a small, well built, thriving place, has several respectable families residing in it, five years since it was a wilderness. The oxen arrived, got off with difficulty. The oxen drew badly; however, with their assistance we got over two other riffles which lay just below. We proceeded about a mile and a half further and encamped on the west bank, having made *ten miles* this day.

September 7, 1803 [Lewis]

Foggy this morning according to custom; set out at half past seven, and in about two hundred paces stuck on a riffle. All hands obliged to get out. Observed the thermometer at sunrise in the air to stand at 47°, the temperature of the river water being 68°—difference of 21 degrees. Got over the riffle, at 45 minutes after eight. Passed Charlestown on the E. shore above the mouth of Buffalo [*Creek?*], over which there is built a handsome wooden bridge. This has the appearance of a handsome little village, containing about 40 houses. This village is three miles below our encampment of last evening. Reached Wheeling, 16 miles distant, at five in the evening. This is a pretty considerable village, contains about 50 houses and is the county town of Ohio (State of Virginia) [*the county seat of Ohio County, Virginia*]. It is situated on the east side of the river on an elevated bank. The landing is good, just below the town and on the same side. Big Wheeling Creek empties itself into the Ohio; on the point formed by this creek and the river stands an old stockade fort, now gone to decay. This town is remarkable for being the point of embarkation for merchants and emigrants who are about to descend the river, particularly if they are late in getting on and the water gets low, as it most commonly is from the beginning of July to the last of September, the water from hence being much deeper and the navigation better than it is from Pittsburgh or any point above it. I went on shore, waited on a Mr. Caldwell, a merchant of that place, to whom I had consigned a part of my goods which I had sent by land from Pittsburgh. Found the articles in good order. Here met with Col. Rodney, one of the commissioners appointed by the government to adjust the land claims in the Mississippi Territory. In his suite was Maj. Claiborne and a young gentleman who was going on to the Territory with a view to commence the practice of the law. He is a pupil of Caesar Rodney of Delaware. Remained all night.

September 8, 1803 [Lewis]

This day wrote to the President, purchased a pirogue, and hired a man to work her. My men were much fatigued and I concluded it would be better to give them a day's rest and let them wash their clothes and exchange their flour for bread or bake their bread in a better manner than they had the means of baking it while traveling. Dined with Col. Rodney and his suite. In the evening they walked down to my boat and partook of some watermelons. I here also met with Dr. Patterson, the son of the professor of mathematics in the University of Philadelphia. He expressed a great desire to go with me. I consented, provided he could get ready by three the next evening. He thought he could and instantly set about it. I told the Doctor that I had a letter of appointment for a Second Lieutenant which I could give him but did not feel myself altogether at liberty to use it as it was given me by the President to be used in the event of Mr. Clark's not consenting to go with me, but as he had I could not use it without the previous consent of the President. However, if he thought proper to go on with me to the Illinois [*i.e., the Illinois territory around the upper Mississippi; Illinois was not yet a state*] where I expected to winter I could obtain an answer from the President by the spring of the year or before the Missouri would be sufficiently open to admit of my ascending it. In the event of the President's not consenting to our wishes, I conceived that the situation of that country was a much more eligible one for a physician than that of Wheeling, particularly as he stated that the prac- tice which he had acquired at Wheeling was not an object: the Doctor was to have taken his medicine with him, which was a small assortment of about 100£ [*100 English pounds*] value.

Remained here all night. The people began to top their corn and collect their fodder.

September 9, 1803 [Lewis]
The Doctor could not get ready. I waited until three this evening and then set out. Had some difficulty getting over a riffle one mile below the town, got on six miles and brought to. I was now informed that by some mistake in the contract between the Corporal and the woman who had engaged to bake the bread for the men at Wheeling the woman would not agree to give up the bread, being 90 pounds, and the bread was left. I instantly dispatched the Corporal and two men for the bread and gave him a dollar to pay the woman for her trouble. About the time we landed it began to rain very hard and continued to rain most powerfully all night with small intervals. Had my pirogues covered with oilcloth, but the rain came down in such torrents

that I found it necessary to have them bailed out frequently in the course of the night. In attending to the security of my goods I was exposed to the rain and got wet to the skin, as I remained until about twelve at night, when I wrung out my saturated clothes, put on a dry shirt, turned into my berth. The rain was excessively cold for the season of the year.

September 10, 1803 [Lewis]

The rain ceased about day, the clouds had not dispersed and looked very much like giving us a repetition of the last evening's frolic. There was but little fog and I should have been able to have set out at sunrise, but the Corporal had not yet returned with the bread. I began to fear that he was piqued with the sharp reprimand I gave him the evening before for his negligence and inattention with respect to the bread and had deserted. In this, however, I was agreeably disappointed. About eight in the morning he came up, bringing with him the two men and the bread, they instantly embarked and we set out. We passed several bad riffles this morning and at 11 o'clock, six miles below our encampment of last evening, I landed on the east side of the river and went on shore to view a remarkable artificial mound of earth called by the people in this neighborhood the Indian grave.

This remarkable mound of earth stands on the east bank of the Ohio 12 miles below Wheeling and about 700 paces from the river. As the land is not cleared, the mound is not visible from the river. This mound gives name to two small creeks, called Little and Big Grave Creeks, which pass about a half a mile on each side of it and fall into the Ohio about a mile distant from each other. The small creek is above. The mound stands on the most elevated ground of a large bottom containing about 4,000 acres of land. The bottom is bounded from N.E. to S.W. by a high range of hills which seem to describe a semicircle around it, of which the river is the diameter, the hills being more distant from the mound than the river. Near the mound to the N. stands a small town lately laid out called Elizabethtown. There are but about six or seven dwelling houses in it as yet. In this town there are several mounds of the same kind as the large one but not near as large. In various parts of this bottom the traces of old entrenchments are to be seen, though they are so imperfect that they cannot be traced in such manner as to make any complete figure; for this inquiry I had not leisure. I shall therefore content myself by giving a description of the large mound and offering some conjectures with regard to the probable purposes for which they were intended by their founders, whoever they may have been.

The mound is nearly a regular cone 310 yards in circumference at its base and 65 feet high, terminating in a blunt point whose diameter is 30 feet. This point is concave, being depressed about five feet in the center. Around the base runs a ditch 60 feet in width which is broken or intersected by a ledge of earth raised as high as the outer bank of the ditch on the N.W. side. This bank is about 30 feet wide and appears to have formed the entrance to the fortified mound. Near the summit of this mound grows a white oak tree whose girth is 13 and a half feet. From the aged appearance of this tree I think its age might reasonably be calculated at 300 years. The whole mound is covered with large timber, sugar tree, hickory, poplar, red and white oak, etc. I was informed that in removing the earth of a part of one of those lesser mounds that stand in the town the skeletons of two men were found and some brass beads were found among the earth near these bones. My informant told me the beads were sent to Mr. Peale's Museum in Philadelphia where he believed they now were.

We got on 24 miles this day. We passed some bad riffles but got over them without the assistance of cattle. Came to on the E. side in deep water and a bold shore. Stayed all night a little above Sunfish Creek.

The mound is now known as Grave Creek Mound and dates from 100 B.C. Peale's Museum in Philadelphia, which was devoted to natural history, had been founded by Charles Willson Peale in 1786 and became a depository for some of the specimens of plants and animals that Lewis and Clark brought back from the West.

September 11, 1803 [Lewis]
Set out about sunrise, passed Sunfish Creek one mile, etc. Entered the long reach, so called from the Ohio running in a straight direction for 18 miles. In this reach there are five islands from three to two miles in length each. Observed a number of squirrels swimming the Ohio and universally passing from the W. to the East shore. They appear to be making to the south; perhaps it may be mast or food which they are in search of but I should rather suppose that it is climate which is their object, as I find no difference in the quantity of mast on both sides of this river, it being abundant on both, except the beechnut, which appears extremely scarce this season. The walnuts and hickory nuts, the usual food of the squirrel, appear in great abundance on

either side of the river. I made my dog take as many each day as I had occasion for; they were fat and I thought them when fried a pleasant food [*the dog went all the way to the Pacific with Lewis and Clark and presumably returned; its name was either Seaman or Scannon, depending on how one reads Lewis's handwriting*]. Many of these squirrels were black; they swim very light on the water and make pretty good speed. My dog was of the Newfoundland breed, very active, strong, and docile. He would take the squirrels in the water, kill them, and swimming bring them in his mouth to the boat. We lay this night below the fifth island in the long reach on the E. side of the river, having come 26 miles.

September 12, 1803 [Lewis]

Set out at sunrise. It began to rain and continued with some intervals until three in the evening. Passed several bad riffles and one particularly at the lower end of the long reach called Wilson's Riffle. Here we were obliged to cut a channel through the gravel with our spade and canoe paddles and then drag the boat through. We were detained about four hours before we accomplished this task and again continued our route and took up on the N.W. shore near a Yankee farmer, from whom I purchased some corn and potatoes for my men and gave him in exchange a few pounds of lead. We came 20 miles this day.

September 13, 1803 [Lewis]

This morning being clear we pursued our journey at sunrise and after passing a few riffles over which we had to lift the boat, we arrived at Marietta, at the mouth of the Muskingum River, at seven o'clock in the evening. Observed many pigeons passing over us pursuing a southeast course [*these were passenger pigeons, which are now extinct; they were killed in huge quantities for food in the 19th century*]. The squirrels still continue to cross the river from N.W. to S.E. Marietta is one hundred miles from Wheeling; lay here all night. Wrote to the President of U.S. Dismissed two of my hands, one of whom by the name of Wilkinson I had engaged at Georgetown, the other, Samuel Montgomery, I engaged at Wheeling. My party from Pittsburgh to McIntosh was 11 strong, from thence to Georgetown 10, from thence to Wheeling 11, from thence to Muskingum 13, from thence to Limestone 12. At Wheeling I engaged Montgomery and a young man came on board and agreed to work his passage. On the same terms I engaged another at Marietta or the mouth of Muskingum. This evening I was visited by Col. Green, the Postmaster at this place. He appears to be much of a gentleman and an excellent republican [*i.e., of the party of Jefferson*].

September 14, 1803 [Lewis]
Set out this morning at 11 o'clock. Was prevented setting out earlier in consequence of two of my men getting drunk and absenting themselves. I finally found them and had them brought on board, so drunk that they were unable to help themselves. Passed several riffles and lay all night on the N.W. shore. Was here informed that there were some instances of the *goiter* in the neighborhood, two women who lived on the bank of the river just below. They had emigrated to that place from the lower part of Pennsylvania and had contracted the disorder since their residence on the Ohio. The *fever* and *ague* and bilious fevers here commence their baneful oppression and continue through the whole course of the river with increasing violence as you approach its mouth [*Lewis is talking here about one disease, malaria, which was common even in New York in the nineteenth century*]. Saw many squirrels this day swimming the river from N.W. to S.E. Caught several by means of my dog.

September 15, 1803 [Lewis]
Set out this morning at sunrise, passed the mouth of the Little Kanawha one mile below our encampment of last evening on the Virginia shore. It is about 60 yards wide at its mouth. There is a considerable settlement on this river. It heads with the Monongahela. Passed the mouths of the little and big Hockhocking [*now simply the Hocking*] and the settlement of Bellepre—*a Yankee settlement.* Passed several bad riffles over which we were obliged to lift the boat.

　　Saw and caught by means of my dog several squirrels attempting to swim the river. One of these, the only instance I have observed, was swimming from the S.E. to the N.W. shore. One of the canoes fell a considerable distance behind; we were obliged to lie to for her coming up, which detained us several hours. It rained very hard on us from seven this morning until about three, when it broke away, and evening was clear with a few flying clouds. Took up on the Virginia shore having made 18 miles this day.

September 16, 1803 [Lewis]
Thermometer this morning in the air 54°, in the water 72°. A thick fog which continued so thick that we did not set out until eight o'clock in the morning.

The day was fair, passed several very bad riffles and among the rest Amberson's Island. While they were getting the boat through this long riffle I went on shore and shot some squirrels. My men were very much fatigued with this day's labor; however, I continued until nearly dark, when we came to on the Virginia shore, having made only 19 miles this day.

September 17, 1803 [Lewis]

The morning was foggy, but being informed by my pilot that we had good water for several miles, I ventured to set out before the fog disappeared. Came on seven miles to the old Town *Bar*, which being a handsome clean place for the purpose I determined to spend the day and to open and dry my goods, which I had found were wet by the rain on the 15th, notwithstanding I had them secured with my oilcloths and a common tent which I had as well and the canoes frequently bailed in the course of the day and night. I found on opening the goods that many of the articles were much injured, particularly the articles of iron, which were rusted very much. My guns, tomahawks, and knives were of this class. I caused them to be oiled and exposed to the sun. The clothing of every description also was opened and aired. We busily employed in this business all hands from ten in the morning until sunset, when I caused the canoes to be reloaded, having taken the precaution to put up all the articles that would admit of that mode of packing in bags of oilcloth which I had provided for that purpose and again returned to their several casks, trunks, and boxes.

My biscuit was much injured. I had it picked and put up in these bags. This work kept me so busy that I ate not anything until after dark, being determined to have everything in readiness for an early start in the morning. The evening was calm, though the wind had blown extremely hard up the river all day. It is somewhat remarkable that the wind on this river, from much observation of my own, and the concurrent observation of those who inhabit its banks, blows or sets up against its current four days out of five during the course of the whole year; it will readily be conceived how much this circumstance will aid the navigation of the river. When the Ohio is in its present low state, between the riffles and in many places for several miles together there is no perceptible current, the whole surface being perfectly dead or taking the direction only which the wind may chance to give it. This makes the passage down this stream more difficult than would at first view be imagined. When it is remembered that the wind so frequently sets up the river, the way the traveler makes in descending therefore is by the dint of hard rowing—or force of the oar or pole.

September 18, 1803 [Lewis]

The morning was clear and having had everything in readiness the overnight we set out before sunrise and at nine in the morning passed Letart Falls, this being nine miles distant from our encampment of the last evening. This rapid is the most considerable in the whole course of the Ohio, except the rapids as they are called opposite to Louisville in Kentucky. The descent at Letart Falls is a little more than four feet in two hundred fifty yards.

SUMMARY

SEPTEMBER 19, 1803 TO MAY 13, 1804

———⊃⊙⊙⊂———

After September 18, Lewis's journal entries break off and do not resume until November 11, when he notes that he has hired George Drouillard (whose last name both he and Clark persist in spelling as Drewyer). Born to a French-Canadian father and a Shawnee mother, Drouillard would become one of the expedition's most capable men, serving as hunter, translator, and scout. He was highly skilled in the Indian sign language. Lewis relied on him heavily. By this time Captain Clark had joined the expedition as well. On November 15 they reached the Mississippi, where the men immediately caught a catfish weighing 128 pounds, with Lewis remarking that he had heard of catfish weighing 175 to 200 pounds. On November 20 they began making their way up the Mississippi toward the mouth of the Missouri. Lewis was practicing now taking sun sights to measure the latitude, which he had learned to do in Philadelphia the previous spring and would continue to do throughout the journey. He also took longitude measurements, but these were less accurate, because whoever was in charge of the chronometer had a tendency to forget to wind it. He taught both these skills to Clark, but throughout the expedition most of the measurements of latitude and longitude were written down by Lewis.

Later in November Lewis stopped keeping daily journal entries, not resuming until April 1805, unless the intervening journals have been lost. He did during this time write descriptive notes of the new species of flora and fauna they found along the way, however, and occasional narrative notes as well; but generally Clark assumed the burden of daily record keeping. Early in December

1803, Lewis left the boat for St. Louis on horseback. Clark took the boats up the Mississippi to the mouth of the Rivière à Dubois, commonly known as Wood River, which empties into the Mississippi on the Illinois side more or less opposite the mouth of the Missouri, and there, on December 13, they began to build their winter camp.

It would be interesting to know more about what happened during the next few months, but the notes and journal entries Lewis and Clark made during this period are sketchy and have no narrative thread to hold them together. Lewis came down the Ohio with between 10 and 13 men; by the time they were ready to start up the Missouri in mid-May the roster included 27 men, not counting Lewis, Clark, and his black slave, York, or the French engagés who would man the pirogues. We do not know when the additional men arrived. In an undated note Clark describes them as "robust, healthy, hardy young men" and indicates that they all came "recommended," but it's also clear from the notes that they were boisterous and difficult to control. When Lewis and Clark were not in camp, as was often the case, they placed Sergeant Ordway in charge, and he could not keep them in line. Men went out on the pretext of hunting and instead wound up in a local whiskey shop and got drunk; when they drank they fought; at least once one of the men loaded up his gun and threatened to kill Sergeant Ordway. There was, perhaps, little to do but hunt and drink, once their cabins had been built.

Lewis and Clark, sometimes separately, sometimes together, were either in St. Louis across the river or in Cahokia, a nearby town on the Illinois side of the Mississippi. Part of their responsibility was to learn as much as they could about the upper reaches of the Missouri from fur traders such as James Mackay and Manuel Lisa, who had been there [Lisa later became a dominant factor in the fur trade on the upper Missouri, establishing a post on the Yellowstone as early as 1807; George Drouillard worked for him and was killed in his service in 1810]. Mackay was especially useful, as he had traded as far up as northeastern Nebraska; he had sent another man, a Welshman named John Thomas Evans, as far as the Mandan villages, and Evans had made a map. Lewis appears to have made a copy of it, and it was the best guide they had. The consensus is that both Lewis and Clark were in St. Louis on March 10 for a ceremony at Government House. With the entire population of St. Louis assembled, the Spanish flag was lowered and the French flag raised, to commemorate the brief three months during which France had recently owned the vast territory of Louisiana (Napoleon having of course acquired it from Spain). Then, amidst salutes from the fort, the French flag was lowered and the flag of the United States of America took up permanent residence on the flagpole. The Louisiana Purchase was complete. The Missouri River, its basin, and the lands drained by western tributaries of the Mississippi was now American territory.

During April and early May preparations at the winter camp seem to have intensified. Traders and merchants came with supplies; local men came to compete in shooting matches with the men, and they invariably lost money to them. There were still discipline problems, but Lewis and Clark were both used to command and knew how to handle men. This was a military organization, with captains, sergeants, corporals, and privates, and they ran it as such. On May 8 they loaded the keelboat and one pirogue; later in the day they manned the keelboat with 20 men at the oars and rowed it a few miles up the Mississippi. On the 11th Drouillard came back to camp with seven French engagés; most of these men had trading experience on the Missouri and knew the river. On Sunday, May 13th, Clark wrote the following in his journal:

I dispatched an express this morning to Capt. Lewis at St. Louis. All our provisions, goods and equipage on board of a boat of 22 oars, a large pirogue of seven oars, a second pirogue of six oars, complete with sails, etc., men complete with powder, cartridges and 100 balls each, all in health and readiness to set out. Boats and everything complete, with the necessary stores of provision and such articles of merchandise as we thought ourselves authorized to procure— though not as much as I think necessary for the multitude of Indians through which we must pass on our road across the Continent.

The next day they set out for the Pacific Ocean.

Clark's roster of expedition members and a map of the confluence of the Missouri and Mississippi Rivers, December 31, 1803–January 3, 1804

MAY 14 TO JUNE 14, 1804

May 14, 1804, Monday [Clark]

Rained the forepart of the day. I determined to go as far as St. Charles, a French village 7 leagues [*21 miles*] up the Missouri, and wait at that place until Capt. Lewis could finish the business he was obliged to attend to at St. Louis and join me by land. By this movement I calculated that if any alterations in the loading of the vessels or other changes were necessary they might be made at St. Charles.

I set out at 4 p.m. in the presence of many of the neighboring inhabitants, and proceeded on under a gentle breeze up the Missouri to the upper point of the first island four miles and camped on the island, which is situated close on the right (or starboard) side and opposite the mouth of a small creek called Coldwater. A heavy rain this afternoon.

May 15, 1804, Tuesday [Lewis]

It rained during the greater part of last night and continued until seven a.m., after which the party proceeded, passed two islands and encamped on the starboard shore at Mr. Fifer's landing opposite an island. The evening was fair. Some wild geese with their young were seen today. The barge ran foul three times today on logs, and in one instance it was with much difficulty they could get her off; happily no injury was sustained, though the barge was several minutes in imminent danger; this was caused by her being too heavily laden in the stern. Persons accustomed to the navigation of the Missouri, and the Mississippi also below the mouth of this river, uniformly take the precaution to load their vessels heaviest in the bow when they ascend the stream in order to avoid the danger incident to running foul of the concealed timber which lies in great quantities in the beds of these rivers.

May 16, 1804, Wednesday [Clark]
A fair morning. Set out at five o'clock. Passed a remarkable coal hill on the larboard side called by the French Carbonere. This hill appears to contain a great quantity of coal. From this hill the village of St. Charles may be seen seven miles distant. We arrived at St. Charles at 12 o'clock. A number of spectators, French and Indians, flocked to the bank to see the party. This village is about one mile in length, situated on the north side of the Missouri at the foot of a hill from which it takes its name, *Petite Cote* or the *Little Hill*. This village contains about 100 houses, most of them small and indifferent, and about 450 inhabitants, chiefly French. Those people appear poor, polite, and harmonious. I was invited to dine with a Mr. Duquette. This gentleman was once a merchant from Canada. From misfortunes added to the loss of a cargo sold to the late Judge Turner he has become somewhat reduced. He has a charming wife, an elegant situation on the hill surrounded by orchards and an excellent garden.

On the evening of the 16th the community of St. Charles held a ball for the expedition, and three men were absent without leave afterward. The next day Clark held a court martial and all three men were found guilty. Two were sentenced to 25 lashes "on their naked back," but sentence was remitted because of good conduct. The third man, John Collins, faced the additional charge of "behaving in an unbecoming manner" at the ball and for speaking "in a language after his return to camp tending to bring into disrespect the orders of the commanding officer." Collins was found guilty and sentenced to 50 lashes, which were administered that evening. Over the next few days Clark had the loads in the boats redistributed, sent a letter to Captain Lewis in St. Louis, received visitors, was invited to another ball, and waited. The following is one of the only narrative entries Lewis made until spring of the next year.

May 20, 1804, Sunday [Lewis]
The morning was fair, and the weather pleasant. At 10 a.m., agreeably to an appointment of the preceding day, I was joined by Capt. Stoddard, Lieuts.

Milford and Worrell, together with Messrs. A. Chouteau, C. Gratiot, and many other respectable inhabitants of St. Louis, who had engaged to accompany me to the village of St. Charles. Accordingly at 12 o'clock, after bidding an affectionate adieu to my hostess, that excellent woman the spouse of Mr. Peter Choteau, and some of my fair friends of St. Louis, we set forward to that village in order to join my friend, companion, and fellow laborer Capt. William Clark, who had previously arrived at that place with the party destined for the discovery of the interior of the continent of North America. The first five miles of our route led through a beautiful high, level and fertile prairie which encircles the town of St. Louis from N.W. to S.E. The lands through which we then passed are somewhat broken, less fertile; the plains and woodlands are here indiscriminately interspersed until you arrive within three miles of the village, when the woodland commences and continues to the Missouri. The latter is extremely fertile. At half after one p.m. our progress was interrupted by the near approach of a violent thunderstorm from the N.W. We concluded to take shelter in a little cabin hard by until the rain should be over; accordingly we alighted and remained about an hour and a half and regaled ourselves with a cold collation we had taken the precaution to bring with us from St. Louis.

The clouds continued to follow each other in rapid succession, insomuch that there was but little prospect of its ceasing to rain this evening; as I had determined to reach St. Charles this evening and knowing that there was now no time to be lost I set forward in the rain, most of the gentlemen continued with me, we arrived at half after six and joined Capt. Clark, found the party in good health and spirits. Supped this evening with Monsr. Charles Tayong, a Spanish Ensign and late commandant of St. Charles. At an early hour I retired to rest on board the barge.

St. Charles is situated on the north bank of the Missouri 21 miles above its junction with the Mississippi, and about the same distance N.W. from St. Louis; it is bisected by one principal street about a mile in length running nearly parallel with the river. The plain on which it stands is narrow, though sufficiently elevated to secure it against the annual inundations of the river, which usually happen in the month of June. In the rear it is terminated by a range of small hills, hence the appellation of *petit Cote*, a name by which this village is better known to the French inhabitants of the Illinois than that of St. Charles. The village contains a chapel, one hundred dwelling houses, and about 450 inhabitants; their houses are generally small and ill constructed; a great majority of the inhabitants are miserably poor, illiterate, and when at home excessively lazy, though they are polite, hospitable, and by no means deficient in point of natural genius. They live in a perfect state of harmony among each other, and place as implicit confidence in the doctrines of their spiritual pastor, the Roman Catholic priest, as they yield passive obedience to the will of their temporal master, the commandant. A small garden of vegetables is the usual extent of their cultivation, and this is commonly imposed on the old men and boys. The men in the vigor of life consider the cultivation of the earth a degrading occupation, and in order to gain the necessary subsistence for themselves and their families, either undertake hunting voyages on their own account, or engage themselves as hirelings to such persons as possess sufficient capital to extend their traffic to the natives of the interior parts of the country. On those voyages in either case they are frequently absent from their families or homes the term of six, twelve, or eighteen months, and always subjected to severe and incessant labor, exposed to the ferocity of the lawless savages, the vicissitudes of weather and climate, and dependent on chance or accident alone for food, raiment or relief in the event of malady. These people are principally the descendants of the Canadian French, and it is not an inconsiderable proportion of them that can boast a small dash of the pure blood of the aborigines of America.

On consulting with my friend Capt. Clark I found it necessary that we should postpone our departure until 2 p.m. the next day and accordingly gave orders to the party to hold themselves in readiness to depart at that hour.

May 21, 1804, Monday [Clark]
All the forepart of the day arranging our party and procuring the different articles necessary for them at this place. Dined with Mr. Duquette and set out at half past three o'clock under three cheers from the gentlemen on the bank and proceeded on to the head of the island (which is situated on the starboard side) three miles. Soon after we set out today a hard wind from the W.S.W. accompanied with a hard rain, which lasted with short intervals all night. Opposite our camp a small creek comes in on the larboard side.

May 22, 1804, Tuesday [Clark]
A cloudy morning. Delayed one hour for four Frenchmen who got liberty to return to arrange some business they had forgotten in town. At six o'clock we proceeded on, passed several small farms on the bank, and a large creek

on the larboard side called Bonhomme. A camp of Kickapoos on the star-board side. Those Indians told me several days ago that they would come on and hunt and by the time I got to their camp they would have some provisions for us. We camped in a bend at the mouth of a small creek. Soon after we came to, the Indians arrived with four deer as a present, for which we gave them two quarts of whiskey.

May 23, 1804, Wednesday [Clark]

We set out early, ran on a log and were detained one hour, proceeded to the mouth of a creek on the starboard side called Osage Woman's Creek, about 30 yards wide, opposite a large island and a settlement. Took in R. and J. Fields who had been sent to purchase corn and butter, etc. Many people came to see us. We passed a large cave on the larboard side (called by the French the *Tavern*) about 120 feet wide, 40 feet deep and 20 feet high. Many different images are painted on the rock at this place. The Indians and the French pay homage. Many names are written on the rock. Stopped about one mile above for Capt. Lewis, who had ascended the cliffs at the said cave, 300 feet high, hanging over the water. The water excessively swift today. We encamped below a small island in the middle of the river, sent out two hunters, one killed a deer.

This evening we examined the arms and ammunition, found the men's arms in the pirogue in bad order. A fair evening. Capt. Lewis near falling from the peninsula of rocks 300 feet, he caught at 20 feet.

May 24, 1804, Thursday [Clark]

Set out early. Passed a very bad part of the river called the Devil's Race Ground. This is where the current sets against some projecting rocks for half a mile on the larboard side. Above this place is the mouth of a small creek. Passed several islands, two small creeks on the starboard side, and passed between an island and the larboard shore—a narrow pass. Above this island is a very bad part of the river. We attempted to pass up under the larboard bank, which was falling in so fast that the evident danger obliged us to cross between the starboard side and a sandbar in the middle of the river. We *hove* up near the head of the sandbar; the sand moving and backing caused us to run on the sand. The swiftness of the current wheeled the boat, broke our tow rope, and was nearly oversetting the boat. All hands jumped out on the upper side and bore on that side until the sand washed from under the boat.

It wheeled on the next bank; by the time she wheeled a third time we got a rope fast to her stern and by the means of swimmers it was carried to shore. We returned to the island where we set out and ascended under the bank, which I have just mentioned as falling in. Here George Drouillard and Willard, two of our men who left us at St. Charles to come on by land, joined us. We camped about 1 mile above where we were so nearly being lost, on the larboard side at a plantation. All in spirits. This place I call the *retrograde* bend as we were obliged to fall back two miles.

May 25, 1804, Friday [Clark]
Rain last night. The river fell several inches. Set out early, passed several islands. Passed Wood River on the larboard side at two miles. Passed creek on the starboard called La Queur [*quiver, says Thwaites*] at five miles. Passed a creek (called Rivière la Poceau) at eight miles, opposite an island on the larboard side. Camped at the mouth of a creek called [*La Charette, says Thwaites*] above a small French village of seven houses and as many families, settled at this place to be convenient to hunt and trade with the Indians. [*This was the last white settlement on the Missouri.*] Here we met with M. Loisel immediately down from Cedar Island in the country of the Sioux 400 leagues up. He gave us a good deal of information and some letters. He informed us that he saw no Indians on the river below the *Poncas*.

The people at this village are poor, houses small. They sent us milk and eggs to eat.

May 26, 1804, Saturday [Clark]
Set out at seven o'clock after a heavy shower of rain. The wind favorable from the E.N.E. Passed a large island called Buffalo Island, separated from the land by a small channel into which Buffalo Creek empties itself on larboard side at three and a half miles. Passed a creek on the larboard side called Shepherd's Creek; passed several islands today. Great deal of deer sign on the bank. One man out hunting, we camped on an island on the starboard side near the southern extreme of Luter Island.

At this point in the journey Lewis wrote out his detachment orders assigning the men to their commands under the various sergeants and instructing them on their duties. We are not printing the list of men under the various commands; these commands changed from time to time. But the duty instructions, with minor omissions, are definitely worth printing.

DETACHMENT ORDERS
May 26, 1804 [Lewis]

The posts and duties of the Sergeants shall be as follows—when the bateau is under way, one Sergeant shall be stationed at the helm, one in the center on the rear of the starboard locker, and one at the bow. The Sergeant at the helm shall steer the boat and see that the baggage on the quarterdeck is properly arranged and stowed away in the most advantageous manner, and see that no cooking utensils or loose lumber of any kind is left on the deck to obstruct the passage between the berths. He will also attend to the compass when necessary.

The Sergeant at the center will command the guard, manage the sails, see that the men at the oars do their duty; that they come on board at a proper season in the morning, and that the boat gets under way in due time. He will keep a good lookout for the mouths of all rivers, creeks, islands and other remarkable places and shall immediately report the same to the commanding officers. He will attend to the issue of spiritous liquors. He shall regulate the halting of the bateau through the day to give the men refreshment, and will also regulate the time of her departure, taking care that no more time than is necessary shall be expended at each halt. It shall be his duty also to post a sentinel on the bank near the boat whenever we come to and halt in the course of the day. At the same time he will (accompanied by two of his guard) reconnoiter the forest around the place of landing to the distance of at least one hundred paces. When we come to for the purpose of encamping at night, the Sergeant of the guard shall post two sentinels immediately on our landing, one of whom shall be posted near the boat, and the other at a convenient distance in rear of the encampment. At night the Sergeant must always be present with his guard, and he is positively forbidden to suffer any man of his guard to absent himself on any pretext whatever. He will at each relief through the night, accompanied by the two men last off their posts, reconnoiter in every direction around the camp to the distance of at least one hundred and fifty paces, and also examine the situation of the boats and pirogues, and see that they lie safe and free from the bank.

It shall be the duty of the *Sergeant at the bow* to keep a good look out for all danger which may approach, either of the enemy, or obstructions which may present themselves to the passage of the boat. Of the first he will notify the Sergeant at the center, who will communicate the information to the commanding officers, and of the second, or obstructions to the boat, he will notify the Sergeant at the helm. He will also report to the commanding officers through the Sergeant at the center all pirogues, boats, canoes, or other craft which he may discover in the river, and all hunting camps or parties of Indians in view of which we may pass. He will at all times be provided with a setting pole and assist the bowsman in poling and managing the bow of the boat. It will be his duty also to give and answer all signals, which may hereafter be established for the government of the pirogues and parties on shore.

The Sergeants will on each morning before our departure relieve each other in the following manner: The Sergeant at the helm will parade the new guard, relieve the Sergeant and the old guard, and occupy the middle station in the boat. The Sergeant of the old guard will occupy the station at the bow, and the Sergeant who had been stationed the preceding day at the bow will place himself at the helm.

The Sergeants in addition to those duties are directed each to keep a separate journal from day to day of all passing occurrences, and such other observations on the country, etc., as shall appear to them worthy of notice.

The Sergeants are relieved and exempt from all labor of making fires, pitching tents or cooking, and will direct and make the men of their several messes perform an equal proportion of those duties.

The guard shall hereafter consist of one Sergeant and six privates and *engagés*.

All details for guard or other duty will be made in the evening when we encamp, and the duty to be performed will be entered on, by the individuals so warned, the next morning. Provision for one day will be issued to the party on each evening after we have encamped; the same will be cooked on that evening by the several messes, and a proportion of it reserved for the next day as no cooking will be allowed in the day while on the march.

Sergeant John Ordway will continue to issue the provisions and make the details for guard or other duty.

The day after tomorrow lyed corn and grease will be issued to the party, the next day pork and flour, and the day following Indian meal and pork; and in conformity to that ration provisions will continue to be issued to the party until further orders. Should any of the messes prefer Indian meal to flour they may receive it accordingly. No pork is to be issued when we have fresh meat on hand.

May 27, 1804, Sunday [Clark]

As we were pushing off this morning two canoes loaded with fur came to from the Omaha nation, living 730 miles above on the Missouri, which place they had left two months ago. At about 10 o'clock four *cajeux* or rafts loaded with furs and peltries came to, one from the *Pawnees*, the others from Grand Osage. They informed us of nothing of consequence. Passed a creek on the larboard side called Ash Creek, 20 yards wide, passed the upper point of a large island on the starboard side, in back of which come in three creeks, one called Otter Creek; here the man we left hunting came in. We camped on a willow island in the mouth of Gasconnade River. George Shannon killed a deer this evening.

"Cajeu" *is a French term describing a raft made usually by tying together two canoes or pirogues side by side.*

May 28, 1804, Monday [Clark]

Rained hard all last night. Some thunder and lightning, hard wind in the forepart of the night from the S.W. Ruben Fields killed a deer. Several hunters out today. I measured the river, found the Gasconnade to be 157 yards wide and 19 feet deep. One of the hunters fell in with six Indians hunting.

Unloaded the large pirogue, on board of which were eight French hands. Found many things wet by their carelessness, put all the articles which were wet out to dry. This day so cloudy that no astronomical observations could be taken. The river began to rise. Examined the men's arms and equipage, all in order.

May 29, 1804, Tuesday [Clark]

Rained last night, cloudy morning. Four hunters sent out with orders to return at 12 o'clock. Took equal altitudes of sun's lower limb. Capt. Lewis observed meridian altitude.

Had the pirogues loaded and all prepared to set out at four o'clock after finishing the observations and all things necessary. Found that one of the hunters had not returned. We determined to proceed on and leave one pirogue to wait for him. Accordingly at half past four we set out and came on four miles and camped on the larboard side above a small creek called Deer Creek. Soon after we came to we heard several guns fire down the river. We answered them by a discharge of a swivel gun on the bow.

May 30, 1804, Wednesday [Clark]
Rained all last night. Set out at six o'clock after a heavy shower and proceeded on, passed a large island opposite a creek on the starboard side,
just above a cave called *Monbrun Tavern* and River, passed a creek on the
larboard side called Rush Creek at four miles. Several showers of rain, the
current very swift, river rising fast. Passed Big Muddy River at 11 miles
on the starboard side, at the lower point of an island. This river is about
50 yards wide.

Camped at the mouth of a creek on the larboard side of about 15 yards
wide called Grindstone Creek, opposite the head of an island and the mouth
of Little Muddy River on the starboard side. A heavy wind accompanied with
rain and hail. We made 14 miles today, the river continues to rise, the country
on each side appears full of water.

May 31, 1804, Thursday [Clark]
Rained the greater part of last night. The wind from the west raised and blew
with great force until five o'clock p.m., which obliged us to lay by. A *cajeu* of
bear skins and peltries came down from the Grand Osage, one Frenchman,
one half-Indian, and a squaw. They had letters from the man Mr. Choteau
sent to that part of the Osage nation settled on the Arkansas River mentioning
that his letter was committed to the flames. The Indians not believing that
the Americans had possession of the country, they disregarded St. Louis and
their supplies, etc. Several rats of considerable size were caught in the woods
today. Capt. Lewis went out to the woods and found many curious plants
and shrubs. One deer killed this evening.

*The rat was no doubt the eastern wood rat, a species not then known to
science. On February 27, 1806, while the expedition was wintering in Fort
Clatsop on the Pacific coast, Lewis wrote the first scientific description of
the animal.*

June 1, 1804, Friday [Clark]
Set out early. A fair morning. Passed the mouth of Bear Creek 25 yards
wide at 6 miles. Several small islands in the river. The wind ahead from the
west, the current exceedingly rapid. Came to on the point of the Osage
River on the larboard side of the Missouri. This Osage River very high; we
felled all the trees in the point to make astronomical observations. Sat up
until 12 o'clock taking observations this night.

June 2, 1804, Saturday [Clark]

I made a surveying angle for the width of the two rivers. The Missouri from the point to the north side is 875 yards wide. The Osage River from the point to the S.E. side is 397 yards wide. The distance between the two rivers at the point of high land (100 feet above the bottom) and 80 poles up the Missouri from the point is 40 poles. On the top of this high land, under which is limestone rock, two mounds or graves are raised. From this point, which commands both rivers, I had a delightful prospect of the Missouri up and down, also the Osage River up.

George Drouillard and John Shields, who we had sent with the horses by land on the north side, joined us this evening much worsted, they being absent seven days depending on their gun, the greater part of the time rain. They were obliged to raft or swim many creeks. Those men gave a flattering account of the country commencing below the first hill on the north side and extending parallel with the river for 30 or 40 miles, the two Muddy Rivers passing through, and some fine springs and streams. Our hunters killed several deer today. Some small salt licks on the S.E. of the Osage River.

June 3, 1804, Sunday [Clark]

The forepart of the day fair. Took meridional altitude of the sun with the octant and glass horizon, adjusted back observation. It was cloudy and the sun's disk much obscured, readings cannot be depended on.

We made other observations in the evening after the return of Capt. Lewis from a walk of three or four miles round. We set out at five o'clock p.m., proceeded on five miles to the mouth of a creek on the larboard side 20 yards wide called Moreau. Passed a creek at three miles which I call *Cupboard Creek*, as it mouths above a rock of that appearance. Several deer killed today. At the mouth of Moreau Creek I saw much sign of war parties of Indians having crossed from the mouth of this creek. I have a bad cold with a sore throat.

June 4, 1804, Monday [Clark]

A fair day. Three men out on the right flank. Passed a large island on the starboard side called Cedar Island; this island has a great deal of cedar on it. Passed a small creek at one mile, 15 yards wide, which we named Nightingale Creek from a bird of that description which sang for us all last night, and is the first of the kind I ever heard. Passed the mouth of Cedar Creek at seven miles on the starboard side about 20 yards wide above some small islands. Passed a creek on the larboard side about 15 yards wide—Mast Creek; here the Sergeant at the helm ran under a bending tree and broke the mast. Some delightful land, with a gentle ascent about the creek, well timbered, oak, ash, walnut, etc. Wind N.W. by W. Passed a small creek called Zancare on the larboard side. At this last point I got out and walked on the larboard side through a rush bottom for one mile and a short distance through nettles as high as my breast. Ascended a hill of about 170 feet to a place where the French report that lead ore has been found. I saw no mineral of that description. Capt. Lewis camped immediately under this hill to wait, which gave me some time to examine the hill. On the top is a mound of about six feet high and about 100 acres of land, on which the large timber is dead. In descending about 50 feet a projecting limestone rock, under which is a cave. At one place on these projecting rocks I went on one which spurred up and hung over the water. From the top of this rock I had a prospect of the river for 20 or 30 miles up. From the cave, which encompassed the hill, I descended by a steep descent to the foot. A very bad part of the river opposite this hill. The river continues to fall slowly. Our hunters killed seven deer today. The land our hunters passed through today on the starboard side was very fine the latter part of today. The high land on the starboard side is about second rate.

North America has no native nightingales. What species of bird Clark actually heard no one knows, although there has been plenty of speculation on the subject.

June 5, 1804, Tuesday [Clark]
After jerking the meat killed yesterday and crossing the hunting party we set out at six o'clock. Passed a small creek on the larboard side I call Lead Creek. Passed a creek on the starboard side of 20 yards wide called Little Good Woman's Creek. On the larboard side a prairie extends from *Lead Creek* parallel with the river to Mine River. At four miles passed the Creek of the Big Rock about 15 yards wide on the larboard side. At 11 o'clock brought to a small caissee [*i.e., a cajeu*] in which were two Frenchmen, from 80 leagues up the Kansas River, where they wintered and caught a great quantity of beaver, the greater part of which they lost by fire from the prairies. Those men inform us that the Kansas Nation are now out in the plains hunting buffalo. They hunted last winter on this river. Passed a projecting rock on which was painted a figure [*in the original journal a drawing of this figure appears here;*

it is a Manitou or spirit figure] and a creek at two miles above called Little Manitou Creek, from the painted rock. This creek 20 yards wide on the larboard side. Passed a small creek on the larboard side opposite a very bad sand bar of several miles in extent, which we named Sand Creek. Here my servant York swam to the sand bar to gather greens for our dinner and returned with a sufficient quantity of wild cresses or tongue grass. We passed up for two miles on the larboard side of this sand and were obliged to return, the water uncertain, the quick sand moving. We had a fine wind, but could not make use of it, our mast being broken. We passed between two small islands in the middle of the current, and round the head of a third. A rapid current for one mile. Camped on the starboard side opposite a large island in the middle of the river. One pirogue did not get up for two hours. Our scout discovered the fresh sign of about 10 Indians. I expect that those Indians are on their way to war against the Osage nation; probably they are the Sauks.

June 6, 1804, Wednesday [Clark]
Mended our mast this morning and set out at seven o'clock under a gentle breeze from S.E. by S. Passed the large island, and a creek called Split Rock Creek at five miles on the starboard side. This creek takes its name from a projecting rock with a hole through a point of the rock. At eight miles passed the mouth of a creek called Saline or Salt Creek on the larboard side. This creek is about 30 yards wide and has so many licks and salt springs on its banks that the water of the creek is brackish. One very large lick is nine miles up on the left side. The water of the spring in this lick is strong, as one bushel of the water is said to make seven pounds of good salt. Passed a large island and several small ones. The water excessively strong, so much so that we camped sooner than the usual time to wait for the pirogue. The banks are falling in very much today. River rose last night a foot.

Capt. Lewis took meridian altitude of the sun with the octant above Split Rock Creek. The country for several miles below is good; on the top of the high land and back is also tolerable land. Some buffalo sign today.

I am still very unwell with a sore throat and headache.

June 7, 1804, Thursday [Clark]
Set out early, passed the head of the island opposite which we camped last night, and breakfasted at the mouth of a large creek on the starboard side of 30 yards wide called Big Manitou. A short distance above the mouth of this

creek are several curious paintings and carvings in the projecting rock of limestone, inlaid with white, red, and blue flint of a very good quality. The Indians have taken of this flint great quantities. We landed at this inscription and found it a den of rattlesnakes. We had not landed three minutes before three very large snakes were observed in the crevices of the rocks and killed. From the mouth of the last mentioned creek Capt. Lewis took four or five men and went to some licks or springs of salt water from two to four miles up the creek on the right side. The waters of those springs are not strong, say from 4 to 600 gallons of water for a bushel of salt. Passed some small willow islands and camped at the mouth of a small river called Good Woman's River. This river is about 35 yards wide and said to be navigable for pirogues several leagues. Capt. Lewis with two men went up the creek a short distance. Our hunters brought in three bears this evening, and informed us that the country through which they passed from the last creek is fine rich land, and well watered.

June 8, 1804, Friday [Clark]
Set out this morning at daylight. Proceeded on the course of last night. Passed two willow islands and a small creek above a rock point on the larboard side at six miles on which there are a number of deer licks. Passed the Mine River at nine miles. This river is about 70 yards wide at its mouth and is said to be navigable for pirogues 80 or 90 miles. The main branch passes near the place where the Little Osage village formerly stood on the Missouri and heads between the Osage and Kansas Rivers. The left hand fork heads with nearer branches of the Osage River. The French inform us that lead ore has been found in different parts of this river. I took Sergeant Floyd and went out four miles below this river. I found the land very good for a mile or one and a half miles back and sufficiently watered with small streams, which lost themselves in the Missouri's bottom. The land rose gradually from the river to the summit of the high country, which is not more than 120 feet above high water mark. We joined the boat and dined on the point above the mouth of this river. Capt Lewis went out above the river and proceeded on one mile, finding the country rich, the weeds and vines so thick and high he came back to the boat. Proceeded on, passed an island and camped at the lower point of an island on the larboard side called the Island of the Mills about four miles above Mine River. At this place I found canteens, axes, pumice stone and peltry hidden and buried (I suppose

by some hunters). None of them (except the pumice stone) was touched by one of our party. Our hunters killed five deer today. Commenced raining soon after we came to, which prevented the party cooking their provisions. Our spies inform us that the country they passed through on starboard side is a fine high bottom, no water.

This day we met three men on a *cajeu* from the river of the Sioux above the Omaha nation. Those men had been hunting 12 months and made about $900 in pelts and furs. They were out of provisions and out of powder. Rained this night.

June 9, 1804, Saturday [Clark]

A fair morning, the river risen a little. We got fast on a snag soon after we set out, which detained us a short time. Passed the upper point of the Island. Several small channels running out of the River below a bluff and prairie (called the Prairie of Arrows) where the river is confined within the width of 300 yards. Passed a creek of eight yards wide called Creek of Arrows. This creek is short and heads in the prairies on the larboard side. Passed a small creek called Blackbird Creek starboard side and one island below and a prairie above on the larboard side. A small lake above the prairie. Opposite the lower point of the second island on the starboard side we had like to have stove our boat. In going round a snag her stern struck a log under water and she swung round on the snag, with her broad side to the current exposed to the drifting timber. By the active exertions of our party we got her off in a few minutes without injury and crossed to the island where we camped. Our hunters lay on the starboard side. The pirogue crossed without seeing them and the banks were too uncertain to send her over. Some wind from the south accompanied with rain this evening. The land on the starboard side is a high rich bottom. The larboard side appears even and of a good quality rising gradually to from 50 to 100 feet.

June 10, 1804, Sunday [Clark]

A hard rain last night. We set out this morning very early. Passed some bad places in the river. Saw a number of goslings this morning. Passed near a bank which was falling in at the time we passed. Passed the two rivers of Charitons which mouth together, above some high land which has a great quantity of stone calculated for whetstones. The first of those rivers is about 30 yards wide and the other is 70 yards wide and heads close to the River des

Moines. The Iowas have a village on the head of this river. They run through an even country and are navigable for pirogues.

Capt. Lewis killed a large buck. Passed a large island called Chicot and camped in a prairie on the larboard side. I walked out three miles, found the prairie composed of good land and plenty of water, rolling and interspersed with points of timber land. Those prairies are not like those, or a number of those, east of the Mississippi void of everything except grass. They abound with hazel grapes and a wild plum of a superior quality, called the Osage plum. It grows on a bush the height of a hazel (and is three times the size of other plums), and they hang in great quantities on the bushes. I saw great numbers of deer in the prairies, the evening is cloudy, our party in high spirits.

June 11, 1804, Monday [Clark]

The N.W. wind blew hard and cold. As this wind was immediately ahead, we could not proceed. We took the advantage of this delay and dried our wet articles, examined provisions, etc. The river beginning to fall. The hunters killed two deer. George Drouillard killed two bears in the prairie; they were not fat. We had the meat jerked and also the venison, which is a constant practice, to have all the fresh meat not used dried in this way.

June 12, 1804, Tuesday [Clark]

Set out early. Passed some bad places, and a small creek on the larboard side called Plum Creek at about one mile. At one o'clock we brought to two *cajeux*, one loaded with furs and peltries, the other with grease, buffalo grease and tallow. We purchased 300 pounds of grease, and, finding that old Mr. Dorion was of the party, we questioned him until it was too late to go further and concluded to camp for the night. Those people informed us nothing of much information.

Concluded to take old Dorion back as far as the Sioux nation with a view to get some of their chiefs to visit the President of the United States, this man being a very confidential friend of those people, he having resided with the nation 20 odd years.

June 13, 1804, Wednesday [Clark]

We set out early. Passed a round bend to the starboard side and two creeks called the Round Bend Creeks. Between those two creeks and behind a small willow island in the bend is a prairie in which the Missouri Indians once lived and the spot where 300 of them fell, a sacrifice to the fury of the Sauks. This nation, once the most numerous nation in this part of the continent, is now reduced to about 30 [*the next word, which is abbreviated in the original, is unclear; Thwaites suggests 30 families*] and that few under the protection of the Otos on the River Platte who themselves are declining. Passed some willow islands and bad sand bars. The hills or high land for several days past, or above the two Charitons, do not exceed 100 feet. Passed a sand rolling where the boat was nearly turned over by her striking and turning on the sand. We came to in the mouth of the Grand River on the starboard side and camped for the night. This river is from 80 to 100 yards wide at its mouth and navigable for pirogues a great distance. This river heads with the River Des Moines. Below its mouth is a beautiful plain of bottomland. The hills rise at a half mile back. The land about this place is either plain or overflow bottom. Capt. Lewis and myself walked to the hill, from the top of which we had a beautiful prospect of surrounding country. In the open prairie we caught a raccoon. Our hunters brought in a bear and deer. We took some lunar observations this evening.

June 14, 1804, Thursday [Clark]
We set out at six o'clock, after a thick fog. Passed through a narrow pass on the starboard side, which forms a large island. Opposite the upper point of this island on the larboard side is one of the worst quick or moving sand bars I have seen. Notwithstanding all our precautions to clear the sands and pass between them (which was the way we were compelled to pass from the immense current and falling banks on the starboard side), the boat struck the point of one. From the active exertions of the men, we prevented her turning. If she had turned she must have overset. We met a *cajeu* from the Pawnee on the River Platte. We detained them two hours with a view of engaging one of the hands to go to the Pawnee nation with a view to get those people to meet us on the river. I went out (shot a deer). We passed a high land and clay bluff on the starboard side called the Snake Bluff from the number of snakes about this place. We passed a creek above the bluff about 18 yards wide. This creek is called Snake Creek, a bad sandbar just below, which we found difficult in passing and camped above. Our hunters came in. George Drouillard gives the following account of a pond about five miles below the starboard side. He heard in this pond a snake making gobbling noises like a turkey. He fired his gun and the noise was increased. He has heard the Indians mention this species of snake. One Frenchman gives a similar account.

SUMMARY

JUNE 15 TO JULY 26, 1804

—◦◦◦—

The snake that Clark wrote about on June 14 was a piece of folklore; no such snake exists. The "rolling sand" Clark speaks of was just that, a kind of rolling sandbar on the river bottom, constantly on the move and very dangerous because it was so unstable. Navigational hazards were, in fact, everywhere; the river was full of driftwood, snags, and sawyers, which were tree limbs, or even whole trees, one end of which was stuck in the river bottom while the other end bobbed in the current with a kind of sawing action. Or else, it bobbed just beneath the surface, where it couldn't be seen, which was far worse. The keelboat was awkward and hard to maneuver. Many times they came within an ace of overturning.

For the men it was punishing work. They were making between 10 and 20 miles a day, although 20 was rare, 10 was common; the boat could make 20 miles only if the wind was behind them and the current, which ran normally about five miles an hour, was slow over that particular stretch. When the wind was on their bow, the men rowed or poled the boat, which was heavily loaded. On July 2 Clark mentions that the current was so strong that "we could with difficulty stem [it] with our 20 oars and all the poles we had." That day they made 11.5 miles. In the worst cases the boat had to be towed from shore. More than once Clark praises his men for their heart, and for their quick thinking when they did run on a snag or a sandbar and the boat started to swing broadside to the current. Many of them were suffering from boils, a few from dysentery, brought on, no doubt, by the diet. They had very few vegetables to eat, and some of the dried meat may have become contaminated. The water they drank came straight from the Missouri;

it's not called the Big Muddy for nothing. On July 6 Clark remarks that "the men sweat more than is common from some cause; I think the Missouri's water is the principal cause." It was hot work; it was hard work. As July wore on and the corps got higher into the plains, it often became necessary to stop from noon until three to rest the men, who were too exhausted to continue.

If the diet didn't cause problems, the ticks and mosquitoes did. Clark mentions them almost every day during the rest of June and July. Some of the bear grease they had bought from the cajeux coming downriver almost certainly went to coating the exposed parts of the body to keep insects off. The captains still faced occasional discipline problems. On June 29 John Collins and Hugh Hall were court-martialed for drinking whiskey from the supplies while on guard duty. They were both found guilty by a jury of their peers; Collins got 100 lashes, while Hall, who didn't open the cask but did join Collins in drinking, got 50. Alexander Willard committed a much more serious offense on July 10 or 11; he fell asleep on guard duty, a very serious crime in the military. Lewis and Clark judged this case themselves, found Willard guilty (Willard claimed that while he did lie down, he didn't fall asleep), and imposed a punishment of 400 lashes, 100 a night for four nights. The punishment was staggering but, as almost every commentator points out, justified. They were in unknown country among a potentially hostile people. A surprise night attack by a Sioux or Pawnee band could have been devastating.

For all the difficulties and complaints, however, Clark gives the impression during this part of the trip that they pale in comparison with the glories of the countryside they are passing through. By June 26 they had come nearly 400 miles and reached the border between what are now the states of Missouri and Kansas, where the general direction of the Missouri turns north by northwest. The word "beautiful" is constantly getting into the journals; Clark exclaims over the "rich fertile soils," the great variety of berries and trees, the abundance of the wildlife; he admires sunsets, and he climbs small rises and admires the view. On the Fourth of July, which they celebrate by shooting off the small cannon mounted on the bow of the boat, he pauses to wonder (in an entry that Moulton prints but that does not appear in Thwaites) at the beauty of what they are seeing: "The plains of this country are covered by a leek-green grass, well calculated for the sweetest and most nourishing hay, interspersed with copses of trees spreading their lofty branches over pools, springs, or brooks of fine water. Groups of shrubs covered with the most delicious fruit are to be seen in every direction, and nature appears to have exerted herself to beautify the scenery by the variety of flowers delicately . . . raised above the grass." He goes on to wonder why "so magnificent a scenery" should appear "in a country thus situated, far removed from the civilized world, to be enjoyed by nothing but the buffalo, elk, deer and bear in which it abounds" [Moulton, Vol. 2, pp. 346-47]. On July 12 Clark writes more on this; they were camping for the day to rest the men and take astronomical readings to determine their latitude. Clark wanders off with five men in a pirogue up the Big Nemaha River, a Missouri tributary, and after a few miles gets out to climb a nearby rise and obtain a view of the country. It is, he says, *"one of the most pleasing prospects I ever beheld, under me a beautiful river of clear water of about 80 yards wide meandering through a level and extensive meadow as far as I could see, the prospect much enlivened by the few trees and shrubs which border the bank of the river."* On a nearby sandstone bluff where Indians had left marks, Clark signed his own name and the date.

Lewis maintains his silence during this period. Whether he was taking notes or not no one knows; if he was, they have been lost. One or two fragments do exist, including one relatively long note that Moulton prints in which he writes about the sand in the Missouri and the problems it causes. He blames the Platte for the strength of the current and for the amount of sand in the Missouri. It was Lewis more often than Clark who spent the day on shore, walking the 10 or 12 miles the boats traveled upstream, sometimes hunting but more often examining the nature of the surrounding countryside and gathering samples of plant life. Lewis was a more gifted naturalist than Clark, who had more experience than Lewis on rivers and was the better boatman.

By July 21 they had reached the Platte, which was a type of river unfamiliar to Americans up to that time: The braided, shallow, sand-filled river was, as they were soon to discover, typical of the prairies and high plains from Nebraska on. Clark and Lewis took six men and paddled up the Platte for about a mile. Nowhere, Clark reports, was it deeper than five or six feet, and it was so full of sand that even for the shallow pirogues it was more or less unnavigable. The Platte was a transition point. Above it lay the upper Missouri and the High Plains, where the nature of the plant life and wildlife changed markedly and the climate became steadily drier. Above it lay the huge bison herds, the vast prairie dog cities, the alkaline soils, the antelope, and the dreaded Sioux. In the lore of the frontier, moving beyond the mouth of the Platte was like crossing the Equator.

They lay over for a week some ten miles above the mouth of the Platte at a place they called Camp White Catfish to rest the men, make repairs to the boats, and perhaps find the Otos. But they were not to be found. The captains sent out Drouillard and Pierre Cruzatte to find them but they found nobody; the Indians were on the plains hunting bison at this season.

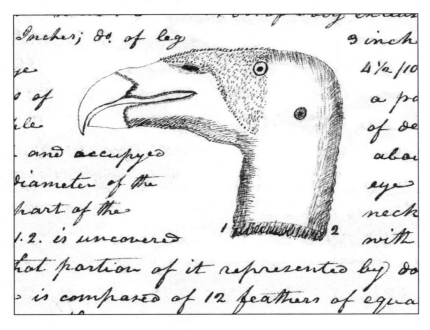

Head of a vulture (Gymnogyps californianus, *California condor*),
February 16, 1806

JULY 27 TO AUGUST 26, 1804

White Catfish Camp, July 27, 1804, Friday [Clark]
A small shower of rain this morning. At 10 o'clock commenced loading the boat and pirogue; had all the oars completely fixed; swam over the two remaining horses to the larboard side with the view of the hunters going on that side. After getting everything complete, we set sail under a gentle breeze from the south and proceeded on, passed an island (formed by a pond fed by springs) on the larboard side of high land covered with timber. In the second bend to the right a large sand island in the river, a high prairie on the starboard side. As we were setting out today one man killed a buck and another cut his knee very bad. Camped in a bend to the larboard side in a copse of trees. A very agreeable breeze from the N.W. this evening. I killed a deer in the prairie and found the mosquitoes so thick and troublesome that it was disagreeable and painful to continue a moment still.

I took one man, R. Fields, and walked on shore with a view of examining some mounds on the larboard side of the river. Those mounds I found to be of different height, shape and size, some composed of sand, some earth and sand, the highest next to the river. All of which covered about 200 acres of land in a circular form. On the side from the river, a low bottom and small pond. The Otos formerly lived here. I did not get to the boat until after night.

July 28, 1804, Saturday [Clark]
Set out this morning early, the wind from the N.W. by N. A dark smoky morning. Some rain. Passed at one mile a bluff on the starboard side, the first high land above the Nodaway approaching the river on that side. An island and creek 15 yards wide on the starboard side above this bluff. As this creek has no name, we call it Indian Knob Creek. Our party on shore came to the river and informed us that they heard firing to the S.W. Below this high land on the starboard side the Iowa Indians formerly lived. Below this old village about five miles we passed some mounds on the larboard side in a bend where the Oto Indians formerly lived. This situation I examined, found it well situated for defense. About 200 or 300 acres of land are covered with mounds.

The flank came in and informed us they heard two guns to the S.W. The high land approaches in the first bend to the left. We camped on the starboard side below the point of an island. G. Drouillard brought in a Missouri Indian that he met with hunting in the prairie. This Indian is one of the few remaining of that nation and lives with the Otos, his camp about four miles from the river. He informs us that the "great gang" of the nation were hunting the buffalo in the plains. His party was small, consisting only of about 20 lodges. [*blank*] miles further another camp where there was a Frenchman who lived in the nation. This Indian appeared sprightly and appeared to make use of the same pronunciation as the Osage, calling a chief Inca.

The word "Inca" has nothing to do with the South American Indian tribe of that name. Linguists have identified it with an Osage word.

July 29, 1804, Sunday [Clark]
Sent a Frenchman, *La Liberté*, with the Indian to the Otos' camp to invite the Indians to meet us on the river above. A dark rainy morning. Wind from the W.N.W. Rained all last night. Set out at five o'clock. Opposite the island—the bend to the right or starboard side is within 20 feet of Indian Knob Creek. The water of this creek is five feet higher than that of the river. Passed the island. We stopped to dine under some high trees near the high land on the larboard side. In a few minutes caught three very large catfish, one nearly white. Those fish are in great plenty on the sides of the river and very fat. A quart of oil came out of the surplus fat of one of these fish. Above this high land and on the starboard side passed much fallen timber, apparently the ravages of a dreadful hurricane which had passed obliquely

across the river from N.W. to S.E. about 12 months since. Many trees were broken off near the ground, the trunks of which were sound and four feet in diameter. About three quarters of a mile above the island on the starboard side a creek comes in called Boyers Creek. This creek is 25 yards wide. One man in attempting to cross this creek on a log let his gun fall in. R. Fields dived and brought it up. Proceeded on to a point on the starboard side and camped.

July 30, 1804, Monday [Clark]
Set out this morning early. Proceeded on to a clear open prairie on the larboard side on a rise of about 70 feet higher than the bottom, which is also a prairie (both forming bluffs to the river) of high grass and plum bushes, grapes, etc. and situated above high water. In a small grove of timber at the foot of the rising ground between those two prairies, and below the bluffs of the high prairie, we came to and formed a camp, intending to wait the return of the Frenchman and Indians. The white horse which we found near the Kansas River died last night.

Posted out our guard and sent out four men. Capt. Lewis and I went up the bank and walked a short distance in the high prairie. This prairie is covered with grass of 10 or 12 inches in height. Soil of good quality. At the distance of about a mile still further back the country rises about 80 or 90 feet higher, and is one continued plain as far as can be seen. From the bluff on the second rise immediately above our camp the most beautiful prospect of the river up and down and the country opposite presented itself which I ever beheld, the river meandering, the open and beautiful plains interspersed with groves of timber, and each point covered with tall timber, such as willow, cottonwood, some mulberry, elm, sycamore, linden and ash. (The groves contain hickory, walnut, coffeenut and oak in addition.)

Two ranges of high land parallel to each other and from 4 to 10 miles distant, between which the river and its bottoms are contained. (From 70 to 300 feet high.)

Joseph Fields killed and brought in an animal called by the French *brarow* [*this was a badger*] and by the Pawnees *cho car tooch*. This animal burrows in the ground and feeds on flesh (prairie dogs), bugs, and vegetables. His shape and size is like that of a beaver, his head, mouth, etc., is like a dog's with short ears, his tail and hair like that of a ground hog but longer and lighter. His internals like the internals of a hog. His skin is thick and loose, his belly is white and the hair short. A white streak from his nose to his shoulders. The toenails of his forefeet are one inch and three quarters long, and feet large; the nails of his hind feet three quarters of an inch long. The hind feet small and toes crooked, his legs are short and when he moves just sufficient to raise his body above the ground. He is of the bear species. We have his skin stuffed.

Jo. and R. Fields did not return this evening. Several men with very bad boils. Catfish are caught in any part of the river. Turkeys, geese and a beaver killed and caught. Everything in prime order. Men in high spirits. A fair still evening. A great number of mosquitoes this evening.

July 31, 1804, Tuesday [Clark]
A fair day, three hunters out. Took meridian altitude. R. and Jo. Fields returned to camp. They killed three deer. The horses strayed off last night. Drouillard killed a buck, one inch of fat on the ribs. R. and Jo. Fields returned without any meat, having been in pursuit of the horses. The Indians not yet arrived. Caught a young beaver alive which is already quite tame. Caught a buffalo fish. The evening very cool. The mosquitoes are yet troublesome.

August 1, 1804, Wednesday [Clark]
A fair morning. Dispatched two men after the horses lost yesterday, one man back to the place from which the messenger was sent for the Otos to see if any Indians had been there since our departure. He returned and informed us that no person had been there since we left it. The prairie which is situated below our camp is above the high water level and rich, covered with grass from five to eight feet high, interspersed with copses of hazel, plums, currants (like those of the U.S.), raspberries and grapes of different kinds. Also producing a variety of plants and flowers not common in the United States: two kinds of honeysuckle, one which grows to a kind of a shrub common about Harrodsburg in Kentucky, the other not so large or tall, which bears a flower in clusters, short and of a light pink color. The leaves differ from any of the other kinds, inasmuch as the leaves are distinct and do not surround the stalk as all the other kinds do.

One elk and three deer killed today, also two beaver caught. The wind rose at 10 o'clock from the W.S.W. and blew a steady and agreeable breeze all day. The mosquitoes very troublesome this evening in the bottom. The Indians not yet arrived. We fear something amiss with our messenger or them.

August 2, 1804, Thursday [Clark]
A very pleasant breeze from the S.E. The two men, Drouillard and Colter, returned with the horses loaded with elk. They found the horses about 12 miles in a southerly direction from camp.

The country through which they passed is similar to what we see from camp. One beaver and a foot of beaver caught in a trap this morning.

At sunset Mr. Fairfong (an Oto interpreter resident with them) and a part of the Oto and Missouri nation came to camp. Among them six were chiefs, not the principal chiefs. Capt. Lewis and myself met them and informed them we were glad to see them and would speak to them tomorrow. Sent them some roasted meat, pork, flour and meal. In return they sent us watermelons. Every man on his guard and ready for anything.

Three fat bucks killed this evening. The 4 quarters of one weighed 147 pounds.

August 3, 1804, Friday [Clark]
Made up a small present for those people in proportion to their consequence, also a package with a medal to accompany a speech for the grand chief. After breakfast we collected the Indians under an awning of our mainsail, in presence of our party paraded, and delivered a long speech to them expressive of our journey, the wishes of our government, some advice to them and directions how they were to conduct themselves. The principal chief for the nation being absent, we sent him the speech, flag, medal and some clothes. After hearing what they had to say delivered a medal of second grade, one for the Otos and one for the Missouri, and four medals of a third grade to the inferior chiefs, two for each tribe. The two parts of the nation, Otos and Missouris, now residing together, are about 250 men, the Otos composing two thirds and the Missouri one third part.

The chiefs all delivered a speech acknowledging their approbation to the speech and promising to pursue the advice and directions given them. They were happy to find that they had fathers which might be depended on, etc.

We gave them a canister of powder and a bottle of whiskey and delivered a few presents to the whole after giving a breech cloth, some paint, quartering [?] and a medal to those we made chiefs. After Capt. Lewis's shooting the air gun a few shots (which astonished the natives), we set out and proceeded on five miles on a direct line, passed a point on the starboard side and around a large sandbar on the larboard side and camped on the upper point. The mosquitoes excessively troublesome this evening. Great appearance of wind and rain to the N.W. We prepared to receive it. The man *Liberté* whom we sent for the Otos has not come up. He left the Otos' town one day before the Indians. This man has either tired his horse or lost himself in the plains. Some Indians are to hunt for him.

The situation of our last camp, Council Bluff or Handsome Prairie (25 days from this to Santa Fe), appears to be a very proper place for a trading establishment and fortification. The soil of the bluff well adapted for brick, great deal of timber above on the two points. Many other advantages of a small nature. And I am told it is central to several nations, viz. one day's march from the Oto town, one day and a half from the great Pawnee village, two days from the Omaha towns, two and a quarter days from the Loups [*otherwise known as the Skiri Pawnee*] village, and convenient to the country through which bands of Sioux hunt. Perhaps no other situation is as well calculated for a trading establishment.

The air is pure and healthy, so far as we can judge.

August 4, 1804, Saturday [Clark]
Set out early. At seven o'clock last night we had a violent wind from the N.W. Some little rain succeeded; the wind lasted with violence for one hour. After the wind it was clear, serene, and cool all night. Proceeded on, passed through between snags which were quite across the river. The channel confined within 200 yards, one side (starboard) a sand point, the other a bend, the banks washing away and trees falling in constantly for one mile. Above this place are the remains of an old trading establishment larboard side where Pierre Cruzatte, one of our hands, stayed two years and traded with the Omahas. A short distance above is a creek, the outlet of three ponds communicating with each other. Those ponds, or rather lakes, are fed by springs and small runs from the hills. A large sand island opposite this creek making out from the larboard point. From the camp of last night to this creek, the river has latterly changed its bed, encroaching on the larboard side. On this sandbar I saw great numbers of wild geese. Passed a small creek on the larboard side about three miles above the last. Both of these creeks are outlets from the

small lakes that receive their water from the small streams running from the high land. Great many pumice stones on the shore of various sizes. The wind blew hard. Reed, a man who went back to camp for his knife, has not joined us. We camped at a beaver house on the larboard side. One buck killed today.

August 5, 1804, Sunday [Clark]

Set out early. Great appearance of wind and rain. I have observed that thunder and lightning is not as common in this country as it is in the Atlantic states. Snakes are not plentiful. One was killed today, large and resembling the rattlesnake, only something lighter. I walked on shore this evening starboard side. In pursuing some turkeys I struck the river twelve miles below within 370 yards. The high water passes through this peninsula and agreeable to the customary changes of the river I concluded that in two years the main current of the river will pass through. In every bend the banks are falling in from the current being thrown against those bends by the sand points, which enlarge; and the soil, I believe, from the unquestionable appearance of the entire bottom from one hill to the other being the mud or ooze of the river at some former period, mixed with sand and clay, easily melts and slips into the river. And the mud mixes with the water and the sand is washed down and lodges on the points.

Great quantities of grapes on the banks. I observe three different kinds at this time ripe. One of the number is large and has the flavor of the purple grape. Camped on the starboard side. The mosquitoes very troublesome. The man who went back after his knife has not yet come up. We have some reason to believe he has deserted.

August 6, 1804, Monday [Clark]

At twelve o'clock last night a violent storm of wind from the N.W. Some rain. One pair of colors lost in the storm from the big pirogue. Set out early and proceeded on, passed a large island on the starboard side. Back of this island Soldier's River mouths. I am told by one of the men that this river is about the size of the Nodaway River, 40 yards wide at the mouth. Reed has not yet come up. Neither has La Liberté, the Frenchman, whom we sent to the Indian camps a few miles below the Council Bluffs.

August 7, 1804, Tuesday [Clark]

Last night at 8 o'clock a storm from the N.W. lasted three quarters of an hour. Set out late this morning. Wind from the north. At one o'clock dispatched George Drouillard, R. Fields, Wm. Bratton and [*Francois*] Labiche back after the deserter Reed with orders if he did not give up peaceably to put him to death, to go to the Otos' village and inquire for La Liberté and bring him to the Omahas' village, also with a speech on the occasion to the Otos and Missouris. And directing a few of their chiefs to come to the Omahas and we would make peace between them and the Omahas and Sioux. A string of wampum and a carrot of tobacco. Proceeded on and camped on the starboard side.

August 8, 1804, Wednesday [Clark]
Set out this morning at the usual time. At two miles passed a bend to the larboard side choked up with snags. Our boat ran on two in turning to pass through. We got through with safety. The wind from N.W. Passed the mouth of a river on the starboard side called by the Sioux Indians Stone River. The French call this river Petite Rivière des Sioux. It is about 80 yards wide and as Mr. Dorion says, who's been on the head of it and the country about, is navigable for pirogues some distance. It runs parallel to the Missouri some distance, then falls down from the N.E. through a rolling open country. The head of this river is nine miles from the River Des Moines, at which place the Des Moines is 80 yards wide. This Little Sioux passes through a lake called D'Esprits which is within 5 leagues of the Des Moines. The said lake is about 20 leagues in circumference and is divided into two by two rocks approaching very near each other. This lake is of various widths, containing many islands. From this lake to the Omaha, four days march. It is said to be near the Dog Plains [*Prairie du Chien*]. One principal branch of the Des Moines is called Cat River. The Des Moines is shoaly.

Capt. Lewis took the meridian altitude of the sun. I took one man and went on shore. The man killed an elk. I fired four times at one and did not kill him, my ball being small, I think, was the reason. The mosquitoes so bad in the prairies that with the assistance of a bush I could not keep them out of my eyes. The boat turned several times today on sandbars. In my absence the boat passed an island 2 miles above the Little Sioux River. On the upper point of the island some hundreds of pelicans were collected. They left three fish on the sand which were very fine. Capt. Lewis killed one and took his dimensions. I joined the boat and we camped on the starboard side. It is worthy of remark that snakes are not plentiful in this part of the Missouri.

August 9, 1804, Thursday [Clark]
The fog being thick detained us until half past seven o'clock, at which time we set out and proceeded on under a gentle breeze from the S.E. I walked on shore, saw an elk, crossed an isthmus of three-fourths of a mile to the river, and returned to the boat. Camped on the larboard side above a beaver den. Mosquitoes very troublesome.

August 10, 1804, Friday [Clark]
Set out early this morning. [*Clark then notes the day's directions and mileages.*] From this island [*the island where they camped that night*] the high hill which the late king of the Omahas was buried on is high and bears west four miles. We camped on this island. Mosquitoes very troublesome. Much elk and beaver sign.

August 11, 1804, Saturday [Clark]
About daylight this morning a hard wind from the N.W. with some rain. Proceeded on around the right of the island.

A hard wind accompanied with rain from the S.E. After the rain was over Capt. Lewis, myself and 10 men ascended the hill on the larboard side, under which were some fine springs, to the top of a high point where the Omahas' king Blackbird was buried four years ago. [*In a note Thwaites adds that this king became powerful by possessing some arsenic, which he threatened to use on anyone who opposed him. He was buried on his horse. In 1832 the artist George Catlin stole his skull, which wound up in the Smithsonian.*] A mound of earth about 12 feet in diameter at the base and six feet high is raised over him turfed, and a pole eight feet high in the center. On this pole we fixed a white flag bound with red, blue and white. This hill is about 300 feet above the water, forming a bluff between that and the water of various heights from 40 to 150 feet. Yellow soft sandstone. From the top of this knoll the river may be seen meandering for 60 or 70 miles. We descended and set out, passing over a sandbar on the south point along the willows to the river opposite a small bayou on the larboard side, which is the conveyance of the high water from a bend which appears near in a northerly direction, having passed a creek in a deep bend to the larboard side called by the Omahas *Wau can di Peeche* (Great Spirit Is Bad). On the creek and hills near it about 400 of the Omahas died with the smallpox.

The mosquitoes very troublesome. Great numbers of herons this evening. I have observed a number of places where the river has once run and is now filled, or is filling up and growing with willows and cottonwood.

August 12, 1804, Sunday [Clark]
Set out early under a gentle breeze from the south. The river wider than usual and shallow. At 12 o'clock we halted to take a meridian altitude of the sun and sent a man back, or I may say across, to the bend of the river where Capt. Lewis took the meridian altitude yesterday [*they had come to an oxbow bend in the Missouri*]. He made it 974 yards across; the distance around the bend is eighteen and three-quarters miles. About four miles above this bend on the larboard side is the commencement of a bluff which extends about four miles on the river, of yellow and brown clay. In some parts of it near the water a soft sandstone is imbedded. On the top, which is from 20 to 150 feet above the water and rises back, it is covered with timber. A few red cedars are on this bluff. The wind came round to the S.E. A prairie wolf came near the bank and barked at us this evening. We made an attempt but could not get him. The animal barks like a large fierce dog. Beaver are very plentiful on this part of the river. I prepared some presents to give the Indians of the Omaha nation. Weiser appointed cook and superintendent of the provisions of Sergeant Floyd's squad. We camped on a sand island in a bend to the starboard side. Mosquitoes very troublesome until the wind rose at one or two o'clock.

August 13, 1804, Monday [Clark]
Set out this morning at light the usual time and proceeded on under a gentle breeze from the S.E.

We formed a camp on a sandbar on the larboard side and detached Sergeant Ordway, Pierre Crusatte, George Shannon, Werner and Carrn [*Thwaites guesses that this refers to someone named Carson, but there was an E. Cann among the* engagés] to the Omaha village with a flag and some tobacco to invite the nation to see and talk with us tomorrow. We took some lunar observations this evening. The air pleasant.

August 14, 1804, Tuesday [Clark]

A fine morning, wind from the S.E. The men sent to the Omaha town last evening have not returned; we conclude to send a spy to know the cause of their delay. At about 12 o'clock the party returned and informed us that they could not find the Indians nor any fresh sign. Those people have not returned from their buffalo hunt. Those people having no houses, no corn, or anything more than the graves of their ancestors to attach them to the old village, continue in pursuit of the buffalo longer than others who had greater attachments to their native village. The ravages of the smallpox (which swept off 400 men and women and children in proportion) have reduced this nation to not exceeding 300 men and left them to the insults of their weaker neighbors, which before were glad to be on friendly terms with them. I am told when this fatal malady was among them they carried their frenzy to very extraordinary lengths, not only burning their village, but they put their wives and children to death with a view of their all going together to some better country. They bury their dead on the tops of high hills and raise mounds on top of them. The cause or way these people took the smallpox is uncertain, the most probable from some other nation by means of a war party.

August 15, 1804, Wednesday [Clark]

I went with ten men to a creek dammed by the beavers about halfway to the village. With some small willows and bark we made a drag and hauled up the creek and caught 318 fish of different kinds, i.e. pike, bass, salmon, perch, red horse, small cat, and a kind of perch called silverfish on the Ohio. I caught a shrimp precisely of the shape, size and flavor of those about New Orleans and the lower part of the Mississippi. This creek, which is only the pass or strait from one beaver pond to another, is crowded with large mussels. Very fat ducks, plover of different kinds, are on these ponds as well as on the river. In my absence Capt. Lewis sent Mr. Dorion, the Sioux interpreter, and three men to examine a fire which threw up an immense smoke from the prairies on the N.E. side of the river and at no great distance from camp. The object of this party was to find some bands of Sioux which the interpreter thought were near the smoke and get them to come in. In the evening this party returned and informed us that the fire arose from some trees which had been left burning by a small party of Sioux who had passed several days ago. The wind setting from that point blew the smoke over our camp. Our party all in health and spirits. The men sent to the Otos and in pursuit of the deserter Reed have not yet returned or joined our party.

No salmon are native to the upper Missouri. The shrimp is almost certainly a crayfish.

August 16, 1804, Thursday [Clark]

A very cool morning, the wind as usual from the N.W. Capt. Lewis took 12 men and went to the pond and creek between camp and the old village and caught upwards of 800 fine fish, 79 pike, 8 salmon, 1 rock, 1 flatback, 127 buffalo and red horse, 4 bass and 490 catfish with many small silverfish. I had a mast made and fixed to the boat today. The party sent to the Otos not yet joined us. The wind shifted around to the S.E. Every evening a breeze rises which blows off the mosquitoes and cools the atmosphere.

August 17, 1804, Friday [Clark]

A fine morning, the wind from the S.E. I collected a grass much resembling wheat in its growth, the grain like rye; also some resembling rye and barley. A kind of timothy, the seed of which branches from the main stalk and is more like flax seed than that of a timothy.

At 6 o'clock this evening Labiche, one of the party sent to the Otos, joined and informed us that the party was behind with one of the deserters, M.B. Reed, and the 3 principal chiefs of the nation. La Liberté they caught but he deceived them and got away. The object of the chiefs coming forward is to make peace with the Omahas through us. As the Omahas are not at home, this great object cannot be accomplished at this time. Set the prairies on fire to bring the Omahas and Sioux if any were near, this being the usual signal.

A cool evening. Two beaver caught today.

August 18, 1804, Saturday [Clark]

A fine morning. Wind from the S.E. In the after part of the day the party with the Indians arrived. We met them under a shade near the boat and after a short talk we gave them provisions to eat and proceeded to the trial of Reed. He confessed that he "deserted and stole a public rifle, shot pouch, powder and balls" and requested we would be as favorable with him as we could consistent with our oaths—which we were and only sentenced him to run the gauntlet four times through the party and that each man with nine switches should punish him and for him not to be considered in future as one of the party.

The three principal chiefs petitioned for pardon for this man. After we explained the injury such men do them by false representation, and explaining the customs of our country, they were all satisfied with the propriety of the sentence and were witness to the punishment. After which we had some talk with the chiefs about the origin of the war between them and the Omahas. It commenced in this way: two of the Missouri tribe residing with the Otoes went to the Omahas to steal horses. They killed them both, which was a cause of revenge on the part of the Missouris and Otoes. They also brought war on themselves nearly in the same way with the Skiri Pawnees. They are greatly in fear of a just revenge from the Pawnees for taking their corn from the Pawnee towns in their absence hunting this summer.

Capt. Lewis's birthday. The evening was closed with an extra gill of whiskey and a dance until 11 o'clock.

This was Lewis's 30th birthday. It may explain the dance.

August 19, 1804, Sunday [Clark]
A fine morning. Wind from the S.E. We prepared a small present for the chiefs and warriors present. The main chief breakfasted with us and begged for a sun glass [*a lens, commonly used to start fires by focusing sunlight*]. Those people are all naked, covered only with breech clouts, blankets, or buffalo robes, the flesh side painted with different colors and figures. At 10 o'clock we assembled the chiefs and warriors, nine in number, under an awning, and Capt. Lewis explained the speech sent to the nation from the Council Bluffs by Mr. Fairfong. The three chiefs and all the men or warriors made short speeches approving the advice and council their great father had sent them, and concluded by giving themselves some credit for their acts.

We then brought out the presents and exchanged the Big Horse's medal and gave him one equal to the one sent to Little Thief and gave all some small articles and eight carrots of tobacco. We gave one small medal to one of the chiefs and a certificate to the others of their good intentions. [*These certificates were printed blanks, the blanks to be filled in by hand with the names of the chiefs they were given to, that were headed "Thomas Jefferson, President of the United States of America." They went on to say that the chief in question was an ally of the United States to whom the government would extend its protection as long as he was willing to acknowledge "the authority of the same."*]

One of those Indians after receiving his certificate delivered it again to me, Big Blue Eyes. The chief petitioned for the certificate again. We would not give the certificate but rebuked them very roughly for having in object goods and not peace with their neighbors. This language they did not like at first, but at length all petitioned for us to give back the certificate to Big Blue Eyes. He came forward and made a plausible excuse. I then gave the certificate to the great chief to bestow it to the most worthy. They gave it to him. We then gave them a dram and broke up the council. The chiefs requested we would not leave them this evening. We determined to set out early in the morning. We showed them many curiosities and the air gun, which they were much astonished at. Those people begged much for whiskey. Sergeant Floyd is taken very bad all at once with a bilious colic. We attempted to relieve him, without success as yet. He gets worse and we are much alarmed at his situation. All attention to him.

August 20, 1804, Monday [Clark]
Sergeant Floyd much weaker and no better. Made Mr. Fairfong the interpreter a few presents and the Indians a canister of whiskey. We set out under a gentle breeze from the S.E. and proceeded on very well. Sergeant Floyd as bad as he can be, no pulse and nothing will stay a moment on his stomach or bowels.

Passed two islands on the starboard side and at the first bluff on the starboard side Sergeant Floyd died with a great deal of composure. Before his death he said to me, "I am going away. I want you to write me a letter." We buried him on the top of the bluff a half mile below a small river, to which we gave his name. He was buried with the honors of war. Much lamented. A cedar post with the name "Sergeant C. Floyd died here 20th of August 1804" was fixed at the head of his grave. This man at all times gave us proofs of his firmness and determined resolution to do service to his country and honor to himself. After paying all the honor to our deceased brother, we camped in the mouth of Floyd's River, about 30 yards wide, a beautiful evening.

The consensus is that Floyd died of a burst appendix and subsequent peritonitis. The river named after him still retains his name. Sergeant Floyd was the only member of the expedition to die during its course.

August 21, 1804, Tuesday [Clark]
We set out very early this morning and proceeded on under a gentle breeze from the S.E. Passed Willow Creek, small, on the starboard side below a bluff of about 170 feet high and one and a half miles above Floyd's River. At one

and a half miles higher and above the bluff passed the Sioux River starboard side. This river is about the size of Grand River and as Mr. Dorion, our Sioux interpreter, says, navigable to the falls 70 or 80 leagues and above these falls still further. The falls are 20 feet or thereabouts and have two principal pitches. It heads with the St. Peters, passing the head of the Des Moines. On the right below the falls a creek comes in which passes through cliffs of red rock which the Indians make pipes of. When the different nations meet at those quarries all is peace. Passed a place in a prairie on the larboard side where the Omahas had a village formerly. The country above the Platte has a great similarity. Camped on the larboard side. Clouds appear to rise in the west and threaten wind. I found a very excellent fruit resembling the red currant. The shrub on which it grows resembles privet and is about the height of a wild plum.

The two men sent with the horses have not joined us as yet.

The creek where the red stone is quarried is now called Pipestone Creek, and it is a national monument. It lies in southwest Minnesota. Only Indians are allowed access to the stone.

August 22, 1804, Friday [Clark]

Set out early, wind from the south. At three miles we landed at a bluff where the two men sent with the horses were waiting with two deer. This bluff contained alum, copperas, cobalt, pyrites, the alum rock soft, and sandstone. Capt. Lewis in proving the quality of these minerals was near poisoning himself by the fumes and taste of the cobalt, which had the appearance of soft isinglass. The copperas and alum are very poisonous. Above this bluff a small creek comes in from the larboard side, passing under the cliffs for several miles. This creek I call Roloje, a name I learned last night. Seven miles above is a cliff of alum stone of a dark brown color, containing also, encrusted in the crevices and shelves of the rock, great quantities of cobalt, cemented shells and a red earth. From this the river bends to the east and is within three or four miles of the River Sioux at the place where that river comes from the high land into the low prairie and passes under the foot of these hills to its mouth.

Capt. Lewis took a dose of salts to work off the effects of the arsenic [*used to test the quality of the ores they had found*]. We camped on the starboard side. Sailed the greater part of this day with a hard wind from the S.E. A great deal of elk sign, and great appearance of wind from the N.W.

Ordered a vote for a Sergeant to choose one of three, which may be the highest number. The highest numbers are Patrick Gass, who had 19 votes, Bratton and Gibson.

The vote to elect a new sergeant was to replace Sergeant Floyd, who had just died.

August 23, 1804, Thursday [Clark]
Set out this morning very early. The two men with the horses did not come up last night. I walked on shore and killed a fat buck. J. Fields sent out to hunt. Came to the boat and informed us that he had killed a buffalo in the plain ahead. Capt. Lewis took 12 men and had the buffalo brought to the boat in the next bend to the starboard side. Two elk swam the river, and were fired at from the boat. R. Fields came up with the horses and brought two deer. One deer killed from the boat. Several prairie wolves seen today. Saw elk standing on the sandbar. The wind blew hard west and raised the sands off the bar in such clouds that we could scarcely see. This sand being fine and very light stuck to everything it touched; and in the plain for half a mile, the distance I was out, every spire of grass was covered with the sand or dust.

We camped on the larboard side above a sand island. One beaver caught.
The buffalo was the first bison the men had killed.

August 24, 1804, Friday [Clark]
Some rain last night, a continuation this morning. We set out at the usual time and proceeded on the course of last night to the commencement of a blue clay bluff of 180 or 190 feet high on the larboard side. These bluffs appear to have been latterly on fire and at this time are too hot for a man to bear his hand in the earth at any depth. Great appearance of coal. An immense quantity of cobalt or a crystallized substance which answers its description is on the face of the bluff. Great quantities of a kind of berry resembling a currant except double the size. It grows on a bush like a privet and the size of a damson, deliciously flavored, and makes delightful tarts. This fruit is now ripe. I took my servant and a French boy and walked on shore. Killed two buck elks and a fawn and intercepted the boat and had all the meat butchered and in by sunset, at which time it began to rain and rained hard. Capt. Lewis and myself walked out and got very wet. A cloudy, rainy night.

In my absence the boat passed a small river called by the Indians White Stone River [*the present Vermillion River*]. This river is about 30 yards wide and runs through a plain or prairie in its whole course. In a northerly direction from the mouth of this creek in an immense plain a high hill is situated, and appears of a conic form. By the different nations of Indians in this quarter it is supposed to be the residence of devils. They are in human form with remarkable large heads and about 18 inches high, they are very watchful, and are armed with sharp arrows with which they can kill at a great distance. They are said to kill all persons who are so hardy as to attempt to approach the hill. They state that tradition informs them that many Indians have suffered by these little people. Among others three Omaha men fell a sacrifice to their merciless fury not many years since. So much do the Omaha, Sioux, Otos and other neighboring nations believe this fable that no consideration is sufficient to induce them to approach the hill.

The hill in question is now known as Spirit Mound.

August 25, 1804, Saturday [Clark]
A cloudy morning. Capt. Lewis and myself concluded to go and see the mound which was viewed with such terror by all the different nations in this quarter. We selected Shields, J. Fields, W. Bratton, Sgt. Ordway, J. Colter, Cann, and Corp. Warfington and Frazer, also G. Drouillard, and dropped down to the mouth of White Stone [*Vermillion*] River, where we left the pirogue with two men, and at 200 yards we ascended a rising ground of about 60 feet. From the top of this high land the country is level and open as far as can be seen, except some few rises at a great distance, and the mound which the Indians call Mountain of *little people* or spirits. This mound appears of a conic form and is N. 20° W. from the mouth of the creek. We left the river at eight o'clock. At four miles we crossed the creek, 23 yards wide, in an extensive valley and continued on. At two miles further our dog was so heated and fatigued we were obliged to send him back to the creek. At 12 o'clock we arrived at the hill. Capt. Lewis much fatigued from heat, the day being very hot and he being in a debilitated state from the precautions he was obliged to take to prevent the effects of the cobalt and mineral substance which had like to have poisoned him two days ago. His want of water, and several of the men complaining of great thirst, determined us to make for the first water, which was the creek in a bend N.E. from the mound about three miles. After a delay of about 1 hour and a half to recruit [*i.e., refresh*] our party, we set out on our return down the creek through the bottom of about one mile in width, and crossed the creek three times to the

place we first struck it, where we gathered some delicious fruit, grapes, plums, and blue currants. After a delay of an hour we set out on our back trail and arrived at the pirogue at sunset. We proceeded on to the place we camped last night and stayed all night.

This mound is situated on an elevated plain in a level and extensive prairie, bearing N. 20° W. from the mouth of White Stone River *nine* miles. The base of the mound is a regular parallelogram, the long side of which is about 300 yards in length, the shorter 60 or 70 yards. From the longer side of the base it rises from the north and south with a steep ascent to the height of 65 or 70 feet, leaving a level plain on the top of 12 feet in width and 90 in length. The north and south part of this mound is joined by two regular rises, each in oval forms of half its height forming three regular rises from the plain. The ascent of each elevated part is as sudden as the principal mound at the narrower sides of its base.

The regular form of this hill would in some measure justify a belief that it owed its origin to the hand of man; but as the earth and loose pebbles and other substances of which it is composed bear an exact resemblance to the steep ground which borders on the creek in its neighborhood, we concluded it was most probably the production of nature.

The only remarkable characteristic of this hill, admitting it to be a natural production, is that it is insulated or separated a considerable distance from any other, which is very unusual in the natural order or disposition of the hills.

The surrounding plain is open, void of timber, and level to a great extent. Hence the wind, from whatever quarter it may blow, drives with unusual force over the naked plains and against this hill; the insects of various kinds are thus involuntarily driven to the mound by the force of the wind, or fly to its leeward side for shelter. The small birds whose food they are consequently resort in great numbers to this place in search of them, particularly the small brown martin, of which we saw a vast number hovering on the leeward side of the hill when we approached it in the act of catching those insects. They were so gentle that they did not quit the place until we had arrived within a few feet of them.

One evidence which the Indians give for believing this place to be the residence of some unusual spirits is that they frequently discover a large assemblage of birds about this mound. That is in my opinion a sufficient proof to produce in the savage mind a confident belief of all the properties which they ascribe to it.

From the top of this mound we beheld a most beautiful landscape. Numerous herds of buffalo were seen feeding in various directions. The plain to North N.W. and N.E. extends without interruption as far as can be seen.

Some high lands to be seen from the mound at a great distance to the N.E., some nearer to the N.W. No woods except on the Missouri's points. If all the timber which is on the White Stone River was on 100 acres it would not be thickly timbered. The soil of the plains is delightful.

Great numbers of birds are seen in the plains, such as blackbirds, wrens, or prairie bird, a kind of lark about the size of a partridge with a short tail. [It is unclear what bird Clark means by this reference.]

The boat under the command of Sgt. Pryor proceeded on in our absence (after jerking the elk I killed yesterday) six miles and camped on the larboard side. R. Fields brought in five deer. George Shannon killed an elk buck. Some rain this evening.

We set the prairies on fire as a signal for the Sioux to come to the river.

August 26, 1804, Sunday [Clark]
Joined the boat at nine o'clock a.m. After jerking the meat killed yesterday and preparing the elk skins for a tow rope, we set out, leaving Drouillard and Shannon to hunt the horses, which were lost, with directions to follow us, keeping on the high lands.

Proceeded on, passed a cliff of white and blue or dark earth of two miles in extent on the larboard side and camped on a sand bar opposite the old village called *Petite Arch*. A small creek falls into the river, 15 yards wide, below the village on the same side, larboard side. This village was built by an Indian chief of the Omaha nation by the name of Petite Arch (or Little Bow). Displeased with the great chief of that nation (Blackbird), he separated with 200 men and built a village at this place. After his death the two villages joined.

Great quantities of grapes, plums of three kinds, two yellow and large, one of which is long, and a third kind, round and red, all well-flavored. Particularly the yellow sort.

[Lewis and Clark]
The commanding officers have thought it proper to appoint Patrick Gass a Sergeant in *the corps of volunteers for North Western Discovery*. He is therefore to be obeyed and respected accordingly.

Sgt. Gass is directed to take charge of the late Sgt. Floyd's mess, and immediately to enter on the discharge of such other duties as by their previous orders have been prescribed for the government of the Sergeants of this corps.

The commanding officers have every reason to hope from the previous faithful services of Sgt. Gass that this expression of their approbation will be still further confirmed by his vigilant attention in future to his duties as Sergeant. The commanding officers are still further confirmed in the high opinion they had previously formed of the capacity, diligence, and integrity of Sgt. Gass, from the wish expressed by a large majority of his comrades for his appointment as Sergeant.

*At 33, Patrick Gass was one of the oldest among the expeditioners and pop-
ular among the men. He was an excellent carpenter who built the winter
quarters the corps used at the Mandan villages and at Fort Clatsop on the
Pacific coast. He was the first member of the expedition to publish his journals, in 1807, and the last to die, in 1870, at the age of 99. On the same day,
August 26, that Gass was made sergeant, the corps left George Drouillard
and Pvt. George Shannon, the youngest member of the expedition, to locate
the horses, which sometimes wandered off. Drouillard returned that night
but Shannon did not, so the next day Lewis and Clark sent two men to find
him. What they found was his trail; Shannon, who evidently believed the
corps was ahead of him, had taken the horses and gone upriver. Shannon
was not a good hunter so John Colter was sent after him with provisions,
but Colter couldn't catch him. He was gone some two weeks. When the corps
finally caught up with him, he was nearly starved. Says Clark, "thus a man
had like to have starved to death in a land of plenty for the want of bullets
or something to kill his meat." Bison had come within 30 yards of his camp.
He survived by eating grapes and a rabbit, which he killed by shooting hard
sticks out of his gun in place of a lead ball. He was out of lead balls. Later
in his life Shannon became a U.S. senator from Missouri.*

*All through the next month the corps proceeded upriver in a state of
growing wonder at the extraordinary abundance of the plains. Everywhere
they looked they found vast herds of bison, deer, elk, and antelope; Lewis*

remarks on the 17th of September that, although it's hard to believe, he could see 3,000 bison "at one view." That same day, when they were laying over to dry out their goods after three days of rain, Lewis tried to get a shot at an antelope and crept within 200 paces of a small group that was standing on a small rise, but the animals were too wary and quick for him to get any closer and took off. When he got to the top of the rise he saw them three miles away. "I think," he says, "I can venture the assertion that the speed of this animal is equal if not superior to that of the finest blooded courser."

They saw their first pronghorn on September 3. Clark called them "goats" (in some parts of the Great Plains people still call them goats); they are antelope-like creatures, but not true antelopes. On the 5th they saw their first mule deer, on the 7th their first prairie dog city, covering some four acres. The corps was fascinated by prairie dogs, killed one, then captured another alive by pouring a great quantity of water down its hole. The following April they sent one live prairie dog to Jefferson with the small party that returned downriver to St. Louis. Remarkably, the creature arrived alive. All through this time they had been seeing what they thought were foxes; in fact they were coyotes. On the 18th Clark killed his first one. The term "coyote" is the Mexican Spanish name for the animal. The corps called them prairie wolves.

The new species filled both Lewis and Clark with amazement and is reflected in the changed tone of their ordinarily quite prosaic accounts of the day's events. Lewis writes long, careful descriptions of the new animals: antelope, bull snake, black-billed magpie, white-tailed jackrabbit. Clark, who is generally rather laconic about the things he observes, cannot help but expand upon his accounts of these animals. It was the numbers of them, however, more than the animals themselves, that were astonishing. As John Logan Allen points out in Passage Through the Garden, his book about the geographical knowledge of the West as Lewis and Clark understood it, the Americans were used to eastern woodland conditions in which game had become relatively scarce. Here game surrounded them on all sides. Only a few of the French engagés with them were familiar with deer, elk, and buffalo in these immense quantities.

On August 27, the day after George Shannon lost his way, an Indian boy appeared on shore at the mouth of the Rivière aux Jacques, now the James River, and swam out to the boats. Then there were two others. They had reached the territory of the Yankton Sioux. The captains sent Pierre

Dorion, who had lived with them for years and had taken a Sioux wife, to their camp on the Jacques to ask the chiefs down for a visit. Although relative latecomers to the plains (their origins lay in the Minnesota forests), the Sioux were already the largest and most dominant tribe on the plains; they controlled access to the upper Missouri. They had already become something of a legend for their fearsomeness. Jefferson thought them so important to the outcome of his expansionist plans that he singled them out in his instructions to Lewis. One of the captains' responsibilities was to persuade some of their chiefs to make the trip to Washington and meet their Great Father. The idea was to awe them into submission with the extent of the power of the United States.

Ethnologists have divided the Sioux into three groups, of which the Yankton (and Yanktonai) Sioux were one. Sioux is a French name for them; they called themselves the Dakota, or "dar co tars" in Clark's inventive spelling. (It's worth mentioning that Clark spelled the word "Sioux" more than 20 different ways in the journals, but almost never correctly.) The two other groups were the Teton Sioux, whom the corps would encounter in a few weeks, and the Santee. Each of these three main groupings broke down further into bands, each with its own name; a band typically consisted of from 100 to 500 warriors, with women and children, who traveled together and had their own chiefs and could be best compared to a movable village. Clark identified 12 such bands in the journals, but his spelling and the difficulty of translating Sioux terms into English has made it difficult to identify these bands precisely.

The meeting with the Yankton Sioux went much like the previous meeting downriver with the Omaha and Missouri. Some 70 Sioux chiefs and warriors appeared on the opposite side of the river on August 29, and on the 30th the corps met with them. Lewis made a speech and gave the same gifts as before: medals, small trade goods, printed "commissions," a little whiskey, carrots of tobacco. Speeches were made in reply. A few of the chiefs promised to make the trip to Washington in the spring. It was evident that the gifts were insufficient. The Yankton wanted guns, powder, ammunition, and whiskey. They had bison to kill and wars to fight; Clark noted that this band was at peace with 8 "nations" but at war with 20 others.

Overall Clark was impressed by them. He writes, "The Sioux are a stout bold-looking people, the young men handsome, and well-made . . . Notwithstanding they live by the bow and arrow, they do not shoot so well as the

Northern Indians. The warriors are very much decorated with paint, porcupine quills and feathers, large leggings and moccasins, all with buffalo robes of different colors. The squaws wore petticoats and a white buffalo robe with the black hair turned back over their necks and shoulders." He goes on to mention a warrior society that held itself apart from the others, "brave active young men who take a vow never to give back, let the danger be what it may. In war parties they always go forward without screening themselves behind trees or anything else." He cites a recent instance where, in crossing the Missouri over the ice, "a hole was in the ice immediately in their course which might easily have been avoided by going around," but the first man disdained to avoid it, walked into it, and was drowned, while the others had to be dragged around the hole by the rest of the party. In a recent battle with the Crow, 18 of 22 of this society had been killed; the four others survived only because they were dragged off by their friends.

On the first of September the corps moved on up the Missouri. On the second they came across natural formations that they mistook for the remains of ancient fortifications, and they spent some time measuring them. The mornings were getting steadily colder, and the wind was often against them. On the 10th of September they discovered on top of a ridge a petrified backbone 45 feet long. Clark thought it the spine of some enormous fish; it was in fact the fossil backbone of a pleisosaur. Some parts of this skeleton are now in the Smithsonian. The river was growing more and more shallow, the sandbars worse. On the 12th the boat got stuck on sand four times; it took the men all day to make four miles. Because of the river's shallowness they decided to redistribute the load in the boat, taking more of the supplies into the two pirogues; this meant that they needed both pirogues to go on. They decided not to send one back, as they had originally planned to do, in the fall, but to wait until the following spring.

On the 20th they came to the Big Bend of the Missouri, where the river makes a loop of 30 miles around a piece of land that is only, at its narrowest point, a mile and a quarter across. Clark added up their mileage to this point and came up with a figure of 1,283 miles from the mouth of the river. That night the sandbar where they were camping collapsed; they got themselves and their gear off just in time. Brants and plovers were heading south now. They were entering ever drier land, with prickly pear cactus now common on the ground, making walking harder. The hunters were complaining that the quantities of harsh mineral salts in the soil were ruining their moccasins. On *the 22nd they passed a fort that had been built by the French trader Regis Loisel a year or two before, with what may have been the first tepees Clark had seen standing nearby. They were entering the country of the Teton Sioux, who were far more belligerent than the Yankton band downriver. They were now entirely in present-day South Dakota.*

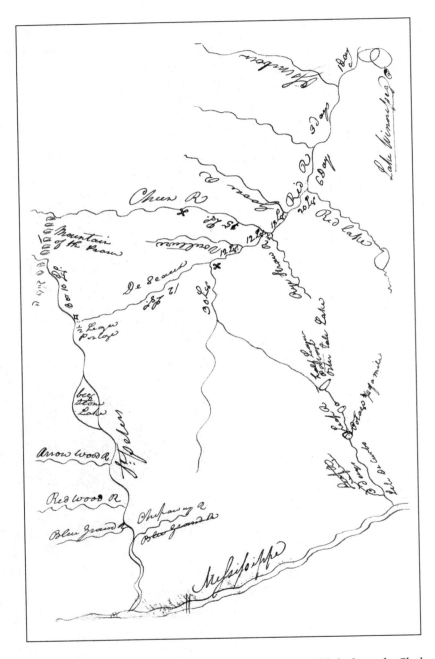

Mississippi River and tributaries (in present-day Minnesota) likely drawn by Clark, winter 1804–05

SEPTEMBER 23 TO NOVEMBER 6, 1804

September 23, 1804, Sunday [Clark]
Set out under a gentle breeze from the S.E. Passed a small island situated in a bend to the larboard side called Goat Island. A short distance above the upper point a creek of 12 yards comes in on the starboard side. We observed a great smoke to the S.W. I walked on shore and observed buffalo in great herds at a distance.

Passed two small willow islands with large sandbars making out from them. Passed Elk Island about two and a half miles long and three-fourths of a mile wide situated near the larboard side covered with cottonwood, the red currants called by the French *gres de beuff* [*buffalo berry*], and grapes.

The river is nearly straight for a great distance, wide and shoal. Passed a creek on the starboard side 16 yards wide we call Reuben Creek, as Reuben Fields found it. Camped on the starboard side below the mouth of a creek on the larboard side. Three Sioux boys came to us, swam the river and informed us that the band of Sioux called the Tetons, of 80 lodges, were camped at the next creek above, and 60 lodges more a short distance above. We gave those boys two carrots of tobacco to carry to their chiefs, with directions to tell them that we would speak to them tomorrow.

Capt. Lewis walked on shore this evening. R. Fields killed a doe goat.

September 24, 1804, Monday [Clark]
Set out early. A fair day, the wind from the E. Passed the mouth of a creek on the larboard side called Creek on High Water. Passed a large island on the larboard side about two miles and one-half long on which Colter had camped and killed four elk. The wind fair from the S.E. We prepared some clothes, a few medals for the chiefs of the Teton band of Sioux we expect to see today at the next river. Observed a great deal of stone on the sides of the hills on the starboard side. We saw one hare today, prepared all things for action in case of necessity. Our pirogues went to the island for the meet. Soon after the man on shore ran up the bank and reported that the Indians had stolen the horse. We soon after met five Indians and anchored out some distance and spoke to them. Informed them we were friends and wished to continue so but were not afraid of any Indians. Some of their young men had taken the horse sent by their Great Father for their chief and we would not speak to them until the horse was returned to us again.

Passed an island about one and a half miles long called Good Humored Island on the starboard side on which we saw several elk. Came to about one and a half miles above off the mouth of a small river about 70 yards wide called by Mr. Evans the Little Missouri River. The tribes of the Sioux called the Teton are camped about two miles up on the N.W. side, and we shall call the river after that nation, *Teton*. This river is 70 yards wide at the mouth of water, and has a considerable current. We anchored off the mouth.

The French pirogue came up early in the day; the other did not get up until the evening, soon after we had come to. I went and smoked with the chiefs who came to see us here. All well. We prepare to speak with the Indians tomorrow, at which time we are informed the Indians will be here. The Frenchman who had for some time been sick began to bleed, which alarmed him. Two-thirds of our party camped on board, the remainder with the guard on shore.

September 25, 1804, off Teton River [Clark]
A fair morning. The wind from the S.E. All well. Raised a flag staff and made an awning or shade on a sandbar in the mouth of the Teton River for the purpose of speaking with the Indians under. The boat crew on board at 70 yards distant from the bar. The 5 Indians which we met last night continued [*with us*]; about 11 o'clock the first and second chiefs came. We gave them some of our provisions to eat, they gave us great quantities of meat, some

of which was spoiled. We feel much at a loss for the want of an interpreter. The one we have can speak but little.

Met in council at 12 o'clock and after smoking, agreeable to the usual custom, Capt. Lewis proceeded to deliver a speech, which we were obliged to curtail for want of a good interpreter. All our party paraded. Gave a medal to the grand chief, called in Indian *Un ton gar Sar bar*, in French *Beuffle noir*, Black Buffalo, said to be a good man; second chief *Torto hon gar*, or the *Partisan—bad*. The third is the *Beuffle de Medicine* [*Buffalo Medicine*], his name is *Tar ton gar wa ker*.

Invited those chiefs on board to show them our boat and such curiosities as were strange to them. We gave them a quarter of a glass of whiskey which they appeared to be very fond of, sucked the bottle after it was out and soon began to be troublesome—one, the second chief, assuming drunkenness as a cloak for his rascally intentions. I went with those chiefs (which left the boat with great reluctance) to shore with a view to reconciling those men to us. As soon as I landed the pirogue three of their young men seized the cable of the pirogue, the chief's soldier [*Sioux "soldiers" were members of a warrior society who performed "police" duties*] hugged the mast, and the second chief was very insolent both in words and gestures, declaring I should not go on, stating he had not received presents sufficient from us. His gestures were of such a personal nature I felt myself compelled to draw my sword. At this motion Capt. Lewis ordered all under arms in the boat. Those with me also showed a disposition to defend themselves and me. The grand chief then took hold of the rope and ordered the young warriors away. I felt myself warm and spoke in very positive terms.

Most of the warriors appeared to have their bows strung and took out their arrows from their quivers. As I was not permitted to return, I sent all the men except 2 interpreters to the boat. The pirogue soon returned with about 12 of our determined men ready for any event. This movement caused a number of the Indians to withdraw at a distance. Their treatment to me was very rough and I think justified roughness on my part. They all left my pirogue and counseled with themselves. The result I could not learn and nearly all went off. After remaining in this situation some time I offered my hand to the first and second chiefs, who refused to receive it. I turned off and went with my men on board the pirogue. I had not progressed more than 10 paces before the first chief, third and second brave men waded in after me. I took them in and went on board.

We proceeded on about one mile and anchored out off a willow island, placed a guard on shore to protect the cooks and a guard in the boat. Fastened the pirogues to the boat. I call this island Bad-Humored Island as we were in a bad humor.

September 26, 1804, Wednesday [Clark]
Set out early, proceeded on and came to by the wish of the chiefs to let their squaws and boys see the boat and suffer them to treat us well. A great number of men, women and children on the banks viewing us. These people show great anxiety. They appear sprightly, generally ill looking and not well made, their legs and arms small generally. They grease and black themselves with coal when they dress, make use of a hawk's feathers about their heads. The men [*wear*] a robe and each a polecat's skin, to hold their *bois roule* [*a mixture of wood bark and tobacco*] for smoking. Fond of dress and show. Badly armed with fusils [*these were a kind of musket*]. The squaws are cheerful, fine looking women, not handsome, high cheeks, dressed in skins, a petticoat and robe which folds back over their shoulder, with long wool. They do all the laborious work and I may say are perfect slaves to the men, as all squaws of nations much at war are, or where the women are more numerous than the men. After coming to, Capt. Lewis and five men went on shore with the chiefs, who appeared disposed to make up and be friendly. After Captain Lewis had been on shore about three hours I became uneasy for fear of some deception and sent a Sergeant to see him and know his treatment, which he reported was friendly. They were preparing for a dance this evening.

They made frequent solicitation for us to remain one night only and let them show their good disposition toward us. We determined to remain. After the return of Capt. Lewis, I went on shore. On landing I was received on an elegant painted buffalo robe and taken to the village by six men and was not permitted to touch the ground until I was put down in the grand council house on a white dressed robe. I saw several Omaha prisoners and spoke to the chiefs. It was necessary to give those prisoners up and become good friends with the Omahas if they wished to follow the advice of their Great Father. I was in several lodges, neatly formed as before mentioned with the *Bois brulé* [*i.e., the Yankton Sioux*] tribe. I was met by about 10 well-dressed young men who took me up in a robe, highly decorated, and set me down by the side of their chief on a dressed robe in a large council house. This house formed a three-quarter circle of skins, well dressed and sewn together. Under this shelter about 70 men sat, forming a circle in front of the chiefs. A place of six feet diameter was clear and the pipe of peace raised on sticks, under which there was swan's down scattered; on each side of the circle two pipes, the flags of Spain and the flag we gave them in front of the grand chief. A large fire was near in which provisions were cooking, in the center about 400 pounds of excellent buffalo beef as a present for us.

Soon after they set me down, the men went for Capt. Lewis, brought him in the same way and placed him also by the chief. In a few minutes an old man rose and spoke, approving what we had done and informing us of their situation, requesting us to take pity on them, which was answered. The great chief then rose with great state to the same purpose as far as we could learn and then with great solemnity took up the pipe of peace, and after pointing it to the heavens, the four quarters of the globe, and the earth, he made some dissertation, lit it, and presented the stem to us to smoke. When the principal chief spoke with the pipe of peace he took in one hand some of the most delicate parts of the dog which was prepared for the feast and made a sacrifice to the flag. After a smoke had taken place, and a short harangue to his people, we were requested to take the meal. [*It included, according to notes added in Nicholas Biddle's hand but whose ultimate source was probably Clark, dog meat, which was a great delicacy to the Sioux, pemmican, and ground potatoes, i.e., a small starchy tuber also known as potato bean. Pemmican was buffalo meat dried and pounded, then mixed with grease and sometimes berries; it lasted almost indefinitely and was a staple food for Plains tribes, especially when traveling.*] We smoked for an hour until dark and all was cleared away. A large fire made in the center, about 10 musicians playing on tambourines, long sticks with deer and goats' hooves tied so as to make a jingling noise and many others of a similar kind. Those men began to sing and beat on the tambourines, the women came forward highly decorated in their way, with the scalps and trophies of war of their father, husband, brothers or near connection and proceeded to dance the war dance, which they did with great cheerfulness until 12 o'clock, when we informed the chiefs that they were fatigued. [*In the field notes that Moulton prints, Clark mentions at this point that the chiefs offered them women, "which we did not accept."*] They then retired and we, accompanied by four chiefs, returned to our boat. They stayed with us all night. Those people have some brave men which they make use of as soldiers.

Those men attend to the police of the village, correct all errors. I saw one of them today whip two squaws who appeared to have fallen out. When he approached, all about appeared to flee with great terror. At night they keep two, three, four, or five men at different distances walking around camp singing the occurrences of the night.

All the men on board 100 paces from shore. Wind from the S.E. moderate. One man very sick on board with a dangerous abscess on his hip. All in spirits this evening.

In this tribe I saw 25 squaws and boys taken 13 days ago in a battle with the Omahas. In this battle they destroyed 40 lodges, killed 75 men, and some boys and children, and took 48 prisoners, women and boys, which they promised both Capt. Lewis and myself shall be delivered up to Mr. Dorion at the *Bois brulé* tribe. Those are a wretched and dejected looking people. The squaws appear low and coarse, but this is an unfavorable time to judge of them.

We gave our Omaha interpreter [*presumably Pierre Cruzatte, whose mother was an Omaha*] some few articles to give those squaws in his name, such as awls, needles, etc.

I saw and ate pemmican, the dog, ground potato made into a kind of hominy, which I thought but little inferior [*presumably to actual hominy*]. I also saw a spoon made of a horn of an animal of the sheep kind. The spoon will hold two quarts. [*This was the bighorn sheep; the corps would see their first one the following spring.*]

September 27, 1804, Thursday
I rose early after a bad night's sleep, found the chiefs all up, and the bank as usual lined with spectators. We gave the two great chiefs a blanket apiece, or rather they took off agreeable with their custom the one they lay on, and each one a peck of corn. After breakfast Capt. Lewis and the chiefs went on shore, as a very large part of their nation was coming in, the disposition of whom I did not know. One of us being sufficient on shore, I wrote a letter to Mr. Pierre Dorion and prepared a medal and some commissions and sent to Capt. Lewis. At two o'clock Capt. Lewis returned with 4 chiefs and a brave man named *War cha pa* or *On His Guard*. When the friends of those people die they run arrows through their flesh above and below their elbows as a testimony of their grief.

After staying about half an hour, I went with them on shore. Those men left the boat with reluctance. I went first to the second chief's lodge, where a crowd came around. After speaking on various subjects I went to a principal man's lodge, from there to the grand chief's lodge. After a few minutes he invited me to a lodge within the circle in which I stayed with all their principal men until the dance began, which was similar to the one of last night performed by their women, with poles on which scalps of their enemies were hung. Some had the guns, spears and war implements of their husbands in their hands.

Capt. Lewis came on shore and we continued until we were sleepy and returned to our boat. The second chief and one principal man accompanied us, those two Indians accompanied me on board in the small pirogue, Capt. Lewis with a guard still on shore. The man who steered not being much accustomed to steer passed the bow of the boat and the pirogue came broadside against the cable and broke it, which obliged me to order in a loud voice all hands up and at their oars. My peremptory order to the men and the bustle of their getting to their oars alarmed the chiefs, together with the appearance of the men on shore as the boat turned. The chief hollered and alarmed the camp or town, informing them that the Omahas were about to attack. In about 10 minutes the bank was lined with armed men, the first chief at their head. About 200 men appeared and after about a half hour returned, all but about 60 men who continued on the bank all night. The chiefs continued all night with us. This alarm I as well as Capt. Lewis considered as the signal of their intentions, which was to stop our proceeding on our journey and if possible to rob us. We were on our guard all night. The misfortune of the loss of our anchor obliged us to lay under a falling bank much exposed to the accomplishment of their hostile intentions. Pierre Cruzatte, our bowman, who could speak Omaha, informed us in the night that the Omaha prisoners had informed him we were to be stopped. We show as little signs of a knowledge of their intentions as possible. All prepared on board for anything which might happen, we kept a strong guard all night in the boat. No sleep.

The Sioux almost certainly did intend to stop them, as they had stopped traders for several years from passing beyond them, wanting to control the trade on the upper Missouri and make themselves the middlemen for all tribes further on. Lewis and Clark did pass, of course, but the Sioux became such a problem subsequently that a new trade route to the Rockies had to be developed, along the valley of the Platte.

September 28, 1804, Friday [Clark]

Made many attempts in different ways to find our anchor but could not, the sand had covered it. From the misfortune of last night our boat was laying at shore in a very unfavorable situation. After finding that the anchor could not be found we determined to proceed on and with great difficulty got the chiefs out of our boat. When we were about setting out the class called the soldiers took possession of the cable. The first chief was still on board and intended to go a short distance up with us. I told him the men of his nation had set on the cable. He went out and told Capt. Lewis, who was at the bow, the men who set on the rope were soldiers and wanted tobacco. Capt. Lewis said he would not agree to be forced into anything. The second chief demanded a flag and tobacco, which we refused to give, stating proper reasons to them for it. After much difficulty, which had nearly reduced us by necessity to hostilities, I threw a carrot of tobacco to the first chief, took the port fire [*a slow burning fuse, used to fire the cannon*] from the gunner. Spoke so as to touch his pride. The chief gave the tobacco to his soldiers and he jerked the rope from them and handed it to the bowsman. We then set out under a breeze from the S.E. About two miles up we observed the third chief on shore beckoning to us. We took him on board. He informed us the rope was held by the order of the second chief, who was a double-spoken man. Soon after we saw a man coming full speed through the plains, left his horse and proceeded across a sandbar near the shore. We took him on board and observed that he was the son of the chief we had on board. We sent by him a talk to the nation, stating the cause of our hoisting the red flag under the white. If they were for peace stay at home and do as we had directed them. If they were for war or were determined to stop us, we were ready to defend ourselves. We halted one hour and a half on the starboard side and made a substitute of stones for an anchor, refreshed our men, and proceeded on about two miles higher up and came to a very small sandbar in the middle of the river and stayed all night. I am very unwell for want of sleep. Determined to sleep tonight if possible. The men cooked and we rested well.

September 29, 1804, Saturday [Clark]

Set out early. Some bad sandbars, proceeded on. At nine o'clock we observed the second chief and two principal men, one man and a squaw on shore. They wished to go up with us as far as the other part of their band, which they said was on the river ahead not far distant. We refused, stating very sufficient reasons and were plain with them on the subject. They were not pleased, observed that they would walk on shore to the place we intended to camp tonight. We observed it was not our wish that they should, for if they did we could not take them or any other Tetons on board except the one we had now with us who might go on shore whenever he pleased. They proceeded on. The chief on board asked for a twist of tobacco for those men. We gave him half a twist, and sent one by them for that part of their band which we did not see, and continued on. Saw great numbers of elk at the mouth of a small creek called No Timber Creek, as no timber appeared to be on it. Above the mouth of this creek the Pawnees had a village five years ago. The second chief came on the sandbar and requested we would put him across the river. I sent a pirogue and crossed him and one man to the starboard side and proceeded on. Came to on a sandbar about a half mile from the main shore and put on it two sentinels. Continued all night at anchor. We substituted large stones for anchors in place of the one we lost. All in high spirits.

September 30, 1804, Sunday [Clark]
Set out this morning early. Had not proceeded on far before we discovered an Indian running after us. He came up with us at seven o'clock and requested to come on board and go up to the Arikaras. We refused to take any of that band on board. If he chose to proceed on shore it was very well. Soon after I discovered on the hills at a great distance great numbers of Indians which appeared to be making to the river above us. We proceeded on under a double-reefed sail, and some rain. At nine o'clock observed a large band of Indians, the same I had before seen on the hills, encamping on the bank of the larboard side. We came to on a sandbar, breakfasted, and proceeded on and cast the anchor opposite their lodges at about 100 yards distant, and informed the Indians, which we found to be a part of the band we had before seen, that we took them by the hand and sent to each chief a carrot of tobacco. As we had been treated badly by some of the band below, after staying two days for them, we could not delay any time, and referred them to Mr. Dorion for a full account of us and to hear our talk, sent by him to the Tetons. Those were very solicitous for us to land and eat with them, that they were friendly, etc. We apologized and proceeded on, sent the pirogue to shore above with the tobacco and delivered it to a soldier of the

chief with us. Several of them ran up the river; the chief on board threw them out a small twist of tobacco and told them to go back and open their ears. They received the tobacco and returned to their lodges. We saw great numbers of white gulls. This day is cloudy and rainy. Refreshed the men with a glass of whiskey after breakfast.

We saw about six miles above two Indians who came to the bank and looked at us about half an hour and went over the hills to the S.W. We proceeded on under a very stiff breeze from the S.E. The stern of the boat got fast on a log and the boat turned and was very near filling before we got her righted, the waves being very high. The chief on board was so frightened at the motion of the boat, which in its rocking caused several loose articles to fall on the deck from the lockers, he ran off and hid himself. We landed. He got his gun and informed us he wished to return, that all things were clear for us to go on, we would not see any more Tetons, etc. We repeated to him what had been said before and advised him to keep his men away, gave him a blanket, a knife and some tobacco, smoked a pipe and he set out. We also set sail and came to at a sandbar, and camped, a very cold evening, all on our guard.

October 1, 1804, Monday [Clark]
The wind blew hard all last night from the S.E. Very cold. Set out early. The wind still hard. Passed a large island in the middle of the river. Opposite the lower point of this island the Arikaras formerly lived in a large town on the larboard side. Above the head of the island about two miles we passed the River Cheyenne (or Dog River). This river comes in from the S.W. and is about 400 yards wide, the current appears gentle, throwing out but little sand, and appears to throw out but little water. The head of this river is not known, a part of the nation of Dog Indians [*Cheyenne; Clark mistakenly believed that the word was a corruption of the French word* chien, *for dog; it was in fact a Sioux word*] who live up this river. The precise distance I can't learn. Above the mouth of this river the sandbars are thick and the water shoal, the river still very wide and falling a little. We are obliged to haul the boat over a sandbar, after making several attempts to pass. The wind so hard we came to and stayed three hours. After it slackened a little we proceeded on round a bend. The wind in the upper part of the day ahead [*i.e., against them*]. Passed a creek on the larboard side which we call the Sentinel. This part of the river has but little timber, the hills not so high. The sandbars more numerous, and

river more than one mile wide, including the sandbars. Passed a small creek above the latter which we call Lookout Creek. Continued on with the wind immediately ahead, and came to on a large sandbar in the middle of the river. We saw a man opposite to our camp on the larboard side which we discovered to be a Frenchman. Among the willows we observed a house. We called to them to come over. A boy came in a canoe and informed us that two French-men were at the house with goods to trade with the Sioux, which he expected down from the Arikaras every day. Several large parties of Sioux set out from the Arikaras for this place to trade with these men.

This Mr. Jean Vallé informs us that he wintered last winter 300 leagues up the Cheyenne River under the Black Mountains. [*These would be the Black Hills in South Dakota; it was also common then to call the Front Range of the Rockies in Wyoming, now known as the Laramie Range, the Black Mountains, a term for them which persisted to the 1840s, when the Oregon Trail began to open up.*] He informs us that this river is very rapid and difficult even for pirogues to ascend and when rising the swells are very high. One hundred leagues up it forks, one fork comes from the S., the other, at 40 leagues above the forks, enters the Black Mountains. The coun-try from the Missouri to the Black Mountains is much like the country on the Missouri, less timber and a greater proportion of cedar.

The Black Mountains, he says, are very high, and some part of them have snow on them in the summer. Great quantities of pine grow on the mountains. A great noise is heard frequently on those mountains. No bea-ver on the Cheyenne River. On the mountains great numbers of goat and a kind of animal with large circular horns. This animal is nearly the size of a small elk. White bear are also plentiful [*the white bear was the grizzly, so-called for the silver hairs on older males*]. The Cheyenne Indians inhabit this river principally, and steal horses from the Spanish settlements to the S.W. This excursion they make in one month. The bottoms and sides of the River Cheyenne are coarse gravel. This Frenchman gives an account of a white-booted turkey, an inhabitant of the Black Mountains [*Moulton spec-ulates that this is the sharp-tailed grouse; Biddle calls it a "prairie cock"*].

We proceeded now from the mouth of this river eleven miles and camped on a sandbar in the river opposite to a trading house. Very windy and cold.

October 2, 1804, Tuesday [Clark]
A violent wind all night from the S.E. Slackened a little and we proceeded

on. Mr. Jean Vallé came on board and proceeded on two miles with us. A very cold morning. Some black clouds flying. The sentinel heard a shot over the hills to the larboard side during the time we were dining on a large sandbar. The after part of this day is pleasant. At two o'clock opposite a wood on the larboard side we observed some Indians on a hill on the starboard side. One came down to the river opposite to us and fired off his gun and beckoned to us to come to. We paid no attention to him. He followed on some distance. We spoke a few words to him; he wished us to go ashore and to his camp, which was over the hill, and consisted of 20 lodges. We excused ourselves, advised him to go and hear our talk of Mr. Dorion. He inquired for traders. We informed him one was in the next bend below and parted. He returned and we proceeded on, passed a large island on the starboard side. Here we expected the Tetons would attempt to stop us and under that idea we prepared ourselves for action, which we expected every moment. Opposite this island on the larboard side a small creek comes in. This island we called the island of Caution. We took in some wood on a favorable situation where we could defend our men on shore and camped on a sandbar half a mile from the main shore. The wind changed to the N.W. and rose very high and cold, which continued. The current of the Missouri is less rapid and contains much less sediment of the same color.

October 3, 1804, Wednesday [Clark]
The N.W. wind blew very hard all night with some rain. A cold morning. We set out at seven o'clock. At 12 o'clock landed on a bare larboard side. Examined the pirogues and forecastle of the boat to see if the mice had done any damage. Several bags cut by them, corn scattered, etc. Some of our clothes also spoiled by them, and papers. At one o'clock an Indian came to the bank starboard side with a turkey on his back. Four others soon joined him. We attempted several channels and could not find water to ascend. Landed on a sandbar and concluded to stay all night and send out and hunt a channel. Some rain this afternoon. Saw brant and white gulls flying southerly in large flocks.

October 4, 1804, Thursday [Clark]
The wind blew all night from the N.W. Some rain. We were obliged to drop down three miles to get a channel sufficiently deep to pass up. Several Indians on the shore, viewing us, called to us to land. One of them gave three yells and skipped a ball [*i.e., skipped a musket ball across the water*] before us.

We paid no attention to him, proceeded on and came to on the larboard side to breakfast. One of those Indians swam across to us, begged for powder. We gave him a piece of tobacco and set him over on a sandbar and set out, the wind hard ahead. Passed an island in the middle of the river about 3 miles in length we call Goodhope Island. At four miles passed a creek on the larboard side about 12 yards wide. Capt. Lewis and three men walked on shore and crossed over to an island situated on the starboard side of the current and near the center of the river. This island is about one and a half miles long and nearly half as wide. In the center of this island was an old village of the Arikaras called *La hoo catt*. It was circular and walled, containing 17 lodges, and it appears to have been deserted about five years. The island contains but little timber. We camped on the sandbar making from this island. The day very cool.

October 5, 1804, Friday [Clark]
Frost this morning. We set out early and proceeded on. Passed a small creek on the larboard side. At seven o'clock heard some yells, proceeded on. Saw three Indians of the Teton band, they called to us to come on shore, begged some tobacco. We answered them as usual and proceeded on. Passed a creek on the starboard side. At three miles above the mouth we saw one white brant [*probably a snow goose*] in a gang of about 30, the others all dark as usual. A description of this kind of goose or brant shall be given hereafter. Saw a gang of goats swimming across the river, out of which we killed four. They were not fat. In the evening passed a small island situated close to the larboard side. At the head of this island a large creek comes in on the larboard side. Saw white brants. We call this creek White Brant Creek. I walked on the island, found it covered with wild rye. I shot a buck, saw a large gang of goats on the hills opposite. One buck killed, also a prairie wolf this evening. The high land not so high as below, river about the same width, the sandbars as numerous, the earth black and many of the bluffs have the appearance of being on fire. We came to and camped on a mud bar making from the starboard side. The evening is calm and pleasant. Refreshed the men with a glass of whiskey.

October 6, 1804, Saturday [Clark]
A cool morning, wind from the north. Set out early, passed a willow island situated near the starboard shore at the upper point of some timber on the

starboard side. Many large round stones near the middle of the river; they appear to have been washed from the hills. Passed a village of about 80 neat lodges covered with earth and picketed around. Those lodges are spacious, of an octagon form, as close together as they can possibly be placed and appear to have been inhabited last spring. From the canoes of skins, mats, buckets found in the lodges, we are of the opinion they were the Arikaras. We found squashes of three different kinds growing in the village. One of our men killed an elk close by this village. I saw two wolves in pursuit of another, which appeared to be wounded and nearly tired. We proceeded on, found the river shoal. We made several attempts to find the main channel between the sandbars and were obliged at length to drag the boat over [a sandbar] to save a league which we must return to get into the deepest channel. We have been obliged to hunt a channel for some time past, the river being divided in many places into a great number of channels. Saw geese, swans, brants and ducks of different kinds on the sandbars today. Capt. Lewis walked on shore, saw great numbers of prairie hens. I observe but few gulls or plover in this part of the river. The *corvos* or magpies are very common in this quarter.

We camped on a large sandbar off the mouth of Beaver or Otter Creek on the starboard side. This creek is about 22 yards wide at the mouth and contains a greater proportion of water than common for creeks of its size.

October 7, 1804, Sunday [Clark]
A cloudy morning. Some little rain, frost last night. We set out early, proceeded on two miles to the mouth of a river on the larboard side and had breakfast. This river when full is 90 yards wide. The water is at this time confined within 20 yards, the current appears gentle. This river throws out but little sand. At the mouth of this river we saw the tracks of white bear, which are very large. I walked up this river a mile. Below the mouth of this river are the remains of an Arikara village or wintering camp, fortified in a circular form of about 60 lodges, built in the same form as those passed yesterday. This camp appears to have been inhabited last winter. Many of their willow and straw mats, baskets and buffalo skin canoes remain entire within the camp. The Arikaras call this river *Sur-war-kar-na* or Park [*it is now known as the Moreau*].

From this river we proceeded on under a gentle breeze from the S.W. At 10 o'clock we saw two Indians on the starboard side. They asked for something to eat and informed us they were part of the Medicine Buffalo lodge on their way to the Arikaras. Passed a willow island in a bend to the starboard side. At five miles passed a willow island on the starboard side. Wind hard from the south. In the evening I walked on an island near the middle of the river called Grouse Island. One of the men killed a she-badger, another man killed a blacktail deer, the largest doe I ever saw (black under her breast). This island is nearly one and a quarter miles square, no timber, high and covered with grass, wild rye, and contains a great number of grouse. We proceeded on a short distance above the island and camped on the starboard side. A fine evening.

October 8, 1804, Monday [Clark]

A cool morning. Set out early, the wind from the N.W. Proceeded on, passed the mouth of a small creek on the larboard side about two and a half miles above Grouse Island. Passed a willow island which divides the current equally. Passed the mouth of a river called by the Arikaras *We tar hoo [now the Grand River]* on the larboard side. This river is 120 yards wide, the water of which at this time is confined within 20 yards, discharging but a small quantity, throwing out mud with a small proportion of sand. Great quantities of the red berries resembling currants are on the river in every bend. Proceeded on, passed a small river of 25 yards wide called Beaver Dam River *[now Oak Creek; they are still in South Dakota]*. This river is entirely choked up with mud, with a stream of one inch in diameter passing through, discharging no sand. At one mile passed the lower point of an island close on the larboard side. Two of our men discovered the Arikara village about the center of the island on the larboard side on the main shore. This island is about three miles long, separated from the larboard side *[of the Missouri]* by a channel of about 60 yards wide, very deep. The island is covered with fields where those people raise their corn, tobacco, beans, etc. Great numbers of them came on the island to see us pass. We passed above the head of the island and Capt. Lewis with two interpreters and two men went to the village. I formed a camp of the French and the guard on shore, with one sentinel on board of the boat at anchor. A pleasant evening. All things arranged both for peace or war. This village is situated about the center of a large island near the larboard side and near the foot of some high, bald, uneven hills. Several Frenchmen came up with Capt. Lewis in a pirogue, one of which is a Mr. Gravelines, a man well versed in the language of this nation, and gave us some information relative to the country, nation, etc.

October 9, 1804, Tuesday [Clark]
A windy rainy night, and cold, so much so we could not speak with the Indians today. The three great chiefs and many others came to see us today. We gave them some tobacco and informed them we would speak tomorrow. The day continued cold and windy, some rain. Sorry canoes of skins passed down from the two villages a short distance above, and many came to view us all day, much astonished at my black servant, who did not lose the opportunity of displaying his powers, strength, etc. This nation never saw a black man before.

Several hunters came in with loads of meat. I observed several canoes made of a single buffalo skin with three squaws cross the river today in waves as high as I ever saw them on this river, quite composed. I have a slight pleurisy this evening, very cold.

The buffalo boats were used wherever there were buffalo to ferry people and goods across rivers; they could be easily made in a day on a framework of sticks, usually willow sticks. Biddle has a note on York that is worth quoting: "By way of amusement he told them that he had once been a wild animal, and caught and tamed by his master; and to convince them showed them feats of strength which added to his looks made him more terrible than we wished him to be."

October 10, 1804, Wednesday [Clark]
A fine morning. Wind from the S.E. At about 11 o'clock the wind shifted to the N.W. We prepare all things ready to speak to the Indians. Mr. Tabeau and Mr. Gravelines came to breakfast with us. The chiefs came from the lower town, but none from the two upper towns, which are the largest. We continue to delay and wait for them. At 12 o'clock dispatched Gravelines to invite them to come down. We have every reason to believe that a jealousy exists between the villages for fear of our making the first chief from the lower village. At one o'clock the chiefs all assembled and after some little ceremony the council commenced. We informed them what we had told the others before, i.e. the Otos and Sioux. Made three chiefs, one for each village. Gave them presents.

After the council was over we shot the air gun, which astonished them much. They then departed and we rested secure all night.

Those Indians were much astonished at my servant. They never saw a black man before, all flocked around him and examined him from top to toe. He carried on the joke and made himself more terrible than we wished him to do. Those Indians were not fond of spirits, liquor of any kind.

October 11, 1804, Thursday [Clark]

A fine morning, the wind from the S.E. At 11 o'clock we met the grand chief in council and he made a short speech thanking us for what we had given him and his nation, promising to attend to the counsel we had given him and informed us the road was open and no one dare shut it, and we might depart at pleasure. At one o'clock we set out for the upper villages three miles distant, the grand chief and nephew on board, proceeded on. At one mile took in the second chief and came to off the second village, separated from the third by a creek. After arranging all matters we walked up with the second chief to his village and sat talking on various subjects until late. We also visited the upper or third village, each of which gave us something to eat in their way; and a few bushels of corn, beans, etc. After being treated by every civility by those people, who are both poor and dirty, we returned to our boat at about 10 o'clock p.m., informing them before we departed that we would speak to them tomorrow at their separate villages. Those people gave us to eat bread made of corn and beans, also corn and beans boiled, a large bean, which they rob from the mice of the prairie, which is rich and very nourishing, also squashes. All tranquility.

October 12, 1804, Friday [Clark]

I rose early. After breakfast we joined the Indians who were waiting on the bank for us to come out and go and counsel. We accordingly joined them and went to the house of the second chief, Pocasse, where there were many chiefs and warriors and where they made us a present of about seven bushels of corn, a pair of leggings, a twist of their tobacco and seeds of two kinds of tobacco. We sat some time before the council commenced. This man spoke at some length declaring his disposition to believe and pursue our counsels, his intention of going to visit his Great Father [*the grand chief did make the trip to Washington but died there; his failure to return adversely affected Arikara relations with whites for years to come*]. He acknowledged the satisfaction in receiving the presents, etc., but raising a doubt as to the safety of passing the nations below, particularly the Sioux. He requested us to take a chief of their nation and make a good peace with the Mandans and nations above. After answering those parts of the second chief's speech which required it, which appeared to give general satisfaction, we went to the village of the third chief and as usual some ceremony took place before he could speak to us on the great subject. This chief spoke very much in the style on nearly the same subjects as the other chief, who sat by his side, but more sincerely and pleasantly. He presented us with about 10 bushels of corn, some beans and squashes, all of which we accepted with much pleasure. After we had answered his speech and given them some account of the magnitude and power of our country, which pleased and astonished them very much, we returned to our boat. The chiefs accompanied us on board, we gave them some sugar, a little salt, and a sun glass, and set two on shore; and the third proceeded on with us to the Mandans. At two o'clock we set out, the inhabitants of the two villages viewing us from the banks. We proceeded on about 9 and a half miles and camped on the starboard side. Some woods passed, the evening clear and pleasant, cool.

This nation is made up of 10 different tribes of the Pawnees [*they belonged, that is, to the same language group, the Caddoan*], who had formerly been separate, but by commotion and war with their neighbors have become reduced and compelled to come together for protection [*it was in fact smallpox, not war, which led to the depletion of their numbers*]. The corruption of the language of those different tribes has so reduced the language that the different villages do not understand all the words of the others. Those people are dirty, kind, poor, and possess extravagant national pride. Not beggarly, they receive what is given with great pleasure, live in warm houses, large and built in an octagon form, forming a cone at the top which is left open for the smoke to pass. Those houses are generally 30 or 40 feet in diameter, covered with earth on poles, with willows and grass to prevent the earth passing through.

Those people express an inclination to be at peace with all nations. The Sioux, who trade the goods which they get of the British traders for their corn, have great influence over the Arikaras, poison their minds and keep them in perpetual dread.

I saw some of the Cheyenne Indians, also a man of a nation under the *Court Nue* [*he means the Black Hills*]. This nation is at war with the Crow Indians and have three children prisoners.

A curious custom with the Sioux as well as the Arikaras is to give handsome squaws to those whom they wish to show some acknowledgements to. The Sioux we got clear of without taking their squaws. They followed us with squaws two days. The Arikaras we put off during the time we were at the towns, but two handsome young squaws were sent by a man to follow us. They came up this evening and persisted in their civilities.

The dress of the men of this nation is simply a pair of moccasins, leggings, flap in front and a buffalo robe, with their hair, arms and ears decorated.

The women wore moccasins, leggings fringed, and a shirt of goat skins, some with sleeves. This garment is long and generally white and fringed, tied at the waist, with a robe, in summer without hair [*i.e., in summer they wear a robe made out of hairless skin*].

October 13, 1804, Saturday [Clark]
One man, J. Newman, confined for mutinous expression. Set out early, proceeded on, passed a camp of Sioux on the starboard side. Those people only viewed us and did not speak one word. The visitors of last evening, all except one, returned, which is the brother of the chief we have on board.

Passed a creek on the starboard side 13 yards wide at 18 miles above the town heading in some ponds a short distance to the N.E. We call it Stone Idol Creek. Passed a large willow and sand island above the mouth of the last creek. At 21 miles above the village passed a creek about 15 yards wide on the larboard side we call after second chief Pocasse. Nearly opposite this creek, a few miles from the river on the starboard side, two stones resembling human persons and one resembling a dog are situated in the open prairie. To those stones the Arikaras pay great reverence, make offerings whenever they pass. Those people have a curious tradition of those stones. One was a man in love, one a girl whose parents would not let them marry. The man, as is customary, went off to mourn, the female followed. The dog went to mourn with them. All turned to stone gradually, commencing at the feet. Those people fed on grapes until they turned and the woman has a bunch of grapes yet in her hand. On the river near the place those are said to be situated we observed a greater quantity of fine grapes than I ever saw at one place.

The river about the island on which the lower Arikara village is situated is narrow and contains a greater proportion of timber than below. The bottoms on both sides are covered with timber, the uplands naked, the current gentle and sandbars confined to the points generally.

We proceeded on under a fine breeze from the S.E. and camped late at the upper part of some woods on the larboard side. Cold and some rain this evening. We sent out hunters, killed one deer.

We tried the prisoner Newman this night by nine of his peers. They did sentence him 75 lashes and disbanded the party. [*He was, in other words, discharged and would be sent back in the spring. A record of the court martial follows this entry. Newman was charged with "having uttered repeated expressions of a highly criminal and mutinous nature, the same having a tendency not only to destroy every principle of military discipline, but also to alienate the affections of the individuals composing this Detachment to their officers, and disaffect them to the service for which they have been so sacredly and solemnly engaged." He was found guilty, stood the 75 lashes, and was indeed returned to St. Louis the following spring, even though he worked hard that winter to redeem himself. He eventually became a trapper, and the Yankton Sioux killed him in 1838.*]

October 14, 1804, Sunday [Clark]
Some rain last night, all wet and cold. We set out early, the rain continued all day. We passed a creek on the larboard side 15 yards wide; this creek we called after the third chief *Piaheto*, or Eagle's Feather. At one o'clock we halted on a sandbar and after dinner executed the sentence of the Court Martial so far as giving the corporal punishment, and proceeded on a few miles, the wind ahead from the N.E. Camped in a cove of the bank on the starboard side. Immediately opposite our camp on the larboard side I observed an ancient fortification, the walls of which appear to be 8 or 10 feet high. The evening wet and disagreeable, the river something wider, more timber on its banks.

The punishment of this day alarmed the Indian chief very much. He cried aloud (or affected to cry). I explained the cause of the punishment and the necessity. He thought examples were also necessary and he himself had made them by death. His nation never whipped even their children, from their birth.

October 15, 1804, Monday [Clark]
Rained all last night. We set out early and proceeded on. At three miles passed an Indian camp on the starboard side. We halted above and about 30 of the Indians came over in their canoes of skins. We ate with them, they

SEPTEMBER 23 TO NOVEMBER 6, 1804 121

gave us meat, in return we gave fishhooks and some beads. About a mile higher we came to on the larboard side at a camp of Arikaras of about eight lodges. We also ate and they gave some meat. We proceeded on. Saw numbers of Indians on both sides passing a creek. Saw many curious hills, high and much the resemblance of a house with a hipped roof. At 12 o'clock it cleared away and the evening was pleasant, wind from the N.E. At sunset we arrived at a camp of Arikaras of 10 lodges on the starboard side. We came to and camped near them. Capt. Lewis and myself went with the chief who accompanied us to the huts of several of the men, all of whom smoked and gave us something to eat, also some meat to take away. Those people were kind and appeared to be much pleased at the attention paid them.

Those people are much pleased with my black servant. Their women very fond of caressing our men.

October 16, 1804, Tuesday [Clark]

Some rain this morning. Two young squaws very anxious to accompany us. Set out with our chief on board by name *Ar ke tar na Shar* or Chief of the Town. A little above our camp on the larboard side passed a circular work where the Cheyenne formerly lived. A short distance above passed a creek which we call Cheyenne Creek, above is a willow island situated near the larboard side, with a large sandbar above and on both sides. Passed a creek above the island on the larboard side called *So-harch* (or Girls') Creek. At two miles higher passed a creek on the larboard side called *Charpart* (or Women's) Creek. Passed an island situated in a bend to the starboard side. This island is about one and a half miles long, covered with timber such as cottonwood. Opposite the lower point a creek comes in on the starboard side called by the Indians *Kee tooch Sar kar nar* (or Place of Beaver). Above the island a small river about 35 yards wide comes in called *War re con ne* or Elk Shed Their Horns. The island is called Carp Island by Evans [*Lewis and Clark had several maps with them; the one made by John Thomas Evans, a fur trader who got as far as the Mandan villages in 1796, was the most detailed for this part of the river and the most useful*]. Wind hard from the N.W. Saw great numbers of goats on the starboard shore. Proceeded on. Capt. Lewis and the Indian chief walked on shore. Soon after, I discovered great numbers of goats in the river and Indians on the shore on each side. As I approached or got nearer I discovered boys in the water killing the goats with sticks and hauling them to shore. Those on the banks shot them with arrows and as they approached the shore would turn them back. Of this gang of goats I counted 58 they had killed on the shore. One of our hunters out with Capt. Lewis killed three goats. We passed the camp on the starboard side and proceeded a half mile and camped on the larboard side. Many Indians came to the boat to see. Some came across late at night. As they approached they hollered and sang. After staying a short time two went for some meat and returned in a short time with fresh and dried buffalo, also goat. Those Indians stayed all night. They sang and were very merry the great part of the night.

October 17, 1804, Wednesday [Clark]
Set out early. A fine morning, the wind from the N.W. After breakfast I walked on shore with the Indian chief and interpreters. Saw buffalo, elk, and great numbers of goats in large gangs. (I am told by Mr. G[*ravelines*] that those animals winter in the Black Mountains and this is about the season they cross from the east of the Missouri to go to that mountain; they return in the spring and pass the Missouri in great numbers.) This chief tells me of a number of their traditions about turtles, snakes, and the power of a particular rock or cave on the next river which informs them of everything. None of those do I think worthwhile mentioning. The wind so hard ahead the boats could not move after 10 o'clock. Capt. Lewis took the altitude of the sun. I killed three deer and the hunters with me killed three also. The Indian shot one but could not get it. I scaffolded up the deer [*i.e., Clark raised it on a temporary scaffold to keep it out of reach of wolves and coyotes*] and returned and met the boat after night on the larboard side about six miles above the place we camped last night. One of the men saw a number of snakes. Capt. Lewis saw a large beaver house starboard side. I caught a whippoorwill, small and not common. The leaves are falling fast. The river wide and full of sandbars. Great numbers of very large stones on the sides of the hills and some rock of a brownish color in the larboard bend below this.

Great numbers of goats are flocking down to the starboard side of the river on their way to the Black Mountains where they winter. Those animals return in the Spring in the same way and scatter in different directions.

October 18, 1804, Thursday [Clark]
Set out early, proceeded on. At six miles passed the mouth of Le Boulet (or Cannonball River) about 140 yards wide on the larboard side. This river heads in the Black Mountains. A fine day. Above the mouth of this river great

numbers of stones, perfectly round with fine grit, are in the bluff and on the shore. The river takes its name from those stones, which resemble cannon-balls. The water of this river is confined within 40 yards. We met two French-men in a pirogue descending from hunting. They complained of the Mandans robbing them of four traps, their fur and several other articles. Those men were in the employ of our Arikara interpreter Mr. Gravelines. They turned and followed us.

Saw great numbers of goats on the starboard side coming to the river. Our hunters killed four of them. Some ran back and others crossed and proceeded on their journey to the Black Mountains. Passed a small river called *Che wah* or Fish River on the starboard side. This river is about 28 yards wide and heads to the N.E. Passed a small creek on the larboard side one mile above the last, and camped on a sandbar on the larboard side. Opposite to us we saw a gang of buffalo bulls which we did not think worthwhile to kill. Our hunters killed four goats, six deer, four elk and a pelican and informed us that they saw in one gang 248 elk. I walked on shore in the evening with a view to see some of those remarkable places mentioned by Evans, none of which I could find. The country in this quarter is generally level and fine. Some high short hills, and some ragged ranges of hills at a distance.

The Arikara Indians inform us that they find no blacktail deer as high up as this place. Those we find are of the fallow deer kind. [*Fallow deer are whitetail deer, the common deer of eastern America.*]

The Arikaras are not fond of spiritous liquors, nor do they appear to be fond of receiving any or thankful for it. [*Biddle adds: "they say we are no friends or we would not give them what makes them fools."*]

October 19, 1804, Friday [Clark]
A fine morning. Wind from the S.E. We set out early under a gentle breeze and proceeded on very well. More timber than common on the banks on this part of the river. Passed a large pond on the starboard side. I walked out on the hills and observed great numbers of buffalo feeding on both sides of the river. I counted 52 gangs of buffalo and three of elk at one view. All the runs which come from the high hills, which are generally about one or two miles from the water, are brackish. [*Drinking this water has the same effect as a laxative.*] Near the hills and the sides of the hills and edges of the streams, the mineral salts appear. I saw some remarkable round hills forming a cone

at top, one about 90 feet, one 60, and several others smaller. The Indian chief says that the calumet bird [*golden eagle*] lives in the holes of those hills. The holes form by water washing away some parts in its passage down from the top. Near one of those knolls, on a point of a hill 90 feet above the lower plain, I observed the remains of an old village which had been fortified. The Indian chief with us tells me a party of Mandans lived there. Here first saw ruins of the Mandan nation. We proceeded on and camped on the larboard side opposite the upper of those conical hills.

Our hunters killed four elk, six deer and a pelican. I saw swans in a pond and killed a fat deer in my walk. Saw above 10 wolves. The day is pleasant.

October 20, 1804, Saturday [Clark]
Set out early this morning and proceeded on, the wind from the S.E. After breakfast I walked out on the larboard side to see those remarkable places pointed out by Evans. I saw the old remains of a village on the side of a hill. The chief with us, *Too né*, tells me the Mandans lived in a number of villages on each side of the river and the troublesome Sioux caused them to move about 40 miles higher up, where they remained a few years and moved to the place they now live. Passed a small creek on the starboard side and one on the larboard side. Passed an island covered with willows lying in the middle of the river, no current on the larboard side. Camped on the larboard side above a bluff containing coal of an inferior quality. This bank is immediately above the old village of the Mandans. The country is fine, the high hills at a distance with gradual ascents. I killed three deer. The timber confined to the bottoms as usual; it's much larger than below. Great numbers of buffalo, elk and deer, goats. Our hunters killed 10 deer and a goat today and wounded a white bear. I saw several fresh tracks of those animals which are three times as large as a man's track. The wind hard all day from the N.E. and East, great numbers of buffalo swimming the river.

I observe wolves near all large gangs of buffalo. When the buffalo move those animals follow and feed on those that are killed by accident or those that are too poor or fat to keep up with the gang.

Moulton prints a note by Lewis of this date indicating that Pierre Cruzatte, out hunting, had wounded a white bear, or grizzly, but then ran away in fear at the "formidable appearance" of the animal and left his gun and tomahawk behind. He retrieved them later. This was the corps's first encounter with a grizzly.

October 21, 1804, Sunday [Clark]

A very cold night. Wind hard from the N.E. Some rain in the night which froze up as it fell. At daylight it began to snow and continued all the forepart of the day. Passed just above our camp a small river on the larboard side called by the Indians *Chiss-Cho-tar*. This river is about 38 yards wide containing a good deal of water. Some distance up this river is situated a stone which the Indians have great faith in and say they see painted on the stone all the calamities and good fortune to happen in the nation and parties who visit it. A tree (an oak) which stands alone near this place about two miles off in the open prairie which has withstood the fire they pay great respect to, make holes and tie strings through the skin of their necks and around this tree to make them brave [*this appears to be a version of the sun dance ceremony*]. All this is the information of Too ne, the chief of the Arikaras who accompanied us to the Mandans. At two miles passed the second village of the Mandans, which was in existence at the same time with the first. This village is at the foot of a hill on the starboard side on a beautiful and extensive plain, at this time covered with buffalo. A cloudy afternoon. I killed a fine buffalo. We camped on the larboard side. Very cold ground, covered with snow. One otter killed.

October 22, 1804, Monday [Clark]

Last night at one o'clock I was violently and suddenly attacked with the rheumatism in the neck, which was so violent I could not move. Capt. Lewis applied a hot stone wrapped in flannel, which gave me some temporary ease. We set out early, the morning cold. At seven o'clock we came to at a camp of Teton Sioux on the larboard side. Those people, 12 in number, were naked and had the appearance of war. We have every reason to believe that they are going or have been to steal horses from the Mandans. They tell two stories. We gave them nothing. After taking breakfast proceeded on. My neck is very painful at times. Spasms.

Camped on the larboard side. Passed an island situated on the larboard side at the head of which we passed a bad place and a Mandan village starboard side. The hunters killed a buffalo bull. They say out of about 300 buffalo which they saw, they did not see one cow. Great deal of beaver sign. Several caught every night.

October 23, 1804, Tuesday [Clark]

A cloudy morning, some snow. Set out early. Passed five lodges, which were deserted, the fires yet burning. We suppose those were the Indians who robbed the two French trappers a few days ago. Those two men are now with us going up with a view to get their property from the Indians through us. Cold and cloudy. Camped on the larboard side of the river.

October 24, 1804, Wednesday [Clark]
Set out early. A cloudy day. Some little snow in the morning. I am something better of the rheumatism in my neck. A beautiful country on both sides of the river, the bottoms covered with wood. We have seen no game on the river today, a proof of the Indians hunting in the neighborhood. Passed an island on the starboard side made by the river cutting through a point, by which the river is shortened several miles. On this island we saw one of the grand chiefs of the Mandans, with five lodges, hunting. This chief met the chief of the Arikaras who accompanied us with great cordiality and ceremony. Smoked the pipe and Capt. Lewis with the interpreter went with the chiefs to his lodges at 1 mile distant. After his return we admitted the grand chief and his brother for a few minutes on our boat. Proceeded on a short distance and camped on the starboard side below the old village of the Mandans and Arikaras. Soon after our landing four Mandans came from a camp above. The Arikara's chief went with them to their camp.

October 25, 1804, Thursday [Clark]
A cold morning. Set out early under a gentle breeze from the S.E. by E. Proceeded on, pass the third old village of the Mandans which has been destroyed for many years. This village was situated on an eminence of about 40 feet above the water on the larboard side. Back for several miles is a beautiful plain. At a short distance above this old village on a continuation of the same eminence was situated the Arikara village, which has been evacuated only six years. About three or four miles above the Arikara villages are three old villages of Mandans near together. Here they lived when the Arikaras came for protection. Afterward moved where they now live. Above this village a large and extensive bottom for several miles in which the squaws raised their corn. But little timber near the villages. On the starboard side below is a point of excellent timber, and in the point several miles above is fine timber. Several parties of Mandans rode to the river on the starboard side to view us. Indeed they are continually in sight, satisfying their curiosity as to our appearance. We are told that the Sioux has latterly fallen in with and stolen the horses of the Big Bellies [*also*

known at the time as the Minitaris, and now generally known as the Hidatsa].
On their way home they [*the Sioux raiders*] fell in with the Assiniboine, who
killed them and took the horses. A Frenchman has latterly been killed by the
Indians on the track to the trading establishment on the Assiniboine River in
the north of this place (or British fort). This Frenchman had lived many years
with the Mandans. We were frequently called on to land and talk to parties of
Mandans on the shore. Wind shifted to the S.W. about 11 o'clock and blew hard
until three o'clock. Clouded up. River full of sandbars and we are at a great loss
to find the channel of the river, frequently run on the sandbars which delays
us much. Passed a very bad riffle of rocks in the evening by taking the larboard
side of a sandbar and camped on a sand point on the starboard side opposite
a high hill on the larboard side. Several Indians came to see us this evening,
amongst others the son of the late great chief of the Mandans. This man has
his two little fingers off. On inquiring the cause, we were told it was customary
for this nation to show their grief by some testimony of pain, and that it was
not uncommon for them to take off two smaller fingers of the hand and sometimes more with other marks of savage affection.

The wind blew very hard this evening from the S.W. Very cold.

R. Fields with the rheumatism in his neck, P. Cruzatte with the same
complaint in his legs. The party otherwise is well. As to myself I feel but slight
symptoms of that disorder at this time.

October 26, 1804, Friday [Clark]

Set out early, wind from the S.W. Proceeded on. Saw numbers of the Mandans on shore. We set the Arikara chief on shore and we proceeded on to
the camp of two of their grand chiefs, where we delayed a few minutes with
the chiefs and proceeded on, taking two of their chiefs on board and some
of the heavy articles of his household, such as earthen pots and corn. Proceeded on. At this camp saw a Mr. McCracken, an Englishman from the
N.W. Company. This man came nine days ago to trade for horses and buffalo
robes. One other man came with him. The Indians continued on the banks
all day. But little wood on this part of the river, many sandbars and bad
places, water much divided between them.

We came to and camped on the larboard side about a half mile below
the first Mandan town on the larboard side. Soon after our arrival many men,
women and children flocked down to see us. Capt. Lewis walked to the village
with the principal chiefs and our interpreters. My rheumatic complaint

increasing, I could not go. If I was well only one would have left the boat and party until we knew the disposition of the Indians. I smoked with the chiefs who came after. Those people appeared much pleased with the corn mill, which we were obliged to use, and was fixed in the boat.

October 27, 1804, Saturday [Clark]
We set out early, came to at the village on the larboard side. This village is situated on an eminence of about 50 feet above the water in a handsome plain. It contains houses in a kind of picket work. The houses are round and very large, containing several families, as also their horses which are tied on one side of the entrance. A description of those houses will be given hereafter. I walked up and smoked a pipe with the chiefs of this village. They were anxious that I would stay and eat with them. My indisposition prevented my eating, which displeased them, until a full explanation took place. I returned to the boat and sent two carrots of tobacco for them to smoke, and proceeded on, passed the second village and camped opposite the village of the *Weter Soon* or ah wah har ways, which is situated on an eminence in a plain on the larboard side. This village is small and contains but few inhabitants. Above this village and also above the Knife River on the same side of the Missouri the Big Bellies' towns are situated. A further description will be given hereafter as also of the town of Mandans on this side of the river, i.e. the starboard side.

A fine warm day. We met with a Frenchman by the name of Jessaume which we employ as an interpreter. This man has a wife and children in the village. Great numbers on both sides flocked down to the bank to view us as we passed.

Capt. Lewis with the interpreter walked down to the village below our camp. After delaying one hour he returned and informed me the Indians had returned to their village. We sent three carrots of tobacco by three young men to the three villages above inviting them to come down and council with us tomorrow. Many Indians came to view us. Some stayed all night in the camp of our party. We procured some information from Mr. Jessaume of the chiefs of the different nations.

The trader named Rene Jessaume had lived among the Mandan for 15 years and spoke the language fluently, but the consensus among historians, and among Jessaume's contemporaries, was that he was not a reliable man. Few people liked him. The journals become confusing at this point with regard to the Hidatsa. There were in all five villages in the vicinity, two Mandan, three Hidatsa; but the Hidatsa were also known collectively by the name Big Bellies, or in French "Gros Ventres"(the name has nothing to do with their anatomy; it comes from the sign language of the Plains, which designated them by the sign for having a big belly). The Mandan, however, did not call them either Hidatsa or Gros Ventres but by a totally different name, Minitari, now in use among some ethnologists as this tribe's name. The three Hidatsa villages were closely linked linguistically, but each belonged to a different subgroup and spoke a slightly different language; they had different chiefs, and they did not necessarily believe that their interests coincided with each other. None of them were as welcoming to the expedition as the Mandans. Lewis and Clark would never have the same kind of relationship with them that they had with the Mandan. The "Weter Soon" village that Clark mentions above was one of the Hidatsa villages, but it was the smallest one, and, as it happens, the most linguistically distinct from the other Hidatsa groups. The captains sometimes called them the Shoe Indians, the Watersoons, the Ahnahaways, and so on. To further confuse the issue, there was another tribe located farther west called the Gros Ventres. They still exist, living mostly in Montana. To distinguish between this tribe and the tribe Lewis and Clark met, the latter are often called the "Gros Ventres of the Plains."

October 28, 1804, Sunday [Clark]
A windy day, fair and clear. Many of the *Gros Ventres* and Watersoons came to see us and hear the council. The wind being so violently hard from the S.W. prevented our going into council. Indeed the chiefs of the Mandans from the lower village could not cross [*the river*]. We made up the presents and entertained several of the curious chiefs who wished to see the boat, which was very curious to them, viewing it as great medicine, as they also viewed my black servant. The Black Cat, grand chief of the Mandans, Capt. Lewis and myself with an interpreter walked up the river about 1 and a half miles. Our views were to examine the situation and timber for a fort. We found the situation good but the timber scarce, or at least small timber such as would not answer us.

We consulted the grand chief in respect to the other chiefs of the different villages. He gave us the names of 12. George Drouillard caught two beaver above our camp last night. We had several presents from the women of corn, boiled hominy, soft corn, etc. I presented a jar to the chief's wife, who received it with much pleasure. Our men very cheerful this evening. We sent the chiefs of the Gros Ventres to smoke a pipe with the grand chief of the Mandans in his village, and told them we would speak tomorrow.

Black Cat was the chief of the second Mandan village, a bit farther upstream; he would become the most trusted of the expedition's friends. The name of his village has been spelled a number of different ways, as with many Indian names. It stood on the same side of the Missouri as Fort Mandan and was within easy walking distance.

October 29, 1804, Monday [Clark]
A fair fine morning. After breakfast we were visited by the old chief of the Big Bellies. [*His name was Caltarcota, but he was also called by many other names: Chokecherry, The Grape, Cherry Grows on a Bush, and so on. He was a chief of the third Hidatsa village.*] This man was old and had transferred his power to his son, who was then out at war against the Snake Indians who inhabit the Rocky Mountains. At 10 o'clock the S.W. wind rose very high. We collected the chiefs and commenced a council under an awning and our sails stretched around to keep out as much wind as possible. We delivered a long speech, the substance of which was similar to what we had delivered to the nations below. The old chief of the Gros Ventres was very restless before the speech was half ended, observed that he could not wait long, that his camp was exposed to the hostile Indians, etc. He was rebuked by one of the chiefs for his uneasiness at such a time as the present. We at the end of the speech mentioned the Arikara who accompanied us to make a firm peace. They all smoked with him (I gave this chief a dollar of American coin as a medal, with which he was much pleased). In council we presented him with a certificate of his sincerity and good conduct, etc. We also spoke about the fur which was taken from two Frenchmen by a Mandan, and informed them of our intentions of sending back the French hands.

After the council we gave the presents with much ceremony and put the medals on the chiefs we intended to make, viz. one for each town, to whom we gave coats, hats and flags, and one grand chief for each nation, to whom we gave medals with the President's likeness. In council we requested them to give us an answer tomorrow or as soon as possible to some points which required their deliberation. After the council was over we shot the air gun, which appeared to astonish the natives much. The greater part of them retired soon after.

The *Arikara* chief, *Ar-ke-tar-na-shar*, came to me this evening and told me he wishes to return to his village and nation. I put him off, saying tomorrow we would have an answer to our talk to our satisfaction and we would send by him a string of wampum informing what had passed here. An iron or steel corn mill which we gave to the Mandans was very thankfully received. The prairie was set on fire (or caught by accident) by a young man of the Mandans; the fire went with such velocity that it burned to death a man and woman who could not get to any place of safety. One man, a woman and child much burnt and several narrowly escaped the flame. A boy, half white, was saved unhurt in the midst of the flame. Those ignorant people say this boy was saved by the Great Spirit medicine because he was white. The cause of his being saved was, a green buffalo skin was thrown over him by his mother, who perhaps had more foresight for the protection of her son and less for herself than those who escaped the flame. The fire did not burn under the skin, leaving the grass around the boy. This fire passed our camp last night about eight o'clock p.m. It went with great rapidity and looked tremendous.

The following chiefs were made in council today:

Mar-too-ton-ha or Lower Village of the Mandans
    First chief *Sha-ha-ka* or Big White
    Second chief *Ka-goh-ha-mi* or *Little Raven*
Roop-tar-hee or Second Village of the Mandans
    First and Grand Chief *Pass-cop-sa-he* or *Black Cat*
    Second chief *Car-gar-no-mok-She* Raven Man Chief
Mah-har-ha Third Village
    Chief Ta-tuck-co-pin-re-ha (White Buffalo Robe Unfolded)
Me-ne-tar-re Me-te har-tar
    First Chief—*Omp-se-ha-ra*. Black Mocassin
    Second chief. *Oh-harh* or *Little Fox.*

We sent the presents intended for the Grand Chief of the *Mi-ne-tar-re* [*this would have been a chief called One Eye, who had a formidable reputation; he was out hunting*], and the presents, flag, and wampum, by the old chief and those intended for the chief of the Lower Village [*i.e., the lower Mandan village*] by a young chief.

Clark then added a list of other subsidiary chiefs who had been "recommended"; we have omitted that list here.

October 30, 1804, Tuesday [Clark]

Two chiefs came to have some talk, one the principal of the lower village, the other the one who thought himself the principal man, and requested to hear some of the speech that was delivered yesterday. They were gratified, and we put the medal on the neck of Big White to whom we had sent clothes yesterday and a flag. Those men did not return from hunting in time to join the council. They were well pleased (second of those is a Cheyenne) [*he had been adopted into the tribe; his name was Big Man*]. I took eight men in a small pirogue and went up the river as far as the first island, about seven miles, to see if a situation could be got on it for our winter quarters, found the wood on the island as also on the point above so distant from the water that I did not think that we could get a good wintering ground there. As all the white men here informed us that wood was scarce as well as game above, we determined to drop down a few miles near wood and game.

On my return found many Indians at our camp, gave the party a dram, they danced, as is very common in the evening, which pleased the savages much. Wind S.E.

October 31, 1804, Wednesday [Clark]

A fine morning. The chief of the Mandans sent a second chief to invite us to his lodge to receive some corn and hear what he had to say. I walked down and with great ceremony was seated on a robe by the side of the chief, he threw a handsome robe over me and after smoking of the pipe with several old men around, the chief spoke.

He said he believed what we had told them, and that peace would be general, which not only gave him satisfaction but all his people. They now could hunt without fear and their women could work in the fields without looking every moment for the enemy, and put off their moccasins at night. As to the Arikaras we will show you that we wish peace with all, and do not make war on any without cause; that chief (pointing to the second) and some brave men will accompany the Arikara chief now with you to his village and nation, to smoke with that people. When you came up the Indians in the neighboring villages, as well as those out hunting when they heard of you, had great expectations of receiving presents. Those hunting, immediately on hearing, returned to the village. And all were disappointed and some dissatisfied. As to himself, he was not much so, but his village was. He would go and see his great father, etc.

He had put before me two of the steel traps which were robbed from the French a short time ago, and about 12 bushels of corn which were brought and put before me by the women of the village. After the chief finished and smoked in great ceremony, I answered the speech, which satisfied them very much, and returned to the boat. Met the principal chief of the third village and the Little Crow, both of which I invited into the cabin and smoked and talked with for about one hour. Soon after those chiefs left us the grand chief of the Mandans came dressed in the clothes we had given him with his two small sons, and requested to see the men dance, which they very readily gratified him in. The wind blew hard all the after part of the day from the N.E. and continued all night to blow hard from that point. In the morning it shifted N.W. Capt Lewis wrote to the N.W. Company's agent on the Assiniboine River about nine days march north of this place.

November 1, 1804, Thursday [Clark]
The wind hard from the N.W. Mr. McCracken, a trader, set out at seven o'clock to the fort on the Assiniboine. By him sent a letter, enclosing a copy of the British Minister's protection [*this was a passport that the British minister to the United States had written asking that any British subjects Lewis and Clark might encounter not be hindered in any way, and to render aid if necessary; the fiction was that the expedition was purely scientific*] to the principal agent of the [*Northwest*] Company. At about 10 o'clock the chiefs of the lower village came and after a short time informed us they wished we would call at their village and take some corn, that they would make peace with the Arikaras. They never made war against them, but after the Arikaras killed their chiefs they killed them like the birds, and were tired of killing them, and would send a chief and some brave men to the Arikaras to smoke with that people. In the evening we set out and fell down to the lower village, where Capt. Lewis got out and continued at the village until after night. I proceeded on and landed on the starboard side at the upper point of the first timber on the starboard side. After landing and continuing all night dropped down to a proper place to build. Capt. Lewis

came down after night, and informed me he intended to return the next morning by the particular request of the chiefs.

We passed the villages on our descent in view of great numbers of the inhabitants.

Moulton prints another version of the Mandan speech of this day from a separate loose sheet of paper, which includes these words: "We were sorry when we heard of your going up but now you are going down we are glad. If we eat you shall eat. If we starve you must starve also. Our village is too far to bring the corn to you, but we hope you will call on us as you pass to the place you intend to stop." They did not, in fact, determine on the site for the winter camp until the next day.

November 2, 1804, Friday [Clark]
This morning at daylight I went down the river with four men to look for a proper place to winter. Proceeded down the river three miles and found a place well supplied with wood, and returned. Capt. Lewis went to the village to hear what they had to say and I fell down, and formed a camp near where a small camp of Indians were hunting. Cut down the trees around our camp. In the evening Capt. Lewis returned with a present of 11 bushels of corn. Our Arikara chief set out, accompanied by one chief and several brave men. He called for some small article which we had given him but as I could not understand him he could not get it. The wind from the S.E., a fine day. Many Indians to view us today.

November 3, 1804, Saturday [Clark]
A fine morning, wind hard from the *West*. We commence building our cabins, send down in a pirogue six men to hunt. Engaged one man [*a French Canadian named Jean Baptiste Lepage; he took the place of John Newman, who had been court-martialed and discharged. Lepage went all the way to the Pacific and back*]. Set the French who intend to return to build a pirogue. Many Indians pass to hunt. Mr. Jessaume with his squaw and children come down to live as interpreter. We receive a horse for our service. In the evening *Ka goh ha me* or Little Raven came and brought us on his squaw about 60 weight [*i.e., 60 lbs.*] of dried buffalo meat, a robe, and pot of meal. They delayed all night. We gave his squaw an ax and a few small articles and himself a piece of tobacco. The men were indulged with a dram this evening. Two beaver caught this morning, and one trap lost.

November 4, 1804, Sunday, Fort Mandan [Clark]
A fine morning. We continued to cut down trees and raise our houses. A Mr. Charbonneau, interpreter for the *Gros Ventre* nation, came to see us and informed us that he came down with several Indians from a hunting expedition up the river to hear what we had told the Indians in council. This man wished to hire on as an interpreter. The wind rose this evening from the east and clouded up. Great numbers of Indian pass hunting and some on the return.

Charbonneau was Toussaint Charbonneau, who had taken two women as wives, both Snake (or Shoshone) Indians, whom he had bought from a Hidatsa who had brought them back from a raiding party into Shoshone territory. One of these wives, the one who went with him on the expedition, was Sacagawea. Charbonneau did not impress the Captains much over the course of the next year, often getting into mishaps, but he could cook well and was evidently a better interpreter than Jessaume. Clark formed a lasting relationship with the family, seeing to the education of the son Sacagawea was soon to bring forth, Jean Baptiste Charbonneau, as if he were his own.

November 5, 1804, Monday [Clark]
I rose very early and commenced raising the two ranges of huts, the timber large and heavy to carry. On hand, sticks [*i.e., bundles of loose wood*], cottonwood and elm, some small ash, our situation sandy. Great numbers of Indians pass to and from hunting. A camp of Mandans a few miles below us caught within two days 100 goats by driving them into a strong pen, directed by a bush fence widening from the pen, etc. The greater part of this day cloudy, wind moderate from the N.W. I have the rheumatism very bad. Capt. Lewis writing all day. We are told by our interpreter that four Assiniboine Indians have arrived at the camps of the Gros Ventres and 50 lodges are coming.

November 6, 1804, Tuesday [Clark]
Last night late we were awoke by the sergeant of the guard to see a northern light, which was light, not red, and appeared to darken and was sometimes nearly obscured, and open, and many times appeared in light streaks, at other times a great space light, containing floating columns which appeared to approach each other and retreat, leaving the lighter space at no time of the same appearance.

This morning I rose at daylight. The clouds to the north appeared black. At eight o'clock the wind began to blow hard from the N.W. and cold, and continued all day. Mr. Joseph Gravelines, our Arikara interpreter, Paul *Primeau, La Jeunesse* and two French boys, who came with us, set out in a small pirogue on their return to the Arikara nation and the Illinois. Mr. Gravelines has instructions to take on the Arikaras in the spring, etc. Continue to build the huts out of cotton timber, this being the only timber we have.

SUMMARY

NOVEMBER 7, 1804 TO APRIL 6, 1805

It took about three weeks to build Fort Mandan and settle in; by November 27 the men had finished daubing the chinks between the logs with mud. The huts were arranged in two rows, standing at an angle to each other and enclosed within a triangular stockade that was 18 feet high, according to Patrick Gass, who would have been in charge of building the fort. The fort was comfortable and warm, as it had to be; temperatures dropped over the winter to as low as 45° below zero, and the wind only made things worse. On February 10 Lewis mentioned it in a note, remarking that the temperature the day before had been lower, but that on this day the wind was high and it felt much colder. They had no way to measure the wind chill factor, but they understood the phenomenon.

One thing the men marveled at over the winter was how well the Indians withstood the cold. On January 10, when the mercury stood at 40° below zero, the Indians came by to borrow a sleigh to go look for a man and a boy who had spent the night outside; they expected to find them frozen to death. The boy, who was about 13 years old, arrived at the fort with only his feet frozen; he had "lain out last night," says Clark, "without fire, with only a buffalo robe to cover him; the dress which he wore was a pair of antelope leggings, which are very thin, and moccasins... Soon after the arrival of the boy, a man came in who had also stayed out without fire, and very thinly clothed. This man was not the least injured."

The Americans would go out to hunt but the cold would force them back inside. They were constantly suffering from frostbite; Clark's servant, York, had a touch of it on his penis. For the Indians frostbite was rarely a problem. The Indian boy with frozen feet lost his toes to frostbite—Lewis and Clark amputated them on January 27—but it seems fair to say that most of the expedition's men would have died if they had been forced to stay out under the same circumstances. "The customs and the habits of those people," Clark remarked, "has inured them to bear more cold than I thought it possible for man to endure."

Lewis and Clark had a great deal more to learn about the Indians. One part of their mission was to divert Indian trade from the North West and Hudson's Bay Companies in Canada to St. Louis and its American traders, and one key to that, from the American point of view, was to rearrange Indian alliances on the upper Missouri to isolate the troublesome Sioux and force them to stop blockading the river and allow the St. Louis traders free access to the Mandan villages and beyond. That was why Lewis and Clark had taken the trouble to bring an Arikara chief to the Mandan villages and persuade them to smoke the peace pipe with the Mandan and negotiate a peace. The Arikara were thought to be subject to the Sioux, prisoners of Sioux policies; if the Arikara could be brought into the orbit of the Mandan it would tend to break the stranglehold the Sioux had on travel up the river. But in fact the Sioux-Arikara relationship was far more symbiotic than Lewis and Clark realized. The Arikara were, like the Mandan, a sedentary agricultural people who raised corn and horses. They traded these with the Sioux for goods such as guns and ammunition, which the Sioux had received for furs traded to the British companies in Canada. It was common for Arikara and Sioux braves to go on warring raids together. Even if the Sioux appeared to be dominant, the two tribes were allies and needed each other.

Trade was also the subject of the day with the representatives of the North West Company who came to the Mandan villages or were already in residence there. Relations with these men were cordial, even friendly, but Lewis and Clark wanted to make it plain that this was now United States territory. The British were operating there on sufferance, and they were not to undermine the American position among the Mandan and Hidatsa, raise the British flag, or give the Mandan competing British honors and medals. Lewis and Clark knew that the trade between the Mandan and the Assiniboine and various Cree groups to the north and Plains tribes to the west and south was long-standing and that the two British companies had a definite edge in the area. The United States was new on the scene and relatively weak in both experience *and authority. But Lewis and Clark were there to open the way, and they would brook no interference.*

Much of the early part of the winter at Fort Mandan was taken up by these concerns. Indians were constantly at the fort, not only to talk but also because the Americans and their ways fascinated them. It was quite common for one or more chiefs to show up on some piece of business and then stay all day and often all night as well. The Mandan liked white men and were quite friendly to them. They loved to watch the corps dance, which was a frequent evening's entertainment, and were amazed that York, who was a big man, could dance as well as the rest. Among the instruments the corps had brought were a fiddle, a tambourine, and a horn of some sort. But the substantive business was trade, and it was confusing to the Mandan, indeed to all the Indians Lewis and Clark met on their journey, that the Americans were not there to trade. Indians were not explorers and had little use for the concept of exploration. They did under-stand trade, however, and they wanted to trade. But Lewis and Clark brought no trade goods: no guns, no ammunition (except for their own use), no clothing, blankets, pots, utensils, and all the rest that could be traded for furs, horses, or whatever else was wanted. Lewis and Clark brought small gifts and symbolic, ceremonial things such as flags and medals and written certificates. The Indians wanted things they could use and were invariably disappointed at what they got: speeches; demonstrations with the air gun; mirrors and beads.

Later on in the winter, however, a trade of sorts did develop. One of the Americans, John Shields, was a skilled blacksmith who could repair guns and make knives and other kinds of weapons. The Indians traded large amounts of corn for battle axes Shields made from a worn-out iron stove. He was constantly at work and kept the expedition in corn. "The blacksmiths," wrote Lewis on the sixth of February, "have proved a happy resource to us in our present situation, as I believe it would have been difficult to have devised any other method to have procured corn from the natives." When the expedition was on its way home in 1806 Shields saw several of his battle axes in the possession of the Nez Perce in what is now Idaho. The Nez Perce had acquired them from Hidatsa traders and were using them in a gambling game.

Feeding the men was a primary concern. The expedition depended on Mandan corn and on whatever game they could shoot. Lewis and Clark were often sending parties out to hunt or leading such parties themselves. A party that went out early in November and hunted some 30 miles downriver came back on November 19 with 32 deer, 12 elk and a buffalo. As the weather got colder it became harder to find game, or game that had any meat on its bones, or to secure the meat before wolves could get to it, and supplies dwindled. On February 4 Clark took 16 men almost 60 miles downriver and hunted for nearly 10 days, killing 40 deer, 3 buffalo bulls, and 19 elk; but much of the meat was unfit for use. He sent the bulk of the meat back on sleds drawn by horses and cached the rest. After he got back himself (walking 30 miles the last day over rough river ice), on the 14th he sent four men back with three horses and two sleds to bring the rest of the meat back, but a Sioux war party of more than a hundred men waylaid them, took two of the horses, and forced the men to give up their knives. The same party also burned one of the caches Clark had set up.

Lewis, some volunteers from the corps, and a number of Indians, 24 men in all, went immediately in pursuit, but the Sioux were too far ahead to be caught. Lewis stayed out for a week, found one cache intact, killed 36 deer and 14 elk, and eventually returned with about 3,000 pounds of meat. They would use it all. The men were burning calories at a prodigious rate.

This was not the first time the expedition had run afoul of a Sioux war party. On November 30 a Mandan crossed the river to tell them that five Mandan had been hunting some 20 miles from the village when they were attacked by a party of Sioux and Arikara. One man was killed, two were wounded, and nine horses were taken. Four Hidatsa of another party were also missing. Lewis and Clark immediately assembled a group of 23 soldiers, crossed the river, and offered their aid to go in pursuit of the Sioux. The Mandan were at first alarmed to see such a large party of well-armed men approach; when it was explained to them what they were about, they politely declined the offer. A chief named Big Man explained to Clark that "the snow is deep and it is cold. Our horses cannot travel through the plains." The Sioux had no doubt retreated to their camps. Perhaps they could go in the spring.

But he also wanted Lewis and Clark to know that he had suspected all along that the Arikara would prove treacherous. The peace the two captains thought they had negotiated between the Mandan and Arikara had fallen apart within weeks. This was another lesson Lewis and Clark had to learn. Peace among Indian tribes was seldom lasting. These were warrior societies; war was a way of life, just as trade was, and it was as complex as trade, too, with shifting alliances, enmities that collapsed once revenge was taken, and private feuds that went on and on. Bands that might trade with one another under certain circumstances might make war on each other in other circumstances. The Mandan and Hidatsa seemed to be at peace with each other, and the peace *seemed permanent. In fact, it was not until January that Hidatsa chiefs came to Fort Mandan to confer with Lewis and Clark, and the captains discovered that the Mandan had been telling the Hidatsa that if they went there the whites would kill them. The Mandan wanted to control relationships with the expedition; they wanted, as James P. Ronda puts it in his book* Lewis and Clark Among the Indians, *a Fort Mandan, not a Fort Hidatsa. Mandan and Hidatsa interests were not identical by any means. None of this was going to end because Lewis and Clark wanted it to end. Chiefs depended for their status on their ability as warriors. For the captains to promote a general peace in the area was unrealistic and betrayed a deep misunderstanding of Indian life. It was also somewhat hypocritical. The whites were living off the corn that they were trading for war axes of their own manufacture.*

But if there were misunderstandings, the winter also produced a great deal of goodwill between the Mandan and the Americans. Acts of kindness on both sides, friendships and mutual respect that developed through trade, and sexual relations all worked to cement a bond between the two groups. Lewis speaks glowingly at one point of Black Cat, the chief of the second Mandan village; "this man," he writes, "possesses more integrity, firmness, intelligence and perspicuity of mind than any Indian I have met with in this quarter." Lewis and Clark in the journals do not speak much about sex between the whites and Indian women, but there was clearly a lot of it. The Indians did not share many of the Western attitudes toward sex. Early in January 1805 Clark described a buffalo dance he had attended across the river at the first Mandan village. The old men, he says, "arrange themselves in a circle and after they smoke a pipe, which is handed them by a young man, dressed up for the purpose, the young men who have their wives back of the circle go to one of the old men with a whining tone and ask the old man to take his wife (who presents herself naked under a robe) . . . The girl then takes the old man (who very often can scarcely walk) and leads him to a convenient place for the business, after which they return to the lodge. If the old man (or a white man) returns to the lodge without gratifying the man and his wife, he offers her again and again." The Plains Indians believed that spiritual power passed between people during the sex act and that the old men, thanks to their long experience as hunters, possessed the power to ensure a successful buffalo hunt.

The expedition, with its cannon and air gun, its odd instruments, its medals and clothing, its keelboat with all its wonders, and most of all the ability to work metal, also possessed great power—great medicine to the Indians who freely offered their women to the whites—and to that strange black creature, York. One of the crew members went to this same buffalo dance. He was given four women. White traders had previously brought syphilis to the Mandan population; by the end of their stay at the fort many of the members of the expedition seem to have contracted it. The treatment of the day was a mercury ointment—which is, of course, no cure; it only allays the symptoms.

There is no evidence that either Lewis or Clark ever had an intimate relationship with an Indian woman on the journey. They were busy men, and leaders, and it may have seemed a bad example to set. Certainly there was never a romance with Sacagawea, as a few romantically inclined historians have wanted to believe. She delivered her child on February 11. The delivery was difficult and Lewis reports that Jessaume suggested they administer "a small portion of the rattle of the rattle-snake, which he assured me had never failed to produce the desired effect, that of hastening the birth of the child." Lewis had a rattle around and Jessaume broke two rings of it into pieces and soaked them in a glass of water. "Whether this medicine was truly the cause or not I shall not undertake to determine," Lewis goes on, "but I was informed that she had not taken it more than ten minutes before she brought forth." Lewis was, however, doubtful about its efficacy.

Sacagawea almost did not accompany the expedition later that spring. A month after the birth of his son, Toussaint Charbonneau decided that he wanted better terms for his services than Lewis and Clark were offering. He would not agree to work, "let our situation be what it may," and he would not stand guard. He wanted the liberty to leave whenever he wished, with whatever provisions he wished. Lewis and Clark would not agree to any such terms and dismissed him. A week later Charbonneau thought better of his decision and asked to be taken back, on the terms the captains had proposed.

The captains were busy by this time getting ready to leave. The hardest job was getting the boats out of the ice; it took weeks of chopping at the ice with axes to get them out. The ice on the Missouri had reached a depth of three feet. When it broke up it could have destroyed the keelboat if the vessel were still in the water. Why the keelboat had spent the winter frozen in the river no one knows. They also had to have new pirogues (or "canoes") built; they were sending the keelboat back downriver, as they had always planned to do, under the command of Corporal Warfington, with maps, samples, and reports intended for the president.

Preparing these reports was a big job; on one occasion Clark says that Lewis was writing all day long. Moulton prints some of this material for the first time, and it's interesting to read. Lewis wrote a long report naming and describing all the tributary rivers they had passed on their way up the Missouri and, from information gathered from the Indians, all those they would be passing west of the Mandan villages. Clark wrote a careful description of everything they knew about every Indian tribe from St. Louis to the Rocky Mountains, and some beyond. It is long, it is thorough, and it is impressive. The botanical, faunal, and mineral collections had to be arranged, preserved, and described. Lewis had to arrange his receipts. Boxes had to be packed with specimens. They were sending back not just the prairie dog but four live magpies and a prairie hen (of these, one magpie and the prairie dog survived).

On April 1 Clark listed the numbers who would go down the Missouri and back to St. Louis: six Americans, three Frenchmen, "and perhaps several Arikara chiefs." The party going upriver in two pirogues and six canoes would consist of Charbonneau and his two wives (only Sacagawea and her baby actually went with Charbonneau), George Drouillard, a Mandan Indian going upstream for a ways, Clark's servant, 26 Americans, and provisions for four months. By April 7 the boats were packed and ready to go, and so were the men. It was on this date as well that Lewis began to write daily entries into his journal.

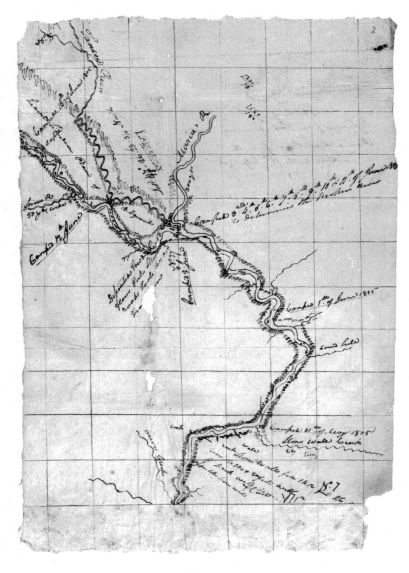

Sketch of the Missouri River from Fort Mandan to the Rocky Mountains,
April 7–July 15, 1805

APRIL 7 TO MAY 9, 1805

April 7, 1805, Fort Mandan [Lewis]
Having on this day at four p.m. completed every arrangement necessary for our departure, we dismissed the barge and crew with orders to return without loss of time to St. Louis. A small canoe with two French hunters accompanied the barge. These men had ascended the Missouri with us the last year as *engagés*. The barge crew consisted of six soldiers and two Frenchmen. Two Frenchmen and an Arikara Indian also take their passage in her as far as the Arikara villages, at which place we expect Mr. Tabeau to embark with his peltry, who in that case will make an addition of two, perhaps four men to the crew of the barge. We gave Richard Warfington, a discharged Corporal, the charge of the barge and crew, and confided to his care likewise our dispatches to the government, letters to our private friends, and a number of articles to the President of the United States. One of the Frenchmen by the name of Gravelines, an honest discreet man and an excellent boatman, is employed to conduct the barge as a pilot. We have therefore every hope that the barge and with her our dispatches will arrive safe at St. Louis. Mr. Gravelines, who speaks the Arikara language extremely well, has been employed to conduct a few of the Arikara chiefs to the seat of government who have promised us to descend in the barge to St. Louis with that view.

At the same moment that the barge departed from Fort Mandan, Capt. Clark embarked with our party and proceeded up the river. As I had used no exercise for several weeks, I determined to walk on shore as far as our encampment of this evening; accordingly I continued my walk on the N. side of the river about six miles, to the upper village of the Mandans, and called on the Black Cat, the great chief of the Mandans. He was not at home. I rested myself a few minutes, and finding that the party had not arrived I returned about two miles and joined them at their encampment on the N. side of the river opposite the lower Mandan village. Our party now consisted of the following individuals: Sgts. John Ordway, Nathaniel Pryor, and Patrick Gass; Privates William Bratton, John Colter, Reuben and Joseph Fields, John Shields, George Gibson, George Shannon, John Potts, John Collins, Joseph Whitehouse, Richard Windsor, Alexander Willard, Hugh Hall, Silas Goodrich, Robert Frazer, Pierre Cruzatte, Jean Baptiste LePage, Francois Labiche, Hugh McNeal, William Werner, Thomas P. Howard, Peter Weiser, and John B. Thompson.

Interpreters, George Drouillard and Toussaint Charbonneau, also a black man by the name of York, servant to Capt. Clark, an Indian woman, wife to Charbonneau, with a young child, and a Mandan man who had promised to accompany us as far as the Snake Indians with a view to bring about a good understanding and friendly intercourse between that nation and his own, the Minitaris and Ahwahharways [*i.e., the Hidatsa subtribe occupying the second Hidatsa village; also known as the Shoe Indians*].

Our vessels consisted of six small canoes, and two large pirogues. This little fleet, although not quite so respectable as those of Columbus or Capt. Cook's, was still viewed by us with as much pleasure as those deservedly famed adventurers ever beheld theirs; and I dare say with quite as much anxiety for their safety and preservation. We were now about to penetrate a country at least two thousand miles in width, on which the foot of civilized man had never trodden; the good or evil it had in store for us was for experiment yet to determine, and these little vessels contained every article by which we were to expect to subsist or defend ourselves. However, as this the state of mind in which we are, generally gives the coloring to events, when the imagination is suffered to wander into futurity, the picture which now presented itself to me was a most pleasing one. Entertaining as I do the most confident hope of succeeding in a voyage which had formed a darling project of mine for the last ten years, I could but esteem this moment of my departure as among the most happy of my life. The party are in excellent health and spirits, zealously attached to the enterprise, and anxious to proceed; not a whisper of murmur or discontent to be heard among them, but all act in unison, and with the most perfect harmony. I took an early supper this evening and went to bed. Capt. Clark, myself, the two interpreters and the woman and child sleep in a tent of dressed skins. This tent is in the Indian style, formed of a number of dressed buffalo skins sewn together with sinews. It is cut in such manner that when folded double it forms the quarter of a circle, and is left open at one side where it may be attached or loosed at pleasure by strings which are sewn to its side to the purpose. To erect this tent, a parcel of ten or twelve poles are provided, four or five of which are attached together at one end; they are then elevated and their lower extremities are spread in a circular manner to a width proportionate to the dimensions of the lodge. In the same position other poles are leaned against those, and the leather is then thrown over them, forming a conic figure.

From this point in the journals until late August both Lewis and Clark were making entries. For the most part only one entry per day will be printed here, almost always the fullest, which in practice means that most of them come from Lewis. If there is something in the second entry which the first does not cover, however, it shall be added to the first.

April 8, 1805, Monday [Lewis]

Set out early this morning. The wind blew hard against us from the N.W. We therefore traveled very slowly. I walked on shore, and visited the Black Cat, took leave of him after smoking a pipe as is their custom, and then proceeded on slowly by land about four miles, where I awaited the arrival of the party. At 12 o'clock they came up and informed me that one of the small canoes was behind in distress. Capt. Clark returned, found she had filled with water and all her loading was wet. We lost half a bag of biscuit and about 30 pounds of powder by this accident. The powder we regard as a serious loss, but we spread it to dry immediately and hope we shall still be able to restore the greater part of it. This was the only powder we had which was not perfectly secure from getting wet. We took dinner at this place, and then proceeded on to our encampment, which was on the N. side opposite to a high bluff. The Mandan man came up after we had encamped and brought with him a woman who was extremely solicitous to accompany one of the men of our party. This, however, we positively refused to permit.

April 9, 1805, Tuesday [Lewis]

Set out as early as it was possible to see this morning and proceeded about five miles where we halted and took breakfast. The Indian man who had promised to accompany us as far as the Snake Indians now informed us of his intention to relinquish the journey and accordingly returned to his village. We saw a great number of brant passing up the river. Some of them were white, except the large feathers in the first and second joint of the wing, which are black. There is no other difference between them and the common gray brant but that of their color. Their note and habits are the same, and they are frequently seen to associate together. I have not yet positively determined whether they are the same, or a different species [*they were snow geese in both their blue and white phases*]. Capt. Clark walked on shore today and informed me on his return that, passing through the prairie, he had seen an animal that precisely resembled the burrowing squirrel, except in point of size, it being only about one-third as large as the squirrel, and that it also burrows. [*It was probably the pocket gopher.*] I have observed in many parts of the plains and prairies the work of an animal of which I could never obtain a view. Their work resembles that of the salamander common to the sand hills of the states of South Carolina and Georgia, and like that animal also it never appears above the ground. The little hillocks which are thrown up by these animals have much the appearance of ten or twelve pounds of loose earth poured out of a vessel on the surface of the plain. In the state they leave them you can discover no hole through which they throw out this earth; but by removing the loose earth gently you may discover that the soil has been broken in a circular manner for about an inch and a half in diameter, where it appears looser than the adjacent surface, and is certainly the place through which the earth has been thrown out, though the operation is performed without leaving any visible aperture.

The bluffs of the river which we passed today were upwards of a hundred feet high, formed of a mixture of yellow clay and sand. Many horizontal strata of carbonated wood, having every appearance of pit coal at a distance, were seen in the face of these bluffs. These strata are of unequal thickness from one to five feet, and appear at different elevations above the water, some of them as much as 80 feet. The hills of the river are very broken and many of them have the appearance of having been on fire at some former period. Considerable quantities of pumice stone and lava appear in many parts of these hills where they are broken and washed down by the rain and melting snow [*this was not pumice; the lignite veins, i.e., the coal, in the hills does catch fire in this area and bakes the clay into a rocklike material that resembles pumice*].

When we halted for dinner the squaw busied herself in searching for the wild artichokes which the mice collect and deposit in large hoards. This operation she performed by penetrating the earth with a sharp stick about some small collections of driftwood. Her labor soon proved successful, and she procured a good quantity of these roots. The flavor of this root resembles that of the Jerusalem artichoke and the stalk of the weed which produces it is also similar, though both the root and stalk are much smaller than the Jerusalem artichoke. The root is white and of an ovate form, from one to three inches in length and usually about the size of a man's finger. One stalk produces from two to four, and sometimes six of these roots.

At a distance of six miles passed a large wintering or hunting camp of the Minitaris on the starboard side. These lodges, about thirty in number, are built of earth and timber in their usual style. Two and a quarter miles higher we passed the entrance of Miry Creek, which discharges itself on the starboard side. This creek is but small, takes its rise in some small lakes near the Mouse River and passes in its course to the Missouri through beautiful, level, and fertile plains entirely destitute of timber. Three miles above the mouth of this creek we passed a hunting camp of the Minitaris, who had prepared a park and were waiting the return of the antelope, which usually pass the Missouri at this season of the year from the Black Hills on the south side to the open plains on the north side of the river. In like manner the antelope repasses the Missouri from north to south in the latter end of autumn and winter in the Black Hills, where there are considerable bodies of woodland. We proceeded on 11 ½ miles further and encamped on the N. side in a most beautiful high extensive open bottom.

April 10, 1805, Wednesday [Lewis]
Set out at an early hour this morning. At the distance of three miles passed some Minitaris who had assembled themselves on the larboard shore to take a view of our little fleet. Capt. Clark walked on shore today for several hours. When he returned he informed me that he had seen a gang of antelope in the plains but was unable to get a shot at them. He also saw some geese and swans. The geese are now feeding in considerable numbers on the young grass which has sprung up in the bottom prairies. The mosquitoes were very

troublesome to us today. The country on both sides of the Missouri from the tops of the river hills is one continued level fertile plain as far as the eye can reach, in which there is not even a solitary tree or shrub to be seen except such as from their moist situations or the steep declivities of hills are sheltered from the ravages of fire. At the distance of 12 miles from our encampment of last night we arrived at the lower point of a bluff on the larboard side. About one and a half miles down this bluff from this point the bluff is now on fire and throws out considerable quantities of smoke, which has a strong sulphurous smell. The appearance of the coal in the bluffs continues as yesterday. At one p.m. we overtook three French hunters who had set out a few days before us with a view of trapping beaver. They had taken 12 since they left Fort Mandan. These people avail themselves of the protection which our numbers will enable us to give them against the Assiniboines who sometimes hunt on the Missouri, and intend ascending with us as far as the mouth of the Yellowstone River and continue their hunt up that river. This is the first essay of a beaver hunter of any description on this river. The beaver these people have already taken are by far the best I have ever seen. The river bottoms we have passed today are wider and possess more timber than usual. The current of the Missouri is but moderate, at least not greater than that of the Ohio in high tide. Its banks are falling in but little; the navigation is therefore comparatively with its lower portion easy and safe. We encamped this evening on a willow point, starboard side, just above a remarkable bend in the river to the S.W. which we called the Little Basin.

April 11, 1805, Thursday [Lewis]
Set out at an early hour. I proceeded with the party, and Capt. Clark with George Drouillard walked on shore in order to procure some fresh meat if possible. We proceeded on about five miles and halted for breakfast, when Capt. Clark and Drouillard joined us. The latter had killed and brought with him a deer, which was at this moment acceptable, as we had had no fresh meat for several days. The country from Fort Mandan to this place is so constantly hunted by the Minitaris that there is but little game. We halted at two p.m. and made a comfortable dinner of venison steak and beavers' tails with the biscuit which got wet on the eighth by the accident of the canoe filling with water before mentioned. The powder which got wet by the same accident, and which we had spread to dry on the baggage of the large pirogue, was now examined and put up; it appears to be almost restored and our loss

is therefore not so great as we had at first apprehended. The country much the same as yesterday. On the sides of the hills and even the banks of the river and sandbars, there is a white substance that appears in considerable quantities on the surface of the earth, which tastes like a mixture of common salt and Glauber's salts. Many of the springs which flow from the base of the river hills are so strongly impregnated with this substance that the water is extremely unpleasant to the taste and has a purgative effect.

Saw some large white cranes pass up the river. These are the largest bird of that genus common to the country through which the Missouri and Mississippi pass. They are perfectly white except the large feathers of the two first joints of the wing, which are black [these were whooping cranes]. We encamped this evening on the starboard shore just above the point of woodland which formed the extremity of the last course of this day. There is a high bluff opposite to us, under which we saw some Indians, but the river is here so wide that we could not speak to them. We suppose them to be a hunting party of the Minitaris. We killed two geese today.

April 12, 1805, Friday [Lewis]
Set out at an early hour. Our pirogue and the canoes passed over to the larboard side in order to avoid a bank, which was rapidly falling in on the starboard. The red pirogue, contrary to my expectation or wish, passed under this bank by means of her tow line where I expected to have seen her carried under every instant. I did not discover that she was about to make this attempt until it was too late for the men to re-embark, and retreating is more dangerous than proceeding in such cases; they therefore continued their passage up this bank, and much to my satisfaction arrived safe above it. This cost me some moments of uneasiness. Her cargo was of much importance to us in our present advanced situation. We proceeded on six miles and came to on the lower side of the entrance of the Little Missouri on the larboard shore in a fine plain, where we determined to spend the day for the purpose of celestial observation. We sent out 10 hunters to procure some fresh meat.

[Lewis then takes a sighting of the sun.]
The night proved so cloudy that I could make no further observations. George Drouillard shot a beaver this morning, which we found swimming in the river a small distance below the entrance of the Little Missouri. The beaver being seen in the day is a proof that they have been but little hunted, as they always keep themselves closely concealed during the day where they

are so. Found a great quantity of small onions in the plain where we encamped; had some of them collected and cooked, found them agreeable. The bulb grows single, is of an oval form, white, and about the size of a small bullet; the leaf resembles that of the chive. The hunters returned this evening with one deer only. The country about the mouth of this river had been recently hunted by the Minitaris and the little game which they had not killed and frightened away was so extremely shy that the hunters could not get in shooting range of them.

The Little Missouri disembogues on the south side of the Missouri 1,693 miles from the confluence of the latter with the Mississippi. It is 134 yards wide at its mouth, and sets in with a bold current, but its greatest depth is no more than two and a half feet. Its navigation is extremely difficult owing to its rapidity, shoals and sandbars. It may, however, be navigated with small canoes a considerable distance. This river passes through the northern extremity of the Black Hills, where it is very narrow and rapid and its banks high and perpendicular. It takes its rise in a broken country west of the Black Hills with the waters of the Yellowstone River, and a considerable distance S.W. of the point at which it passes the Black Hills. The country through which it passes is generally broken and the highlands possess but little timber. There is some timber in its bottom-lands, which consists of cottonwood, red elm, with a small proportion of small ash and box elder. The underbrush is willow, red wood (sometimes called red or swamp willow), the red berry [i.e., buffalo berry], and choke cherry. The country is extremely broken about the mouth of this river, and as far up on both sides as we could observe it from the tops of some elevated hills, which stand between these two rivers about three miles from their junction. The soil appears fertile and deep; it consists generally of a dark rich loam intermixed with a small proportion of fine sand. This river in its course passed near the N.W. side of the Turtle Mountain, which is said to be no more than four or five leagues distant from its entrance in a straight direction, a little to the S. of west. This mountain and the Knife River have therefore been laid down too far S.W. [He was referring to the map Clark had prepared at Fort Mandan, based on information from Indian informants.] The color of the water, the bed of the river, and its appearance in every respect resembles the Missouri; I am therefore induced to believe that the texture of the soil of the country in which it takes its rise, and that through which it passes, is similar to the country through which the Missouri passes after leaving the woody country, or such as we are now in.

On the side of a hill not distant from our camp I found some of the dwarf cedar of which I preserved a specimen. This plant [*creeping juniper*] spreads its limbs along the surface of the earth, where they are sometimes covered and always put forth a number of roots on the underside, while on the upper there are a great number of small shoots which with their leaves seldom rise higher than six or eight inches. They grow so close as perfectly to conceal the earth. It is an evergreen; the leaf is much more delicate than the common cedar, and its taste and smell the same. I have often thought that this plant would make very handsome edgings to the borders and walks of a garden; it is quite as handsome as box and would be much more easily propagated. The appearance of the Glauber's salts and carbonated wood still continue.

Clark notes that they had examined the canoes and already found mice chewing holes in the bags of corn and parched meal stored there.

April 13, 1805, Saturday [Lewis]
Being disappointed in my observations of yesterday for longitude, I was unwilling to remain at the entrance of the river another day for that purpose, and therefore determined to set out early this morning, which we did accordingly. The wind was in our favor after nine a.m. and continued favorable until three p.m. We therefore hoisted both the sails in the white pirogue, consisting of a small square sail and spritsail, which carried her at a pretty good gait until about two in the afternoon, when a sudden squall of wind struck us and turned the pirogue so much on the side as to alarm Charbonneau, who was steering at the time. In this state of alarm he threw the pirogue with her side to the wind, when the spritsail gibing was as near oversetting the pirogue as it was possible to have missed. The wind, however, abating for an instant, I ordered Drouillard to the helm and the sails to be taken in, which was instantly executed and the pirogue being steered before the wind was again placed in a state of security. This accident was very near costing us dearly. Believing this vessel to be the most steady and safe, we had embarked on board of it our instruments, papers, medicine and the most valuable part of the merchandise which we had still in reserve as presents for the Indians. We had also embarked on board ourselves, with three men who could not swim and the squaw with the young child, all of whom, had the pirogue overset, would most probably have perished, as the waves were high and the pirogue

upwards of 200 yards from the nearest shore. However, we fortunately escaped and pursued our journey under the square sail, which shortly after the accident I directed to be again hoisted. Our party caught three beaver last evening, and the French hunters seven. As there was much appearance of beaver just above the entrance of the Little Missouri these hunters concluded to remain some days; we therefore left them without the expectation of seeing them again.

Just above the entrance of the Little Missouri the great Missouri is upwards of a mile in width, though immediately at the entrance of the former it is not more than 200 yards wide and so shallow that the canoes passed it with setting poles. At the distance of nine miles passed the mouth of a creek on the starboard side which we called Onion Creek from the quantity of wild onions which grow in the plains on its borders. Capt. Clark, who was on shore, informed me that this creek was 16 yards wide a mile and a half above its entrance, discharges more water than creeks of its size usually do in this open country, and that there was not a stick of timber of any description to be seen on its borders or the level plain country through which it passes. At the distance of 10 miles further we passed the mouth of a large creek discharging itself in the center of a deep bend. Of this creek and the neighboring country, Capt. Clark, who was on shore, gave me the following description. "This creek I took to be a small river from its size and the quantity of water which it discharged. I ascended it one and a half miles and found it the discharge of a pond or small lake, which had the appearance of having formerly been the bed of the Missouri. Several small streams discharge themselves into this lake. The country on both sides consists of beautiful level and elevated plains, ascending as they recede from the Missouri; there were a great number of swans and geese in this lake and near its borders I saw the remains of 43 temporary Indian lodges, which I presume were those of the Assiniboines who are now in the neighborhood of the British establishments on the Assiniboine River."

This lake and its discharge we call Goose Egg from the circumstance of Capt. Clark shooting a goose while on her nest in the top of a lofty cottonwood tree, from which we afterwards took one egg. The wild geese frequently build their nests in this manner. At least we have already found several in trees, nor have we as yet seen any on the ground, or sandbars, where I had supposed from previous information that they most commonly deposited their eggs. Saw some buffalo and elk at a distance today but killed none of them. We found a number of the carcasses of the buffalo lying along shore, which had been drowned by falling through the ice in winter and lodged on shore by the high water when the river broke up about the first of this month. We saw also many tracks of the white bear [*once again, this is the grizzly bear*] of enormous size along the river shore and about the carcasses of the buffalo, on which I presume they feed. We have not as yet seen one of these animals, though their tracks are so abundant and recent. The men as well as ourselves are anxious to meet with some of these bears. The Indians give a very formidable account of the strength and ferocity of this animal, which they never dare to attack but in parties of six, eight, or ten persons; and are even then frequently defeated with the loss of one or more of their party. The savages attack this animal with their bows and arrows and the indifferent guns with which the traders furnish them. With these they shoot with such uncertainty and at so short a distance that they frequently miss their aim and fall a sacrifice to the bear. Two Minitaris were killed during the last winter in an attack on a white bear. This animal is said more frequently to attack a man on meeting with him, than to flee from him. When the Indians are about to go in quest of the white bear, previous to their departure they paint themselves and perform all those superstitious rites commonly observed when they are about to make war upon a neighboring nation.

Observed more bald eagles on this part of the Missouri than we have previously seen. Saw the small hawk, frequently called the sparrow hawk, which is common to most parts of the United States. Great quantities of geese are seen feeding in the prairies. Saw a large flock of white brant or geese with black wings pass up the river; there were a number of gray brant with them; from their flight I presume they proceed much further still to the N.W. We have never been able yet to shoot one of these birds and cannot therefore determine whether the gray brant found with the white are their brood of the last year or whether they are the same with the gray brant common to the Mississippi and lower part of the Missouri. We killed two antelope today which we found swimming from the S. to the N. side of the river; they were very poor. We encamped this evening on the starboard shore in a beautiful plain, elevated about 30 feet above the river.

April 14, 1805, Sunday [Lewis]
One of the hunters saw an otter last evening and shot at it, but missed it. A dog came to us this morning, which we supposed to have been lost by the

Indians who were recently encamped near the lake that we passed yesterday. The mineral appearances of salts, coal and sulfur, together with burnt hills and pumice stone, still continue. While we remained at the entrance of the Little Missouri, we saw several pieces of pumice stone floating down that stream, a considerable quantity of which had lodged against a point of driftwood a little above its entrance.

Capt. Clark walked on shore this morning and on his return informed me that he had passed through the timbered bottoms on the north side of the river and had extended his walk several miles back on the hills. In the bottomlands he had met with several uninhabited Indian lodges built with the boughs of the elm, and in the plains he met with the remains of two large encampments of a recent date, which from the appearance of some hoops of small kegs seen near them we concluded that they must have been the camps of the Assiniboines, as no other nation who visit this part of the Missouri ever indulge themselves with spirituous liquor. Of this article the Assiniboines are passionately fond, and we are informed that it forms their principal inducement to furnish the British establishments on the Assiniboine River with the dried and pounded meat and grease which they do. They also supply those establishments with a small quantity of fur, consisting principally of the large and small wolves and the small fox skins. These they barter for small kegs of rum which they generally transport to their camps at a distance from the establishments, where they revel with their friends and relations as long as they possess the means of intoxication. Their women and children are equally indulged on those occasions and are all seen drunk together. So far is a state of intoxication from being a cause of reproach among them that with the men it is a matter of exultation that their skill and industry as hunters has enabled them to get drunk frequently. In their customs, habits and dispositions these people very much resemble the Sioux from whom they have descended. The principal inducement with the British fur companies for continuing their establishments on the Assiniboine River is the buffalo meat and grease they procure from the Assiniboines and Crees, by means of which they are enabled to supply provision to their engagés on their return from Rainy Lake to the English River and the Athabaska country where they winter. Without such resource those voyagers would frequently be straitened for provision, as the country through which they pass is but scantily supplied with game and the rapidity with which they are compelled to travel in order to reach their winter stations would leave them but little leisure to search for food while on their voyage.

The Assiniboines have so recently left this neighborhood that the game is scarce and very shy. The river continues wide, and not more rapid than the Ohio in an average state of its current. The bottoms are wide and low, the moister parts containing some timber; the upland is extremely broken, consisting of high gaulded [i.e., bare] knobs as far as the eye can reach on either side, and entirely destitute of timber. On these hills many aromatic herbs are seen, resembling in taste, smell and appearance the sage, hyssop, wormwood, southernwood, and two other herbs which are strangers to me: the one resembling the camphor in taste and smell, rising to the height of two or three feet; the other, about the same size, has a long, narrow, smooth, soft leaf of an agreeable smell and flavor. Of this last the antelope is very fond; they feed on it, and perfume the hair of their foreheads and necks with it by rubbing against it. The dwarf cedar and juniper is also found in great abundance on the sides of these hills. Where the land is level it is uniformly fertile, consisting of a dark loam intermixed with a proportion of fine sand. It is generally covered with a short grass resembling very much the blue grass. The mineral appearances still continue. Considerable quantities of bituminous water, about the color of strong lye, trickles down the sides of the hills. This water partakes of the taste of Glauber's salts and slightly of alum.

While the party halted to take dinner today Capt. Clark killed a buffalo bull; it was meager, and we therefore took the marrowbones and a small proportion of the meat only. Near the place we dined on the larboard side there was a large village of burrowing squirrels. I have remarked that these animals generally select a southeasterly exposure for their residence, though they are sometimes found in the level plains. Passed an island, above which two small creeks fall in on the larboard side. The upper creek is the largest, which we called Charbonneau's Creek after our interpreter, who encamped several weeks on it with a hunting party of Indians. This was the highest point to which any white man had ever ascended, except two Frenchmen who, having lost their way, had straggled a few miles further, though to what place precisely I could not learn.

I walked on shore above this creek and killed an elk, which was so poor that it was unfit for use; I therefore left it, and joined the party at their encampment on the starboard shore a little after dark. On my arrival Capt. Clark informed me that he had seen two white bears pass over the hills shortly after I fired, and that they appeared to run nearly from the place where I shot. The larboard shore on which we walked was very broken and the hills in many places had the appearance of having slipped down in masses of several acres of land in surface. We saw many geese feeding on the tender grass in the prairies and several of their nests in the trees. We have not in a single instance found the nest of this bird on or near the ground. We saw a number of magpies, their nests and eggs. Their nests are built in trees and are composed of small sticks, leaves and grass, open at top, and much in the style of the large blackbird common to the United States. The egg is of a bluish brown color, freckles with reddish brown spots. One of the party killed a large hooting owl. I observed no difference between this bird and those of the same family common to the United States, except that this appeared to be more booted and more thickly clad with feathers.

April 15, 1805, Monday [Lewis]
Set out at an early hour this morning. I walked on shore, and Capt. Clark continued with the party, it being an invariable rule with us not to be both absent from our vessels at the same time. I passed through the bottoms of the river on the starboard side. They were partially covered with timber and were very extensive, level and beautiful. In my walk, which was about six miles, I passed a small rivulet of clear water making down from the hills, which on tasting, I discovered to be in a small degree brackish. It possessed less of the Glauber's salts, or alum, than those little streams from the hills usually do. In a little pond of water formed by this rivulet where it entered the bottom, I heard the frogs crying for the first time this season; their note was the same with that of the small frogs which are common to the lagoons and swamps of the United States. I saw great quantities of geese feeding in the bottoms, of which I shot one. Saw some deer and elk, but they were remarkably shy. I also met with great numbers of grouse or *prairie hens*, as they are called by the English traders of the N.W. These birds appeared to be mating; the note of the male is kuck, kuck, kuck, coo, coo, coo. The first part of the note both male and female use when flying. The male also drums something like the pheasant, but by no means as loud.

After breakfast Capt. Clark walked on the starboard shore, and on his return in the evening gave me the following account of his ramble: "I ascended to the high country, about nine miles [*Clark in his entry for the day says three miles*] distant from the Missouri. The country consists of beautiful, level and fertile plains, destitute of timber. I saw many little drains which took their rise in the river hills, from whence as far as I could see they run to the N.E." These streams we suppose to be the waters of the Mouse River, a branch of the Assiniboine which the Indians informed us approaches the Missouri very nearly, about this point. "I passed," continued he, "a creek about 20 yards wide, which falls into the Missouri; the bottoms of this creek are wide, level, and extremely fertile, but almost entirely destitute of timber. The water of this creek as well as all those creeks and rivulets which we have passed since we left Fort Mandan was so strongly impregnated with salts and other mineral substances that I was incapable of drinking it. I saw the remains of several camps of the Assiniboines, near one of which, in a small ravine, there was a park which they had formed of timber and brush, for the purpose of taking the antelope. It was constructed in the following manner: a strong pound was first made of timbers, on one side of which there was a small aperture, sufficiently large to admit an antelope; from each side of this aperture, a curtain was extended to a considerable distance, widening as they receded from the pound."

We passed a rock this evening standing in the middle of the river, and the bed of the river was formed principally of gravel. We encamped this evening on a sand point on the larboard side. A little above our encampment the river was confined to a channel of 80 yards in width.

April 16, 1805, Tuesday [Lewis]
Set out very early this morning. Capt. Clark walked on shore this morning and killed an antelope, rejoined us at half after eight a.m. He informed me that he had seen many buffalo, elk and deer in his absence, and that he had met with a great number of old hornets' nests in the woody bottoms through which he had passed. The hills of the river still continue extremely broken for a few miles back, when it becomes a fine level country of open fertile lands. Immediately on the river there are many fine, level, extensive and extremely fertile high plains and meadows. I think the quantity of timbered land on the river is increasing. The mineral appearances still continue. I met with several stones today that had the appearance of wood first carbonated and then petrified by the water of the river, which I have discovered has that effect on many vegetable substances when exposed to its influence for a length of time. I believe it to be the strata of coal seen in those hills which causes

the fire and burnt appearances frequently met with in this quarter. Where those burnt appearances are to be seen in the face of the river bluffs, the coal is seldom seen, and when you meet with it in the neighborhood of the strata of burnt earth, the coal appears to be precisely at the same height, and is nearly of the same thickness, together with the sand and a sulfurous substance which usually accompanies it. There was a remarkable large beaver caught by one of the party last night. These animals are now very abundant. I have met with several trees which have been felled by them 20 inches in diameter. Bark is their only food and they appear to prefer that of the cottonwood and willow, as we have never met with any other species of timber on the Missouri which had the appearance of being cut by them. We passed three small creeks on the starboard side. They take their rise in the river hills at no great distance. We saw a great number of geese today, both in the plains and on the river. I have observed but few ducks; those we have met with are the mallard and blue-winged teal.

April 17, 1805, Wednesday [Lewis]
A delightful morning, set out at an early hour. The country through which we passed today was much the same as that described of yesterday; there was more appearance of burnt hills, furnishing large quantities of lava and pumice stone. Of the latter some pieces were seen floating down the river. Capt. Clark walked on shore this morning on the starboard side and did not join us until half after six in the evening. He informed me that he had seen the remains of the Assiniboine encampments in every point of woodland through which he had passed. We saw immense quantities of game in every direction around us as we passed up the river, consisting of herds of buffalo, elk and antelope with some deer and wolves. Though we continue to see many tracks of the bear we have seen but very few of them, and those are at a great distance generally running from us. I therefore presume that they are extremely wary and shy; the Indian account of them does not correspond with our experience so far. One black bear passed near the pirogues on the 16th and was seen by myself and the party but he so quickly disappeared that we did not shoot at him.

At the place we halted to dine on the larboard side we met with a herd of buffalo of which I killed the fattest as I conceived among them; however, on examining it I found it so poor that I thought it unfit for use and only took the tongue. The party killed another which was still more lean. Just before we encamped this evening we saw some tracks of Indians who had passed about 24 hours; they left four rafts of timber on the starboard side, on which they had passed. We supposed them to have been a party of the Assiniboines who had been to war against the Rocky Mountain Indians, and then on their return. Capt. Clark saw a curlew today. There were three beaver taken this morning by the party. The men prefer the flesh of this animal to that of any other which we have, or are able to procure at this moment. I eat very heartily of the beaver myself and think it excellent, particularly the tail and liver. We had a fair wind today which enabled us to sail the greater part of the distance we have traveled; encamped on the larboard shore the extremity of the last course.

April 18, 1805, Thursday [Lewis]
A fine morning, set out at an early hour. One beaver caught this morning by two traps, having a foot in each. The traps belonged to different individuals, between whom a contest ensued which would have terminated, most probably, in a serious encounter had not our timely arrival at the place prevented it. After breakfast this morning, Capt. Clark walked on the starboard shore, while the party were ascending by means of their tow lines. I walked with them on the bank, found a species of pea bearing a yellow flower, and now in bloom. It seldom rises more than six inches high; the leaf and stalk resembles that of the common garden pea; the root is perennial. I also saw several parcels of buffalo hair hanging on the rose bushes, which had been bleached by exposure to the weather and become perfectly white. It has every appearance of the wool of the sheep, though much finer and more silky and soft. I am confident that an excellent cloth may be made of the wool of the buffalo. The buffalo I killed yesterday had cast his long hair and the pile which remained was very thick, fine, and about two inches in length. I think this animal would have furnished about five pounds of wool. We were detained today from one to five p.m. in consequence of the wind, which blew so violently from the north that it was with difficulty we could keep the canoes from filling with water, although they were along shore. I had them secured by placing the pirogues on the outside of them in such manner as to break the waves off them. At five we proceeded and shortly after met with Capt. Clark, who had killed an elk and a deer and was waiting our arrival. We took the meat on board and continued our march until nearly dark, when we came to on the starboard side under a bold, well-timbered bank which sheltered

us from the wind, which had abated but not yet ceased. Here we encamped, it being the extremity of the last course of the day.

April 19, 1805, Friday [Lewis]
The wind blew so hard this morning from N.W. that we dared not to venture our canoes on the river. Observed considerable quantities of dwarf juniper on the hillsides. It seldom rises higher than three feet. The wind having placed ourselves in a safe harbor. The party killed one elk and a beaver today. The beaver of this part of the Missouri are larger, fatter, more abundant and better clad with fur than those of any other part of the country that I have yet seen; I have remarked also that their fur is much darker.

   Clark adds that they saw a "great deal of sign of the large bear."

April 20, 1805, Saturday [Lewis]
The wind continued to blow tolerably hard this morning but by no means as violently as it did yesterday. We determined to set out and accordingly departed a little before seven. I walked on shore on the north side of the river, and Capt. Clark proceeded with the party. The river bottoms through which I passed about seven miles were fertile and well covered with cottonwood, some box elder, ash and red elm. The underbrush, willow, rose bushes, honeysuckle, red willow, gooseberry, currant and serviceberry and in the open grounds along the foot of the river hills, immense quantities of hyssop. In the course of my walk I killed two deer, wounded an elk and a deer. Saw the remains of some Indian hunting camps, near which stood a small scaffold of about seven feet high on which were deposited two dog sleighs with their harness. Underneath this scaffold a human body was lying, well rolled in several dressed buffalo skins and near it a bag of the same material, containing sundry articles belonging to the deceased, consisting of a pair of moccasins, some red and blue earth, beaver's nails, instruments for dressing the buffalo skin, some dried roots, several plats of the sweet grass, and a small quantity of Mandan tobacco. I presume that the body, as well as the bag containing these articles, had formerly been placed on the scaffold, as is the custom of these people, but had fallen down by accident. Near the scaffold I saw the carcass of a large dog not yet decayed, which I suppose had been killed at the time the human body was left on the scaffold. This was no doubt the reward which the poor dog had met with for performing the friendly office to his mistress of transporting her corpse to the place of

deposit. It is customary with the Assiniboines, Mandans, Minitaris, etc., who scaffold their dead, to sacrifice the favorite horses and dogs of their deceased relations, with a view of their being serviceable to them in the land of spirits. I have never heard of any instances of human sacrifices on those occasions among them.

The wind blew so hard that I concluded it was impossible for the pirogues and canoes to proceed and therefore returned and joined them about three in the evening. Capt. Clark informed me that soon after setting out, a part of the bank of the river fell in near one of the canoes and had very nearly filled her with water. The wind became so hard and the waves so high that it was with infinite risk he had been able to get as far as his present station. The white pirogue and several of the canoes had shipped water several times but happily our stores were but little injured. Those which were wet we put out to dry and determined to remain until the next morning. We sent out four hunters who soon added three elk, four geese, and two deer to our stock of provisions. The party caught six beaver today which were large and in fine order. The buffalo, elk and deer are poor at this season, and of course are not very palatable. However our good health and appetites make up every necessary deficiency, and we eat very heartily of them. Encamped on the starboard side under a high, well-timbered bank.

April 21, 1805, Sunday [Lewis]
Set out at an early hour this morning. Capt. Clark walked on shore; the wind, though ahead, was not violent. The country through which we passed is very similar in every respect to that through which we have passed for several days. We saw immense herds of buffalo, elk, deer and antelope. Capt. Clark killed a buffalo and four deer in the course of his walk today; and the party with me killed three deer, two beaver, and four buffalo calves. The latter we found very delicious. I think it equal to any veal I ever tasted. The elk now begin to shed their horns. Passed one large and two small creeks on the larboard side, though neither of them discharges any water at present. The wind blew so hard this evening that we were obliged to halt several hours. We reached the place of encampment after dark, which was on the larboard side a little above White Earth River [*now called the Little Muddy*], which discharges itself on the starboard side. Immediately at the mouth of this river it is not more than 10 yards wide, being choked up by the mud of the Missouri; though after leaving the bottomlands of this river, or even sooner, it becomes

a bold stream of 60 yards wide and is deep and navigable. The course of this river as far as I could see from the top of *Cut Bluff* was due north. It passes through a beautiful, level and fertile valley about five miles in width. I think I saw about 25 miles up this river and did not discover one tree or bush of any description on its borders. The valley was covered with elk and buffalo. Saw a great number of geese today as usual, also some swans and ducks.

April 22, 1805, Monday [Lewis]
Set out at an early hour this morning; proceeded pretty well until breakfast, when the wind became so hard ahead that we proceeded with difficulty even with the assistance of our tow lines. The party halted and Capt. Clark and myself walked to the White Earth River, which approaches the Missouri very near at this place, being about four miles above its entrance. We found that it contained more water than streams of its size generally do at this season. The water is much clearer than that of the Missouri. The banks of the river are steep and not more than ten or twelve feet high; the bed seems to be composed of mud altogether. The salts which have been before mentioned as common on the Missouri appear in great quantities along the banks of this river, which are in many places so thickly covered with it that they appear perfectly white. Perhaps it has been from this white appearance of its banks that the river has derived its name. This river is said to be navigable nearly to its source, which is at no great distance from the Saskatchewan, and I think from its size and the direction which it seems to take, and the latitude of its mouth, that there is very good ground to believe that it extends as far north as latitude 50 degrees [*an important consideration to the United States, as the Louisiana Purchase included all the lands drained by the Missouri and its tributaries. The farther north any tributary originated, the farther north the border with Canada would run. But the White Earth River rises in North Dakota, not Canada*].

This stream passes through an open country generally. The broken hills of the Missouri about this place exhibit large irregular and broken masses of rocks and stones, some of which, though 200 feet above the level of the water, seem at some former period to have felt its influence, for they appear smooth as if worn by the agitation of the water. This collection consists of white and grey granite, a brittle black rock, flint, limestone, freestone, some small specimens of an excellent pebble and occasionally broken strata of a stone which appears to be petrified wood. It is of a black color and makes excellent whetstones. Coal or carbonated wood, pumice stone, lava and other mineral appearances still continue. The coal appears to be of better quality. I exposed a specimen of it to the fire and found that it burned tolerably well; it afforded but little flame or smoke, but produced a hot and lasting fire.

I ascended to the top of the cut bluff this morning, from whence I had a most delightful view of the country, the whole of which, except the valley formed by the Missouri, is void of timber or underbrush, exposing to the first glance of the spectator immense herds of buffalo, elk, deer, and antelope feeding in one common and boundless pasture. We saw a number of beaver feeding on the bark of the trees along the verge of the river, several of which we shot, found them large and fat. Walking on shore this evening I met with a buffalo calf, which attached itself to me and continued to follow close at my heels until I embarked and left it. It appeared alarmed at my dog, which was probably the cause of its so readily attaching itself to me. Capt. Clark informed me that he saw a large drove of buffalo pursued by wolves today, that they at length caught a calf which was unable to keep up with the herd. The cows only defend their young so long as they are able to keep up with the herd and seldom return any distance in search of them.

April 23, 1805, Tuesday [Lewis]
Set out at an early hour this morning. About nine a.m. the wind arose, and shortly after became so violent that we were unable to proceed; in short it was with much difficulty and some risk that I was able to get the canoes and pirogues into a place of tolerable safety, there being no timber on either side of the river at this place. Some of the canoes shipped water and wet several parcels of their lading, which I directed to be opened and aired. We remained until five in the evening, when, the wind abating in some measure, we reloaded and proceeded. Shortly after we were joined by Capt. Clark, who had walked on shore this morning, and passing through the bottomlands had fallen on the river some miles above; concluding that the wind had detained us, he came down the river in search of us. He had killed three blacktailed or mule deer, and a buffalo calf in the course of his ramble. These hard winds, being so frequently repeated, become a serious source of detention to us. Encamped on the starboard side.

April 24, 1805, Wednesday [Lewis]
The wind blew so hard during the whole of this day that we were unable to

move. Notwithstanding that we were sheltered by high timber from the effects of the wind, such was its violence that it caused the waves to rise in such a manner as to wet many articles in the small canoes before they could be unloaded. We sent out some hunters who killed four deer and two elk, and caught some young wolves of the small kind [*i.e., coyote cubs*]. Sore eyes are a common complaint among the party. I believe it originates from the immense quantities of sand, which is driven by the wind from the sandbars of the river in such clouds that you are unable to discover the opposite bank of the river in many instances. The particles of this sand are so fine and light that they are easily supported by the air and are carried by the wind for many miles, at a distance exhibiting every appearance of a column of thick smoke. So penetrating is this sand that we cannot keep any article free from it; in short we are compelled to eat, drink, and breathe it very freely. My pocket watch is out of order; she will run only a few minutes without stopping. I can discover no radical defect in her works and must therefore attribute it to the sand, with which she seems plentifully charged, notwithstanding her cases are double and tight.

April 25, 1805, Thursday [Lewis]
The wind was more moderate this morning, though still hard; we set out at an early hour. The water froze on the oars this morning as the men rowed. About 10 o'clock a.m. the wind began to blow so violently that we were obliged to lie to. My dog had been absent during the last night and I was fearful we had lost him altogether; however, much to my satisfaction he joined us at eight o'clock this morning. The wind had been so unfavorable to our progress for several days past, and seeing but little prospect of a favorable change, knowing that the river was crooked, from the report of the hunters who were out yesterday, and believing that we were at no very great distance from the Yellowstone River, I determined, in order as much as possible to avoid detention, to proceed by land with a few men to the entrance of that river and make the necessary observations to determine its position, which I hoped to effect by the time that Capt. Clark could arrive with the party. Accordingly I set out at 11 o'clock on the larboard side, accompanied by four men. We proceeded about four miles, when falling in with some buffalo I killed a yearling calf, which was in good order; we soon cooked and made a hearty meal of a part of it, and renewed our march. Our route lay along the foot of the river hills. When we had proceeded

about four miles I ascended the hills, from whence I had a most pleasing view of the country, particularly of the wide and fertile valleys formed by the Missouri and the Yellowstone Rivers, which, occasionally unmasked by the wood on their borders, disclose their meanderings for many miles in their passage through these delightful tracts of country. I could not discover the junction of the river immediately, they being concealed by the woods; however, sensible that it could not be distant, I determined to encamp on the bank of the Yellowstone River, which made its appearance about two miles south of me. The whole face of the country was covered with herds of buffalo, elk and antelope; deer are also abundant, but keep themselves more concealed in the woodland. The buffalo, elk and antelope are so gentle that we pass near them while feeding without appearing to excite any alarm among them, and when we attract their attention, they frequently approach us more nearly to discover what we are, and in some instances pursue us a considerable distance apparently with that view.

In our way to the place I had determined to encamp, we met with two large herds of buffalo, of which we killed three cows and a calf. Two of the former were but lean; we therefore took their tongues and a part of their marrow-bones only. I then proceeded to the place of our encampment with two of the men, taking with us the calf and marrowbones, while the other two remained, with orders to dress the cow that was in tolerable order, and hang the meat out of the reach of the wolves, a precaution indispensable to its safekeeping, even for a night. We encamped on the bank of the Yellowstone River, two miles south of its confluence with the Missouri. On rejoining Capt. Clark the 26th in the evening, he informed me that at five p.m. after I left him the wind abated in some measure and he proceeded a few miles further and encamped.

April 26, 1805, Friday [Lewis]
This morning I dispatched Joseph Fields up the Yellowstone River with orders to examine it as far as he could conveniently and return the same evening; two others were directed to bring in the meat we had killed last evening, while I proceeded down the river with one man in order to take a view of the confluence of this great river with the Missouri, which we found to be two miles distant on a direct line northwest from our encampment. The bottomland on the lower side of the Yellowstone River near its mouth for about one mile in width appears to be subject to inundation, while that on

the opposite side of the Missouri and the point formed by the junction of these rivers is of the common elevation, say from 12 to 18 feet above the level of the water, and of course not liable to be overflown except in extreme high water, which does not appear to be very frequent. There is more timber in the neighborhood of the junction of these rivers, and on the Missouri as far below as the White Earth River, than there is on any part of the Missouri above the entrance of the Cheyenne River to this place. The timber consists principally of cottonwood, with some small elm, ash and box elder. The undergrowth on the sandbars and verge of the river is the small-leafed willow; the low bottoms, rose bushes which rise to three or four feet high, the red-berry, serviceberry, and the redwood [*the red willow, not the California redwood tree*]. The high bottoms are of two descriptions, either timbered or open. The first lies next to the river and its underbrush is the same with that of the low timbered bottoms, with the addition of the broad-leafed willow, gooseberry, choke cherry, purple currant, and honeysuckle bushes. The open bottoms border on the hills, and are covered in many parts by the wild hyssop, which rises to the height of two feet. I observe that the antelope, buffalo, elk and deer feed on this herb. The willow of the sandbars also furnish a favorite winter food to these animals as well as to the grouse, the porcupine, hare, and rabbit. About 12 o'clock I heard the discharge of several guns at the junction of the rivers, which announced to me the arrival of the party with Capt. Clark. I afterwards learned that they had fired on some buffalo which they met with at that place, and of which they killed a cow and several calves; the latter are now fine veal. I dispatched one of the men to Capt. Clark requesting him to send up a canoe to take down the meat we had killed and our baggage to his encampment, which was accordingly complied with. After I had completed my observations in the evening I walked down and joined the party at their encampment on the point of land formed by the junction of the rivers, found them all in good health and much pleased at having arrived at this long-wished-for spot, and in order to add in some measure to the general pleasure which seemed to pervade our little community, we ordered a dram to be issued to each person. This soon produced the fiddle and they spent the evening with much hilarity, singing and dancing, and seemed as perfectly to forget their past toils, as they appeared regardless of those to come. In the evening, the man I had sent up the river this morning returned and reported that he had ascended it about eight miles on a straight line; that he found it crooked, meandering from side to side of the valley formed by it, which is from four to five miles wide. The current of the river gentle, and its bed much interrupted and broken by sandbars. At the distance of five miles he passed a large island well covered with timber, and three miles higher a large creek falls in on the southeast side above a high bluff in which there are several strata of coal. The country bordering on this river as far as he could perceive, like that of the Missouri, consisted of open plains. He saw several of the big-horned animals in the course of his walk, but they were so shy that he could not get a shot at them. He found a large horn of one of these animals, which he brought with him. The bed of the Yellowstone River is entirely composed of sand and mud, not a stone of any kind to be seen in it near its entrance. Capt. Clark measured these rivers just above their conflu-ence, found the bed of the Missouri 520 yards wide, the water occupying 330, its channel deep. The Yellowstone River including its sandbar, 858 yards of which the water occupied 297 yards; the deepest part 12 feet; it was falling at this time and appeared to be nearly at its summer tide.

The Indians inform that the Yellowstone River is navigable for pirogues and canoes nearly to its source in the Rocky Mountains, and that in its course near these mountains it passes within less than half a day's march of a navigable part of the Missouri. Its extreme sources are adjacent to those of the Missouri, River Platte, and I think probably with some of the south branch of the Columbia River. The first part of this course lies through a mountainous rocky country, though well timbered and in many parts fertile; the middle, and much the most extensive portion of the river, lies through a delightful, rich and fertile country, well covered with timber, interspersed with plains and meadows, and well watered; it is somewhat broken in many parts. The lower portion consists of fertile open plains and meadows almost entirely, though it possesses a considerable proportion of timber on its borders. The current of the upper portion is extremely rapid, that of the middle and lower portions much more gentle than the Missouri. The water of this river is turbid, though it does not possess as much sedi-ment as that of the Missouri. This river in its course receives the waters of many large tributary streams principally from the southeast, of which the most considerable are the Tongue and Bighorn Rivers. The former is much the largest and heads with the River Platte and Bighorn River [*this was wrong; the Bighorn is the larger river. The information on their contiguity at the source with the Platte is wrong as well; the Platte rises in Colorado*], as does the latter with the Tongue River and the River Platte. A sufficient quantity of limestone may be readily procured for building near the junction of the Missouri and Yellowstone Rivers. I could observe no regular strata of it, though it lies on the sides of the river hills in large irregular masses, in considerable quantities; it is of a light color, and appears to be of an excellent quality.

April 27, 1805, Saturday [Lewis]
This morning I walked through the point formed by the junction of the rivers. The woodland extends about a mile, when the rivers approach each other within less than half a mile. Here a beautiful level low plain commences and extends up both rivers for many miles, widening as the rivers recede from each other, and extending back half a mile to a plain about 12 feet higher than itself. The low plain appears to be a few inches higher than high water mark and of course will not be liable to be overflown—though where it joins the high plain a part of the Missouri when at its great height passes through a channel of 60 or 70 yards wide and falls into the Yellowstone River. On the Missouri about 2 and a half miles from the entrance of the Yellowstone River, and between this high and low plain, a small lake is situated about 200 yards wide extending along the edge of the high plain parallel with the Missouri about one mile. On the point of the high plain at the lower extremity of this lake I think would be the most eligible site for an establishment.

Between this low plain and the Yellowstone River there is an extensive body of timbered land extending up the river for many miles. This site recommended is about 400 yards distant from the Missouri and about double that distance from the River Yellowstone. From it the high plain, rising very gradually, extends back about three miles to the hills, and continues with the same width between these hills and the timbered land on the Yellowstone River, up that stream, for seven or eight miles, and is one of the handsomest plains I ever beheld. On the Missouri side the hills circumscribe its width, and at the distance of three miles up that river from this site it is not more than 400 yards wide. Capt. Clark thinks that the lower extremity of the low plain would be most eligible for this establishment. It is true that it is much nearer both rivers, and might answer very well, but I think it rather too low to venture a permanent establishment, particularly if built of brick or other durable materials, at any considerable expense; for so capricious and versatile are these rivers that it is difficult to say how long it will be until they direct the force of their currents against this narrow part of the low plain, which, when they do, must shortly yield to their influence. In such case only a few years would be necessary for the annihilation of the plain, and with it the fortification.

I continued my walk on shore. At 11 a.m. the wind became very hard from N.W. insomuch that the pirogues and canoes were unable either to proceed or pass the river to me. I was under the necessity therefore of shooting a goose and cooking it for my dinner. The wind abated about four p.m. and the party proceeded, though I could not conveniently join them until night. Although game is very abundant and gentle, we only kill as much as is necessary for food. I believe that two good hunters could conveniently supply a regiment with provisions. For several days past we have observed a great number of buffalo lying dead on shore, some of them entire and others partly devoured by the wolves and bears. Those animals either drowned during the winter in attempting to pass the river on the ice or by swimming across at present to bluff banks which they were unable to ascend, and feeling themselves too weak to return, remain and perish for the want of food. In this situation we met with several little parties of them. Beaver are very abundant; the party kill several of them every day. The eagles, magpies, and geese have their nests in trees adjacent to each other; the magpie particularly appears fond of building near the eagle, as we scarcely see an eagle's nest unaccompanied with two or three magpies' nests within a short distance. The bald eagles are more abundant here than I ever observed them in any part of the country.

April 28, 1805, Sunday [Lewis]
Set out this morning at an early hour; the wind was favorable and we employed our sails to advantage. Capt. Clark walked on shore this morning and I proceeded with the party. The country through which we passed today is open as usual and very broken on both sides near the river hills; the bottoms are level, fertile, and partially covered with timber. The hills and bluffs exhibit their usual mineral appearances, some burnt hills but no appearance of pumice stone; coal is in great abundance and the salts still increase in quantity. The banks of the river and sandbars are encrusted with it in many places and appear perfectly white, as if covered with snow or frost.

The woods are now green, though the plains and meadows appear to abate of the verdure those below exhibited some days past. We passed three small runs today, two falling in on the starboard side and one on the larboard side; they are but small, afford but little water and head a few miles back in the hills. We saw great quantities of game today, consisting of the common and mule deer, elk, buffalo, and antelope; also four brown bear, one of which was fired on and wounded by one of the party but we did not get it. The beaver have cut great quantities of timber, saw a tree nearly three feet in diameter that had been felled by them. Capt. Clark in the course of his walk killed a deer and a goose, and saw three black bear. He thinks the bottoms are not so wide as they have been for some days past.

April 29, 1805, Monday [Lewis]
Set out this morning at the usual hour; the wind was moderate; I walked on shore with one man. About eight a.m. we fell in with two brown or yellow bear, both of which we wounded. One of them made his escape; the other after my firing on him pursued me seventy or eighty yards, but fortunately had been so badly wounded that he was unable to pursue so closely as to prevent my charging my gun. We again repeated our fire and killed him. It was a male not fully grown. We estimated his weight at 300 pounds, not having the means of ascertaining it precisely. The legs of this bear are somewhat longer than those of the black, as are its talons and tusks incomparably larger and longer. The testicles, which in the black bear are placed pretty well back between the thighs and contained in one pouch like those of the dog and most quadrupeds, are in the yellow or brown bear placed much further forward and are suspended in separate pouches from two to four inches asunder. [*Thwaites in his edition makes no attempt to explain this anatomical oddity; Moulton, however, notes that no other grizzly bear with its testicles placed in this position has ever been discovered, and concludes that Lewis was mistaken in his observation.*] Its color is yellowish brown, the eyes small, black, and piercing; the front of the forelegs near the feet is usually black; the fur is finer, thicker and deeper than that of the black bear. These are all the particulars in which this animal appeared to me to differ from the black bear. It is a much more furious and formidable animal and will frequently pursue the hunter when wounded. It is astonishing to see the wounds they will bear before they can be put to death. The Indians may well fear this animal, equipped as they generally are with their bows and arrows or indifferent fuzees, but in the hands of skillful riflemen they are by no means as formidable or dangerous as they have been represented.

Game is still very abundant; we can scarcely cast our eyes in any direction without perceiving deer, elk, buffalo or antelope. The quantity of wolves appears to increase in the same proportion. They generally hunt in parties of six, eight, or ten. They kill a great number of antelope at this season. The antelope are yet meager and the females are big with young. The wolves take them most generally in attempting to swim the river; in this manner my dog caught one, drowned it, and brought it on shore; they are but clumsy swimmers, though on land when in good order they are extremely fleet and durable. We have frequently seen the wolves in pursuit of the antelope in the plains. They appear to decoy a single one from a flock, and then pursue it, alternately relieving each other until they take it. On joining Capt. Clark he informed me that he had seen a female and faun of the big-horned animal, and that they ran for some distance with great apparent ease along the side of the river bluff where it was almost perpendicular. Two of the party fired on them while in motion without effect. We took the flesh of the bear on board and proceeded. Capt. Clark walked on shore this evening, killed a deer, and saw several of the big-horned animals. There is more appearance of coal today than we have yet seen; the strata are 6 feet thick in some instances. The earth has been burnt in many places, and always appears in strata on the same level with the strata of coal. We came to this evening in the mouth of a little river which falls in on the starboard side. This stream is about 50 yards wide from bank to bank; the water occupies about 15 yards. The banks are of earth only, abrupt, though not high. The bed is of mud principally. Capt. Clark, who was up this stream about three miles, informed me that it continued about the same width, that its current was gentle, and it appeared navigable for pirogues. It meanders through an extensive, fertile, and beautiful valley as far as could be seen about N. 30° W. There was but one solitary tree to be seen on the banks of this river after it left the bottom of the Missouri. The water of this river is clear, with a brownish yellow tint. Here the highlands recede from the Missouri, leaving the valley formed by the river from seven to eight miles wide, and rather lower than usual. This stream my friend Capt. Clark named Martha's River, in honor of Miss M.F. [*her identity remains unknown; it is now called Big Muddy*].

April 30, 1805, Tuesday [Clark]
The wind blew hard from the N.E. all last night. We set out at sunrise; the

wind blew hard the greater part of the day and part of the time favorably. We did not lie by today on account of the wind. I walked on shore today, our interpreter and his squaw followed. In my walk the squaw found and brought me a bush something like the currant, which she said bore a delicious fruit and that great quantities grew on the Rocky Mountains. This shrub was in bloom, has a yellow flower with a deep cup. The fruit when ripe is yellow and hangs in bunches like cherries. Some of those berries yet remained on the bushes. The bottoms above the mouth of the last river are extensive, level and fertile land and covered with indifferent timber in the points. The upland appears to rise gradually. I saw great numbers of antelope, also scattering buffalo, elk, deer, wolves, geese, ducks and crows. I killed two geese which we dined on today. Capt. Lewis walked on shore and killed an elk this evening, and we came to and camped on the starboard side. The country on both sides has a beautiful appearance.

May 1, 1805, Wednesday [Lewis]
Set out this morning at an early hour. The wind being favorable we used our sails, which carried us on at a good pace until about 12 o'clock, when the wind became so high that the small canoes were unable to proceed. One of them, which separated from us just before the wind became so violent, is now lying on the opposite side of the river, being unable to rejoin us in consequence of the waves, which during those gusts run several feet high. We came to on the larboard shore in a handsome bottom well stocked with cottonwood timber; here the wind compelled us to spend the balance of the day. We sent out some hunters who killed a buffalo, an elk, a goat and two beaver. Game is now abundant. The country appears much more pleasant and fertile than that we have passed for several days; the hills are lower, the bottoms wider and better stocked with timber, which consists principally of cottonwood, not however of large size. The undergrowth willow on the verge of the river and sandbars, rose bushes, red willow and the broad-leafed willow in the bottom lands. The high country on either side of the river is one vast plain, entirely destitute of timber, but is apparently fertile, consisting of a dark, rich, mellow-looking loam. John Shields sick today with the rheumatism. Shannon killed a bird of the plover kind, weight one pound [*this was the American avocet, which was known to science, if not to Lewis, who gave it a new name, the "Missouri plover"; we omit Lewis's long description of the bird that follows in the text*].

May 2, 1805, Thursday [Lewis]

The wind continued violent all night, nor did it abate much of its violence this morning, when at daylight it was attended with snow, which continued to fall until about 10 a.m. Being about one inch deep, it formed a singular contrast with the vegetation, which was considerably advanced. Some flowers had put forth in the plains and the leaves of the cottonwood were as large as a dollar. Sent out some hunters, who killed two deer, three elk and several buffalo. On our way this evening we also shot three beaver along the shore. These animals in consequence of not being hunted are extremely gentle. Where they are hunted they never leave their lodges in the day. The flesh of the beaver is esteemed a delicacy among us. I think the tail a most delicious morsel; when boiled it resembles in flavor the fresh tongues and sounds [*i.e., the air bladders*] of the codfish and is usually sufficiently large to afford a plentiful meal for two men.

Joseph Fields, one of the hunters who was out today, found several yards of scarlet cloth which had been suspended on the bough of a tree near an old Indian hunting camp, where it had been left as a sacrifice to the deity by the Indians, probably of the Assiniboine nation, it being a custom with them, as well as all the nations inhabiting the waters of the Missouri so far as they are known to us, to offer or sacrifice in this manner to the deity whatever they may be possessed of which they think most acceptable to him, and, very honestly making their feelings the test of those of the deity, offer him the article which they most prize themselves. This being the most usual method of worshiping the Great Spirit, as they term the deity, is practiced on interesting occasions, or to produce the happy eventuation of the important occurrences incident to human nature, such as relief from hunger or malady, protection from their enemies or the delivering them into their hands, and with such as cultivate, to prevent the river's overflowing and destroying their crops, etc. Sacrifices of a similar kind are also made to the deceased by their friends and relatives.

The air was very piercing this evening. The water froze on the oars as they rowed. The wind dying at five p.m. we set out. Everything which is incomprehensible to the Indians they call *big medicine,* and is the operation of the presence and power of the *Great Spirit.* This morning one of the men shot the Indian dog that had followed us for several days; he would steal their cooked provision.

May 3, 1805, Friday [Lewis]

The morning being very cold we did not set out as early as usual; ice formed on a kettle of water one quarter of an inch thick. The snow has melted generally in the bottoms, but the hills still remain covered. On the larboard side at the distance of two miles we passed a curious collection of bushes which had been tied up in the form of a fascine and standing on end in the open bottom [*a fascine was a large bundle of sticks; the old Latin term for it is* fasces]. It appeared to be about 30 feet high and ten or twelve feet in diameter. This we supposed to have been placed there by the Indians as a sacrifice for some purpose. The wind continued to blow hard from the west but not so strong as to compel us to lie by.

Capt. Clark walked on shore and killed an elk, which he caused to be butchered by the time I arrived with the party. Here we halted and dined, it being about 12 o'clock, our usual time of halting for that purpose. After dinner Capt. Clark pursued his walk, while I continued with the party, it being a rule which we had established never to be absent at the same time from the party. The plains or high lands are much less elevated than they were, not being more than from 50 to 60 feet above the river bottom, which is also wider than usual, being from five to nine miles in width; traces of the ancient beds of the river are visible in many places through the whole extent of this valley.

Since the hills have become lower the appearance of the strata of coal, burnt hills and pumice stone have in a great measure ceased; I saw none today. We saw vast quantities of buffalo, elk, deer, principally of the long-tailed kind, antelope or goats, beaver, geese, ducks, brant and some swans. Near the entrance of the river mentioned in the tenth course of this day, we saw an unusual number of porcupines, from which we determined to call the river after that animal, accordingly denominated it *Porcupine River*. This stream discharges itself into the Missouri on the starboard side 2,000 miles above the mouth of the latter. It is a beautiful bold running stream, 40 yards wide at its entrance; the water is transparent, it being the first of this description that I have yet seen discharge itself into the Missouri. Before it enters a large sandbar through which it discharges itself into the Missouri, its banks and bottom are formed of a stiff blue and black clay. It appears to be navigable for canoes and pirogues at this time and I have no doubt but it might be navigated with boats of a considerable size in high water. Its banks appear to be from 8 to 10 feet high and seldom overflow.

From the quantity of water furnished by this river, the appearance of the country, the direction it pursues, and the situation of its entrance, I have but little doubt but it takes its source not far from the main body of the Saskatchewan River, and that it is probably navigable 150 miles, perhaps not very distant from that river. Should this be the case, it would afford a very favorable communication to the Athabaska country, from whence the British N.W. Company derive so large a portion of their valuable furs.

Capt. Clark, who ascended this river several miles and passed it above where it entered the hills, informed me on his return that he found the general width of the bed of the river about one hundred yards. Where he passed the river the bed was 112 yards wide, the water was knee deep and 38 yards in width. The river, which he could observe from the rising grounds for about 20 miles, bore a little to the east of north. There was a considerable portion of timber in the bottomlands of this river. Capt. Clark also met with limestone on the surface of the earth in the course of his walk. He also saw a range of low mountains at a distance to the W. of N., their direction [*i.e., the direction the range ran in*] being N.W. The country in the neighborhood of this river, and as far as the eye can reach, is level, fertile, open and beautiful beyond description. One quarter of a mile above the entrance of this river a large creek falls in which we called *2000 Mile Creek*. I sent Reuben Fields to examine it. He reported it to be a bold running stream, its bed 30 yards wide. We proceeded about three miles above this creek and encamped on the starboard shore. I walked out a little distance and met with two porcupines, which were feeding on the young willow which grows in great abundance on all the sandbars. This animal is exceedingly clumsy and not very watchful. I approached so near one of them before it perceived me that I touched it with my espontoon [*a spear carried by infantrymen until the late 18th century; it had a small metal crosspiece below the head and could be used as a rifle support*]. Found the nest of a wild goose among some driftwood on the river from which we took three eggs. This is the only nest we have met with on driftwood. The usual position is the top of a broken tree, sometimes in the forks of a large tree, but almost invariably from 15 to 20 feet or upwards high.

May 4, 1805, Saturday [Lewis]
We were detained this morning until about nine o'clock in order to repair the rudder irons of the red pirogue, which were broken last evening in landing.

We then set out, the wind hard against us. I walked on shore this morning; the weather was more pleasant, the snow has disappeared. The frost seems to have affected the vegetation much less than could have been expected. The leaves of the cottonwood, the grass, the box elder, willow and the yellow flowering pea seem to be scarcely touched. The rose bushes and honeysuckle seem to have sustained the most considerable injury. The country on both sides of the Missouri continues to be open, level, fertile and beautiful as far as the eye can reach, which from some of the eminences is not short of 30 miles. The river bottoms are very extensive and contain a much greater proportion of timber than usual; the forepart of this day the river was bordered with timber on both sides, a circumstance which is extremely rare and the first which has occurred of anything like the same extent since we left the Mandans. In the after part of the day we passed an extensive beautiful plain on the starboard side which gradually ascended from the river. I saw immense quantities of buffalo in every direction, also some elk, deer and goats. Having an abundance of meat on hand, I passed them without firing on them; they are extremely gentle. The bull buffalo particularly will scarcely give way to you. I passed several in the open plain within 50 paces. They viewed me for a moment as something novel and then very unconcernedly continued to feed. Capt. Clark walked on shore this evening and did not rejoin us until after dark. He struck the river several miles above our camp and came down to us. We saw many beaver, some which the party shot; we also killed two deer today. Much sign of the brown bear.

Passed several old Indian hunting camps in the course of the day. One of them contained two large lodges, which were fortified with old driftwood and fallen timber. This fortification consisted of a circular fence of timber laid horizontally lapping on and overlaying each other to the height of five feet. These pounds are sometimes built from 20 to 30 feet in diameter and covered over with the trunks and limbs of old timber. The usual construction of the lodges we have lately passed is as follows. Three or more strong sticks the thickness of a man's leg or arm and about 12 feet long are attached together at one end by a withe of small willows; these are then set on end and spread at the base, forming a circle of 10, 12, or 14 feet in diameter. Sticks of driftwood and fallen timber of convenient size are now placed with one end on the ground and the other resting against those, which are secured together at top by the withe and which support and give the form to the whole. Thus the sticks are laid on until they make it as thick as they design, usually about three ranges, each piece breaking or filling up the interstice of the two beneath it, the whole forming a conic figure about 10 feet high with a small aperture in one side which answers as a door. Leaves, bark and straw are sometimes thrown over the work to make it more complete, but at best it affords a very imperfect shelter, particularly without straw, which is the state in which we have most usually found them.

May 5, 1805, Sunday [Lewis]
A fine morning. I walked on shore until after eight a.m. when we halted for breakfast and in the course of my walk killed a deer, which I carried about a mile and a half to the river; it was in good order. Soon after setting out the rudder irons of the white pirogue were broken by her running foul on a sawyer; she was, however, refitted in a few minutes with some tugs of rawhide and nails. As usual saw a great quantity of game today, buffalo, elk and goats or antelope feeding in every direction. We kill whatever we wish; the buffalo furnish us with fine veal and fat beef. We also have venison and beaver tails when we wish them. The flesh of the elk and goat are less esteemed, and certainly are inferior. We have not been able to take any fish for some time past. The country is as yesterday beautiful in the extreme.

Saw the carcasses of many buffalo lying dead along the shore partially devoured by the wolves and bear. Saw a great number of white brant, also the common brown brant, geese of the common kind and a small species of goose, which differs considerably from the common Canadian goose. Their neck, head and beak are considerably thicker, shorter and larger than the other in proportion to their size; they are also more than a third smaller, and their note is more like that of the brant or a young goose which has not perfectly acquired his notes. In all other respects they are the same in color, habits and the number of feathers in the tail. They frequently also associate with the large geese when in flocks. But I never saw them paired off with the large or common goose. The white brant associate in very large flocks. They do not appear to be mated or paired off as if they intended to raise their young in this quarter, I therefore doubt whether they reside here during the summer for that purpose. This bird is about the size of the common brown brant or two-thirds of the common goose. It is not so long by six inches from point to point of the wings when extended as the other. The beak, head and neck are also larger and stronger. Their beaks, legs and feet are of a reddish or flesh-colored white. The eye is of a moderate size, the pupil of a deep sea green encircled with a ring of yellowish brown. It has sixteen feathers of equal length in the tail. Their note differs but little from the common brant, their flesh much the same, and in my opinion preferable to the goose. The flesh is dark. They are entirely of a beautiful pure white except the large feathers of the first and second joints of the wings, which are jet black. Form and habits are the same with the other brant. They sometimes associate and form one common flock.

Capt. Clark found a den of young wolves in the course of his walk today and also saw a great number of those animals. They are very abundant in this quarter, and are of two species. The small wolf or burrowing dogs of the prairies are the inhabitants almost invariably of the open plains; they usually associate in bands of ten or twelve, sometimes more, and burrow near some pass or place much frequented by game. Not being able alone to take a deer or goat they are rarely ever found alone but hunt in bands. They frequently watch and seize their prey near their burrows. In these burrows they raise their young and to them they also resort when pursued. When a person approaches them they frequently bark, their note being precisely that of the small dog. They are of an intermediate size between that of the fox and dog, very active, fleet and delicately formed, the ears large, erect and pointed, the head long and pointed more like that of the fox; tail long and bushy. The hair and fur also resembles the fox though much coarser and inferior. They are of a pale reddish brown color. The eye of a deep sea green color, small and piercing. Their talons are rather longer than those of the ordinary wolf or that common to the Atlantic states, none of which are to be found in this quarter, nor I believe above the River Platte. The large wolf found here is not as large as those of the Atlantic states. They are lower and thicker made, shorter legged. Their color, which is not affected by the seasons, is a gray or blackish brown and every intermediate shade from that to a cream-colored white. These wolves resort to the woodlands and are also found in the plains, but never take refuge in the ground or burrow so far as I have been able to inform myself. We scarcely see a gang of buffalo without observing a parcel of those faithful shepherds on their skirts in readiness to take care of the maimed and wounded. The large wolf never barks, but howls as those of the Atlantic states do.

Capt. Clark and Drouillard killed the largest brown bear this evening which we have yet seen. It was a most tremendous looking animal, and extremely hard to kill notwithstanding he had five balls through his lungs and five others in various parts. He swam more than half the distance across the river to a sandbar and it was at least 20 minutes before he died. He did not attempt to attack, but fled and made the most tremendous roaring from the moment he was shot. We had no means of weighing this monster; Capt. Clark thought he would weigh 500 lbs. For my own part I think the estimate too small by 100 lbs. He measured 8 feet 7 ½ inches from the nose to the extremity of the hind feet, 5 feet 10 ½ inches around the breast, 1 foot 11 inches around the middle of the arm, and 3 feet 11 inches around the neck. His talons, which were five in number on each foot, were 4 ⅜ inches in length. He was in good order; we therefore divided him among the party and made them boil the oil and put it in a cask for future use. The oil is as hard as hog's lard when cool, much more so than that of the black bear. This bear differs from the common black bear in several respects. Its talons are much longer and more blunt, its tail shorter, its hair, which is of a reddish or bay brown, is longer, thicker and finer than that of the black bear. His liver, lungs and heart are much larger even in proportion with his size; the heart particularly was as large as that of a large ox. His maw was also ten times the size of the black bear, and was filled with flesh and fish. His testicles were pendant from his belly and placed four inches asunder in separate bags or pouches. This animal also feeds on roots and almost every species of wild fruit.

The party killed two elk and a buffalo today, and my dog caught a goat, which he overtook by superior fleetness; the goat it must be understood was with young and extremely poor. A great number of these goats are devoured by the wolves and bears at this season when they are poor and passing the river from S.W. to N.E. They are very inactive and easily taken in the water. A man can outswim them with great ease. The Indians take them in great numbers in the river at this season and in autumn when they repass to the S.W.

May 6, 1805, Monday [Lewis]
The morning being fair and pleasant and wind favorable we set sail at an early hour and proceeded on very well the greater part of the day. The country still continues level, fertile and beautiful, the bottoms wide and well timbered, comparatively speaking, with other parts of the river. No appearance of burnt hills, pumice stone or coal, the salts of tartar or vegetable salts continue to appear on the river banks, sandbars, and in many parts of the plains, most generally in the little ravines at the base of the low hills. Passed three streams

today which discharged themselves on the larboard side; the first of these we call Little Dry Creek. It contained some water in standing pools but discharged none. The second, 50 yards wide, no water, we called Big Dry Creek. The third is the bed of a conspicuous river 200 yards wide, which we called Little Dry River. The banks of these streams are low and bottoms wide with but little timber; their beds are almost entirely formed of a fine brown sand intermixed with a small proportion of little pebbles, which were either transparent, white, green, red, yellow or brown. These streams appeared to continue their width without diminution as far as we could perceive them, which with respect to the river was many miles. They had recently discharged their waters. From the appearance of these streams, and the country through which they passed, we concluded that they had their sources in level, low, dry plains, which probably is the character of the country for a great distance west of this, or to the vicinity of the Black Hills, that the country being low on the same level nearly and in the same parallel of latitude, that the rains in the spring of the year (in a few days) suddenly melt the snow at the same time and cause for a few days a vast quantity of water to find its way to the Missouri through those channels. By reference to the diary of the weather [*Lewis and Clark kept a daily weather diary that was tabulated monthly; we have not included it in this edition*] it will be perceived that there is scarcely any rain during the summer, autumn and winter in this open country distant from the mountains.

Fields still continues unwell. Saw a brown bear swim the river above us; he disappeared before we could get in reach of him. I find that the curiosity of our party is pretty well satisfied with respect to this animal. The formidable appearance of the male bear killed on the 5th, added to the difficulty with which they die when even shot through the vital parts, has staggered the resolution of several of them. Others, however, seem keen for action with the bear. I expect these gentlemen [*Lewis is referring to the bears*] will give us some amusement shortly as they soon begin now to copulate. Saw a great quantity of game of every species common here. Capt. Clark walked on shore and killed two elk; they were not in very good order, we therefore took a part of the meat only. It is now only amusement for Capt. Clark and myself to kill as much meat as the party can consume. I hope it may continue thus through our whole route, but this I do not much expect. Two beaver were taken in traps this morning and one since shot by one of the party. Saw numbers of these animals peeping at us as we passed out of their holes, which they form of a cylindrical shape by burrowing in the face of the abrupt banks of the river.

May 7, 1805, Tuesday [Lewis]
A fine morning, set out at an early hour. The driftwood begins to come down in consequence of the river's rising; the water is somewhat clearer than usual, a circumstance I did not expect on its rise. At 11 a.m. the wind became so hard that we were compelled to lie by for several hours. One of the small canoes by the bad management of the steersman filled with water and had very nearly sunk. We unloaded her and dried the baggage. At one we proceeded on, the wind having in some measure abated. The country we passed today on the north side of the river is one of the most beautiful plains we have yet seen. It rises gradually from the river bottom to the height of 50 or 60 feet, then becoming level as a bowling green extends back as far as the eye can reach. On the south side the river hills are more broken and much higher, though some little distance back the country becomes level and fertile. No appearance of burnt hills, coal or pumice stone; that of salts still continues. Vegetation appears to have advanced very little since the 28th ultimo.

We continue to see a great number of bald eagles. I presume they must feed on the carcasses of dead animals, for I see no fishing hawks to supply them with their favorite food. The water of the river is so turbid that no bird which feeds exclusively on fish can subsist on it; from its mouth to this place I have neither seen the blue crested fisher nor a fishing hawk. This day we killed three buffalo, one elk and eight beaver. Two of the buffalo killed by Capt. Clark near our encampment of this evening were in good order, dressed them and saved the meat. The elk I killed this morning, thought it fat, but on examination found it so lean that we took the tongue, marrowbones and skin only.

May 8, 1805, Wednesday [Lewis]
Set out at an early hour under a gentle breeze from the east. A black cloud which suddenly sprang up at the S.E. soon overshadowed the horizon. At eight a.m. it gave us a slight sprinkle of rain; the wind became much stronger but not so much as to detain us. We nooned it just above the entrance of a large river which disembogues on the starboard side. I took the advantage of this leisure moment and examined the river about three miles; I found it generally 150 yards wide, and in some places 200. It is deep, gentle in its

current and affords a large body of water; its banks, which are formed of a dark rich loam and blue clay, are abrupt and about 12 feet high. Its bed is principally mud. I have no doubt but it is navigable for boats, pirogues and canoes, for the latter probably a great distance. The bottoms of this stream are wide, level, fertile and possess a considerable portion of timber, principally cottonwood. From the quantity of water furnished by this river it must water a large extent of country. Perhaps this river also might furnish a practicable and advantageous communication with the Saskatchewan River; it is sufficiently large to justify a belief that it might reach to that river if its direction be such. The water of this river possesses a peculiar whiteness, being about the color of a cup of tea with the admixture of a tablespoonful of milk. From the color of its water we called it Milk River. (We think it possible that this may be the river called by the Minitaris *the river which scolds at all others.*) Capt. Clark, who walked this morning on the larboard shore, ascended a very high point opposite to the mouth of this river; he informed me that he had a perfect view of this river and the country through which it passed for a great distance (probably 50 or 60 miles), that the country was level and beautiful on both sides of the river, with large herds of buffalo distributed throughout; that the river from its mouth bore N.W. for 12 or 15 miles, when it forked, the one taking a direction nearly north, and the other to the west of northwest. From the appearance of the valleys and the timber on each of these streams Capt. Clark supposed that they were about the same size. Great appearance of beaver on this river, and I have no doubt but what they continue abundant, there being plenty of cottonwood and willow, the timber on which they subsist.

The country on the larboard side of the river is generally high broken hills, with much broken gray, black, and brown granite scattered on the surface of the earth in a confused manner. The wild liquorice is found on the sides of these hills in great abundance. At a little distance from the river there is no timber to be seen on either side; the bottom lands are not more than one-fifth covered with timber; the timber as below is confined to the borders of the river. In future it will be understood that there is no timber of any description on the upland unless particularly mentioned; and also that one-fifth of the bottomlands being covered with timber is considered a large proportion.

The white apple is found in great abundance in this neighborhood; it is confined to the highlands principally. The *white apple*, so called by the French *engagés*, is a plant which rises to the height of six or nine inches, rarely exceeding a foot. It puts forth from one to four and sometimes more stalks from the same root, but is most generally found with one only, which is branched but not diffusely, is cylindrical and villous [*i.e., hairy*]; the leafstalks, cylindrical, villous, and very long compared with the height of the plant, though they gradually diminish in length as they ascend, and are irregular in point of position; the leaf, digitate, from three to five in number, oval, one inch long, absolutely entire and cottony: the whole plant of a pale green, except the under disk of the leaf which is of a white color from the cottony substance with which it is covered. The radix a tuberous bulb, generally ova formed, sometimes longer and more rarely partially divided or branching; always attended with one or more radicles at its lower extremity which sink from four to six inches deep. The bulb covered with a rough, black, tough, thin rind which easily separates from the bulb, which is a fine white substance, somewhat porous, spongy and moist and rather tough before it is dressed. The center of the bulb is penetrated with a small, tough string or ligament, which passing from the bottom of the stem terminates in the extremity of the radicle, which last is also covered by a prolongation of the rind which envelops the bulb. The bulb is usually found at the depth of four inches and frequently much deeper.

This root forms a considerable article of food with the Indians of the Missouri, who for this purpose prepare them in several ways. They are esteemed good at all seasons of the year, but are best from the middle of July to the latter end of autumn, when they are sought and gathered by the provident part of the natives for their winter store. When collected they are stripped of their rind and strung on small thongs or cords and exposed to the sun or placed in the smoke of their fires to dry. When well dried they will keep for several years, provided they are not permitted to become moist or damp. In this situation they usually pound them between two stones placed on a piece of parchment until they reduce it to a fine powder. Thus prepared, they thicken their soup with it; sometimes they also boil these dried roots with their meat without breaking them. When green they are generally boiled with their meat, sometimes mashing them or otherwise as they think proper. They also prepare an agreeable dish with them by boiling and mashing them and adding the marrow grease of the buffalo and some berries, until the whole be of the consistency of a hasty pudding. They also eat this root roasted and frequently make hearty meals of it raw without sustaining any inconvenience or injury therefrom. The white or brown bears feed very much on this root, which their talons assist them to procure very readily. The white apple appears to me to be a tasteless insipid food of itself, though I have no doubt but it is a very healthy and moderately nutritious food. I have no doubt but our epicures would admire this root very much. It would serve them in their ragouts and gravies instead of the truffles morella.

We saw a great number of buffalo, elk, common and black-tailed deer, goats, beaver and wolves. Capt. Clark killed a beaver and a wolf, the party killed three beaver and a deer. We can send out at any time and obtain whatever species of meat the country affords in as large quantity as we wish. We saw where an Indian had recently grained, or taken the hair off of a goat skin. We do not wish to see those gentlemen just now as we presume they would most probably be the Assiniboines and might be troublesome to us. Capt. Clark could not be certain but thought he saw the smoke and some Indian lodges at a considerable distance up the Milk River.

Clark adds that it was Sacagawea who was gathering the white apple roots; she gave him some to eat.

May 9, 1805, Thursday [Lewis]
Set out at an early hour; the wind being favorable we used our sails and proceeded very well. The country in appearance is much as yesterday, with this difference, that the land appears more fertile, particularly the larboard hills, which are not so stony and less broken. The timber has also in some measure declined in quantity. Today we passed the bed of the most extraordinary river that I ever beheld. It is as wide as the Missouri is at this place or half a mile wide and not containing a single drop of running water, some small standing pools being all the water that could be perceived. It falls in on the larboard side. I walked up this river about three miles and ascended an eminence from which I could perceive it many miles; its course is about south for 10 or 12 miles, when it veers around to the E. of S.E. as far as I could see. The valley of this river is wide and possesses but a scanty proportion of timber. The hills which border it are not very high nor is the country very broken. It is what may properly be designated a wavy or rolling country interspersed with some handsome level plains. The banks are low and abrupt, seldom more than six or eight feet above the level of the bed, yet show but little appearance of being overflown; they are of black or yellow clay or a rich sandy loam. The bed is entirely composed of a light

brown sand, the particles of which as well as that of the Missouri are remarkably fine.

This river I presume must extend back as far as the Black Hills and probably is the channel through which a great extent of plains country discharges its superfluous waters in the spring season. It had the appearance of having recently discharged its water; and from the watermark it did not appear that it had been more than two feet deep at its greatest height. This stream (if such it can properly be termed) we called Big Dry River. About a mile below this river on the same side a large creek falls in, also dry at present. The mineral salts and quartz appear in large quantities in this neighborhood. The sand of the Missouri from its mouth to this place has always possessed a mixture of granulated talc; I now think most probably that it is this quartz.

Capt. Clark killed two bucks and two buffalo; I also killed one buffalo which proved to be the best meat, it was in tolerable order. We saved the best of the meat, and from the cow I killed we saved the necessary materials for making what our right-hand cook, Charbonneau, calls the *boudin blanc,* and immediately set him about preparing them for supper. This white pudding we all esteem one of the greatest delicacies of the forest; it may not be amiss therefore to give it a place. About six feet of the lower extremity of the large gut of the buffalo is the first morsel that the cook makes love to. This he holds fast at one end with the right hand, while with the forefinger and thumb of the left he gently compresses it and discharges what he says *is not good to eat,* but of which in the sequel we get a moderate portion. The muscle lying underneath the shoulder blade next the back, and fillets are next sought; these are kneaded up very fine with a good portion of kidney suet. To this composition is then added a just proportion of pepper and salt and a small quantity of flour. Thus far advanced, our skillful operator Charbonneau seizes his receptacle, which has never once touched the water, for that would entirely destroy the regular order of the whole procedure. You will not forget that the side you now see is that covered with a good coat of fat provided the animal be in good order. The operator seizes the receptacle I say, and tying it fast at one end turns it inwards and begins now with repeated evolutions of the hand and arm, and a brisk motion of the finger and thumb, to put in what he says is *bon pour manger* [*good to eat*]; thus by stuffing and compressing he soon distends the receptacle to the utmost limits of its power of expansion, and in the course of its longitudinal progress it drives from the other end of the receptacle a much larger portion of the [*blank*] than was previously discharged by the finger and thumb of the left hand in a former part of the operation.

Thus when the sides of the receptacle are skillfully exchanged, the outer for the inner, and all is completely filled with something good to eat, it is tied at the other end, but not any cut off, for that would make the pattern too scant. It is then baptized in the Missouri with two dips and a flirt, and bobbed into the kettle, from whence, after it be well boiled, it is taken and fried with bear's oil until it becomes brown, when it is ready to assuage the pangs of a keen appetite such as travelers in the wilderness are seldom at a loss for.

We saw a great quantity of game today, particularly of elk and buffalo. The latter are now so gentle that the men frequently throw sticks and stones at them in order to drive them out of the way. We also saw this evening immense quantities of timber cut by the beaver, which appeared to have been done the preceding year. In one place particularly they had cut all the timber down for three acres in front and on nearly one back from the river and had removed a considerable proportion of it. The timber grew very thick and some of it was as large as a man's body. The river for several days has been as wide as it is generally near its mouth, though it is much shallower or I should begin to despair of ever reaching its source. It has been crowded today with many sandbars; the water also appears to become clearer. It has changed its complexion very considerably. I begin to feel extremely anxious to get in view of the Rocky Mountains.

I killed four plover this evening of a different species from any I have yet seen. It resembles the gray or whistling plover more than any other of this family of birds. It is about the size of the yellow-legged or large gray plover common to the lower part of this river as well as most parts of the Atlantic states, where they are sometimes called the jack curlew. The eye is moderately large, black with a narrow ring of dark yellowish brown; the head, neck, upper part of the body and coverts of the wings are of a dove-colored brown, which when the bird is at rest is the predominant color. The breast and belly are of a brownish white; the tail is composed of 12 feathers of three inches, being of equal length; of these the two in the center are black, with traverse bars of yellowish brown; the others are a brownish white. The large feathers of the wings are white-tipped with black. The beak is black, two and a half inches in length, slightly tapering, straight, of a cylindrical form and bluntly or roundly pointed. The chaps are of equal length, and nostrils narrow, longitudinal and connected. The feet and legs are smooth and of a greenish brown; it has three long toes and a short one on each foot. The long toes are unconnected with a web, and the short one is placed very high up the leg behind, insomuch that it does not touch the ground when the bird stands erect. The notes of this bird are louder and more various than any other of this family that I have seen. [*Lewis has just described the willet for the first time.*]

The willet was not the only new species Lewis would meticulously describe in the next month. On May 17 Clark came close to stepping on a prairie rattlesnake; that evening Lewis wrote a description of it. A week earlier he had written a description of the mule deer, noting how it differed from what he called the "common" or eastern white-tailed deer. One of the most interesting differences was its behavior. When the eastern deer is alarmed, Lewis says, it heads for the nearest cover. The mule deer does just the opposite; it seeks out open country. They were seeing their first bighorn sheep as well, and on May 25 they killed their first specimens, three of them, in the Missouri Breaks. The men had all been amazed at the animals' ability to navigate the precipitous slopes along this stretch of the Missouri, and at their elusiveness. The head of one that they shot, with its massive horns, weighed 27 pounds. Clark found the flesh to be dark and inferior to that of the deer, but it was better than eating antelope.

The most amazing animal of all, however, was the grizzly bear. The men were seeing them, shooting them, or running from them, almost every day. On the 11th of May, Bratton wounded a grizzly badly; it came after him anyway and he ran to the river "making signs and hollering as if in distress." Lewis and seven other men went after the beast, followed its trail, and found it hiding in a thicket. Two bullets through the skull put it to rest. "We now found that Bratton had shot him through the center of the lungs, notwithstanding which he had pursued him near half a mile and had returned more than double that distance and with his talons had prepared himself a bed in the earth of about 2 feet deep and five long and was perfectly alive when we found him." And then he adds:

> these bears being so hard to die rather intimidates us all; I must confess that I do not like the gentlemen and had rather fight two Indians than one bear. There is no other chance to conquer them by a single shot but by shooting them through the brains, and this becomes difficult in consequence of two large muscles which cover the sides of the forehead and the sharp projection of the center of the frontal bone, which is also of a pretty good thickness. The fleece and skin were as much as two men could possibly carry.

The next day Lewis walked alone on shore, which he liked to do, carrying his rifle and espontoon and thinking about his chances should he meet a grizzly. He felt himself "more than an equal match for a brown bear provided I get him in open woods or near the water, but feel myself a little diffident with respect to an attack in the open plains." He resolved to act only on the defensive. The rifles the men carried were effective, but they were muzzle-loaders. To reload took precious seconds and the animals did not run off when they were wounded; they ran at you.

Two days later, May 14, some of the men spotted a grizzly lying in the open some 300 yards from the river. Six of them went after him, "all good hunters," as Lewis remarks. They got within 40 yards without being detected, then four men fired more or less at once while the two others reserved their fire. None of the four missed, yet

> in an instant this monster ran at them with open mouth; the two who had reserved their fire discharged their pieces at him as he came towards them, both of them struck him, one only slightly and the other fortunately broke his shoulder; this however only retarded his motion for a moment. The men, unable to reload their guns, took to flight, the bear pursued and had very nearly overtaken them before they reached the river. Two of the party betook themselves to a canoe and the others separated and concealed themselves among the willows, reloaded their pieces, each discharged his piece at him as they had an opportunity. They struck him several times again but the guns served only to direct the bear to them. In this

manner he pursued two of them separately so close that they were obliged to throw aside their guns and pouches and throw themselves into the river, although the bank was nearly 20 feet perpendicular. So enraged was this animal that he plunged into the river only a few feet behind the second man he had compelled to take refuge in the water, when one of those who still remained on shore shot him through the head and finally killed him.

When they cut the animal up they found that eight balls "had passed through him in different directions."

The 14th was a bad day overall for the corps: They almost lost the white pirogue, its contents, and those of its crew who could not swim. It was one of those rare occasions when both captains were on shore at the same time; they could only watch helplessly as their expedition came close to ending in front of their eyes. Charbonneau was at the helm, he was "perhaps the most timid waterman in the world," in Lewis's words, the pirogue was under sail, when a sudden gust of wind "struck her obliquely"; Charbonneau mishandled the boat and she went on her side. "In this pirogue," says Lewis, "were embarked our papers, instruments, books, medicine, a great part of our merchandise and in short almost every article indispensably necessary to further the views, or ensure the success of the enterprise." The boat lay on its side, filling with water, while the men cut down the sail. Charbonneau was helpless during the event, crying to God for mercy (he couldn't swim). Only Pierre Cruzatte's intervention—he told Charbonneau that if he didn't grab the helm immediately and "do his duty," he would kill him on the spot—saved the boat from filling completely and sinking. Lewis was so alarmed that he dropped his gun and was going to try to swim out to the boat, but then he thought better of it. Through it all Sacagawea stayed calm; she was in the rear and gathered up the articles that were floating out into the river. It took a full day to dry out what had been saved from the boat. They lost some of their medicines, garden seeds, a small quantity of gunpowder, and a few cooking utensils. "The Indian woman," said Lewis, "to whom I ascribe equal fortitude and resolution with any person on board at the time of the accident, caught and preserved most of the light articles which were washed overboard."

Close calls seemed to be endemic. Just three days later, on the 17th, while the captains were sleeping in what they describe as their "lodge" (i.e., the tepee they were using instead of a tent), a large tree leaning over them caught fire, no doubt from the high wind blowing embers from the campfire into the air. The guard roused them and they moved the lodge; a few minutes later a large part of the top of the tree fell right where the lodge had stood. "Had we been a few minutes later," Lewis remarks, "we should have been crushed to atoms." Burning atoms at that. On the night of the 28th a buffalo bull came up out of the river into the sleeping camp, stepped right into the white pirogue and bent York's rifle out of shape, then rampaged in terror through the camp, narrowly missing the heads of sleeping men as the guard tried to get it out of the way; it then charged the captains' tepee, only to be driven in another direction by Lewis's dog. Luckily no one was hurt, but the white pirogue was slightly damaged. Lewis decided that it was attended by "some evil genii."

Their greatest enemy, however, was neither fire nor bear nor stray buffalo. It was the wind. It blew very hard most of the time—the word they use most often to describe it is "violent"—and it blew against them. Some days it blew so hard that they gave up and stayed put; they could not paddle upstream against it nor could they tow the boats because the waves were too high. Many days they made only a few miles before they had to quit; and on other days they waited until late before it abated enough that they could move. The country was dry, furthermore, so the wind blew up huge clouds of dust and sand; it was so bad on the 21st of May that they "could neither cook, eat, nor sleep."

The river current was strong, too. The Missouri was not yet a swift mountain stream, but it was running fast from the spring melt. They were using the towrope most days, pulling the boats upstream. They had only one actual hemp rope; otherwise they were using lines made out of elk skin, nine strips of it woven together into cords. Towing the boats was difficult, exhausting work. The towropes themselves were damp and rotten, and they frequently broke. Often the banks of the river were stony and bruising to walk on. If the banks were too steep, the men had to walk in the water, sometimes breast high, and it was cold. Some mornings it was so cold that the water froze on the oars. It isn't hard to imagine what walking in water that cold would be like. It is hard to imagine making 20 miles or more a day that way.

When they reached the Missouri Breaks late in May, towing the boats became truly nightmarish. The river narrows through the breaks, and the broken nature of the country has left small rapids in the river itself and large deposits of stone along its banks. They had to double up on the towing crews to get the boats through some of these areas. Lewis, writing on the 29th of May, describes the difficulties:

This day we proceeded with more labor and difficulty than we have yet experienced; in addition to the embarrassments of the rapid current, riffles, and rocky points, which were as bad if not worse than yesterday, the banks and sides of the bluff were more steep than usual and were now rendered so slippery by the late rain that the men could scarcely walk.

The cord is our only dependence for the current is too rapid to be resisted with the oar and the river too deep in most places for the pole. The earth and stone also falling from these immense high bluffs render it dangerous to pass under them. The wind was also hard and against us. Our cords broke several times today but happily without injury to the vessels. We had slight showers of rain through the course of the day; the air was cold and rendered more disagreeable by the rain.

Two days later the conditions were even worse.

The obstructions of rocky points and riffles still continue as yesterday. At those places the men are compelled to be in the water even to their armpits, and the water is yet very cold, and so frequent are those points that they are one fourth of their time in the water. Added to this, the banks and bluffs along which they are obliged to pass are so slippery and the mud so tenacious that they are unable to wear their moccasins, and in that situation they drag the heavy burden of a canoe and walk occasionally for several hundred yards over the sharp fragments of rocks which tumble from the cliffs and garnish the borders of the river. In short their labor is incredibly painful and great, yet those faithful fellows bear it without a murmur.

On June 3 Lewis remarked that many of the men "have their feet so mangled and bruised with the stones and rough ground over which they passed barefoot that they can scarcely walk or stand." They were now in prickly pear country, too. The spines pierced moccasins. The prickly pears were so plentiful on the ground, Lewis says, that it required "half the traveler's attention to avoid them."

Yet hardly a day passes that Lewis does not remark on the beauty of the country. They were moving through eastern Montana, which gets something like

10 inches of rain a year. The air was so dry that the wooden case that held Lewis's sextant was shrinking and coming apart at the seams, and landscape features at great distances looked much closer than they actually were. The vegetation became sparser and more desert-like; Clark remarked at one point that there was hardly any grass anymore and what there was, was short. The ground cover was mostly aromatic herbs and prickly pear. Cottonwoods and willow continued to grow in the river bottoms, but the timber, too, was diminishing in size and quantity.

Lewis loved this country, and describes it lovingly. His journal entries often say that the landscape is level as far as the eye can see, and he finds this enchanting. It thrills him that he can see so far and so clearly. Just after they entered the Missouri Breaks, on May 26, Lewis climbed one of the river hills to see what he could see. He found the climb fatiguing, he later wrote, but "I thought myself well repaid for any labor, as from this point I beheld the Rocky Mountains for the first time. I could only discover a few of the most elevated points above the horizon." He was clearly happy at the view. "These points of the Rocky Mountains were covered with snow and the sun shone on it in such manner as to give me the most plain and satisfactory view." He must have known he was the first American to see them. But they also gave him pause:

> While I viewed these mountains I felt a secret pleasure in finding myself so near the head of the heretofore conceived boundless Missouri; but when I reflected on the difficulties which this snowy barrier would most probably throw in my way to the Pacific, and the sufferings and hardships of myself and party in them, it in some measure counterbalanced the joy I had felt in the first moments in which I gazed on them. But as I have always held it a crime to anticipate evils I will believe it a good comfortable road until I am compelled to believe differently.

The mountains he was seeing were the Bear Paws, in fact, not the Rockies, but the passage remains a touching one.

They had entered the Missouri Breaks just a day or two before, so Lewis already knew that it was hardly a comfortable road. Yet even here in this broken, desolate country he finds much to admire, and when the corps got to the White Cliffs area of the breaks on May 31, he became positively rapturous. His description of it, in fact, has become a classic of Romantic landscape description, and his words deserve to be quoted at length:

The bluffs of the river rise to the height of from 2 to 300 feet and in most places nearly perpendicular; they are formed of remarkable white sandstone which is sufficiently soft to give way readily to the impression of water . . . The water in the course of time in descending from those hills and plains on either side of the river has trickled down the soft sand cliffs and worn it into a thousand grotesque figures, which with the help of a little imagination and an oblique view at a distance are made to represent elegant ranges of lofty freestone buildings, having their parapets well stocked with statuary. Columns of various sculpture both grooved and plain are also seen supporting long galleries in front of those buildings. In other places on a much nearer approach and with the help of less imagination we see the remains or ruins of elegant buildings, some columns standing and almost entire with their pedestals and capitals, others retaining their pedestals but deprived by time or accident of their capitals, some lying prostrate and broken, others in the form of vast pyramids of conic structure bearing a series of other pyramids on their tops becoming less as they ascend and finally terminating in a sharp point. Niches and alcoves of various forms and sizes are seen at different heights as we pass . . . The thin strata of hard freestone intermixed with the soft sandstone seems to have aided the water in forming this curious scenery. As we passed on it seemed as if those scenes of visionary enchantment would never have an end; for here it is too that nature presents to the view of the traveler vast ranges of walls of tolerable workmanship. So perfect indeed are those walls that I should have thought that nature had attempted here to rival the human art of masonry had I not recollected that she had first begun her work.

Visionary enchantment indeed. It is remarkable that Lewis could see the landscape this way while he and his men were struggling to haul the boats past it on bruised, bleeding feet. Clark nowhere exhibits such a tendency; he is much more practical-minded than Lewis, capable of seeing that the country is beautiful but far less expansive in his appreciation of it. Yet they worked together very effectively as a team, and the men who followed them did so with complete confidence in their joint authority. No evidence exists that they ever had an argument, or even disagreed in any substantial way about what particular course of action to take.

They were about to meet an important test of their ability as leaders. The corps emerged from the breaks toward the first of June; on the third they reached the Marias River, for which they were totally unprepared. Coming in from the north, it was clearly a major stream. It looked like the Missouri—turbid, loaded with sediment, a whitish brown in color—while the river coming in from the southwest was relatively clear, like a mountain river, and the Indians back at Fort Mandan had said nothing about a major river coming in from the north in this general location. Which way, then, should they go? Up the right-hand fork, which the men immediately and unanimously decided must be the Missouri, because it had all the features of the river they had become so familiar with over the last year? Or should they go up the left-hand fork, coming out of the southwest?

It was a critical decision. The men knew that the headwaters of the Missouri lay in the mountains. They also knew that once they portaged around the Great Falls of the Missouri, the river was navigable; this they knew from what the Indians had told them. It was the route west. They knew of no other river that was. Go up the wrong river and they would have to backtrack, perhaps hundreds of miles, wasting so much time that it would bring the expedition, in effect, to an end; they would never get over the mountains and to the Pacific before winter came. Go up the right river and they had a good chance of making it.

Their first act was to send a canoe up each branch, three men in a canoe, to see what they could see, and other men to explore the country immediately surrounding them. "Their accounts," says Lewis, "were by no means satisfactory nor did the information we acquired bring us nigher to the decision . . . or determine us which stream to take." The next day, June 4, Lewis and Clark themselves set out on foot with small parties of men, each to travel a day and a half up each branch, Lewis taking the northern branch, Clark the southern. It rained most of that night and traveling conditions were terrible, but they kept on. Clark gave up first, coming back on June 6, having traveled some 50 miles upstream. By the 6th Lewis was convinced that the north fork was not the Missouri; it bore too far north. He sent some men up to look for a rise from which they could take the river's bearing while the others built rafts to descend the river back to camp. His party had traveled some 70 miles upstream. It rained and stormed that night, and they had no shelter. The rafts were too hazardous so they decided to walk the whole way. On the 7th rain fell all night again and Lewis, then one of his men, almost fell off a cliff; they had to wade a good part of the time, the water to their chests. Conditions were nearly as bad as in the Missouri Breaks. They did not finally return until five in the afternoon on June 8.

But "the whole of my party to a man," he writes, "were fully persuaded that this river was the Missouri." Lewis demurred. "Being fully of opinion that it was neither the main stream nor that which it would be advisable for us to take, I determined to give it a name." He called it Maria's River, in honor of a cousin, Maria Wood, whom he may have been interested in romantically. It retains the name to this day.

On June 9 the captains sat down, looked over their maps, and decided to take the south fork. Only Clark agreed with Lewis that the south fork was the true Missouri. Pierre Cruzatte, "who had been an old Missouri navigator and who from his integrity, knowledge, and skill as a waterman had acquired the confidence of every individual of the party, declared it as his opinion that the N. fork was the true, genuine Missouri and could be no other." The rest of the party still all agreed with Cruzatte; they were afraid the south fork "would soon terminate in the mountains and leave us at a great distance from the Columbia."

Nevertheless, reports Lewis, with a sense of gratification we can only imagine, "they said very cheerfully that they were ready to follow us anywhere we thought proper to direct." However wrong they believed their captains to be, they refused to challenge them. They would go. In the event, of course, Lewis and Clark were right. The Missouri bends to the southwest here.

The party rested for a day or two and prepared a cache for some of their supplies; they would travel as lightly as possible from now on. Shields fixed the air gun and some of the other men's arms; he was, says Lewis, an invaluable man. They cached the pirogue among the trees on a small island, and Lewis left his brand on the trees to warn any Indians who might come by not to harm the boat. They prepared a cache and Cruzatte showed them how to do so. Lewis, it was decided, would set out on foot with a few men the next day up the south fork while Clark finished the caching and came later by boat. Lewis set out on the 11th and almost at once became ill with dysentery. He ordered some tea made from the twigs of the chokecherry, then drank it; the next day he felt weak, but much better. He was not so weak that he couldn't make 27 miles that day on foot. The Rockies were now plainly visible to the west. Clark set out on the 12th and made 18 miles. They were on their way again. We rejoin them on June 13, 1805, as they head for the Great Falls of the Missouri, their next ordeal.

Captains Lewis and Clark holding a council with Oto and Omaha Indians.
From the journals of Patrick Gass.

JUNE 13 TO JULY 2, 1805

June 13, 1805, Thursday [Lewis]

This morning we set out about sunrise after taking breakfast off our venison and fish. We again ascended the hills of the river and gained the level country. The country through which we passed for the first six miles, though more rolling than that we had passed yesterday, might still with propriety be deemed a level country. Our course as yesterday was generally S.W. The river from the place we left it appeared to make a considerable bend to the south. From the extremity of this rolling country I overlooked a most beautiful and level plain of great extent or at least 50 or 60 miles; in this there were infinitely more buffalo than I had ever before witnessed at a view. Nearly in the direction I had been traveling, or S.W., two curious mountains presented themselves of square figures, the sides rising perpendicularly to the height of 250 feet, and appeared to be formed of yellow clay. Their tops appeared to be level plains. These inaccessible heights appeared like the ramparts of immense fortifications; I have no doubt but with very little assistance from art they might be rendered impregnable [*these were evidently the first buttes Lewis had seen*].

Fearing that the river bore to the south and that I might pass the falls if they existed between this and the Snowy Mountains I altered my course nearly to the south, leaving those isolated hills to my right and proceeded through the plain. I sent Fields on my right and Drouillard and Gibson on my left with orders to kill some meat and join me at the river, where I should halt for dinner. I had proceeded on this course about two miles with Goodrich at some distance behind me when my ears were saluted with the agreeable sound of a fall of water, and advancing a little further I saw the spray arise above the plain like a column of smoke, which would frequently disappear again in an instant, caused, I presume, by the wind, which blew pretty hard from the S.W. I did not, however, lose my direction to this point, which soon began to make a roaring too tremendous to be mistaken for any cause short of the Great Falls of the Missouri. Here I arrived about 12 o'clock, having traveled by estimate about 15 miles. I hurried down the hill, which was about 200 feet high and difficult of access, to gaze on this sublimely grand spectacle. I took my position on the top of some rocks about 20 feet high opposite the center of the falls. This chain of rocks appears once to have formed a part of those over which the waters tumbled, but in the course of time has been separated from it to the distance of 150 yards, lying parallel to it and forming an abutment against which the water, after falling over the precipice, beats with great fury. This barrier extends on the right to the perpendicular cliff which forms that border of the river, but to the distance of 120 yards next to the cliff it is but a few feet above the level of the water, and here the water in very high tides appears to pass in a channel of 40 yards next to the higher part of the ledge of rocks. On the left it extends within 80 or 90 yards of the larboard cliff, which is also perpendicular. Between this abrupt extremity of the ledge of rocks and the perpendicular bluff the whole body of water passes with incredible swiftness. Immediately at the cascade the river is about 300 yards wide; about 90 or 100 yards of this next the larboard bluff is a smooth, even sheet of water falling over a precipice of at least eighty feet. The remaining part of about 200 yards on my right forms the grandest sight I ever beheld. The height of the fall is the same as the other but the irregular and somewhat projecting rocks below receive the water in its passage down and break it into a perfect white foam which assumes a thousand forms in a moment, sometimes flying up in jets of sparkling foam to the height of 15 or 20 feet that are scarcely formed before large rolling bodies of the same beaten and foaming water are thrown over and conceal them. In short the rocks seem to be most happily fixed to present a sheet of the whitest beaten froth for 200 yards in length and about 80 feet perpendicular.

The water after descending strikes against the abutment before mentioned, or that on which I stand, and seems to reverberate, and being met by the more impetuous current they roll and swell into half-formed billows of great height, which rise and again disappear in an instant. This abutment of rock defends a handsome little bottom of about three acres, which is diversified and agreeably shaded with some cottonwood trees. In the lower extremity of the bottom there is a very thick grove of the same kind of trees which are small. In this wood there are several Indian lodges formed of sticks. A few small cedars grow near the ledge of rocks where I rest. Below the point of these rocks at a small distance the river is divided by a large rock which rises several feet above the water and extends downward with the stream for about 20 yards. About a mile before the water arrives at the pitch it descends very rapidly and is confined on the larboard side by a perpendicular cliff of about 100 feet. On the starboard side it is also perpendicular for about three hundred yards above the pitch, where it is broken by the discharge of a small ravine, down which the buffalo have a large beaten road to the water, for it is but in very few places that these animals can obtain water near this place owing to the steep and inaccessible banks.

I see several skeletons of the buffalo lying in the edge of the water near the starboard bluff which I presume have been swept down by the current and precipitated over this tremendous fall. About 300 yards below me there is another abutment of solid rock with a perpendicular face and about 60 feet high which projects from the starboard side at right angles to the distance of 134 yards and terminates the lower part nearly of the bottom before mentioned, there being a passage around the end of this abutment between it and the river of about 20 yards. Here the river again assumes its usual width, soon spreading to near 300 yards, but still continues its rapidity. From the reflection of the sun on the spray or mist which rises from these falls there is a beautiful rainbow produced which adds not a little to the beauty of this majestically grand scenery.

After writing this imperfect description I again viewed the falls and was so much disgusted with the imperfect idea which it conveyed of the scene that I determined to draw my pen across it and begin again, but then reflected that I could not perhaps succeed better than penning the first impressions of the mind. I wished for the pencil of Salvator Rosa or the pen of Thomson [*Rosa was known for his wilderness landscapes; Thomson was the author of a then famous poem called "The Seasons," which is full of natural description*], that I might be enabled to give to the enlightened world some just idea of this truly magnificent and sublimely grand object, which has from the commencement of time been concealed from the view of civilized man; but this was fruitless and vain. I most sincerely regretted that I had not brought a camera obscura with me by the assistance of which even I could have hoped to have done better, but alas, this was also out of my reach. [*The camera obscura was used by painters in the 18th and 19th centuries to help them draw scenes from the outside world, which were projected through a pinhole, upside down, onto a wall opposite.*] I therefore with the assistance of my pen only endeavored to trace some of the stronger features of this scene, by the assistance of which and my recollection, aided by some able pencil, I hope still to give to the world some faint idea of an object which at this moment fills me with such pleasure and astonishment, and which of its kind I will venture to assert is second to but one in the known world [*the "one" he refers to is no doubt Niagara Falls, already a famous tourist attraction*]. I retired to the shade of a tree where I determined to fix my camp for the present and dispatch a man in the morning to inform Capt. Clark and the party of my success in finding the falls and settle in their minds all further doubts as to the Missouri.

The hunters now arrived loaded with excellent buffalo meat and informed me that they had killed three very fat cows about three-quarters of a mile hence. I directed them after they had refreshed themselves to go back and butcher them and bring another load of meat each to our camp, determining to employ those who remained with me in drying meat for the party against their arrival. In about two hours or at four o'clock p.m. they set out on this duty, and I walked down the river about three miles to discover if possible some place to which the canoes might arrive or at which they might be drawn on shore in order to be taken by land above the falls, but returned without effecting either of these objects. The river was one continued scene of rapids and cascades, which I readily perceived could not be encountered with our canoes, and the cliffs still retained their perpendicular structure and were from 150 to 200 feet high. In short the river appears here to have worn a channel in the process of time through a solid rock. On my return I found the party at camp. They had butchered the buffalo and brought in some more meat as I had directed. Goodrich had caught half a dozen very fine trout and a number of both species of the white fish. These trout are from 16 to 23 inches in length, precisely resemble our mountain or speckled trout in form and the position of their fins, but the specks on these are of a deep black instead of the red or gold color of those common to the United States. These are furnished long sharp teeth on the palate and tongue and have generally a small dash of red on each side behind the front ventral fins. The flesh is of a pale yellowish red, or when in good order of a rose red [*this is the first description of the cut-throat trout*].

I am induced to believe that the brown, the white and the grizzly bear of this country are the same species, only differing in color from age or more probably from the same natural cause that many other animals of the same family differ in color. One of those which we killed yesterday was of a cream-colored white while the other in company with it was of the common bay or reddish brown, which seems to be the most usual color of them. The white one appeared from its talons and teeth to be the youngest; it was smaller than the other, and although a monstrous beast we supposed that it had not yet attained its growth and that it was a little upwards of two years old. The young cubs which we have killed have always been of a brownish white, but none of them as white as that we killed yesterday. One other that we killed some time since, which I mentioned sunk under some driftwood and was lost, had a white stripe or list of about eleven inches wide entirely around his body just behind the shoulders, and was much darker than these bears usually are. The grizzly bear we have never yet seen. I have seen their talons in possession of the Indians and from their form I am persuaded if there is any difference between this species and the brown or white bear it is very inconsiderable. There is no such animal as a black bear in this open country or of that species generally denominated the black bear.

My fare is really sumptuous this evening: buffalo humps, tongues and marrowbones, fine trout, parched meal, pepper and salt, and a good appetite. The last is not considered the least of the luxuries.

Clark reports on this day that they made 13 miles, the river was shallow and full of stones, Sacagawea was very sick, so was one of his crew, and three men had swellings (possibly abscesses, which were common among the men).

June 14, 1805, Friday [Lewis]
This morning at sunrise I dispatched Joseph Fields with a letter to Capt. Clark and ordered him to keep sufficiently near the river to observe its situation in order that he might be enabled to give Capt. Clark an idea of the point at which it would be best to halt to make our portage. I set one man about preparing a scaffold and collecting wood to dry the meat. Sent the others

to bring in the balance of the buffalo meat, or at least the part which the wolves had left us, for those fellows are ever at hand and ready to partake with us the moment we kill a buffalo; and there is no means of putting the meat out of their reach in those plains. The two men shortly after returned with the meat and informed me that the wolves had devoured the greater part of the meat.

About ten o'clock this morning while the men were engaged with the meat I took my gun and espontoon and thought I would walk a few miles and see where the rapids terminated above, and return to dinner. Accordingly I set out and proceeded up the river about S.W. After passing one continued rapid and three small cascades of about four or five feet each at the distance of about five miles I arrived at a fall of about 19 feet; the river is here about 400 yards wide. This pitch, which I called the Crooked Falls [*so it is called to this day*], occupies about three-fourths of the width of the river, commencing on the south side, extends obliquely upwards about 150 yards, then forming an acute angle extends downwards nearly to the commencement of four small islands lying near the N. shore. Among these islands and between them and the lower extremity of the perpendicular pitch, being a distance of 100 yards or upwards, the water glides down the side of a sloping rock with a velocity almost equal to that of its perpendicular ascent. Just above this rapid the river makes a sudden bend to the right, or northwardly. I should have returned from hence, but hearing a tremendous roaring above me I continued on my route across the point of a hill a few hundred yards further and was again presented by one of the most beautiful objects in nature, a cascade of about fifty feet perpendicular stretching at right angles across the river from side to side to the distance of at least a quarter of a mile. Here the river pitches over a shelving rock, with an edge as regular and straight as if formed by art, without a nick or break in it. The water descends in one even and uninter-rupted sheet to the bottom, where dashing against the rocky bottom rises into foaming billows of great height and rapidly glides away, hissing, flashing and sparkling as it departs. The spray rises from one extremity to the other to 50 feet. I now thought that if a skillful painter had been asked to make a beautiful cascade that he would most probably have presented the precise image of this one; nor could I for some time determine on which of those two great cataracts to bestow the palm, on this or that which I had discovered yesterday. At length I determined between these two great rivals for glory that this was *pleasingly beautiful*, while the other was *sublimely grand*. I had scarcely infixed my eyes from this pleasing object before I discovered another fall above at the distance of half a mile; thus invited I did not once think of returning but hurried thither to amuse myself with this newly discovered object. I found this to be a cascade of about 14 feet possessing a perpendicular pitch of about 6 feet. This was tolerably regular, stretching across the river from bank to bank, where it was about a quarter of a mile wide. In any other neighborhood but this, such a cascade would probably be extolled for its beauty and magnificence, but here I passed it by with but little attention, determining as I had proceeded so far to continue my route to the head of the rapids if it should even detain me all night. At every rapid, cataract and cascade I discovered that the bluffs grew lower or that the bed of the river rose nearer to a level with the plains. Still pursuing the river with its course about S.W., passing a continued scene of rapids and small cascades, at the distance of two and a half miles I arrived at another cataract of 26 feet. This is not immediately perpendicular, a rock about one-third of its descent seems to protrude to a small distance and receives the water in its passage downwards and gives a curve to the water, though it falls mostly with a regular and smooth sheet. The river is near 600 yards wide at this place, a beautiful level plain on the south side only a few feet above the level of the pitch. On the north side where I am the country is more broken and immediately behind me near the river is a high hill. Below this fall at a little distance a beautiful little island, well timbered, is situated about the middle of the river. In this island on a cottonwood tree an eagle has placed her nest. A more inaccessible spot I believe she could not have found, for neither man nor beast dare pass those gulfs which separate her little domain from the shores. The water is also broken in such manner as it descends over this pitch that the mist or spray rises to a considerable height. This fall is certainly much the greatest I ever beheld except those two which I have mentioned below. It is incomparably a greater cataract and a more noble, interesting object than the celebrated falls of Potomac or Schuylkill.

Just above this is another cascade of about five feet, above which the water as far as I could see began to abate of its velocity, and I therefore determined to ascend the hill behind me, which promised a fine prospect of the adjacent country, nor was I disappointed on my arrival at its summit. From hence I overlooked a most beautiful and extensive plain reaching from the river to the base of the snow-clad mountains to the S. and southwest. I also observed the Missouri stretching its meandering course to the south through this plain to a great distance filled to its even and grassy brim. Another large river flowed in on its western side about four miles above me and extended itself through a level and fertile valley of three miles in width a great distance to the N.W., rendered more conspicuous by the timber which garnished its borders. In these plains and more particularly in the valley just below me immense herds of buffalo are feeding. The Missouri just above this hill makes a bend to the south where it lies a smooth, even and unruffled sheet of water of nearly a mile in width bearing on its watery bosom vast flocks of geese which feed at pleasure in the delightful pasture on either border. The young geese are now completely feathered except the wings, which both in the young and old are yet deficient.

After feasting my eyes on this ravishing prospect and resting myself a few minutes I determined to proceed as far as the river which I saw discharge itself on the west side of the Missouri, convinced that it was the river which the Indians call Medicine River and which they informed us fell into the Missouri just above the falls. I descended the hills and directed my course to the bend of the Missouri, near which there was a herd of at least a thousand buffalo; here I thought it would be well to kill a buffalo and leave him until my return from the river and if I then found that I had not time to get back to camp this evening to remain all night here, there being a few sticks of driftwood lying along shore which would answer for my fire, and a few scattering cottonwood trees a few hundred yards below which would afford me at least the semblance of a shelter.

Under this impression I selected a fat buffalo and shot him very well, through the lungs. While I was gazing attentively on the poor animal discharging blood in streams from his mouth and nostrils, expecting him to fall every instant, and having entirely forgotten to reload my rifle, a large white, or rather brown bear, had perceived and crept on me within 20 steps before I discovered him. In the first moment I drew up my gun to shoot, but at the same instant recollected that she was not loaded and that he was too near for me to hope to perform this operation before he reached me, as he was then briskly advancing on me. It was an open level plain, not a bush within miles nor a tree within less than 300 yards of me. The riverbank was sloping and not more than three feet above the level of the water. In short there was no place by means of which I could conceal myself from this monster until I could charge my rifle. In this situation I thought of retreating in a brisk walk as fast as he was advancing until I could reach a tree about 300 yards below me, but I had no sooner turned myself about but he pitched at me, open mouthed and at full speed. I ran about 80 yards and found he gained on me fast. I then ran into the water. The idea struck me to get into the water to such depth that I could stand and he would be obliged to swim, and that I could in that situation defend myself with my espontoon. Accordingly I ran hastily into the water about waist deep and faced about and presented the point of my espontoon. At this instant he arrived at the edge of the water within about 20 feet of me. The moment I put myself in this attitude of defense he suddenly wheeled about as if frightened, declined the combat on such unequal grounds, and retreated with quite as great precipitation as he had just before pursued me. As soon as I saw him run off in that manner I returned to the shore and charged my gun, which I had still retained in my hand throughout this curious adventure. I saw him run through the level open plain about three miles till he disappeared in the woods on Medicine River. During the whole of this distance he ran at full speed, sometimes appearing to look behind him as if he expected pursuit.

I now began to reflect on this novel occurrence and endeavored to account for this sudden retreat of the bear. I at first thought that perhaps he had not smelt me before he arrived at the water's edge so near me, but I then reflected that he had pursued me for about 80 or 90 yards before I took to the water and on examination saw the ground torn with his talons immediately on the impression of my steps. The cause of his alarm still remains with me mysterious and unaccountable. So it was and I felt myself not a little gratified that he had declined the combat.

My gun reloaded, I felt confident once more in my strength and determined not to be thwarted in my design of visiting Medicine River, but determined never again to suffer my piece to be longer empty than the time she necessarily required to charge her. I passed through the plain nearly in the direction which the bear had run to Medicine River, found it a handsome stream, about 200 yards wide with a gentle current, apparently deep, its waters clear, and its banks, which were formed principally of dark brown and blue clay, were about the height of those of the Missouri or from three to five feet. Yet they had not the appearance of being overflown, a circumstance which I did not expect so immediately in the neighborhood of the mountains, from whence I should have supposed that sudden and immense torrents would issue at certain seasons of the year. But the reverse is absolutely the case. I am therefore compelled to believe that the Snowy Mountains yield their waters slowly, being partially affected every day by the influence of the sun only, and never suddenly melted down by hasty showers of rain.

Having examined Medicine River I now determined to return, having by my estimate about 12 miles to walk. I looked at my watch and found it was half after six p.m. In returning through the level bottom of Medicine River and about 200 yards distant from the Missouri, my direction led me directly to an animal that I at first supposed was a wolf; but on nearer approach, or about 60 paces distant, I discovered that it was not. Its color was a brownish yellow, it was standing near its burrow, and when I approached it thus directly, it couched itself down like a cat, looking immediately at me as if it designed to spring on me. I took aim at it and fired. It instantly disappeared in its burrow; I loaded my gun and examined the place, which was dusty, and saw the track from which I am still further convinced that it was of the tiger kind [*most Lewis and Clark scholars think it was a wolverine*]. Whether I struck it or not I could not determine, but I am almost confident that I did. My gun is true and I had a steady rest by means of my espontoon, which I have found very serviceable to me in this way in the open plains.

It now seemed to me that all the beasts of the neighborhood had made a league to destroy me, or that some fortune was disposed to amuse herself at my expense, for I had not proceeded more than 300 yards from the burrow of this tiger cat before three bull buffalo, which were feeding with a large herd about half a mile from me on my left, separated from the herd and ran full speed towards me. I thought at least to give them some amusement and altered my direction to meet them. When they arrived within a hundred yards they made a halt, took a good view of me and retreated with precipitation. I then continued my route homewards past the buffalo which I had killed, but did not think it prudent to remain all night at this place, which really from the succession of curious adventures wore the impression on my mind of enchantment. At some times for a moment I thought it might be a dream, but the prickly pears which pierced my feet very severely once in a while, particularly after it grew dark, convinced me that I was really awake and that it was necessary to make the best of my way to camp. It was some time after dark before I returned to the party. I found them extremely uneasy for my safety; they had formed a thousand conjectures, all of which equally foreboding my death, which they had so far settled among them, that they had already agreed on the route which each should take in the morning to search for me. I felt myself much fatigued, but ate a hearty supper and took a good night's rest. The weather being warm I had left my leather overshirt and had worn only a yellow flannel one.

A full day. Clark was having his own troubles, struggling upriver against a rapid current, the canoes taking in water frequently. Sacagawea was still quite sick; her case, said Clark, is "somewhat dangerous." Two men had toothaches, these two and another man had tumors (abscesses), and they made only ten miles. But Lewis's letter reached him, and the party now knew for certain that this was the Missouri.

June 15, 1805, Saturday [Lewis]

This morning the men again were sent to bring in some more meat which Drouillard had killed yesterday and continue the operation of drying it. I amused myself in fishing and sleeping away the fatigues of yesterday. I caught a number of very fine trout, which I made Goodrich dry. Goodrich also caught about two dozen and several small catfish of a yellow color which would weigh about four pounds. The tails were separated with a deep angular niche like that of the white catfish of the Missouri, from which indeed they differed only in color. When I awoke from my sleep today I found a large rattlesnake coiled on the leaning trunk of a tree under the shade of which I had been lying at the distance of about ten feet from him. I killed the snake and found that he had 176 scuta on the abdomen and 17 half-formed scuta on the tail. It was of the same kind which I had frequently seen before. They do not differ in their colors from the rattlesnake common to the Middle Atlantic states, but considerably in the form and figures of those colors. This evening after dark Joseph Fields returned and informed me that Capt. Clark had arrived with the party at the foot of a rapid about five miles below, which he did not think proper to ascend and would wait my arrival there. I had discovered from my journey yesterday that a portage on this side of the river will be attended by much difficulty in consequence of several deep ravines which intersect the plains nearly at right angles with the river to a considerable distance, while the south side appears to be a delightful smooth unbroken plain. The bearings of the river also make it probable that the portage will be shorter on that side than on this. I directed Fields to return early in the morning to Capt. Clark and request him to send up a party of men for the dried meat, which we had made. I find a very heavy dew on the grass about my camp every morning, which no doubt proceeds from the mist of the falls, as it takes place nowhere in the plains nor on the river except here.

Clark was struggling upriver still, Sacagawea was still sick and dispirited, and Clark says "the fatigue which we have to encounter is incredible, the men in the water from morning until night hauling the cord and boats, walking on sharp rocks and round slippery stones which alternately cut their feet and throw them, place was crawling with rattlesnakes, too." That night they could not find enough wood to build a good fire.

June 16, 1805, Sunday [Lewis]
J. Fields set out early on his return to the lower camp. At noon the men arrived and shortly after I set out with them to rejoin the party. We took with us the dried meat, consisting of about 600 pounds, and several dozen of dried trout. About two p.m. I reached the camp, found the Indian woman extremely ill and much reduced by her indisposition. This gave me some concern as well for the poor object herself, then with a young child in her arms, as from the consideration of her being our only dependence for a friendly negotiation with the Snake Indians, on whom we depend for horses to assist us in our portage from the Missouri to the Columbia River. I now informed Capt. Clark of my discoveries with respect to the most proper side for our portage, and of its great length, which I could not estimate at less than 16 miles. Capt. Clark had already sent two men this morning to examine the country on the south side of the river; he now passed over with the party to that side and fixed a camp about a mile below the entrance of a creek where there was a sufficient quantity of wood for fuel, an article which can be obtained but in few places in this neighborhood. After discharging the loads four of the canoes were sent back to me, which by means of strong ropes we hauled above the rapid and passed over to the south side, from whence, the water not being rapid, we can readily convey them into the creek by means of which we hope to get them on the high plain with more ease. One of the small canoes was left below this rapid in order to pass and repass the river for the purpose of hunting as well as to procure the water of the sulfur spring, the virtues of which I now resolved to try on the Indian woman. This spring is situated about 200 yards from the Missouri on the N.E. side nearly opposite to the entrance of a large creek; it discharges itself into the Missouri over a precipice of rock about 25 feet, forming a pretty little cataract. The water is as transparent as possible, strongly impregnated with sulfur, and I suspect iron also, as the color of the hills and bluffs in the neighborhood indicate the existence

of that metal. The water to all appearance is precisely similar to that of Bowyer's Sulfur Spring in Virginia.

Capt. Clark determined to set out in the morning to examine and survey the portage, and discover the best route. As the distance was too great to think of transporting the canoes and baggage on the men's shoulders, we selected six men and ordered them to look out some timber this evening, and early in the morning to set about making a parcel of truck wheels in order to convey our canoes and baggage over the portage. We determined to leave the white pirogue at this place and substitute the iron boat [*this was an experimental boat, an iron frame on which Lewis hoped to stretch elk skins instead of using wood planking, that the corps had brought all the way from Pennsylvania for just this purpose*], and also to make a further deposit of a part of our stores. In the evening the men who had been sent out to examine the country made a very unfavorable report. They informed us that the creek just above us, and two deep ravines still higher up, cut the plain between the river and the mountain in such a manner that in their opinion a portage for the canoes on this side was impracticable. Good or bad we must make the portage. Notwithstanding this report I am still convinced from the view I had of the country the day before yesterday that a good portage may be had on this side, at least much better than on the other, and much nearer also.

I found that two doses of barks and opium which I had given her since my arrival had produced an alteration in her pulse for the better [*Lewis has returned to the subject of Sacagawea*]; they were now much fuller and more regular. I caused her to drink the mineral water altogether. When I first came down I found that her pulse were scarcely perceptible, very quick, frequently irregular and attended with strong nervous symptoms, that of the twitching of the fingers and leaders of the arm. Now the pulse had become regular, much fuller, and a gentle perspiration had taken place. The nervous symptoms have also in a great measure abated, and she feels herself much freer from pain. She complains principally of the lower region of the abdomen. I therefore continued the cataplasms of bark and laudanum [*these would have been poultices of the bark of the South American cinchona tree, used to treat malaria, and tincture of opium*] which had been previously used by my friend Capt. Clark. I believe her disorder originated principally from an obstruction of the menses in consequence of taking cold. I determined to remain at this camp in order to make some celestial observations, restore the sick woman, and have all matters in a state of readiness to commence the portage immediately on the return of Capt. Clark, who now furnished me with the daily occurrences which had taken place with himself and party since our separation.

June 17, 1805, Monday [Lewis]
Capt. Clark set out early this morning with five men to examine the country and survey the river and portage as had been concerted last evening. I set six men at work to prepare four sets of truck wheels with couplings, tongues and bodies, that they might either be used without the bodies for transporting our canoes, or with them in transporting our baggage. I found that the elk skins I had prepared for my boat were insufficient to complete her, some of them having become damaged by the weather and being frequently wet. To make up this deficiency I sent out two hunters this morning to hunt elk. The balance of the party I employed first in unloading the white pirogue, which we intend leaving at this place, and bring the whole of our baggage together and arranging it in proper order near our camp. This duty being completed I employed them in taking five of the small canoes up the creek, which we now call Portage Creek, about one and three-quarter miles; here I had them taken out to lie in the sun to dry. From this place there is a gradual ascent to the top of the high plain to which we can now take them with ease. The bluffs of this creek below and those of the river above its entrance are so steep that it would be almost impracticable to have gotten them on the plain. We found much difficulty in getting the canoes up this creek to the distance we were compelled to take them in consequence of the rapids and rocks which obstruct the channel of the creek. One of the canoes overset and was very near injuring two men essentially. Just above the canoes the creek has a perpendicular fall of five feet and the cliffs again become very steep and high. We were fortunate enough to find one cottonwood tree just below the entrance of Portage Creek that was large enough to make our carriage wheels about 22 inches in diameter—fortunate, I say, because I do not believe that we could find another of the same size perfectly sound within 20 miles of us. The cottonwood which we are obliged to employ in the other parts of the work is extremely ill calculated for it, being soft and brittle. We have made two axletrees of the mast of the white pirogue, which I hope will answer tolerably well, though it is rather small.

The Indian woman much better today. I have still continued the same course of medicine; she is free from pain, clear of fever, her pulse regular, and eats as heartily as I am willing to permit her of broiled buffalo well seasoned with pepper and salt and rich soup of the same meat; I think therefore that there is every rational hope of her recovery. Saw a vast number of buffalo feeding in every direction around us in the plains, others coming down in large herds to water at the river. The fragments of many carcasses of these poor animals daily pass down the river mangled, I presume, in descending those immense cataracts above us. As the buffalo generally go in large herds to water and the passages to the river about the falls are narrow and steep, the hinder part of the herd press those in front out of their depth and the water instantly takes them over the cataracts, where they are instantly crushed to death without the possibility of escaping. In this manner I have seen ten or a dozen disappear in a few minutes. Their mangled carcasses lie along the shores below the falls in considerable quantities and afford fine amusement for the bears, wolves, and birds of prey. This may be one reason, and I think not a bad one, either, that the bear are so tenacious of their right of soil in this neighborhood.

Clark, meanwhile, was examining the route of the portage and the falls and rapids, at which he was, he says, astonished. He, too, saw the buffalo going down to water at the river and being driven in by those behind them. He himself "in descending the cliffs to take the height of the fall was near slipping into the water, at which place I must have been sucked under in an instant, and with difficulty and great risk I ascended again, and descended the cliff lower down . . . and took the height with as much accuracy as possible with a spirit level."

June 18, 1805, Tuesday [Lewis]

This morning I employed all hands in drawing the pirogue on shore in a thick bunch of willow bushes some little distance below our camp, fastened her securely, drove out the plugs of the gage holes of her bottom and covered her with bushes and driftwood to shelter her from the sun. I now selected a place for a cache and set three men at work to complete it and employed all others except those about the wagons in overhauling, airing, and repacking our Indian goods, ammunition, provision and stores of every description which required inspection. Examined the frame of my iron boat and found all the parts complete except one screw, which the ingenuity of Shields can readily replace, a resource which we have very frequent occasion for. About 12 o'clock the hunters returned; they had killed 10 deer but no elk. I begin to fear that we shall have some difficulty in procuring skins for the boat. I would prefer those of the elk because I believe them more durable and strong than those of the buffalo, and that they will not shrink so much in drying.

We saw a herd of buffalo come down to water at the sulfur spring this evening; I dispatched some hunters to kill some of them, and a man also for a cask of mineral water. The hunters soon killed two of them in fine order and returned with a good quantity of the flesh, having left the remainder in a situation that it will not spoil, provided the wolves do not visit it. The wagons are completed this evening, and appear as if they would answer the purpose very well if the axletrees prove sufficiently strong. The wind blew violently this evening, as it frequently does in open country where there is not a tree to break or oppose its force. The Indian woman is recovering fast. She sat up the greater part of the day and walked out for the first time since she arrived here. She eats heartily and is free from fever or pain. I continued the same course of medicine and regimen, except that I added one dose of 15 drops of the oil of vitriol today about noon.

Lewis then describes a species of gooseberry he had come across and remarks on the number of grasshoppers he has seen. Clark was exploring the falls and both measuring and admiring them; he also discovered what is now called Giant Springs, marveling at the volume of water coming out of it. He went on to above Medicine River, killing some buffalo. Alexander Willard was attacked by a grizzly and "very near being caught"; the bear pursued him to within 40 yards of camp, having followed Clark after he killed a buffalo and come across Willard. John Colter was still out so Clark and three hunters went after the bear, only to find that it had already chased Colter into the water. They got Colter out safely but didn't get a clean shot at the bear.

June 19, 1805, Wednesday [Lewis]
This morning I sent over several men for the meat which was killed yesterday; a few hours after, they returned with it. The wolves had not discovered it. I also dispatched George Drouillard, Reuben Fields and George Shannon on the north side of the Missouri with orders to proceed to the entrance of Medicine River and endeavor to kill some elk in that neighborhood. As there is more timber on that river than the Missouri I expect that the elk are more plentiful. The cache completed today. The wind blew violently the greater part of the day. The Indian woman was much better this morning. She walked out and gathered a considerable quantity of the white apples of which she ate so heartily in their raw state, together with a considerable quantity of dried fish, without my

knowledge, that she complained very much and her fever again returned. I rebuked Charbonneau severely for suffering her to indulge herself with such food, he being privy to it and having been previously told what she must only eat. I now gave her broken doses of diluted niter until it produced perspiration and at 10 p.m. 30 drops of laudanum, which gave her a tolerable night's rest.

I amused myself in fishing several hours today and caught a number of both species of the white fish, but no trout or catfish. I employed the men in making up our baggage in proper packages for transportation, and waxed the stoppers of my powder canisters anew. Had the frame of my iron boat cleansed of rust and well greased. In the evening the men mended their moccasins and prepared themselves for the portage. After dark my dog barked very much and seemed extremely uneasy, which was unusual with him. I ordered the sergeant of the guard to reconnoiter with two men, thinking it possible that some Indians might be about to pay us a visit, or perhaps a white bear. He returned soon after and reported that he believed the dog had been baying at a buffalo bull which had attempted to swim the river just above our camp but had been beaten down by the stream, landed a little below our camp on the same side and run off.

Clark looked for the troublesome grizzly the next day but could not find it, then went back to examine the best route for the portage. On his way he lost some of his notes, which blew away in the wind. The next entry is in Clark's words.

June 20, 1805, Thursday [Clark]
A cloudy morning, a hard wind all night and this morning. I direct stakes to be cut to stick up in the prairie to show the way for the party to transport the baggage, etc. We set out early on the portage [*he means the portage route*]. Soon after we set out it began to rain and continued a short time. We proceeded on through a tolerable level plain and found the hollow of a deep ravine to obstruct our route, as it could not be passed with canoes and baggage for some distance above the place we struck it. I examined it for some time and finding it late determined to strike the river and take its course and distance to camp, which I accordingly did. The wind hard from the S.W. A fair afternoon. The river on both sides cut with ravines, some of which pass through steep cliffs into the river. The country above the falls and up the Medicine River is level, with low banks, a chain of mountains to the west, some part of which, particularly those to the N.W. and S.W., are covered with snow and appear very high. I saw a rattlesnake in an open plain two miles

from any creek or wood. When I arrived at camp found all well with great quantities of meat. The canoes Capt. Lewis had carried up the one and three-quarters miles to a good place to ascend the bank and taken up. Not having seen the Snake Indians or knowing in fact whether to calculate on their friendship or hostility, we have conceived our party sufficiently small, and therefore have concluded not to dispatch a canoe with a part of our men to St. Louis as we had intended early in the Spring. We fear also that such a measure might discourage those who would in such case remain and might possibly hazard the fate of the expedition. We have never hinted to any one of the party that we had such a scheme in contemplation, and all appear perfectly to have made up their minds to succeed in the expedition or perish in the attempt. We all believe that we are about to enter on the most perilous and difficult part of our voyage, yet I see no one repining; all appear ready to meet those difficulties which await us with resolution and becoming fortitude.

We had a heavy dew this morning. The clouds near those mountains rise suddenly and discharge their contents partially on the neighboring plains; the same cloud discharges hail in one part, hail and rain in another and rain only in a third, all within the space of a few miles; and on the mountains to the south and S.E. of us sometimes snow. At present there is no snow on those mountains; that which covered them a few days ago has all disappeared. The mountains to the N.W. and west of us are still entirely covered, are white and glitter with the reflection of the sun.

I do not believe that the clouds that prevail at this season of the year reach the summits of those lofty mountains; and if they do the probability is that they deposit snow only, for there has been no perceptible diminution of the snow which they contain since we first saw them. I have thought it probable that these mountains might have derived their appellation of *Shining Mountains* from their glittering appearance when the sun shines in certain directions on the snow which covers them.

During the time of my being on the plains and above the falls I, as also all my party, repeatedly heard a noise which proceeded from a direction a little to the N. of west, as loud and resembling precisely the discharge of a piece of ordinance of six pounds at the distance of five or six miles. I was informed of it several times by the men, J. Fields particularly, before I paid any attention to it, thinking it was thunder most probably which they had mistaken. At length, walking in the plains yesterday near the most extreme S.E. bend of the river above the falls, I heard this *noise* very distinctly. It was perfectly calm, clear, and not a cloud to be seen. I halted and listened atten-tively about two hours, during which time I heard two other discharges, and took the direction of the sound with my pocket compass, which was as nearly west from me as I could estimate from the sound. I have no doubt but if I had leisure I could find from whence it issued. I have thought it probable that it might be caused by running water in some of the caverns of those immense mountains, on the principal of the blowing caverns [*he is referring to Blowing Cave in Virginia, which emits air currents*]; but in such case the sounds would be periodical and regular, which is not the case with this, being sometimes heard once only and at other times several discharges in quick succession. It is heard also at different times of the day and night. I am at a great loss to account for this phenomenon. I well recollect hearing the Mini-taris say that those Rocky Mountains make a great noise, but they could not tell me the cause, neither could they inform me of any remarkable substance or situation in these mountains which would authorize a conjecture of a probable cause of this noise. [*No one knows now what causes it, although it is still heard in the area.*]

It is probable that the large river just above those Great Falls which heads in the direction of the noise has taken its name *Medicine River* from this unaccountable rumbling sound, which like all unaccountable things with the Indians of the Missouri is called medicine. The Arikaras inform us of the Black Mountains making a similar noise and many other wonderful tales of those Rocky Mountains and those Great Falls.

Lewis was back in camp waiting for Clark to return, having game killed to be stored there for the use of the men in making the portage so that they would not have to hunt for their food during it, and seeing to Sacagawea, who was much better. The buffalo were coming down in vast numbers to the river to drink. We return to Lewis now.

June 21, 1805, Friday [Lewis]
This morning I employed the greater part of the men in transporting a part of the baggage over Portage Creek to the top of the high plain about three miles in advance on the portage. I also had one canoe carried on truck wheels to the same place and put the baggage in it, in order to make an early start in the morning, as the route of our portage is not yet entirely settled, and it would be inconvenient to remain in the open plain all night at a distance from water, which would probably be the case if we did not

set out early, as the latter part of the route is destitute of water for about eight miles.

Having determined to go to the upper part of the portage tomorrow in order to prepare my boat and receive and take care of the stores as they were transported, I caused the iron frame of the boat and the necessary tools, my private baggage and instruments, to be taken as a part of this load, also the baggage of Joseph Fields, Sergeant Gass, and John Shields, whom I had selected to assist me in constructing the leather boat. Three men were employed today in shaving the elk skins which had been collected for the boat. The balance of the party were employed in cutting the meat we had killed yesterday into thin fletches and drying it, and in bringing in the balance of what had been left over the river with three men last evening. I readily perceived several difficulties in preparing the leather boat, which are the want of convenient and proper timber, bark, skins, and above all that of pitch to pay her seams, a deficiency that I really know not how to surmount unless it be by means of tallow and pounded charcoal, which mixture has answered a very good purpose on our wooden canoes heretofore.

I have seen for the first time on the Missouri at these falls a species of fishing ducks with white wings, brown and white body and the head and part of the neck adjoining of a brick red, and the beak narrow, which I take to be the same common to James River, the Potomac and Susquehanna [*i.e., the merganser, either the female red-breasted or the female common species*]. Immense numbers of buffalo coming to the river as usual. The men who remained over the river last night killed several mule deer, and Willard who was with me killed a young elk. The wind blew violently all day. The growth of the neighborhood, what little there is, consists of the broad-and-narrow-leaved cottonwood, box elder, the large or sweet willow, the narrow and broad-leaved willow. The sweet willow has not been common to the Missouri below this or the entrance to Maria's River; it here attains to the same size and in appearance is much the same as in the Atlantic states. The undergrowth consists of rosebushes, gooseberry and currant bushes, honeysuckle small, and the redwood, the inner bark of which the *engagés* are fond of smoking mixed with tobacco.

June 22, 1805 [Lewis]
This morning early Capt. Clark and myself with all the party except Sgt. Ordway, Charbonneau, Goodrich, York and the Indian woman set out to pass the

portage with the canoe and baggage to the White Bear Islands, where we intend that this portage shall end [*the islands, so named because of Lewis's experience with the grizzly there, and where they had established the portage camp, were about 16 miles upriver*]. Capt. Clark piloted us through the plains. About noon we reached a little stream about eight miles on the portage where we halted and dined. We were obliged here to renew both axletrees and the tongues and hounds of one set of wheels, which took us no more than two hours. These parts of our carriage had been made of cottonwood and one axletree of an old mast, all of which proved deficient and had broken down several times before we reached this place. We have now renewed them with the sweet willow and hope that they will answer better. After dark we had reached within half a mile of our intended camp when the tongues gave way and we were obliged to leave the canoe. Each man took as much of the baggage as he could carry on his back and proceeded to the river, where we formed our encampment much fatigued. The prickly pears were extremely troublesome to us, sticking our feet through our moccasins. Saw a great number of buffalo in the plains, also immense quantities of little birds and the large brown curlew. The latter is now setting; it lays its eggs, which are of a pale blue with black specks, on the ground without any preparation of a nest. There is a kind of lark here that much resembles the bird called the Oldfield Lark with a yellow breast and a black spot on the croup, though this differs from ours in the form of the tail, which is pointed, being formed of feathers of unequal length. The beak is somewhat longer and more curved and the note differs considerably. However in size, action, and colors there is no perceptible difference, or at least none that strikes my eye. [*This was the western meadowlark, a Lewis and Clark discovery; the Oldfield Lark is the eastern meadowlark.*]

After reaching our camp we kindled our fires and examined the meat which Capt. Clark had left, but found only a small proportion of it; the wolves had taken the greatest part. We ate our suppers and soon retired to rest.

Clark noted that "we determined to employ every man, cooks and all, on the portage after today."

June 23, 1805, Sunday [Lewis]

This morning early I selected a place for the purpose of constructing my boat near the water under some shady willows. Capt. Clark had the canoe and baggage brought up, after which we breakfasted and nearly consumed the meat which he had left here. He now set out on his return with the party.

I employed the three men with me in the forenoon clearing away the brush and forming our camp, and putting the frame of the boat together. This being done I sent Shields and Gass to look out for the necessary timber, and with J. Fields descended the river in the canoe to the mouth of the Medicine River in search of the hunters whom I had dispatched thither on the 19th inst. and from whom we had not heard a sentence. I entered the mouth of the Medicine River and ascended it about half a mile, when we landed and walked up the starboard side, frequently whooping as we went on in order to find the hunters. At length after ascending the river about five miles we found Shannon, who had passed the Medicine River and fixed his camp on the larboard side, where he had killed seven deer and several buffalo and dried about 600 pounds of buffalo meat—but had killed no elk. Shannon could give me no further account of R. Fields and Drouillard than that he had left them about noon on the 19th at the Great Falls and had come on the mouth of Medicine River to hunt elk as he had been directed, and never had seen them since.

The evening being now far spent I thought it better to pass the Medicine River and remain all night at Shannon's camp. I passed the river on a raft which we soon constructed for the purpose. The river is here about 80 yards wide, is deep and but a moderate current. The banks low as those of the Missouri above the falls, yet never appear to overflow.

As it will give a better view of the transactions of the party, I shall on each day give the occurrences of both camps during our separation as I afterwards learned those of the lower camp from Capt. Clark. On his return today he cut off several angles of the route by which we came yesterday, shortened the portage considerably, measured it and set up stakes throughout as guides to mark the route. He returned this evening to the lower camp in sufficient time to take up two of the canoes from Portage Creek to the top of the plain about a mile in advance. This evening the men repaired their moccasins, and put on double soles to protect their feet from the prickly pears. During the late rains the buffalo have trodden up the prairie very much, which having now become dry, the sharp points of earth as hard as frozen ground stand up in such abundance that there is no avoiding them. This is particularly severe on the feet of the men who have not only their own weight to bear in treading on those hacklelike points but have also the addition of the burden which they draw and which in fact is as much as they can possibly move with. They are obliged to halt and rest frequently for a few minutes; at every halt these poor fellows tumble down and are so much fatigued that many of them are asleep in an instant. In short their fatigues are incredible; some are limping from the soreness of their feet, others faint and unable to stand for a few minutes, with heat and fatigue, yet no one complains, all go with cheerfulness. In the evening Reuben Fields returned to the lower camp and informed Capt. Clark of the absence of Shannon, with respect to whom they were extremely uneasy. Fields and Drouillard had killed several buffalo at the bend of the Missouri above the falls and had dried a considerable quantity of meat. They had also killed several deer but no elk.

Clark's entry for the day amplifies on the difficulty of hauling the heavy wagons across this terrain. "The men have to haul," he says, "with all their strength, weight, and art, many times catching the grass and knobs and stones with their hands to give them more force in drawing on the canoes and loads, and notwithstanding the coolness of the air in high perspiration. At every halt, those not employed in repairing the course [?] are asleep in a moment . . . To state the fatigues of this party would take up more of the journal than other notes, which I find scarcely time to set down." Clark now measured the portage at more than 18 miles, much of it level but at least a mile and a half up a gradual hill and a quarter of a mile a difficult, rough, steep ascent. There were several gullies to cross, and a creek.

June 24, 1805, Monday [Lewis]

Supposing that Drouillard and R. Fields might possibly be still higher up Medicine River, I dispatched J. Fields up the river with orders to proceed about four miles and then return whether he found them or not and join Shannon at this camp. I set out early and walked down the southwest side of the river and sent Shannon down the opposite side to bring the canoe over to me and put me across the Missouri. Having landed on the larboard side of the Missouri I sent Shannon back with the canoe to meet J. Fields and bring the dried meat at that place to the camp at the White Bear Islands, which he accomplished and arrived with Fields this evening. The party also arrived this evening with two canoes from the lower camp. They were wet and fatigued, gave them a dram. R. Fields came with them and gave me an account of his and Drouillard's hunt and informed me that Drouillard was still at their camp with the meat they had dried. The iron frame of my boat is 36 feet long, 41½ feet in the beam and 26 inches in the hole.

This morning early Capt. Clark had the remaining canoe drawn out of the water and divided the remainder of our baggage into three parcels, one of which he sent today by the party with two canoes. The Indian woman is now perfectly recovered. Capt. Clark came a few miles this morning to see the party under way and returned. On my arrival at the upper camp this morning I found that Sgt. Gass and Shields had made but slow progress in collecting timber for the boat. They complained of great difficulty in getting straight or even tolerably straight sticks of 4½ feet long. We were obliged to make use of the willow and box elder, the cottonwood being too soft and brittle. I kept one of them collecting timber while the other shaved and fitted it. I have found some pine logs among the driftwood near this place, from which I hope to obtain as much pitch as will answer to pay the seams of the boat. I directed Frazer to remain in order to sew the hides together and form the covering for the boat.

Clark notes for this day that his feet were "very sore from the walk over ruts, stones and hills and through the level plain for six days preceding, carrying my pack and gun." It hailed that day, he adds, then it rained for about an hour, but hardly wet the earth; while on the other side of the river streams were discharging "immense torrents of water into the river." The following entry is Clark's.

June 25, 1805, Tuesday [Clark]
A fair warm morning. Clouded and a few drops of rain at five o'clock a.m. Fair. I feel myself a little unwell with a looseness, etc. Put out the stores to dry and set Charbonneau to cook for the party against their return—he being the only man left on this side with me. I had a little coffee for breakfast, which was to me a necessity, as I had not tasted any since last winter. The wind from the N.W. and warm. This country has a romantic appearance, river enclosed between high and steep hills cut to pieces by ravines, but little timber and that confined to the rivers and creeks; the Missouri has but a few scattering trees on its borders, and only one solitary cottonwood tree in sight of my camp. The wood which we burn is driftwood which is broken to pieces in passing the falls, not one large tree longer than about eight or ten feet to be found drifted below the falls. The plains are inferior in point of soil to those below, more stone on the sides of the hills, grass but a few inches high and but few flowers in the plains, great quantities of choke cherries, gooseberries, red and yellow berries, and red and purple currants on the edges of water courses, in bottoms and damp places. About my camp the cliffs or bluffs are a hard red or reddish brown earth containing iron. We catch great quantities

of trout, and a kind of mussel, flat backs and a soft fish resembling a shad and a few catfish. At five o'clock the party returned, fatigued as usual, and proceeded to mend their moccasins. G. Shannon and R. Fields, two of the men who were sent up the Medicine River to hunt elk. They killed no elk, several buffalo and deer, and report that the river is 120 yards wide and about 8 feet deep, some timber on its borders. A powerful rain fell on the party on their route yesterday, wet some few articles, and caused the route to be so bad, wet and deep they could with difficulty proceed. Capt. Lewis and the men with him much employed with the iron boat in fitting it for the water.

Dispatched one man to George Drouillard's camp below Medicine River for meat. A fair afternoon. Great numbers of buffalo water opposite to my camp every day. It may be here worthy of remark that the sails were hoisted in the canoes as the men were drawing them and the wind was a great relief to them, being sufficiently strong to move the canoes on the trucks. This is sailing on dry land in every sense of the word. Sgt. Pryor sick. The party amused themselves with dancing until 10 o'clock, all cheerfulness and good humor. They all tied up their loads to make an early start in the morning.

Lewis reports that Fields had had an encounter with a grizzly.

He had seen two white bear near the river a few miles above and in attempting to get a shot at them had stumbled upon a third, which immediately made at him, being only a few steps distant. In running in order to escape from the bear he had leapt down a steep bank of the river on a stony bar, where he fell, cut his hand, bruised his knees and bent his gun. Fortunately for him the bank hid him from the bear when he fell and by that means he had escaped. This man has been truly unfortunate with these bears; this is the second time he has narrowly escaped from them.

Cruzatte, he tells us, was the violinist for the dances; he played very well.

June 26, 1805, Wednesday [Lewis]
The mosquitoes are extremely troublesome to us. This morning early I dispatched J. Fields and Drouillard in one of the canoes up the river to hunt elk. Set Frazer at work to sew the skins together for the covering of the boat. Shields and Gass I sent over the river to search a small timbered bottom on that side opposite to the islands for timber and bark; and to myself I assign the duty of cook as well for those present as for the party, which I expect again to arrive from the lower camp. I collected my wood and water, boiled a large quantity of excellent dried buffalo meat and made each man a large

suet dumpling by way of a treat. About four p.m. Shields and Gass returned with a better supply of timber than they had yet collected though not by any means enough. They brought some bark principally of the cottonwood, which I found was too brittle and soft for the purpose; for this article I find my only dependence is the sweet willow, which has a tough and strong bark. Shields and Gass had killed seven buffalo in their absence, the skins of which and a part of the best of the meat they brought with them. If I cannot procure a sufficient quantity of elk skins I shall substitute those of the buffalo. Late in the evening the party arrived with two more canoes and another portion of the baggage. Whitehouse, one of them much heated and fatigued on his arrival, drank a very heart draught of water and was taken almost instantly extremely ill. His pulse was very full and I therefore bled him plentifully, from which he felt great relief. I had no other instrument with which to perform this operation but my penknife; however it answered very well. The wind being from S.E. today and favorable, the men made considerable progress by means of their sails.

At the lower camp. The party set out very early from this place and took with them two canoes and a second allotment of baggage, consisting of parched meal, pork, powder, lead, axes, tools, biscuit, portable soup, some merchandise and clothing. Capt. Clark gave Sgt. Pryor a dose of salts this morning and employed Charbonneau in rendering the buffalo tallow which had been collected there; he obtained a sufficient quantity to fill three empty kegs. Capt. Clark also selected the articles to be deposited in the cache, con-sisting of my desk, which I had left for that purpose and in which I had left some books, my specimens of plants, minerals, etc., collected from Fort Mandan to that place. Also two kegs of pork, half a keg of flour, two blun-derbusses, half a keg of fixed ammunition and some other small articles belonging to the party which could be dispensed with. Deposited the swivel [*the swivel gun*] and carriage under the rocks a little above the camp near the river. Great numbers of buffalo continue to water daily opposite the camp. The antelope continue scattered and separate in the plains. The females with their young only, of which they generally have two, and the males alone.

June 27, 1805, Thursday [Lewis]
The party returned early this morning for the remaining canoe and baggage. Whitehouse was not quite well this morning. I therefore detained him and about 10 a.m. set him at work with Frazer sewing the skins together for the

boat. Shields and Gass continued the operation of shaving and fitting the horizontal bars of wood in the sections of the boat; the timber is so crooked and indifferent that they make but little progress. For myself I continued to act the part of cook in order to keep all hands employed. Some elk came near our camp and we killed two of them. At one p.m. a cloud arose to the S.W. and shortly after came on attended with violent thunder, lightning and hail. [*Lewis wrote about the hail in his weather diary for this month, which Moulton prints, and noted that the hail was more than an inch deep on the ground and individual hailstones were as large as pigeon's eggs. When the hail struck the ground it would bounce ten or twelve feet in the air. Some of the hailstones were seven inches around. Anyone caught in the open in such a storm could be badly hurt.*]

Soon after this storm was over Drouillard and J. Fields returned. They were about four miles above us during the storm; the hail was of no uncommon size where they were. They had killed nine elk and three bears during their absence. One of the bears was the largest by far that we have yet seen; the skin appears to me to be as large as a common ox. While hunting they saw a thick brushy bottom on the bank of the river where from the tracks along the shore they suspected that there were bears concealed. They therefore landed without making any noise and climbed a leaning tree and placed themselves on its branches about 20 feet above the ground. When thus securely fixed they gave a whoop and this large bear instantly rushed forward to the place from whence he had heard the human voice issue. When he arrived at the tree he made a short pause and Drouillard shot him in the head. It is worthy of remark that these bears never climb. The forefeet of this bear measured nine inches across and the hind feet eleven and three-quarters inches in length exclusive of the talons and seven inches in width. A bear came within 30 yards of our camp last night and ate up about 30 weight [*i.e., pounds*] of buffalo suet which was hanging on a pole. My dog seems to be in a constant state of alarm with these bears and keeps barking all night. Soon after the storm this evening the water on this side of the river became of a deep crimson color, which I presume proceeded from some stream above and on this side. There is a kind of soft red stone in the bluffs and bottoms of the gullies in this neighborhood which forms this coloring matter.

At the lower camp. Capt. Clark completed a draught of the river with the courses and distances from the entrance of the Missouri to Fort Mandan, which we intend depositing here in order to guard against accidents. Sgt. Pryor is somewhat better this morning. At four p.m. the party returned from the upper camp; Capt. Clark gave them a drink of grog; they prepared for the labor of the next day. Soon after the party returned it began to rain accompanied by some hail and continued a short time. A second shower fell late in the evening accompanied by a high wind from N.W. The mangled carcasses of several buffalo passed down the river today which had no doubt perished in the falls.

June 28, 1805, Friday [Lewis]
Set Drouillard to shaving the elk skins, Fields to make the cross stays for the boat. Frazer and Whitehouse continue their operation with the skins, Shields and Gass finish the horizontal bars of the sections, after which I sent them in search of willow bark, a sufficient supply of which they now obtained to line the boat. Expecting the party this evening I prepared a supper for them but they did not arrive. Not having quite enough elk skins, I employed three buffalo hides to cover one section. Not being able to shave these skins I had them singed pretty closely with a blazing torch; I think they will answer tolerably well.

The white bears have become so troublesome to us that I do not think it prudent to send one man alone on an errand of any kind, particularly where he has to pass through the brush. We have seen two of them on the large island opposite to us today but are so much engaged that we could not spare the time to hunt them but will make a frolic of it when the party return and drive them from these islands. They come close around our camp every night but have never yet ventured to attack us and our dog gives us timely notice of their visits. He keeps constantly patrolling all night. I have made the men sleep with their arms by them as usual for fear of accidents. The river is now about nine inches higher than it was on my arrival.

Lower camp. Early this morning Capt. Clark dispatched the remaining canoe with some baggage to the top of the plain above Portage Creek three miles in advance. Some others he employed in carrying the articles to the cache and depositing them and others to mend the carriages, which were somewhat out of repair. This being accomplished he loaded the two carriages with the remaining baggage and set out with all the party and proceeded on with much difficulty to the canoe in the plain. Portage Creek had risen considerably and the water was of a deep crimson color and ill-tasting. On his arrival at the canoe he found there was more baggage than he could possibly take on one load on the two sets of trucks and therefore left some barrels of pork and flour and a few heavy boxes of ammunition which could not well be injured, and proceeded with the canoe and one set of trucks loaded with baggage to Willow Run, where he encamped for the night, and killed two buffalo to sustain the party. Soon after his arrival at Willow Run he experienced a hard shower of rain which was succeeded by a violent wind from the S.W. off the Snowy Mountains, accompanied with rain. The party being cold and wet, he administered the consolation of a dram to each.

June 29, 1805, Saturday [Lewis]
This morning we experienced a heavy shower of rain for about an hour, after which it became fair. Not having seen the large fountain of which Capt. Clark spoke I determined to visit it today as I could better spare this day from my attention to the boat than probably any other when the work would be further advanced. Accordingly after setting the hands at their several employments I took Drouillard and set out for the fountain and passed through a level beautiful plain for about six miles when I reached the break of the river hills. Here we were overtaken by a violent gust of wind and rain from the S.W. attended with thunder and lightning. I expected a hail storm probably from this cloud and therefore took refuge in a little gully where there were some broad stones with which I purposed protecting my head if we should have a repetition of the scene of the 27th, but fortunately we had but little hail and that not large. I sat very composedly for about an hour without shelter and took a copious drenching of rain.

After the shower was over I continued my route to the fountain which I found much as Capt. Clark had described and think it may well be retained on the list of prodigies of this neighborhood, towards which nature seems to have dealt with a liberal hand, for I have scarcely experienced a day since my first arrival in this quarter without experiencing some novel occurrence among the party or witnessing the appearance of some uncommon object. I think this fountain the largest I ever beheld, and the handsome cascade which it affords over some steep and irregular rocks in its passage to the river adds not a little to its beauty. It is about 25 yards from the river, situated in a pretty little level plain, and has a sudden descent of about six feet in one part of its course. The water of this fountain is extremely transparent and cold; nor is it impregnated with lime or any other extraneous matter which I can discover, but is very pure and pleasant. Its waters mark their passage as Capt. Clark observes for a considerable distance down the Missouri, notwithstanding its rapidity and force. The waters of the fountain boil up with such force near its center that its surface in that part seems even higher than the surrounding earth, which is a firm handsome turf of fine green grass.

After amusing myself about 20 minutes in examining the fountain I found myself so chilled with my wet clothes that I determined to return and accordingly set out. On our way to camp we found a buffalo dead which we had shot as we came out and took a parcel of the meat to camp. It was in very good order; the hump and tongue of a fat buffalo I esteem great delicacies. On my arrival at camp I was astonished not to find the party yet arrived, but then concluded that probably the state of the prairies had detained them, as in the wet state in which they are at present the mud sticks to the wheels in such manner that they are obliged to halt frequently and cleanse them.

Transaction and occurrences which took place with Capt. Clark and party today. Shortly after the rain which fell early this morning he found it impossible from the state of the plains for the party to reach the upper extremity of the portage with their present load and therefore sent back almost all of the party to bring the baggage which had been left behind yesterday. He determined himself to pass by the way of the river to camp in order to supply the deficiency of some notes and remarks which he had made as he first ascended the river but which he had unfortunately lost. Accordingly he left one man at Willow Run to guard the baggage and took with him his black man, York. Charbonneau and his Indian woman also accompanied Capt. Clark. On his arrival at the falls he perceived a very black cloud rising in the west which threatened immediate rain. He looked about for a shelter but could find none without being in greater danger of being blown into the river should the wind prove as violent as it sometimes is on those occasions in these plains.

At length about one quarter of a mile above the falls he discovered a deep ravine where there were some shelving rocks under which he took shelter near the river with Charbonneau and the Indian woman, laying their guns, compass, etc. under a shelving rock on the upper side of the ravine where they were perfectly secure from the rain. The first shower was moderate, accompanied by a violent rain the effects of which they did but little feel. Soon after a most violent torrent of rain descended, accompanied with hail. The rain appeared to descend in a body and instantly collected in the ravine and came down in a rolling torrent with irresistible force, driving rocks, mud, and everything before it which opposed its passage. Capt. Clark fortunately discovered it a moment before it reached them and, seizing his gun and shot pouch with his left hand, with the right he assisted himself up the steep bluff, shoving occasionally the Indian woman before him who had her child in her arms. Charbonneau had the woman by the hand endeavoring to pull her up the hill but was so much frightened that he remained frequently motionless. But for Capt. Clark both himself and his woman and child must have perished. So sudden was the rise of the water that before Capt. Clark could reach his gun and begin to ascend the bank it was up to his waist and wet the watch; and he could scarcely ascend faster than it arose till it had obtained the depth of 15 feet with a current tremendous to behold. One moment longer and it would have swept them into the river just above the great cataract of 87 feet, where they must have inevitably perished. Charbonneau lost his gun, shot pouch, horn, tomahawk, and my wiping rod; Capt. Clark his umbrella and compass.

They fortunately arrived on the plains safe, where they found the black man, York, in search of them; York had separated from them a little while before the storm in pursuit of some buffalo and had not seen them enter the ravine. When this gust came on he returned in search of them and not being able to find them for some time was much alarmed. The bier [*a kind of mosquito netting*] in which the woman carries her child and all its clothes were swept away as they lay at her feet, she having time only to grasp her child; the infant was therefore very cold and the woman also, who had just recovered from a severe indisposition, was wet and cold. Capt. Clark therefore relinquished his intended route and returned to the camp at Willow Run in order also to obtain dry clothes for himself and directed them to follow him.

On Capt. Clark's arrival at camp he found that the party dispatched for the baggage had returned in great confusion and consternation, leaving their loads in the plains. The men, who were all nearly naked and had no covering on the head were sorely mauled with the hail, which was so large and driven with such force by the wind that it knocked many of them down, one particularly as many as three times. Most of them were bleeding freely and complained of being much bruised. Willow Run raised about 6 feet with this rain and the plains were so wet they could do nothing more this evening. Capt. Clark gave the party a dram to console them in some measure for their general defeat.

Clark adds to this that the compass was "a serious loss, as we have no other large one."

June 30, 1805, Sunday [Lewis]
We had a heavy dew this morning which is a remarkable event. Frazer and Whitehouse still continue their operation of sewing the skins together. I set Shields and Gass to shaving bark and Fields continued to make the cross braces. Drouillard and myself rendered a considerable quantity of tallow and cooked. I begin to be extremely impatient to be off, as the season is now wasting apace. Nearly three months have now elapsed since we left Fort Mandan and not yet reached the Rocky Mountains. I am therefore fully persuaded that we shall not reach Fort Mandan again this season if we even return from the ocean to the Snake Indians.

Wherever we find timber there is also beaver; Drouillard killed two today. There are a number of large bats or goatsuckers here. I killed one of them and found that there was no difference between them and those common to the United States. I have not seen the leather-winged bat for some time nor are there any of the small goatsuckers in this quarter of the country. We have not the whippoorwill either. This last is by many persons in the United States confounded with the large goatsucker or night hawk as it is called in the Eastern states, and are taken for the same bird. It is true that there is a great resemblance but they are distinct species of the goatsucker. Here the one exists without the other. The large goatsucker lays its eggs in these open plains without the preparation of a nest. We have found their eggs in several instances. They lay only two before they set nor do I believe that they raise more than one brood in a season; they have now just hatched their young.

This evening the bark was shaved and the leather covering for the sections were also completed and I had them put into the water, in order to toughen the bark, and prepare the leather for sewing on the sections in the morning. It has taken 28 elk skins and 4 buffalo skins to complete her. The cross bars are also finished this evening. We have therefore only the way strips now to obtain in order to complete the wood work, and this I fear will be a difficult task. The party has not returned from the lower camp. I am therefore fearful that some uncommon accident has happened.

Occurrences with Capt. Clark and party. This morning Capt. Clark dispatched two men to kill some small buffalo, two others to the falls to search for the articles lost yesterday, one he retained to cook and sent the others for the baggage left in the plains yesterday. The hunters soon returned loaded with meat. Those sent for the baggage brought it up in a few hours. He then set four men at work to make axletrees and repair the carriages. The others he employed in conveying the baggage over the run on their shoulders, it having now fallen to about three feet of water. The men complained much today of the bruises and wounds which they had received yesterday from the hail. The two men sent to the falls returned with the compass, which they found covered in the mud and sand near the mouth of the ravine. The other articles were irrecoverably lost. They found that part of the ravine in which Capt. Clark had been sitting yesterday filled with huge rocks. At 11 a.m. Capt. Clark dispatched the party with a load of the baggage as far as the six mile stake, with orders to deposit it there and return with the carriages, which they did accordingly. They experienced a heavy gust of wind this evening from the S.W. after which it was a fair afternoon. More buffalo than usual were seen around their camp. Capt. Clark assured me that he believes he saw at least ten thousand at one view.

July 1, 1805, Monday [Lewis]
This morning I set Frazer and Whitehouse to sewing the leather on the sides of the sections of the boat, Shields and J. Fields to collect and split light wood and prepare a pit to make tar. Gass I set at work to make the way strips out of some willow limbs which, though indifferent, were the best which could be obtained. Drouillard and myself completed the operation of rendering the tallow; we obtained about 100 pounds. By evening the skins were all attached to their sections and I returned them again to the water. All matters are now in readiness to commence the operation of putting the parts of the boat together in the morning. The way strips are not yet ready but will be done in time as I have obtained the necessary timber. The difficulty in obtaining the necessary materials has retarded my operations in forming this boat, [*making it*] extremely tedious and troublesome; and as it was a novel piece of mechanism to all who were employed, my constant attention was necessary to every part of the work. This, together with the duties of chief cook, has kept me pretty well employed. At three p.m. Capt. Clark arrived with the party, all very much fatigued. He brought with him all the baggage except what he had deposited yesterday at the six mile stake, for which the party were too much fatigued to return this evening. We gave them a dram and

suffered them to rest from their labors this evening. I directed Bratton to assist in making the tar tomorrow, and selected several others to assist in putting the boat together.

The day has been warm and the mosquitoes troublesome, of course. The bears were about our camp all last night; we have therefore determined to beat up their quarters tomorrow, and kill them or drive them from their haunts about this place.

July 2, 1805, Tuesday [Lewis]

A shower of rain fell very early this morning after which we dispatched the men for the remaining baggage at the six mile stake. Shields and Bratton setting their tar kiln, Sgts. Pryor and Gass at work on the way strips and myself and all other hands engaged in putting the boat together, which we accomplished in about three hours. I then set four men at work sewing the leather over the cross bars of iron on the inner side of the boat, which form the ends of the sections. About two p.m. the party returned with the baggage, all well pleased that they had completed the laborious task of portage.

The mosquitoes uncommonly troublesome. The wind hard from the S.W. all day. I think it possible that these almost perpetual S.W. winds proceed from the agency of the Snowy Mountains and the wide, level, and untimbered plains which stretch themselves along their bases for an immense distance, i.e. that the air coming in contact with the snow is suddenly chilled and condensed, thus becoming heavier than the air beneath in the plains. It glides down the sides of these mountains and descends to the plains, where by the constant action of the sun on the face of an untimbered country there is a partial vacuum formed for its reception. I have observed that the winds from this quarter are always the coldest and most violent which we experience, yet I am far from giving full credit to my own hypothesis on this subject. If, however, I find on the opposite side of these mountains that the winds take a contrary direction I shall then have more faith.

After I had completed my observation of equal altitudes today Capt. Clark, myself, and 12 men passed over to the large island to hunt bear. The brush in that part of it where the bears frequent is an almost impenetrable thicket of the broad-leaved willow; this brush we entered in small parties of three or four together and searched in every part. We found one only, which made at Drouillard and he shot him in the breast at the distance of about 20 feet. The ball fortunately passed through his heart, the stroke knocked the bear down and gave Drouillard time to get out of his sight. The bear changed his course; we pursued him about a hundred yards by the blood and found him dead. We searched the thicket in every part but found no other, and therefore returned. This was a young male and would weigh about 400 pounds. The water of the Missouri here is in most places about 10 feet deep.

After our return, in moving some of the baggage, we caught a large rat. It was somewhat larger than the common European rat, of lighter color, the body and outer part of the legs and head of a light lead color, the belly and inner side of the legs white, as were also the feet and ears. The toes were longer and the ears much larger than the common rat; the ears uncovered with hair. The eyes were black and prominent, the whiskers very long and full. The tail was rather longer than the body and covered with fine fur of the same length and color of the back. The fur was very silky, close and short. I have frequently seen the nests of these rats in cliffs of rocks and hollow trees but never before saw one of them. They feed very much on the fruit and seed of the prickly pear—or at least I have seen large quantities of the hulls of that fruit lying about their holes and in their nests. [*Thwaites calls this the Rocky Mountain rat. Its common name now is the pack rat; it was then new to science.*]

The exhausting 18-mile portage around the Great Falls of the Missouri had delayed the corps for weeks. Now they were faced with still further delay as the elk- and buffalo-hide skin of the iron-frame boat, what the men called the Experiment, slowly dried out. It was not enough to cover the boat with hides; the hides had to be made watertight, particularly at the seams, where they were sewn together. As they dried, the hides shrank, pulling at the holes the needles had made and stretching them open.

In the East, Lewis would have used pitch from pitch pines to coat the seams and make them watertight. No pitch pines grew within hundreds of miles of the Great Falls. Lewis had to find some other means of coating the boat. He had the men pound powdered charcoal into a mixture of beeswax and buffalo tallow. They built small fires under the boat to dry it out. It took days. Everybody was anxious to get going. Clark must have looked skeptically on; at least one scholar has suggested that he never believed the Experiment would work in the first place, and he had already scouted out a grove of cottonwood some miles upstream where he thought the trees were large enough to make canoes.

Meanwhile the men passed the time either working on the boat or hunting. The few men who had not yet seen the Great Falls themselves went back downriver to see them. On July 4, Lewis and Clark passed out the last of the liquor to celebrate the nation's birthday, and they all ate well, with Lewis remarking that they "had no just cause to covet the sumptuous feasts of our countrymen on this day."

The next day the boat was still not dry; on July 6 it rained, keeping the boat wet. The men made clothing for themselves. Clark went back downriver and measured the falls precisely with his instruments; Lewis wrote a description of a kit fox, otherwise known as the swift fox. Not until July 8, at noon, could Lewis begin to coat the boat with his mixture of grease and charcoal. On July 9 they put it in the water. "She lay like a perfect cork," said Lewis hopefully. And if it had worked it would have saved the day.

So light five men could "carry her with the greatest ease," the Experiment was 36 feet long and had a carrying capacity of 8,000 pounds. Despite all they had cached, they still had a great deal of food and equipment to take with them. They needed something more than the six canoes they had. That evening they discovered that the wax and tallow composition they had applied to the boat was separating from the skin "and she leaked in such manner that she would not answer. I need not add," says Lewis, "that this circumstance mortified me not a little." Indeed. They had waited a full week while the boat dried out and the composition was applied. Now they would have to leave it behind.

It took another five days, from July 10 through July 14, to get all the men, baggage, and canoes from their camp at the White Bear Islands up to the grove, some 23 miles on (but only eight miles overland, so much did the river twist and turn), where Clark had found the trees and was busy digging two more canoes, one 25 feet long, one 33, out of the largest two cottonwood trees they could find. The wind was against them once again, and the current was swift—a presage of the labor that still faced them getting the corps up the Missouri to the Three Forks. Mosquitoes were a plague, and now they had to deal with buffalo gnats, insects that did not bite but got constantly into their eyes. Lewis and everyone else were "excessively anxious to be moving on." The season was aging fast.

On July 13 Lewis left White Bear Island camp for the last time and walked up to Clark's camp. On the way he passed a large abandoned Indian lodge in tepee form but 216 feet in circumference at the base. They were in Blackfeet territory now, although they hadn't seen an Indian of any tribe for months. The lodge may have been a ceremonial Sun Dance lodge.

Lewis remarked during the course of the day on how much meat the corps required to keep going: "It requires 4 deer, an elk and a deer, or one buffalo, to supply us plentifully 24 hours. Meat now forms our food principally as we reserve our flour, parched meal and corn as much as possible for the Rocky Mountains which we are shortly to enter, and where from the Indian account game is not very abundant." Where, as he knew, they would sometimes have to fast.

Finally, on July 15, 1805, 12 days after they had completed the portage from the cottonwood grove, the corps got going again. The eight canoes were heavily laden, so to lighten the load, Lewis walked on shore with two of his men who were sick; the captains, he noted, "find it extremely difficult to keep the baggage of many of our men within reasonable bounds; they will be adding bulky articles of but little use or value to them," though he doesn't say what they were. They made 20 miles that day.

The next day Lewis took George Drouillard with him on foot toward the mountains to make observations, to determine latitude and longitude; it took time to make these observations and he could get there faster on foot than by canoe. The river was becoming even more winding and shallower. On the way they saw signs of Snake or Shoshone Indians, but not the Indians themselves. Finding the Shoshone was now their main priority. They needed horses and guides to get over the Rockies to the Columbia. The Shoshone could provide both, and Sacagawea was a Shoshone. They were among mountains now, in the foothills of the Rockies, passing land features for which the Minitari had given them no names. They named one river after Robert Smith, the secretary of the Navy, another after Henry Dearborn, secretary of war; they named smaller streams after members of the corps.

Clark set out on foot with Joseph Fields, York, and John Potts on July 18 to go ahead and try to make contact with the Shoshone. The captains were afraid that the sound of guns from the hunting that was constantly necessary to feed the men would frighten them away. The sound of guns to the Shoshones would normally mean a Blackfeet raiding party was in the area; the Blackfeet were their enemies. The Shoshone had very few guns; they were at a distinct disadvantage because of it, forced to flee into the mountains at the appearance of the Blackfeet or their other enemies. Clark's smaller party would make much less noise, even though they, too, had to hunt.

On July 19 Lewis and the corps entered the Gates of the Mountains, the narrow ravine, a little under six miles long, that he named and that still bears the name.

He writes,

This evening, we entered much the most remarkable cliffs that we have yet seen. These cliffs rise from the water's edge on either side perpendicularly to the height of 1,200 feet. Every object here wears a dark and gloomy aspect. The towering and projecting rocks in many places seem ready to tumble on us . . . The river appears to have worn a passage just the width of its channel or 150 yards. It is deep from side to side nor is there in the first three miles of this distance a spot except one of a few yards in extent on which a man could rest the sole of his foot.

It was new country to the men. These were Easterners who had never seen such mountains, many of them still covered with snow in midsummer; they had never been in a ravine this narrow with such steep cliffs on either side. The usually eloquent Lewis has yet to find the language to describe the scene.

Clark, meanwhile, was over these mountains and into the valley beyond. He was seeing Indian sign, but no Indians. He made 30 miles on July 19, in country so full of prickly pear that it was nearly impossible to walk; that evening he pulled 17 prickly pear spines out of his feet. The next day, the 20th, both Lewis and Clark noted meadow fires that were too large to be accidental; they had been seen, and the Shoshone were warning other members of the tribe that they were a possible Blackfeet raiding party. Clark left his own sign—clothes, linens, paper—to show the Indians that they were white men, not Blackfeet. Clark and his men were growing exhausted, their feet a total mess.

Lewis was struggling upriver, using the setting poles and towropes mostly. The beaver, thousands of them, had totally transformed the nature of the river; it was full of narrow channels threading around and through large islands, doubling or tripling the miles they had to pole or pull the canoes upstream, compared to the miles on foot. And this was a mountain river now. The current was swift. Getting eight heavily laden canoes upriver was exhausting work. The men were beginning to complain.

On July 21 Clark decided to camp by the river, rest his men, and wait for Lewis to come up with the party. The next day Lewis caught up with them. Sacagawea was recognizing the country now; "this is the river on which her relations live," Lewis writes, and "the Three Forks are at no great distance."

When the captains got together that evening Clark, even with his sore feet, insisted on going ahead on foot the next day, taking different people this time: Frazer and both the Fields brothers, and then Charbonneau, who begged to go with them. It was important to Clark that he go on; he decided to go on, and Lewis forbore to contradict him. It was a moment of tension between the two men. It passed. On the 23rd, the next day, Clark walked 25 miles ahead, while Lewis continued the labor of moving upstream.

On the 24th Lewis found the words to describe the country. The mountains, he says,

> seem to rise in some places like an amphitheater, one range above another as they recede from the river until the most distant and lofty have their tops clad with snow. The adjacent mountains commonly rise so high as to conceal the more distant and lofty mountains from our view. I fear every day that we shall meet with some considerable falls or obstruction in the river notwithstanding the information of the Indian woman to the contrary, who assures us that the river continues much as we see it. I can scarcely form an idea of a river running to a great extent through such a rough mountainous country without having its stream interspersed by some difficult and dangerous rapids or falls.

But there were no such rapids or falls—only the river, so difficult to navigate. He remarks that the labor of his men is "excessively great." He sometimes takes the pole himself, to relieve one of them. Clark made 30 miles that day; he saw a wild horse in the distance but couldn't get close to it.

On July 25 Clark reached the Three Forks and immediately moved on, some 25 more miles, up the westernmost of the forks, what they would name a few days later the Jefferson River. Lewis was two days behind him; the men were suffering now not only from prickly pear, mosquitoes, and buffalo gnats but also from a species of grass, the seeds of which had sharp points and bristles that got into their moccasins and were extremely painful. The weather was hot and dry.

On the 26th Clark went another 12 miles up the Jefferson, then turned back to the Three Forks to explore the middle fork, which they named the Madison River, after James Madison, then secretary of state. On the way back to the Three Forks he drank some cold spring water, too much of it at once, and he was soon sick from it. Nevertheless he managed to save Charbonneau's life. Crossing the river, Charbonneau, who could not swim, was nearly swept away by the strong current, but Clark grabbed him. The next day, after exploring up the Madison some miles, he got back to the Three Forks, sick and feverish, at three in the afternoon. Lewis had arrived at nine that morning. The captains decided to rest their men for a couple of days, then move on.

They were getting nervous about not finding the Shoshone. Lewis worries,

> If we do not find them, or some other nation who have horses I fear the successful issue of our voyage will be very doubtful or at all events much more difficult in its accomplishment. We are now several hundred miles within the bosom of this wild and mountainous country, where game may rationally be expected shortly to become scarce and subsistence precarious, without any information with respect to the country, not knowing how far these mountains continue or where to direct our course to pass them to advantage or intercept a navigable branch of the Columbia.

They were, in short, in completely unknown country. There's no other word for it: They were lost. It must have been reassuring to give names to the Three Forks of the Missouri. They named the east fork the Gallatin, after Albert Gallatin, secretary of the treasury.

The corps rested until the 30th of July. The men explored a little, and they made clothes; they had all, said Lewis, become leather workers and tailors. Sacagawea told Lewis about the Hidatsa raid that occurred in this area that had brought her to the Mandan villages in the first place. Lewis was surprised at how little emotion she showed, either at the memory of the raid or at being in her own country again. "If she has enough to eat and a few trinkets to wear," he remarks, "I believe she would be perfectly content anywhere." The men captured a young sandhill crane that could not fly yet, and Lewis, after amusing himself with it a while, released it.

No one could know it then but they were in a fateful place. The Three Forks would become the heart of the fur trade in just a few short years. In pursuit of beaver, indeed, John Potts would lose his life to the Blackfeet two years later, in 1807, near the Three Forks, and John Colter would escape on this same occasion only by running for his life. Three years later George Drouillard would die nearby, too, again at the hands of Blackfeet warriors. No one was thinking about the fur trade now, however. They were thinking about finding the Shoshone.

Lewis and Clark shooting at bear. From the journals of Patrick Gass.

AUGUST 1 TO AUGUST 17, 1805

August 1, 1805, Thursday [Lewis]

This morning we set out early and proceeded on tolerably well until eight o'clock, by which time we had arrived within a few miles of a mountain through which the river passes. We halted on the starboard side and took breakfast, after which or at half after 8 a.m. as had been previously concerted between Capt. Clark and myself I set out with three men in search of the Snake Indians or Shoshones. Our route lay over a high range of mountains on the north side of the river. Capt. Clark recommended this route to me, no doubt from a belief that the river as soon as it passed this chain of mountains bore to the N. of W., he having on the 26th ultimo ascended these mountains to a position from whence he discovered a large valley passing between the mountains which bore to the N.W. and presumed that the river passed in that direction. This however proved to be the passage of a large creek which discharged itself into the river just above this range of mountains, the river bearing to the S.W. We were therefore thrown several miles out of our route.

As soon as we discovered our error we directed our course to the river, which we at length gained about two p.m., much exhausted by the heat of the day, the roughness of the road and the want of water. The mountains are extremely bare of timber, and our route lay through the steep and narrow hollows of the mountains exposed to the intense heat of the midday sun

246 THE ESSENTIAL LEWIS AND CLARK

without shade or scarcely a breath of air. To add to my fatigue in this walk of about 11 miles, I had taken a dose of Glauber's salts in the morning in consequence of a slight dysentery with which I had been afflicted for several days. Being weakened by the disorder and the operation of the medicine I found myself almost exhausted before we reached the river. I felt my spirits much revived on our near approach to the river at the sight of a herd of elk, of which Drouillard and myself soon killed a couple. We then hurried to the river and allayed our thirst. I ordered two of the men to skin the elk and bring the meat to the river, while myself and the other prepared a fire and cooked some of the meat for our dinner. We made a comfortable meal on the elk, and left the balance of the meat and skins on the bank of the river for Capt. Clark and party. This supply will no doubt be acceptable to them, as they had had no fresh meat when I left them for almost two days except one beaver, game being very scarce and shy above the forks. We had seen a few deer and antelope but had not been fortunate enough to kill any of them.

As I passed these mountains I saw a flock of the black or dark brown pheasants [*the blue grouse; this would be the first description of this bird, which Lewis compares to the ruffed grouse of the East. We omit his description of it*]. I also saw near the top of the mountain among some scattering pine a blue bird about the size of the common robin [*it was the pinyon jay; this is its first description*]. Its action and form are somewhat that of the jay bird; it never rests long in any position but is constantly flying or hopping from spray to spray. I shot at one of them but missed it. Their note is loud and frequently repeated both flying and when at rest and is char ah, char ah, char ah, as nearly as letters can express it. After dinner we resumed our march and my pack felt much lighter than it had done about two hours before. We traveled about six miles further and encamped on the starboard bank of the river, making a distance of 17 miles for this day. The mosquitoes were troublesome but I had taken the precaution of bringing my bier [*again, a kind of mosquito netting*].

Shortly after I left Capt. Clark this morning he proceeded on and passed through the mountains; they formed tremendous cliffs of ragged and nearly perpendicular rocks. The lower part of this rock is of the black granite before mentioned and the upper part a light-colored freestone. These cliffs continue for nine miles and approach the river very closely on either side. He found the current very strong. Capt. Clark killed a bighorn on these cliffs, which himself and the party dined on. After passing this range of mountains he entered this beautiful valley in which we also were; it is from six to eight miles wide. The river is crooked and crowded with islands, its bottoms wide, fertile, and covered with fine grass from nine inches to two feet high and possesses but a scant proportion of timber, which consists almost entirely of a few narrow-leaved cottonwood trees distributed along the verge of the river.

In the evening Capt. Clark found the elk I had left him and ascended a short distance above to the entrance of a large creek which falls in on the starboard and encamped opposite to it on the larboard side. He sent out the two Fields to hunt this evening and they killed five deer, which with the elk again gave them a plentiful store of fresh provisions. This large creek we called Fields' Creek after Reuben Fields, one of our party. On the river above the mountains which Capt. Clark passed today he saw some large cedar trees and some juniper also. Just at the upper side of the mountain there is a bad rapid; here the tow line of our canoe broke in the shoot of the rapids and swung on the rocks and had very nearly overset. A small distance above this rapid a large bold creek falls in on the larboard side which we called Frazer's Creek after Robt. Frazer. They saw a large brown bear feeding on currants but could not get a shot at him.

August 2, 1805, Friday [Lewis]
We resumed our march this morning at sunrise; the day was fair and wind from the N.W. Finding that the river still bore to the south I determined to pass it if possible in order to shorten our route; this we effected by wading the river about five miles above our encampment of the last evening. We found the current very rapid, waist deep, and about 90 yards wide, bottom smooth, pebble with a small mixture of coarse gravel. This is the first time that I ever dared to wade the river, though there are many places between this and the forks where I presume it might be attempted with equal success. The valley along which we passed today, and through which the river winds its meandering course, is from six to eight miles wide and consists of a beautiful level plain with but little timber and that confined to the verge of the river. The land is tolerably fertile and is either black or a dark yellow loam, covered with grass from nine inches to two feet high. The plain ascends gradually on either side of the river to the bases of two ranges of high mountains, which lie parallel to the river and prescribe the limits of the plains. The tops of these mountains are yet covered partially with snow,

while we in the valley are nearly suffocated with the intense heat of the midday sun. The nights are so cold that two blankets are not more than sufficient covering.

Soon after passing the river this morning Sgt. Gass lost my tomahawk in the thick brush and we were unable to find it. I regret the loss of this useful implement; however accidents will happen in the best families, and I consoled myself with the recollection that it was not the only one we had with us. The bones of the buffalo and their excrement of an old date are to be met with in every part of this valley but we have long since lost all hope of meeting with that animal in these mountains. We met with great quantities of currants today, two species of which were red, others yellow, deep purple and black; also black gooseberries and serviceberries now ripe and in great perfection. We feasted sumptuously on our wild fruits, particularly the yellow currant and the deep purple serviceberries, which I found to be excellent. The serviceberry grows on a small bush and differs from ours only in color, size, and superior excellence of its flavor. It is somewhat larger than ours.

On our way we saw an abundance of deer, antelope—of the former we killed two. We also saw many tracks of the elk and bear. No recent appearance of Indians. The Indians in this part of the country appear to construct their lodges with the willow boughs and brush; they are small, of a conic figure, and have a small aperture on one side through which they enter. We continued our route up this valley on the larboard side of the river until sunset, at which time we encamped on the larboard bank of the river, having traveled 24 miles. We had brought with us a good stock of venison, of which we ate a hearty supper. I feel myself perfectly recovered of my indisposition, and do not doubt being able to pursue my route tomorrow with the same comfort I have done today. We saw some very large beaver dams today in the bottoms of the river, several of which were five feet high and overflowed several acres of land. These dams are formed of willow brush, mud and gravel and are so closely interwoven that they resist the water perfectly. The base of this work is thick and rises nearly perpendicularly on the lower side, while the upper side or that within the dam is gently sloped. The brush appears to be laid in no regular order yet acquires a strength by the irregularity with which they are placed by the beaver that it would puzzle the ingenuity of man to give them.

Capt. Clark continued his route early this morning. The rapidity of the current was such that his progress was slow; in short it required the utmost exertion of the men to get on, nor could they resist this current by any other means than that of the cord and pole. In the course of the day they passed some villages of burrowing squirrels, saw a number of beaver dams and the inhabitants of them, many young ducks, both of the mallard and the red headed fishing duck [*mergansers*], geese, several rattlesnakes, black woodpeckers, and a large gang of elk. They found the river much crowded with islands both large and small and passed a small creek on the starboard side which we called *Birth* Creek [*in honor of Clark's birthday, August 1*]. Capt. Clark discovered a tumor rising on the inner side of his ankle this evening which was painful to him. They encamped in a level bottom on the larboard side.

August 3, 1805, Saturday [Lewis]
Set out early this morning, or before sunrise, still continued our march through the level valley on the larboard side of the river. The valley much as yesterday only rather wider; I think it is 12 miles wide, though the plains near the mountains rise higher and are more broken with some scattering pine near the mountain. In the leveler parts of the plain and river bottoms, which are very extensive, there is no timber except a scant proportion of cottonwood near the river. The underwood consists of the narrow-leaved or small willow, the small honeysuckle, rosebushes, currant, serviceberry, and gooseberry bushes, also a small species of birch in but small quantities, the leaf of which is oval, finely indented, small and of a deep green color. The stem is simple, ascending and branching, and seldom rises higher than 10 or 12 feet. The mountains continue high on either side of the valley and are but scantily supplied with timber. Small pine appears to be the prevalent growth. It is of the pitch kind, with a short leaf. At 11 a.m. Drouillard killed a doe and we halted about two hours and breakfasted, and then continued our route until night without halting, when we arrived at the river in a level bottom which appeared to spread to a greater extent than usual. From the appearance of the timber I supposed that the river forked above us and resolved to examine this part of the river minutely tomorrow.

This evening we passed through a high plain for about eight miles covered with prickly pears and bearded grass, though we found this even better walking than the wide bottoms of the river, which we passed in the evening. These, although apparently level, from some cause which I know not, were formed into myriads of deep holes as if rooted up by hogs. These the grass covered so thick that it was impossible to walk without the risk of falling down at every step. Some parts of these bottoms also possess excellent turf or peat, I believe of many feet deep. The mineral salts also frequently mentioned on the Missouri we saw this evening in these uneven bottoms. We saw many deer, antelope, ducks, geese, some beaver and great appearance of their work, also a small bird and the curlew as usual.

We encamped on the riverbank on the larboard side, having traveled by estimate 23 miles. The fish of this part of the river are trout and a species of scale fish of a white color and a remarkable small long mouth, which one of our men informs us are the same with the species called in the Eastern states *bottlenose*. The snowy region of the mountains and for some distance below has no timber or herbage of any kind; the timber is confined to the lower and middle regions.

Capt. Clark set out this morning as usual. He walked on shore a small distance this morning and killed a deer. In the course of his walk he saw a track which he supposed to be that of an Indian from the circumstance of the large toes turning inward. He pursued the track and found that the person had ascended a point of a hill from which his camp of the last evening was visible; this circumstance also confirmed the belief of its being an Indian who had thus discovered them and ran off. They found the river as usual much crowded with islands, the current more rapid and much more shallow than usual. In many places they were obliged to double-man the canoes and drag them over the stone and gravel. This morning they passed a small creek on the starboard at the entrance of which Reuben Fields killed a large panther [*mountain lion*]. We called the creek after that animal, Panther Creek. They also passed a handsome little stream on the larboard which is formed of several large springs which rise in the bottoms and along the base of the mountains with some little rivulets from the melting snows. The beaver have formed many large dams on this stream. They saw some deer, antelope and the common birds of the country. In the evening they passed a very bad rapid where the bed of the river is formed entirely of solid rock and encamped on an island just above. The panther which Fields killed measured seven and a half feet from the nose to the extremity of the tail. It is precisely the same animal common to the western part of our country [*i.e., to the western part of the then United States*]. The men were compelled to be a great proportion of their time in the water today; they have had a severe day's labor and are much fatigued.

August 4, 1805, Sunday [Lewis]

Set out very early this morning and steered S.E. by E. four miles, when we passed a bold running creek 12 yards wide, the water of which was clear and very cold. It appears to be formed by four drains from the snowy mountains to our left. After passing this creek we changed our direction to S.E., passing obliquely across a valley which bore E., leaving the valley we had pursued for the two preceding days. At the distance of three miles we passed a handsome little river which meanders through this valley; it is about 30 yards wide, affords a considerable quantity of water and appears as if it might be navigated some miles. The current is not rapid nor the water very clear; the banks are low and the bed formed of stone and gravel. I now changed my route to S.W., passed a high plain which lies between the valleys and returned to the south valley, in passing which I fell in with a river about 45 yards wide, gravely bottom, gentle current, waist deep and water of a whitish blue tinge. This stream we waded and continued our route down it to the entrance of the river just mentioned about three-quarters of a mile. Still continuing down we passed the entrance of the creek about two miles lower down; and at the distance of three miles further arrived at its junction with a river 50 yards wide which comes from the S.W. and falling into the south valley runs parallel with the middle fork about 12 miles before it forms a junction.

I now found that our encampment of the last evening was about one and a half miles above the entrance of this large river on starboard. This is a bold, rapid and clear stream, its bed so much broken and obstructed by gravelly bars and its waters so much subdivided by islands that it appears to me utterly impossible to navigate it with safety. The middle fork is gentle and possesses about two-thirds as much water as this stream. Its course so far as I can observe it is about S.W., and from the opening of the valley I believe it still bears more to the west above. It may be safely navigated. Its water is much warmer than the rapid fork and its water more turbid, from which I conjecture that it has its sources at a greater distance in the mountains and passes through a more open country than the other. [*Lewis had reached the forks of the Jefferson. The river is formed from the confluence of what are now known as the Ruby River, the Beaverhead, and, a little farther on, the Big Hole River. Lewis and Clark named the two tributary rivers the Wisdom River and the Philanthropy River, while they retained the name Jefferson for the middle fork, the main part of the river.*]

Under this impression I wrote a note to Capt. Clark, recommending his taking the middle fork, provided he should arrive at this place before my return, which I expect will be the day after tomorrow. This note I left on a pole at the forks of the river, and having refreshed ourselves and eaten heartily of some venison which we killed this morning, we continued our route up the rapid fork on the starboard side, resolving to pursue this stream until noon tomorrow and then pass over to the middle fork and come down it to their junction, or until I meet Capt. Clark. I have seen no Indian sign in the course of my route as yet.

Charbonneau complains much of his leg, and is the cause of considerable detention to us. We encamped on the riverbank near the place at which it leaves the valley and enters the mountain, having traveled about 23 miles. We saw some antelope, deer, cranes, geese, and ducks of the two species common to this country. The summer duck has ceased to appear, nor do I believe it is an inhabitant of this part of the country. The timber is as heretofore, though there is more in this valley on the rapid fork than we have seen in the same extent on the river since we entered this valley. The Indians appear on some parts of the river to have destroyed a great proportion of the little timber which there is by setting fire to the bottoms.

This morning Capt. Clark set out at sunrise and sent two hunters ahead to kill some meat. At eight a.m. he arrived at my camp of the second inst., where he breakfasted; here he found a note which I had left for him at that place informing him of the occurrences of my route, etc. The river continued to be crowded with islands, rapid and shoaly. These shoals or riffles succeeded each other every three or four hundred yards; at those places they are obliged to drag the canoes over the stone, there not being water enough to float them, and between the riffles the current is so strong that they are compelled to have recourse to the cord, and being unable to walk on the shore for the brush, wade in the river along the shore and haul them by the cord. This has increased the pain and labor extremely; their feet soon get tender and sore by wading and walking over the stones. These are also so slippery that they frequently get severe falls. Being constantly wet soon makes them feeble also. Their hunters killed two deer today, and some geese and ducks were killed by those who navigated the canoes. They saw deer, antelope, cranes, beaver, otter, etc. Capt. Clark's ankle became so painful to him that he was unable to walk. This evening they encamped on the starboard side in a bottom of cottonwood timber all much fatigued.

August 5, 1805, Monday [Lewis]

As Charbonneau complained of being unable to march far today I ordered him and Sgt. Gass to pass the rapid river near our camp and proceed at their leisure through the level bottom to a point of high timber about seven miles distant on the middle fork which was in view. I gave them my pack, that of Drouillard, and the meat which we had, directing them to remain at that place until we joined them. I took Drouillard with me and continued my route up the starboard side of the river about four miles and then waded it, found it so rapid and shallow that it was impossible to navigate it. Continued up it on the larboard side about one and a half miles further when the mountains put in close on both sides and arose to great height, partially covered with snow. From hence the course of the river was to the east of north. I took advantage of a high projecting spur of the mountain, which with some difficulty we ascended to its summit in about half an hour. From this eminence I had a pleasing view of the valley through which I had passed many miles below and the continuation of the middle fork through the valley equally wide above me to the distance of about 20 miles, when that also appeared to enter the mountains and disappeared to my view. However the mountains which terminate the valley in this direction appeared much lower than those up either of the other forks. On the rapid fork they appeared still to rise, the one range towering above another as far as I could perceive them. The middle fork as I suspected does bear considerably to the west of south and the gap formed by it in the mountains after the valley terminates is in the same direction. Under these circumstances I did not hesitate in believing the middle fork the most proper for us to ascend.

About south from me the middle fork approached within about five miles. I resolved to pass across the plains to it and return to Gass and Charbonneau; accordingly we set out and descended the mountain among some steep and difficult precipices of rocks. Here Drouillard missed his step and had a very dangerous fall. He sprained one of his fingers and hurt his leg very much.

In 15 or 20 minutes he was able to proceed and we continued our route to the river where we had designed to intercept it. I quenched my thirst and rested a few minutes, examined the river and found it still very navigable. An old Indian road, very large and plain, leads up this fork, but I could see no tracks except those of horses, which appeared to have passed early in the spring. As the river made a great bend to the southeast we again ascended the high plain and steered our course as straight as we could to the point where I had directed Gass and Charbonneau to remain. We passed the plain, regained the bottom and struck the river about three miles above them. By this time it was perfectly dark and we whooped but could hear no tidings of them. We had struck the river at the point of timber to which I had directed them, but they, having mistaken a point of woods lower down, had halted short of the place. We continued our route after dark down the bottom through thick brush of the pulpy-leaved thorn and prickly pears for about two hours when we arrived at their camp. They had a small quantity of meat left which Drouillard and I ate, it being the first we had tasted today. We had traveled about 25 miles. I soon lay down and slept very soundly until morning. I saw no deer today nor any game except a few antelope, which were very shy. The soil of the plains is a light yellow clay, very meager and intermixed with a large proportion of gravel, producing nothing except the twisted or bearded grass, sedge and prickly pears. The drier parts of the bottoms are also much more indifferent in point of soil to those below and are covered with the southernwood pulpy-leaved thorn and prickly pears with but little grass. The moist parts are fertile and covered with fine grass and sand rushes.

This morning Capt. Clark set out at sunrise and dispatched Joseph and Reuben Fields to hunt. They killed two deer, on one of which the party breakfasted. The river today they found straighter and more rapid even than yesterday, and the labor and difficulty of navigation was proportionately increased; they therefore proceeded but slowly and with great pain, as the men had become very languid from working in the water and many of their feet swollen and so painful that they could scarcely walk. At four p.m. they arrived at the confluence of the two rivers where I had left the note. This note had unfortunately been placed on a green pole which the beaver had cut and carried off together with the note. The possibility of such an occurrence never once occurred to me when I placed it on the green pole. This accident deprived Capt. Clark of any information with respect to the country and supposing that the rapid fork was most in the direction which it was proper we should pursue, or west, he took that stream and ascended it with much difficulty about a mile and encamped on an island that had been lately overflown and was yet damp. They were therefore compelled to make beds of brush to keep themselves out of the mud. In ascending this stream for about a quarter of a mile it scattered in such a manner that they were obliged to cut a passage through the willow brush which leaned over the little channels and united their tops. Capt. Clark's ankle is extremely painful to him this evening; the tumor has not yet matured, he has a slight fever. The men were so much fatigued today that they wished much that navigation was at an end that they might go by land.

August 6, 1805, Tuesday [Lewis]
We set out this morning very early on our return to the forks. Having nothing to eat I sent Drouillard to the woodlands to my left in order to kill a deer, sent Sgt. Gass to the right with orders to keep sufficiently near to discover Capt. Clark and the party should they be on their way up that stream, and with Charbonneau I directed my course to the main forks through the bottom, directing the others to meet us there. About five miles above the forks I heard the whooping of the party to my left and changed my route towards them. On my arrival I found that they had taken the rapid fork and learned from Capt. Clark that he had not found the note which I had left for him at that place and the reasons which had induced him to ascend this stream. It was easiest and more in our direction, and appeared to contain as much water. He had, however, previously to my coming up with him, met Drouillard who informed him of the state of the two rivers and was on his return. One of their canoes had just overset and all the baggage was wet, the medicine box among other articles, and several articles lost, a shot pouch and horn with all the implements for one rifle, lost and never recovered. I walked down to the point where I waited their return. On their arrival found that two other canoes had filled with water and wet their cargoes completely. Whitehouse had been thrown out of one of the canoes as she swung in a rapid current and the canoe had rubbed him and pressed him to the bottom as she passed over him and had the water been two inches shallower must inevitably have crushed him to death. Our parched meal, corn, Indian presents, and a great part of our most valuable stores were wet and much damaged on this occasion.

To examine, dry, and arrange our stores was the first object; we therefore passed over to the larboard side opposite to the entrance of the rapid fork where there was a large gravelly bar that answered our purposes; wood was also convenient and plentiful. Here we fixed our camp, unloaded all our canoes, and opened and exposed to dry such articles as had been wet. A part of the load of each canoe consisted of the leaden canisters of powder which were not in the least injured, though some of them had remained upwards of an hour under water. About 20 pounds of powder which we had in a tight keg, or at least one which we thought sufficiently so, got wet and entirely spoiled. This would have been the case with the other had it not been for the expedient which I had fallen on of securing the powder by means of the lead, having the latter formed into canisters which were filled with the necessary proportion of powder to discharge the lead when used, and those canisters well secured with corks and wax. In this country the air is so pure and dry that any vessel, however well seasoned the timber may be, will give way or shrink unless it is kept full of some liquid. We found that three deer skins which we had left at a considerable height on a tree were taken off, which we supposed had been done by a panther.

We sent out some men to hunt this evening; they killed three deer and four elk, which gave us a plentiful supply of meat once more. Shannon had been dispatched up the rapid fork this morning to hunt by Capt. Clark before he met with Drouillard or learned his mistake in the rivers. When he returned he sent Drouillard in search of him, but he rejoined us this evening and reported that he had been several miles up the river and could find nothing of him. We had the trumpet sounded and fired several guns but he did not join us this evening. I am fearful he is lost again. This is the same man who was separated from us 15 days as we came up the Missouri and subsisted nine days of that time on grapes only.

Whitehouse is in much pain this evening with the injury one of his legs sustained from the canoe today at the time it upset and swung over him. Capt. Clark's ankle is also very painful to him. We should have given the party a day's rest somewhere near this place had not this accident happened, as I had determined to take some observations to fix the latitude and longitude of these forks. Our merchandise, medicine etc. are not sufficiently dry this evening. We covered them securely for the evening. Capt. Clark had ascended the river about nine miles from this place before he met with Drouillard.

We believe that the N.W. or rapid fork is the drain of the melting snows of the mountains, and that it is not as long as the middle fork and does not at all seasons of the year supply anything like as much water as the other and that about this season it rises to its greatest height. This last appears from the apparent bed of the river which is now overflown and the water in many places spreads through old channels which have their bottoms covered with grass that has grown this season and is such as appears on the parts of the bottom not inundated. We therefore determined that the middle fork was that which ought of right to bear the name we had given to the lower portion or *River Jefferson*, and called the bold, rapid and clear stream *Wisdom*, and the more mild and placid one which flows in from the S.E. *Philanthropy*, in commemoration of two of those cardinal virtues which have so eminently marked that deservedly celebrated character through life.

August 7, 1805, Wednesday [Clark]
A fine morning. Put out our stores to dry and took equal altitudes with the sextant. As our stores were a little exhausted and one canoe became unnecessary we determined to leave one. We hauled her up in the bushes on the lower side of the main fork and fastened her so that the water could not float her off. The country in this quarter is as follows: a valley of five or six miles wide enclosed between two high mountains, the bottom rich, some small timber on the islands and bushes on the edges of the river. Some bogs and very good turf in different places in the valley, some scattering pine and cedar on the mountains in places, other parts naked except grass and stone. We proceeded up the main, middle, or S.E. fork, passed a camp on the larboard side above the mouth of a bold running stream 12 yards wide, which we call *Turf* Creek from the number of bogs and quantity of turf in its waters. This creek runs through an open plain for several miles, taking its rise in a high mountain to the N.E. The River Jefferson above Wisdom is gentle, crooked and about 40 yards wide, containing but little timber, some few cotton, willow, and birch, and the shrubs common to the country and before mentioned. At five o'clock a thunderstorm from the N.W. accompanied with rain which lasted about 40 minutes. Dispatched R. Fields to hunt Shannon, who was out hunting on Wisdom River at the time I returned down that stream, and has made on up the river expecting us to follow him up that river. One deer killed this evening. All those streams contain immense numbers of beaver, otter, muskrats, etc.

Lewis, who stayed behind to take latitude and longitude readings, noted the disappearance of the buffalo gnats and the appearance of various kinds of biting flies. The mosquitoes, however, were less troublesome.

August 8, 1805, Thursday [Lewis]
We had a heavy dew this morning. As one canoe had been left we had now more hands for the chase; game being scarce, it requires more hunters to

supply us. We therefore dispatched four this morning. We set out at sunrise and continued our route up the river, which we find much more gentle and deep than below the entrance of Wisdom River. It is from 35 to 45 yards wide, very crooked, many short bends constituting large and general bends, insomuch that, although we travel briskly and a considerable distance, yet it takes us only a few miles on our general course or route. There is but very little timber on this fork, principally the underbrush frequently mentioned. I observe a considerable quantity of the buffalo clover in the bottoms. The sunflower, flax, green sword, thistle and several species of the rye grass, some of which rise to the height of three or four feet. There is a grass also with a soft smooth leaf that bears its seeds very much like the timothy but it does not grow very luxuriant or appear as if it would answer so well as the common timothy for meadows. I preserved some of its seeds which are now ripe, thinking perhaps it might answer better if cultivated. At all events it is at least worth the experiment. It rises about three feet high.

On a direct line about two miles above our encampment of this morning we passed the entrance of Philanthropy River which discharges itself by two channels a small distance asunder. This river from its size and S. Eastwardly course no doubt heads with Madison's River in the snowy mountains visible in that direction. At noon Reuben Fields arrived and reported that he had been up Wisdom River some miles above where it entered the mountain and could find nothing of Shannon. He had killed a deer and an antelope. Great quantities of beaver, otter, and muskrats in these rivers. Two of the hunters we sent out this morning returned at noon, had killed each a deer and an antelope. We used the setting poles today almost altogether. We encamped on the larboard side where there was but little timber, were obliged to use willow brush for fuel; the rosebushes and briars were very thick. The hunters brought in another deer this evening. The tumor on Capt. Clark's ankle has discharged a considerable quantity of matter but is still much swollen and inflamed and gives him considerable pain. Saw a number of geese, ducks and some cranes today. The former begin to fly.

The evening again proved cloudy, much to my mortification, and prevented my making any lunar observations. The Indian woman recognized the point of a high plain to our right which she informed us was not very distant from the summer retreat of her nation on a river beyond the mountains which runs to the west. This hill she says her nation calls the Beaver's Head from a conceived resemblance of its figure to the head of that animal.

She assures us that we shall either find her people on this river or on the river immediately west of its source, which from its present size cannot be very distant. As it is now all important with us to meet with those people as soon as possible, I determined to proceed tomorrow with a small party to the source of the principal stream of this river and pass the mountains to the Columbia, and down that river until I found the Indians. In short it is my resolution to find them or some others who have horses if it should cause me a trip of one month, for without horses we shall be obliged to leave a great part of our stores, of which it appears to me that we have a stock already sufficiently small for the length of the voyage before us.

August 9, 1805, Friday [Lewis]

The morning was fair and fine; we set out at an early hour and proceeded on very well. Some parts of the river more rapid than yesterday. I walked on shore across the land to a point which I presumed they would reach by eight a.m., our usual time of halting. By this means I acquired leisure to accomplish some writings which I conceived from the nature of my instructions necessary lest any accident should befall me on the long and rather hazardous route I was now about to take. The party did not arrive and I returned about a mile and met them; here they halted and we breakfasted; I had killed two fine geese on my return. While we halted here Shannon arrived and informed us that having missed the party the day on which he set out he had returned the next morning to the place from whence he had set out or first left them, and not finding them that he had supposed that they were above him; that he then set out and marched one day up Wisdom River, by which time he was convinced that they were not above him, as the river could not be navigated; he then returned to the forks and had pursued us up this river. He brought the skins of three deer which he had killed which he said were in good order. He had lived very plentifully this trip but looked a good deal worried with his march. He informed us that Wisdom River still kept its course obliquely down the Jefferson River as far as he was up it.

Immediately after breakfast I slung my pack and set out accompanied by Drouillard, Shields and McNeal, who had been previously directed to hold themselves in readiness for this service. I directed my course across the bottom to the starboard plain, left the Beaver's Head about two miles to my left and intercepted the river about eight miles from the point at which I had left it. I then waded it and continued my route to the point where I could observe that it entered the mountain, but not being able to reach that place, changed my direction to the river, which I struck some miles below the mountain, and encamped for the evening, having traveled 16 miles. We passed a handsome little stream formed by some large springs that rise in this wide bottom on the larboard side of the river. We killed two antelope on our way and brought with us as much meat as was necessary for our suppers and breakfast the next morning. We found this bottom fertile and covered with taller grass than usual. The river very crooked, much divided by islands, shallow, rocky in many places and very rapid, insomuch that I have my doubts whether the canoes could get on or not, or if they do it must be with great labor.

Capt. Clark proceeded after I left him as usual, found the current of the river increasing in rapidity towards evening. His hunters killed two antelope only. In the evening it clouded up and we experienced a slight rain attended with some thunder and lightning. The mosquitoes very troublesome this evening. There are some soft bogs in these valleys covered with turf. The earth of which this mud is composed is white or bluish white and appears to be argillaceous.

Clark noted that he would have taken this trip in Lewis's place had he been able to march, but "the raging fury" of the boil on his ankle prevented him.

August 10, 1805, Saturday [Lewis]
We set out very early this morning and continued our route through the wide bottom on the larboard side of the river. After passing a large creek at about five miles we fell in with a plain Indian road which led towards the point that the river entered the mountain. We therefore pursued the road. I sent Drouillard to the right to kill a deer which we saw feeding and halted on the river under an immensely high perpendicular cliff of rocks where it entered the mountain. Here we kindled a fire and waited for Drouillard. He arrived in about an hour and a half or at noon with three deer skins and the flesh of one of the best of them. We cooked and ate a hasty meal and departed, returning a short distance to the Indian road which led us the best way over the mountains, which are not very high but are rugged and approach the river closely on both sides just below these mountains. I saw several bald eagles and two large white-headed fishing hawks. Both these birds were the same common to our country. From the number of rattlesnakes about the cliffs at which we halted we called them the Rattlesnake Cliffs. This serpent

is the same before described with oval spots of yellowish brown. The river below the mountains is rapid, rocky, very crooked, much divided by islands and withal shallow. After it enters the mountains its bends are not so circuitous and its general course more direct, but it is equally shallow, less divided, more rocky and rapid.

We continued our route along the Indian road, which led us sometimes over the hills and again in the narrow bottoms of the river, till at the distance of 15 miles from the Rattlesnake Cliffs we arrived in a handsome, open and level valley where the river divided itself nearly into two equal branches. Here I halted and examined those streams and readily discovered from their size that it would be vain to attempt the navigation of either any further.

Here also the road forked, one leading up the valley of each of these streams. I therefore sent Drouillard on one and Shields on the other to examine these roads for a short distance and to return and compare their information with respect to the size and apparent plainness of the roads, as I was now determined to pursue that which appeared to have been the most traveled this spring. In the meantime I wrote a note to Capt. Clark informing him of the occurrences which had taken place, recommending it to him to halt at this place until my return and informing him of the route I had taken, which from the information of the men on their return seemed to be in favor of the S.W. or left-hand fork, which is rather the smallest.

Accordingly I put up my note on a dry willow pole at the forks and set out up the S.W. fork. After proceeding about one and a half miles I discovered that the road became so blind that it could not be that which we had followed to the forks of the Jefferson River, neither could I find the tracks of the horses which had passed early in the spring along the other. I therefore determined to return and examine the other myself, which I did, and found that the same horses had passed up the west fork, which was rather the largest, and more in the direction that I wished to pursue. I therefore did not hesitate about changing my route but determined to take the western road. I now wrote a second note to Capt. Clark informing him of this change and sent Drouillard to put it with the other at the forks and waited until he returned.

There is scarcely any timber on the river above the Rattlesnake Cliffs, nor is there anything larger than willow brush in sight of these forks. Immediately in the level plain between the forks and about half a mile distant from them stands a high rocky mountain, the base of which is surrounded by the level plain; it has a singular appearance. The mountains do not appear very high in any direction, though the tops of some of them are partially covered with snow. This convinces me that we have ascended to a great height since we have entered the Rocky Mountains, yet the ascent has been so gradual along the valleys that it was scarcely perceptible by land. I do not believe that the world can furnish an example of a river running to the extent which the Missouri and Jefferson Rivers do through such a mountainous country and at the same time being so navigable as they are. If the Columbia furnishes us such another example, a communication across the continent by water will be practicable and safe. But this I can scarcely hope from a knowledge of its having in its comparatively short course to the ocean the same number of feet to descend which the Missouri and Mississippi have from this point to the Gulf of Mexico. [*Lewis means that the rivers will be necessarily full of rapids and falls; he was correct.*]

The valley of the west fork through which we passed for four miles bore a little to N. of west and was about 1 mile wide, hemmed in on either side by rough mountain and steep cliffs of rock. At 4 and a half miles this stream enters a beautiful and extensive plain about ten miles long and from five to six in width. This plain is surrounded on all sides by a country of rolling or high wavy plains through which several little rivulets extend their wide valleys quite to the mountains which surround the whole in an apparent circular manner, forming one of the handsomest coves I ever saw, of about 16 or 18 miles in diameter. Just after entering this cove the river bends to the N.W. and runs close under the starboard hills. Here we killed a deer and encamped on the starboard side and made our fire of dry willow brush, the only fuel which the country produces. There are not more than three or four cottonwood trees in this extensive cove and they are but small. The uplands are covered with prickly pears and twisted or bearded grass and are but poor; some parts of the bottomlands are covered with grass and tolerably fertile, but much the greater proportion is covered with prickly pears, sedge, twisted grass, the pulpy-leaved thorn, southernwood, wild sage, etc., and like the uplands is very inferior in point of soil. We traveled by estimate 30 miles today, that is 10 to the Rattlesnake Cliffs, 15 to the forks of Jefferson River, and five to our camp in the cove. At the apparent extremity of the bottom above us two perpendicular cliffs of considerable height stand on either side of the river and appear at this distance like a gate; it is about 10 miles due west.

Capt. Clark set out at sunrise this morning and pursued his route, found the river not rapid but shallow, also very crooked. They were obliged to drag the canoes over many riffles in the course of the day. They passed the point which the natives call the Beaver's Head. It is a steep rocky cliff of 150 feet high near the starboard side of the river. Opposite to it at the distance of 300 yards is a low cliff of about 50 feet which is the extremity of a spur of the mountains about four miles distant on the larboard. At four p.m. they experienced a heavy shower of rain attended with hail, thunder and lightning which continued about an hour. The men defended themselves from the hail by means of the willow bushes but all the party got perfectly wet. After the shower was over they pursued their march and encamped on the starboard side. Only one deer killed by their hunters today, though they took up another by the way which had been killed three days before by Joseph Fields and hung up near the river.

August 11, 1805, Sunday [Lewis]
We set out very early this morning, but the track which we had pursued last evening soon disappeared. I therefore resolved to proceed to the narrow pass on the creek about 10 miles west in hopes that I should again find the Indian road at the place. Accordingly I passed the river, which was about 12 yards wide and barred in several places entirely across by beaver dams, and proceeded through the level plain directly to the pass. I now sent Drouillard to keep near the creek to my right and Shields to my left, with orders to search for the road, which if they found they were to notify me by placing a hat in the muzzle of their gun. I kept McNeal with me. After having marched in this order for about five miles I discovered an Indian on horseback about two miles distant coming down the plain towards us. With my glass I discovered from his dress that he was of a different nation from any that we had yet seen, and was satisfied of his being a Shoshone. His arms were a bow and quiver of arrows; he was mounted on an elegant horse without a saddle, and a small string, which was attached to the underjaw of the horse, answered as a bridle. I was overjoyed at the sight of this stranger and had no doubt of obtaining a friendly introduction to his nation, provided I could get near enough to him to convince him of our being white men. I therefore proceeded towards him at my usual pace. When I had arrived within about a mile he made a halt, which I did also; and unloosing my blanket from my pack, I made him the signal of friendship

known to the Indians of the Rocky Mountains and those of the Missouri, which is by holding the mantle or robe in your hands at two corners and then throwing it up in the air higher than the head, bringing it to the earth as if in the act of spreading it, thus repeating three times. This signal of the robe has arisen from a custom among all those nations of spreading a robe or skin for their guests to sit on when they are visited.

This signal had not the desired effect. He still kept his position and seemed to view Drouillard and Shields, who were now coming in sight on either hand, with an air of suspicion. I would willingly have made them halt but they were too far distant to hear me and I feared to make any signal to them lest it should increase the suspicion in the mind of the Indian of our having some unfriendly design upon him.

I therefore hastened to take out of my sack some beads, a looking glass, and a few trinkets which I had brought with me for this purpose and, leaving my gun and pouch with McNeal, advanced unarmed towards him. He remained in the same steadfast posture until I arrived within about 200 paces of him, when he turned his horse about and began to move off slowly from me. I now called to him in as loud a voice as I could command, repeating the word *tab-ba-bone*, which in their language signifies *white man* [*Lewis obviously had this word from either Sacagawea or Charbonneau, but it is by no means clear that the Shoshone had a word for "white man," having never met one; scholars have been trying for some time to figure out what this word might actually have meant*]. But looking over his shoulder he still kept his eye on Drouillard and Shields, who were still advancing, neither one of them having sagacity enough to recollect the impropriety of advancing when they saw me thus in parley with the Indian. I now made a signal to these men to halt. Drouillard obeyed but Shields, who afterwards told me that he did not observe the signal, still kept on. The Indian halted again and turned his horse about as if to wait for me, and I believe he would have remained until I came up with him had it not been for Shields, who still pressed forward.

When I arrived within about 150 paces I again repeated the word tab-ba-bone and held up the trinkets in my hands and stripped up my shirtsleeve to give him an opportunity of seeing the color of my skin and advanced leisurely toward him. But he did not remain until I got nearer than about 100 paces, when he suddenly turned his horse about, gave him the whip, leaped the creek and disappeared in the willow brush in an instant, and with him vanished all my hopes of obtaining horses for the present.

I now felt quite as much mortification and disappointment as I had pleasure and expectation at the first sight of this Indian. I felt sorely chagrined at the conduct of the men, particularly Shields, to whom I principally attributed this failure in obtaining an introduction to the natives. I now called the men to me and could not forebear upbraiding them a little for their want of attention and imprudence on this occasion. They had neglected to bring my spyglass, which in haste I had dropped in the plain with the blanket where I made the signal before mentioned. I sent Drouillard and Shields back to search for it; they soon found it and rejoined me. We now set out on the track of the horse, hoping by that means to be led to an Indian camp, the trail of inhabitants of which, should they abscond, we should probably be enabled to pursue to the body of the nation to which they would now probably fly for safety. This route led us across a large island framed by nearly an equal division of the creek in this bottom. After passing to the open ground on the north side of the creek we observed that the track made out toward the high hills about 3 miles distant in that direction. I thought it probable that their camp might be among those hills and that they would reconnoiter us from the tops of them, and that if we advanced hastily towards them that they would become alarmed and probably run off. I therefore halted in an elevated situation near the creek, had a fire kindled of willow brush, cooked and took breakfast.

During this leisure I prepared a small assortment of trinkets consisting of some moccasin awls, a few strands of several kinds of beads, some paint, a looking glass, etc., which I attached to the end of a pole and planted it near our fire in order that, should the Indians return in search of us, they might from this token discover that we were friendly and white persons. Before we had finished our meal a heavy shower of rain came on with some hail which continued about 20 minutes and wet us to the skin. After this shower we pursued the track of the horse, but as the rain had raised the grass which he had trodden down it was with difficulty that we could follow it. We pursued it, however, about four miles, it turning up the valley to the left under the foot of the hills. We passed several places where the Indians appeared to have been digging roots today and saw the fresh tracks of eight or ten horses, but they had been wandering about in such a confused manner that we not only lost the track of the horse which we had been pursuing but could make nothing of them. In the head of this valley we passed a large bog covered with tall grass and moss in which were a great number of springs of cold pure water. We now turned a little to the left along the foot of the high hills and arrived at a small branch on which we encamped for the night, having traveled in different directions about 20 miles and about 10 from the camp of last evening on a direct line. After meeting with the Indian today I fixed a small flag of the U.S. to a pole which I made McNeal carry, and planted in the ground where we halted or encamped.

This morning Capt. Clark dispatched several hunters ahead. The morning being rainy and wet, he did not set out until after an early breakfast. He passed a large island which he called the 3,000 Mile Island from the circumstance of its being that distance from the entrance of the Missouri by water. A considerable proportion of the bottom on the larboard side is a bog covered with tall grass and many parts would afford fine turf. The bottom is about eight miles wide and the plains which succeed it on either side extend about the same distance to the base of the mountains. They passed a number of small islands and bayous on both sides which cut and intersect the bottoms in various directions. Found the river shallow and rapid, insomuch that the men were compelled to be in the water a considerable proportion of the day dragging the canoes over the shoals and riffles. They saw a number of geese, ducks, beaver and otter, also some deer and antelope. The men killed a beaver with a setting pole and tomahawked several otter. The hunters killed three deer and an antelope. Capt. Clark observed some bunches of privet near the river. There are but few trees in this bottom and those small narrow-leaved cottonwood. The principal growth is willow with the narrow leaf and currant bushes. They encamped this evening on the upper point of a large island near the starboard shore.

August 12, 1805, Monday [Lewis]
This morning I sent Drouillard out as soon as it was light to try and discover what route the Indians had taken. He followed the track of the horse we had pursued yesterday to the mountain where it had ascended, and returned to me in about an hour and a half. I now determined to pursue the base of the mountains which form this cove to the S.W. in the expectation of finding some Indian road which leads over the mountains. Accordingly I sent Drouillard to my right and Shields to my left with orders to look out for a road or the fresh tracks of horses, either of which I should first meet with I had determined to pursue.

At the distance of about four miles we passed four small rivulets near each other on which we saw some recent bowers or small conic lodges formed with willow brush. Near them the Indians had gathered a number of roots from the manner in which they had torn up the ground; but I could not discover the root which they seemed to be in search of. I saw several large hawks that were nearly black. Near this place we fell in with a large and plain Indian road which came into the cove from the N.E. and led along the foot of the mountains to the S.W., obliquely approaching the main stream which we had left yesterday. This road we now pursued to the S.W. At five miles it passed a stout stream which is a principal fork of the main stream and falls into it just above the narrow pass between the two cliffs before mentioned and which we now saw below us. Here we halted and breakfasted on the last of our venison, having yet a small piece of pork in reserve.

After eating we continued our route through the low bottom of the main stream along the foot of the mountains on our right. The valley for five miles further in a S.W. direction was from two to three miles wide. The main stream now, after discarding two streams on the left in this valley, turns abruptly to the west through a narrow bottom between the mountains. The road was still plain; I therefore did not despair of shortly finding a passage over the mountains and of tasting the waters of the great Columbia this evening. We saw an animal that we took to be of the fox kind, as large or rather larger than the small wolf of the plains. Its colors were a curious mixture of black, reddish brown and yellow. Drouillard shot at him from about 130 yards and knocked him down but he recovered and got out of our reach. It is certainly a different animal from any that we have yet seen. We also saw several of the heathcock [this was the sage grouse] with a long pointed tail and a uniform dark brown color but could not kill one of them. They are much larger than the common dunghill fowl and in their habits and manner of flying resemble the grouse or prairie hen.

At the distance of four miles further the road took us to the most distant fountain of the waters of the mighty Missouri in search of which we have spent so many toilsome days and restless nights. Thus far I had accomplished one of those great objects on which my mind has been unalterably fixed for many years. Judge then of the pleasure I felt in allaying my thirst with this pure and ice-cold water, which issues from the base of a low mountain or hill of a gentle ascent for half a mile. The mountains are high on either hand of this gap at the head of this rivulet through which the road passes. Here I halted a few minutes and rested myself. Two miles below McNeal had exultingly stood with a foot on each side of this little rivulet and thanked his god that he had lived to bestride the mighty and heretofore deemed endless Missouri. After refreshing ourselves we proceeded on to the top of the dividing ridge [*Lewis was here standing on Lemhi Pass*] from which I discovered immense ranges of high mountains still to the west of us with their tops partially covered with snow. I now descended the mountain about three-quarters of a mile which I found much steeper than on the opposite side, to a handsome bold running creek of cold clear water. Here I first tasted the water of the great Columbia River [*the modern name for this creek is Horseshoe Bend Creek and its waters do eventually flow into the Columbia*]. After a short halt of a few minutes we continued our march along the Indian road, which led us over steep hills and deep hollows to a spring on the side of a mountain, where we found a sufficient quantity of dry willow brush for fuel. Here we encamped for the night, having traveled about 20 miles. As we had killed nothing during the day we now boiled and ate the remainder of our pork, having yet a little flour and parched meal. At the creek on this side of the mountain I observed a species of deep purple currant lower in its growth, the stem more branched and leaf doubly as large as that of the Missouri. The leaf is covered on its under disk with a hairy pubescence. The fruit is of the ordinary size and shape of the currant and is supported in the usual manner, but is acid and very inferior in point of flavor.

This morning Capt. Clark set out early. Found the river shoaly, rapid, shallow, and extremely difficult. The men in the water almost all day. They are getting weak, sore and much fatigued; they complained of the fatigue to which the navigation subjected them and wished to go by land. Capt. Clark encouraged them and pacified them. One of the canoes was very near over-setting in a rapid today. They proceeded but slowly. At noon they had a thunderstorm which continued about half an hour. Their hunters killed three deer and a fawn. They encamped in a smooth plain near a few cottonwood trees on the larboard side.

August 13, 1805, Tuesday [Lewis]
We set out very early on the Indian road, which still led us through an open broken country in a westerly direction. A deep valley appeared to our left at the base of a high range of mountains which extended from S.E. to N.W., having their sides better clad with pine timber than we had been accustomed to see. The mountains and their tops were also partially covered with snow. At the distance of five miles the road, after leading us down a long descending

valley for two miles, brought us to a large creek about 10 yards wide. This we passed and on rising the hill beyond it had a view of a handsome little valley to our left of about a mile in width, through which, from the appearance of the timber, I conjectured that a river passed. I saw near the creek some bushes of the white maple, the sumac of the small species with the winged rib, and a species of honeysuckle much in its growth and leaf like the small honey-suckle of the Missouri, only rather larger and it bears a globular berry as large as a garden pea and as white as wax. This berry is formed of a thin smooth pellicle which envelopes a soft white mucilaginous substance in which there are several small brown seeds irregularly scattered or intermixed without any shell or perceptible membranous covering.

We had proceeded about four miles through a wavy plain parallel to the valley or river bottom when at the distance of about a mile we saw two women, a man and some dogs on an eminence immediately before us. They appeared to view us with attention and two of them after a few minutes sat down as if to wait our arrival. We continued our usual pace towards them. When we had arrived within half a mile of them I directed the party to halt and, leaving my pack and rifle, I took the flag which I unfurled and advanced singly towards them. The women soon disappeared behind the hill. The man continued until I arrived within a hundred yards of him and then likewise absconded, though I frequently repeated the word *tab-ba-bone* sufficiently loud for him to have heard it. I now hastened to the top of the hill where they had stood but could see nothing of them. The dogs were less shy than their masters; they came about me pretty close. I therefore thought of tying a handkerchief about one of their necks with some beads and other trinkets and then let them loose to search for their fugitive owners, thinking by this means to convince them of our pacific disposition towards them, but the dogs would not suffer me to take hold of them; they also soon disappeared. I now made a signal for the men to come on; they joined me and we pursued the back track of these Indians, which led us along the same road which we had been traveling. The road was dusty and appeared to have been much traveled lately both by men and horses. These prairies are very poor, the soil is of a light yellow clay, intermixed with small smooth gravel, and produces little else but prickly pears and bearded grass about three inches high. The prickly pear are of three species, that with a broad leaf common to the Mis-souri, that of a globular form also common to the upper part of the Missouri and more especially after it enters the Rocky Mountains, also a third peculiar to this country. It consists of small, circular, thick leaves with a much greater number of thorns. These thorns are stronger and appear to be barbed. The leaves grow from the margin of each other as in the broad-leaved pear of the Missouri, but are so slightly attached that when the thorn touches your moccasin it adheres and brings with it the leaf, covered in every direction with many others. This is much the most troublesome plant of the three.

We had not continued our route more than a mile when we were so fortunate as to meet with three female savages. The short and steep ravines which we passed concealed us from each other until we arrived within 30 paces. A young woman immediately took to flight, an elderly woman and a girl of about 12 years old remained. I instantly laid by my gun and advanced towards them. They appeared much alarmed but saw that we were too near for them to escape by flight; they therefore seated themselves on the ground, holding down their heads as if reconciled to die, which they expected no doubt would be their fate. I took the elderly woman by the hand and raised her up, repeated the word *tab-ba-bone* and stripped up my shirtsleeve to show her my skin to prove to her the truth of the assertion that I was a white man, for my face and hands, which have been constantly exposed to the sun, were quite as dark as their own. They appeared instantly reconciled, and the men coming up I gave these women some beads, a few moccasin awls, some pewter looking-glasses and a little paint. I directed Drouillard to request the old woman to recall the young woman who had run off to some distance by this time, fearing she might alarm the camp before we approached and must so exasperate the natives that they would perhaps attack us without inquiring who we were. The old woman did as she was requested and the fugitive soon returned almost out of breath. I bestowed an equivalent portion of trinkets on her with the others. I now painted their tawny cheeks with some vermilion, which with this nation is emblematic of peace.

After they had become composed I informed them by signs that I wished them to conduct us to their camp, that we were anxious to become acquainted with the chiefs and warriors of their nation. They readily obeyed and we set out, still pursuing the road down the river. We had marched about two miles when we met a party of about 60 warriors mounted on excellent horses who came in nearly full speed. When they arrived I advanced towards them with the flag, leaving my gun with the party about 50 paces behind me.

The chief and two others who were a little in advance of the main body spoke to the women, and they informed them who we were and exultingly showed the presents which had been given them. These men then advanced and embraced me very affectionately in their way, which is by putting their left arm over your right shoulder clasping your back, while they apply their left cheek to yours and frequently vociferate the word *âh-hí-e, âh-hí-e,* that is, I am much pleased, I am much rejoiced. Both parties now advanced and we were all caressed and besmeared with their grease and paint till I was heartily tired of the national hug. I now had the pipe lit and gave them smoke; they seated themselves in a circle around us and pulled off their moccasins before they would receive or smoke the pipe. This is a custom among them, as I afterwards learned, indicative of a sacred obligation of sincerity in their profession of friendship, given by the act of receiving and smoking the pipe of a stranger—or which is as much as to say that they wish they may always go barefoot if they are not sincere, a pretty heavy penalty if they are to march through the plains of their country.

After smoking a few pipes with them I distributed some trifles among them, with which they seemed much pleased, particularly with the blue beads and vermilion. I now informed the chief that the object of our visit was a friendly one, that after we should reach his camp I would undertake to explain to him fully those objects, who we were, from whence we had come and whither we were going; that in the meantime I did not care how soon we were in motion, as the sun was very warm and no water at hand. They now put on their moccasins and the principal chief, Ca-me-âh-wait, made a short speech to the warriors. I gave him the flag, which I informed him was an emblem of peace among white men and now that it had been received by him it was to be respected as the bond of union between us. I desired him to march on, which he did, and we followed him; the dragoons moved on in squadron in our rear. After we had marched about a mile in this order he halted them and gave a second harangue, after which six or eight of the young men rode forward to their encampment and no further regularity was observed in the order of march. I afterwards understood that the Indians we had first seen this morning had returned and alarmed the camp. These men had come out armed *cap a pie* for action, expecting to meet with their enemies the Minitaris of Fort de Prairie, whom they call Pâh'-kees [*the modern designation is Atsina*]. They were armed with bows, arrows and shields, except three whom I observed with small pieces such as the N.W. Company furnish the natives with, which they had obtained from the Rocky Mountain Indians on the Yellowstone River, with whom they are at peace.

On our arrival at their encampment on the river in a handsome level and fertile bottom at the distance of four miles from where we had first met them, they introduced us to a lodge made of willow brush and an old leather lodge which had been prepared for our reception by the young men which the chief had dispatched for that purpose. Here we were seated on green boughs and the skins of antelope. One of the warriors then pulled up the grass in the center of the lodge, forming a small circle of about two feet in diameter. The chief next produced his pipe and native tobacco and began a long ceremony of the pipe when we were requested to take off our moccasins, the chief having previously taken off his as well as all the warriors present. This we complied with. The chief then lit his pipe at the fire kindled in this little magic circle, and standing on the opposite side of the circle uttered a speech of several minutes in length, at the conclusion of which he pointed the stem to the four cardinal points of the heavens, first beginning at the east and ending with the north. He now presented the pipe to me as if desirous that I should smoke, but when I reached my hand to receive it, he drew it back and repeated the same ceremony three times, after which he pointed the stem first to the heavens, then to the center of the magic circle, smoked himself with three whiffs, and held the pipe until I took as many as I thought proper. He then held it to each of the white persons and then gave it to be consumed by his warriors.

This pipe was made of a dense semitransparent green stone, very highly polished, about two and a half inches long and of an oval figure, the bowl being in the same direction with the stem. A small piece of burned clay is placed in the bottom of the bowl to separate the tobacco from the end of the stem and is of an irregularly rounded figure not fitting the tube perfectly close in order that the smoke may pass. Their tobacco is of the same kind as that used by the Minitaris, Mandans and Arikaras of the Missouri. The Shoshones do not cultivate this plant, but obtain it from the Rocky Mountain Indians and some of the bands of their own nation who live further south.

I now explained to them the objects of our journey. All the women and children of the camp were shortly collected about the lodge to indulge themselves with looking at us, we being the first white persons they had ever seen. After the ceremony of the pipe was over I distributed the remainder of the small articles I had brought with me among the women and children. By this time it was late in the evening and we had not tasted any food since the evening before. The chief informed us that they had nothing but berries to eat and gave us some cakes of serviceberries and choke cherries which had been dried in the sun. Of these I made a hearty meal, and then walked to the river, which I found about 40 yards wide, very rapid, clear and about 3 feet deep, the banks low and abrupt, as those of the upper part of the Missouri, and the bed formed of loose stones and gravel.

Cameahwait informed me that this stream discharged itself into another doubly as large at the distance of half a day's march which came from the S.W. But he added on further inquiry that there was but little more timber below the junction of those rivers than I saw here, and that the river was confined between inaccessible mountains, was very rapid and rocky, insomuch that it was impossible for us to pass either by land or water down this river to the great lake where the white men lived, as he had been informed. This was unwelcome information, but I still hoped that this account had been exaggerated with a view to detain us among them. As to timber, I could discover not any that would answer the purpose of constructing canoes or in short more than was barely necessary for fuel, consisting of the narrow-leaved cottonwood and willow, also the red willow, choke cherry, serviceberry and a few currant bushes such as were common on the Missouri.

These people had been attacked by the Minitaris of Fort de Prairie this spring and about 20 of them killed and taken prisoners. On this occasion they lost a great part of their horses and all their lodges except that which they had erected for our accommodation. They were now living in lodges of a conic figure made of willow brush. I still observe a great number of horses feeding in every direction around their camp and therefore entertain but little doubt but we shall be enabled to furnish ourselves with an adequate number to transport our stores, even if we are compelled to travel by land over these mountains. On my return to my lodge an Indian called me into his bower and gave me a small morsel of the flesh of an antelope boiled, and a piece of a fresh salmon roasted, both of which I ate with a very good relish. This was the first salmon I had seen and perfectly convinced me that we were on the waters of the Pacific Ocean. The course of this river is a little to the north of west as far as I can discover it, and is bounded on each side by a range of high mountains, though those on the E. side are lowest and more distant from the river.

This evening the Indians entertained us with their dancing nearly all night. At 12 o'clock I grew sleepy and retired to rest, leaving the men to amuse themselves with the Indians. I observe no essential difference between the music and manner of dancing among this nation and those of the Missouri. I was several times awoken in the course of the night by their yells but was too much fatigued to be deprived of a tolerable sound night's repose.

This morning Capt. Clark set out early, having previously dispatched some hunters ahead. It was cool and cloudy all the forepart of the day. At eight a.m. they had a slight rain. They passed a number of shoals over which they were obliged to drag the canoes, the men in the water three-fourths of the day. They passed a bold running stream seven yards wide on the larboard side just below a high point of limestone rocks. This stream we call McNeal's Creek after Hugh McNeal, one of our party. This creek heads in the mountains to the east and forms a handsome valley for some miles between the mountains. They killed one deer only today. Saw a number of otter, some beaver, antelope, ducks, geese and cranes. They caught a number of fine trout as they have every day since I left them. They encamped on the larboard side in a smooth level prairie near a few cottonwood trees, but were obliged to make use of the dry willow brush for fuel.

August 14, 1805, Wednesday [Lewis]
In order to give Capt. Clark time to reach the forks of the Jefferson River I concluded to spend this day at the Shoshone camp and obtain what information I could with respect to the country. As we had nothing but a little flour and parched meal to eat except the berries with which the Indians furnished us, I directed Drouillard and Shields to hunt a few hours and try to kill something. The Indians furnished them with horses and most of their young men also turned out to hunt. The game which they principally hunt is the antelope, which they pursue on horseback and shoot with their arrows. This animal is so extremely fleet and durable that a single horse has no possible chance to overtake them or run them down. The Indians are therefore obliged to have recourse to stratagem; when they discover a herd of the antelope they separate and scatter themselves to the distance of five or six miles in different directions around them, generally selecting some commanding eminence for a stand. Some one or two now pursue the herd at full speed over the hills, valleys, gullies and the sides of precipices that are tremendous to view. Thus after running them from five to six or seven miles the fresh horses that were in waiting head them and drive them back, pursuing them as far or perhaps further, quite to the other extreme of the

hunters, who now in turn pursue on their fresh horses, thus worrying the poor animals down and finally killing them with their arrows. Forty or fifty hunters will be engaged for half a day in this manner and perhaps not kill more than two or three antelope. They have but few elk or black-tailed deer, and the common red deer they cannot take, as they secrete themselves in the brush when pursued, and they have only the bow and arrow, which is a very slender dependence for killing any game except such as they can run down with their horses.

I was very much entertained with a view of this Indian chase; it was after a herd of about 10 antelope and about 20 hunters. It lasted about two hours and considerable part of the chase was in view from my tent. About one p.m. the hunters returned, they had not killed a single antelope, and their horses were foaming with sweat. My hunters returned soon after and had been equally unsuccessful. I now directed McNeal to make me a little paste with the flour and added some berries to it, which I found very palatable.

The means I had of communicating with these people was by way of Drouillard, who understood perfectly the common language of gesticulation or signs, which seems to be universally understood by all the nations we have yet seen. It is true that this language is imperfect and liable to error, but is much less so than would be expected. The strong parts of the idea are seldom mistaken. [*At this point Thwaites moves the following conversation between Lewis and Cameahwait to the entry for August 20, following an interlined memorandum in Clark's handwriting, but it obviously belongs here, in chronological order, and that is how we print it.*]

I now prevailed on the chief to instruct me with respect to the geography of this country. This he undertook very cheerfully, by delineating the rivers on the ground. But I soon found that his information fell far short of my expectation or wishes. He drew the river on which we now are, to which he placed two branches just above us, which he showed me from the openings of the mountains were in view. He next made it discharge itself into a large river which flowed from the S.W. about ten miles below us, then continued this joint stream in the same direction of this valley or N.W. for one day's march, and then inclined it to the west for two more days' march. Here he placed a number of heaps of sand on each side which he informed me represented the vast mountains of rock eternally covered with snow through which the river passed. The perpendicular and even jutting rocks so closely hemmed in the river that there was no possibility of passing along the shore;

the bed of the river was obstructed by sharp pointed rocks and the rapidity of the streams was such that the whole surface of the river was beaten into perfect foam as far as the eye could reach [*the chief is describing the Salmon River, often called the River of No Return*]. The mountains were also inaccessible to man or horse. He said that this being the state of the country in that direction, himself nor none of his nation had ever been further down the river than these mountains. I then inquired about the state of the country on either side of the river but he could not inform me. He said there was an old man of his nation a day's march below who could probably give me some information of the country to the N.W. and referred me to an old man then present for that to the S.W.

The chief further informed me that he had understood from the pierced nose Indians [*the Nez Perce*] who inhabit this river below the Rocky Mountains that it ran a great way toward the setting sun and finally lost itself in a great lake of water which was ill-tasting, and where the white men lived. I next commenced my inquiries of the old man to whom I had been referred for information relative to the country S.W. of us. This he depicted with horrors and obstructions scarcely inferior to that just mentioned. He informed me that the band of this nation to which he belonged resided at the distance of 20 days' march from hence not far from the white people [*almost certainly, Spaniards are meant*], with whom they traded for horses, mules, cloth, metal, beads and the shells which they wear as ornament, being those of a species of pearl oyster [*more probably, most authorities agree, abalone shell*]. That the course to his relations was a little to the west of south. That in order to get to his relations the first seven days we should be obliged to climb over steep and rocky mountains where we could find no game to kill nor anything but roots such as a fierce and warlike nation lived on, whom he called the broken moccasins or moccasins with holes [*no one is certain what tribe is meant by this reference*], and who, he said, inhabited those mountains and lived like the bears of other countries among the rocks and fed on roots or the flesh of such horses as they could take or steal from those who passed through their country. That in passing this country the feet of our horses would be so much wounded with the stones many of them would give out. The next part of the route was about 10 days through a dry and parched sandy desert in which there was no food at this season for either man or horse, and in which we must suffer, if not perish, for the want of water. That the sun had now dried up the little pools of water which exist through this desert plain in the spring season and had also scorched all the grass. That no animal inhabited this plain on which we could hope to subsist [*the old man is talking about the Snake River country; the desert he refers to is the arid Snake River plains area of southern Idaho*]. That about the center of this plain a large river passed from S.E. to N.W. which was navigable but afforded neither salmon nor timber. That beyond this plain three or four days' march his relations lived in a country tolerably fertile and partially covered with timber on another large river which ran in the same direction as the former. That this last discharged itself into a large river on which many numerous nations lived with whom his relations were at war, but whether this last discharged itself into the great lake or not he did not know. That from his relations it was yet a great distance to the great or stinking lake, as they call the ocean. That the way which such of his nation as had been to the stinking lake traveled was up the river on which they lived and over to that on which the white people lived, which last they knew discharged itself into the ocean, and that this was the way which he would advise me to travel if I was determined to proceed to the ocean, but he would advise me to put off the journey until the next spring, when he would conduct me.

I thanked him for his information and advice and gave him a knife, with which he appeared to be much gratified. From this narrative I was convinced that the streams of which he had spoken as running through the plains and that on which his relations lived were southern branches of the Columbia, heading with the rivers Apostles and Colorado, and that the route he had pointed out was to the Vermilion Sea or Gulf of California [*there was no River of the Apostles, although it appeared on various conjectural maps of the West, and Lewis was wrong about any branch of the Columbia heading near the sources of the Colorado*]. I therefore told him that this route was more to the south than I wished to travel, and requested to know if there was no route on the left of this river on which we now are, by means of which I could intercept it below the mountains through which it passes; but he could not inform me of any except that of the barren plain, which he said joined the mountain on that side and through which it was impossible for us to pass at this season, even if we were fortunate enough to escape from the broken moccasin Indians.

I now asked Cameahwait by what route the Pierced Nose Indians, who he informed me inhabited this river below the mountains, came over to the Missouri. This he informed me was to the north, but added that the road was a very bad one, as he had been informed by them, and that they had suffered excessively with hunger on the route, being obliged to subsist for many days on berries alone, as there was no game in that part of the mountains, which were broken, rocky, and so thickly covered with timber that they could scarcely pass. However, knowing that Indians had passed, and did pass, at this season on that side of this river to the same below the mountains, my route was instantly settled in my own mind, provided the account of this river should prove true on an investigation of it, which I was determined should be made before we would undertake the route by land in any direction. I felt perfectly satisfied, that if the Indians could pass these mountains with their women and children, we could also pass them; and that if the nations on this river below the mountains were as numerous as they were stated to be that they must have some means of subsistence which it would be equally in our power to procure in the same country. They informed me that there was no buffalo on the west side of these mountains, that the game consisted of a few elk, deer and antelope, and that the natives subsisted on fish and roots principally.

In this manner I spent the day smoking with them and acquiring what information I could with respect to their country. They informed me that they could pass to the Spaniards by the way of the Yellowstone River in 10 days. I can discover that these people are by no means friendly to the Spaniards. Their complaint is that the Spaniards will not let them have firearms and ammunition, that they put them off by telling them that if they suffer them to have guns they will kill each other, thus leaving them defenseless and an easy prey to their bloodthirsty neighbors to the east of them, who, being in possession of firearms, hunt them up and murder them without respect to sex or age and plunder them of their horses on all occasions. They told me that to avoid their enemies who were eternally harassing them, they were obliged to remain in the interior of these mountains at least two-thirds of the year, where they suffered as we then saw great hardships for the want of food, sometimes living for weeks without meat and only a little fish, roots and berries. But this, added Cameahwait, with his fierce eyes and lank jaws grown meager for the want of food, would not be the case if we had guns. We could then live in the country of buffalo and eat as our enemies do and not be compelled to hide ourselves in these mountains and live on roots and berries as the bears do. We do not fear our enemies when placed on an equal footing with them. I told them that the Minitaris, Mandans and Arikaras of the Missouri had promised us to desist from making war on them and that we would endeavor to find the means of making the Minitaris of Fort de Prairie, or as they call them Pakhees, desist from waging war against them also. That after our finally returning to our homes towards the rising sun, white men would come to them with an abundance of guns and every other article necessary to their defense and comfort, and that they would be enabled to supply themselves with these articles on reasonable terms in exchange for the skins of the beaver, otter and ermine so abundant in their country. They expressed great pleasure at this information and said they had been long anxious to see the white men that traded guns, and that we might rest assured of their friendship and that they would do whatever we wished them.

I now told Cameahwait that I wished him to speak to his people and engage them to go with me tomorrow to the forks of the Jefferson River where our baggage was by this time arrived with another chief and a large party of white men who would wait my return at that place. That I wish them to take with them about 30 spare horses to transport our baggage to this place, where we would then remain some time among them and trade with them for horses, and finally concert our future plans for getting on to the ocean and of the trade which would be extended to them after our return to our homes.

He complied with my request and made a lengthy harangue to his village. He returned in about an hour and a half and informed me that they would be ready to accompany me in the morning. I promised to reward them for their trouble. Drouillard, who had had a good view of their horses, estimated them at 400. Most of them are fine horses. Indeed many of them would make a figure on the south side of the James River or the land of fine horses. I saw several with Spanish brands on them, and some mules, which they informed me they had also obtained from the Spaniards. I also saw a bridle bit of Spanish manufacture, and sundry other articles which I have no doubt were obtained from the same source.

Notwithstanding the extreme poverty of these poor people they are very merry; they danced again this evening until midnight. Each warrior keeps one or more horses tied by a cord to a stake near his lodge both day and night and is always prepared for action at a moment's warning. They fight on horseback altogether. I observe that the large flies are extremely troublesome to the horses as well as ourselves.

The morning being cold and the men stiff and sore from the exertions of yesterday, Capt. Clark did not set out this morning until 7 a.m. The river was so crooked and rapid that they made but little way. At one mile he passed a bold running stream on starboard which heads in a mountain to the north, on which there is snow. This we called Track Creek. It is four yards wide and three feet deep. At seven miles they passed a stout stream which heads in some springs under the foot of the mountains on larboard. The river near the mountain they found one continued rapid, which was extremely laborious and difficult to ascend. This evening Charbonneau struck his Indian woman, for which Capt. Clark gave him a severe reprimand. Joseph and Reuben Fields killed four deer and an antelope, Capt. Clark killed a buck. Several of the men have lamed themselves by various accidents in working the canoes through this difficult part of the river, and Capt. Clark was obliged personally to assist them in this labor. They encamped this evening on the larboard side near the Rattlesnake Cliff.

August 15, 1805, Thursday [Lewis]
This morning I arose very early and as hungry as a wolf. I had eaten nothing yesterday except one scant meal of the flour and berries, which did not appear to satisfy my appetite as they appeared to do those of my Indian friends. I found on inquiry of McNeal that we had only about two pounds of flour remaining. This I directed him to divide into two equal parts and to cook the one half this morning in a kind of pudding with the berries as he had done yesterday and reserve the balance for the evening. On this new-fashioned pudding four of us breakfasted, giving a pretty good allowance also to the chief, who declared it the best thing he had tasted for a long time. He took a little of the flour in his hand, tasted and examined it very scrutinizingly, and asked me if we made it of roots. I explained to him the manner in which it grew. I hurried the departure of the Indians. The chief addressed them several times before they would move; they seemed very reluctant to accompany me. I at length asked the reason and he told me that some foolish persons among them had suggested the idea that we were in league with the Pahkees and had come on in order to decoy them into an ambuscade where their enemies were waiting to receive them, but that for his part he did not believe it. I readily perceived that our situation was not entirely free from danger, as the transition from suspicion to the confirmation of the fact would not be very difficult in the minds of these

ignorant people who have been accustomed from their infancy to view every stranger as an enemy.

I told Cameahwait that I was sorry to find that they had put so little confidence in us, that I knew they were not acquainted with white men and therefore could forgive them. That among white men it was considered disgraceful to lie or entrap an enemy by falsehood. I told him if they continued to think thus meanly of us that they might rely on it, no white men would ever come to trade with them or bring them arms and ammunition and that if the bulk of his nation still entertained this opinion I still hoped that there were some among them that were not afraid to die, that were men and would go with me and convince themselves of the truth of what I had asserted. That there was a party of white men waiting my return either at the forks of the Jefferson River or a little below, coming on to that place in canoes loaded with provisions and merchandise.

He told me for his own part he was determined to go, that he was not afraid to die. I soon found that I had touched him on the right string; to doubt the bravery of a savage is at once to put him on his mettle. He now mounted his horse and harangued his village a third time, the purport of which as he afterwards told me was to inform them that he would go with us and convince himself of the truth or falsity of what we had told him even if he was certain he should be killed, that he hoped there were some of them who heard him who were not afraid to die with him and if there were to let him see them mount their horses and prepare to set out. Shortly after this harangue he was joined by six or eight only and with these I smoked a pipe and directed the men to put on their packs, being determined to set out with them while I had them in the humor. At half after 12 we set out. Several of the old women were crying and imploring the Great Spirit to protect their warriors as if they were going to inevitable destruction. We had not proceeded far before our party was augmented by ten or twelve more, and before we reached the creek which we had passed in the morning of the 13th it appeared to me that we had all the men of the village and a number of women with us. This may serve in some measure to illustrate the capricious disposition of those people, who never act but from the impulse of the moment. They were now very cheerful and gay, and two hours ago they looked as surly as so many imps of Saturn.

When we arrived at the spring on the side of the mountain where we had encamped on the 12th the chief insisted on halting to let the horses graze, with which I complied and gave the Indians smoke. They are excessively fond of the pipe, but have it not much in their power to indulge themselves with even their native tobacco, as they do not cultivate it themselves. After remaining about an hour we again set out, and by engaging to make compensation to four of them for their trouble obtained the privilege of riding with an Indian myself and a similar situation for each of my party. I soon found it more tiresome riding without stirrups than walking and of course chose the latter, making the Indian carry my pack. About sunset we reached the upper part of the level valley of the cove, which I now called Shoshone Cove. The grass being burned on the north side of the river, we passed over to the south and encamped near some willow brush about four miles above the narrow pass between the hills, noticed as I came up this cove. The river was here about six yards wide, and frequently dammed up by the beaver. I had sent Drouillard forward this evening before we halted to kill some meat but he was unsuccessful and did not rejoin us until after dark. I now cooked and among six of us ate the remaining pound of flour stirred in a little boiling water.

Capt. Clark delayed again this morning until after breakfast, when he set out and passed between low and rugged mountains which had a few pine trees distributed over them. The cliffs are formed of limestone and a hard black rock intermixed. No trees on the river, the bottoms narrow, river crooked, shallow, shoaly and rapid. The water is as cold as that of the best springs in our country. The men as usual suffered excessively with fatigue and the coldness of the water, to which they were exposed for hours together. At the distance of 6 miles by water they passed the entrance of a bold creek on starboard side 10 yards wide and three feet three inches deep, which we called Willard's Creek after Alexander Willard, one of our party. At four miles by water from their encampment of last evening they passed a bold branch which tumbled down a steep precipice of rocks from the mountains on the larboard. Capt. Clark was very near being bitten twice today by rattlesnakes; the Indian woman also narrowly escaped. They caught a number of fine trout. Capt. Clark killed a buck which was the only game killed today. The venison has an uncommon bitter taste which is unpleasant. I presume it proceeds from some article of their food, perhaps the willow, on the leaves of which they feed very much. They encamped this evening on the larboard side near a few cottonwood trees about which there were the remains of several old Indian brush lodges.

In a separate entry that Moulton prints, Clark calculated his mileage from August 7 through August 14 and came up with the figure of 111 miles by water—and 41 miles on a direct course overland.

August 16, 1805, Friday [Lewis]

I sent Drouillard and Shields before this morning in order to kill some meat, as neither the Indians nor ourselves had anything to eat. I informed the chief of my view in this measure, and requested that he would keep his young men with us lest by their whooping and noise they should alarm the game and we should get nothing to eat, but so strongly were their suspicions excited by this measure that two parties of discovery immediately set out, one on each side of the valley, to watch the hunters as I believe to see whether they had not been sent to give information of their approach to an enemy that they still persuaded themselves were lying in wait for them. I saw that any further effort to prevent their going would only add strength to their suspicion and therefore said no more. After the hunters had gone about an hour we set out. We had just passed through the narrows when we saw one of the spies coming up the level plain under whip. The chief paused a little and seemed somewhat concerned. I felt a good deal so myself and began to suspect that by some unfortunate accident perhaps some of their enemies had straggled hither at this unlucky moment; but we were all agreeably disappointed on the arrival of the young man to learn that he had come to inform us that one of the white men had killed a deer. In an instant they all gave their horses the whip and I was taken nearly a mile before I could learn what were the tidings; as I was without stirrups and an Indian behind me the jostling was disagreeable. I therefore reined up my horse and forbid the Indian to whip him, who had given him the lash at every jump for a mile, fearing he should lose a part of the feast. The fellow was so uneasy that he left me the horse, dismounted and ran on foot at full speed, I am confident, a mile.

When they arrived where the deer was, which was in view of me, they dismounted and ran in tumbling over each other like a parcel of famished dogs, each seizing and tearing away a part of the intestines, which had been previously thrown out by Drouillard, who killed it. The scene was such when I arrived that had I not had a pretty keen appetite myself I am confident I should not have tasted any part of the venison shortly. Each one had a piece of some description and all eating most ravenously. Some were eating the kidneys, the melt [*i.e., the spleen*], and liver, the blood running from the corners of their mouths; others were in a similar situation with the paunch and guts, but the exuding substance in this case from their lips was of a different description. One of the last who attracted my attention particularly had been fortunate in his allotment or rather active in the division; he had provided himself with about nine feet of the small guts, one end of which he was chewing on while with his hands he was squeezing the contents out at the other. I really did not until now think that human nature ever presented itself in a shape so nearly allied to the brute creation. I viewed these poor starved devils with pity and compassion.

I directed McNeal to skin the deer and reserved a quarter; the balance I gave the chief to be divided among his people. They devoured the whole of it nearly without cooking. I now bore obliquely to the left in order to intercept the creek where there was some brush to make a fire, and arrived at this stream where Drouillard had killed a second deer. Here nearly the same scene was encored. A fire being kindled, we cooked and ate and gave the balance of the two deer to the Indians, who ate the whole of them, even to the soft parts of the hooves. Drouillard joined us at breakfast with a third deer. Of this I reserved a quarter and gave the balance to the Indians. They all appeared now to have filled themselves and were in a good humor. This morning early, soon after the hunters set out, a considerable part of our escort became alarmed and returned. Twenty-eight men and three women only continued with us.

After eating and suffering the horses to graze about two hours we renewed our march and towards evening arrived at the lower part of the cove. Shields killed an antelope on the way, a part of which we took and gave the remainder to the Indians. Being now informed of the place at which I expected to meet Capt. Clark and the party, they insisted on making a halt, which was complied with. We now dismounted and the chief with much ceremony put tippets about our necks such as they themselves wore. I readily perceived that this was to disguise us and owed its origin to the same cause already mentioned. To give them further confidence I put my cocked hat with feather on the chief; and my over shirt being of the Indian form, my hair disheveled and skin well browned with the sun, I wanted no further addition to make me a complete Indian in appearance. The men followed my example and we were soon completely metamorphosed. I again repeated to them the possibility of the party not having arrived at the place where I expected they were, but assured them they could not be far below, lest by not finding them at the forks their suspicions might arise to such height as to induce them to return precipitately.

We now set out and rode briskly within sight of the forks, making one of the Indians carry the flag that our own party should know who we were. When we arrived in sight at the distance of about two miles I discovered to my mortification that the party had not arrived, and the Indians slackened their pace. I now scarcely knew what to do and feared every moment when they would halt altogether. I now determined to restore their confidence, cost what it might, and therefore gave the chief my gun and told him that if his enemies were in those bushes before him that he could defend himself with that gun, that for my own part I was not afraid to die and if I deceived him he might make what use of the gun he thought proper, or in other words that he might shoot me. The men also gave their guns to other Indians, which seemed to inspire them with more confidence. They sent their spies before them at some distance and when I drew near the place I thought of the notes which I had left and directed Drouillard to go with an Indian man and bring them to me, which he did. The Indian seeing him take the notes from the stake on which they had been placed, I now had recourse to a stratagem in which I thought myself justified by the occasion, but which I must confess sat a little awkward. It had its desired effect. After reading the notes, which were the same I had left, I told the chief that when I had left my brother chief with the party below where the river entered the mountain, we both agreed not to bring the canoes higher up than the next forks of the river above us, wherever this might happen, that there he was to wait my return, should he arrive first, and that in the event of his not being able to travel as fast as usual from the difficulty of the water, he was to send up to the first forks above him and leave a note informing me where he was, that this note was left here today and that he informed me that he was just below the mountains and was coming on slowly up, and added that I should wait here for him. But if they did not believe me I should send a man at any rate to the chief and they might also send one of their young men with him, and myself and two others would remain with them at this place.

This plan was readily adopted and one of the young men offered his services; I promised him a knife and some beads as a reward for his confidence in us. Most of them seemed satisfied but there were several that complained of the chief's exposing them to danger unnecessarily and said that we told different stories; in short a few were much dissatisfied. I wrote a note to Capt.

Clark by the light of some willow brush and directed Drouillard to set out early, being confident that there was not a moment to spare. The chief and five or six others slept about my fire and the others hid themselves in various parts of the willow brush to avoid the enemy, who they were fearful would attack them in the course of the night.

I now entertained various conjectures myself with respect to the cause of Capt. Clark's detention and was even fearful that he had found the river so difficult he had halted below the Rattlesnake Bluffs. I knew that if these people left me they would immediately disperse and secrete themselves in the mountains, where it would be impossible to find them or at least in vain to pursue them, and that they would spread the alarm to all other bands within our reach and of course we should be disappointed in obtaining horses, which would vastly retard and increase the labor of our voyage and I feared might so discourage the men as to defeat the expedition altogether. My mind was in reality quite as gloomy all this evening as the most affrighted Indian. But I affected cheerfulness to keep the Indians so who were about me. We finally lay down and the chief placed himself by the side of my mosquito bier.

I slept but little, as might be well expected, my mind dwelling on the state of the expedition, which I have ever held in equal estimation with my own existence, and the fate of which appeared at this moment to depend in a great measure upon the caprice of a few savages who are ever as fickle as the wind. I had mentioned to the chief several times that we had with us a woman of his nation who had been taken prisoner by the Minitaris, and that by means of her I hoped to explain myself more fully than I could do by signs. Some of the party had also told the Indians that we had a man with us who was black and had short curling hair. This had excited their curiosity very much. And they seemed quite as anxious to see this monster as they were the merchandise which we had to barter for their horses.

At seven a.m. Capt. Clark set out after breakfast. He changed the hands in some of the canoes; they proceeded with more ease than yesterday, yet they found the river still rapid and shallow, insomuch that they were obliged to drag the large canoes the greater part of the day. The water excessively cold. In the evening they passed several bad rapids. Considerable quantities of the buffalo clover grows along the narrow bottoms through which they passed. There was no timber except a few scattering small pine on the hills. Willow, serviceberry and currant bushes were the growth of the river bottoms. They gathered considerable quantities of serviceberries, and caught some trout. One deer was killed by the hunters, who slept out last night and did not join the party until 10 a.m. Capt. Clark sent the hunters this evening up to the forks of the river, which he discovered from an eminence; they must have left this place but a little time before we arrived. This evening they encamped on the larboard side only a few miles below us and were obliged like ourselves to make use of small willow brush for fuel. The men were much fatigued and exhausted this evening.

August 17, 1805, Saturday [Lewis]
This morning I arose very early and dispatched Drouillard and the Indian down the river. Sent Shields to hunt. I made McNeal cook the remainder of our meat, which afforded a slight breakfast for ourselves and the chief. Drouillard had been gone about two hours when an Indian who had straggled some little distance down the river returned and reported that the white men were coming, that he had seen them just below. They all appeared transported with joy, and the chief repeated his fraternal hug. I felt quite as much gratified at this information as the Indians appeared to be. Shortly after Capt. Clark arrived with the interpreter Charbonneau and the Indian woman, who proved to be a sister of the chief Cameahwait. [*Lewis does not expand on this, but the Biddle version of the journals—Biddle had the advantage of having talked with Clark when he was preparing his text—does; Sacagawea did not recognize her brother until she began interpreting for the captains, and then, suddenly seeing who he was, "jumped up, and ran and embraced him, throwing over him her blanket, and weeping profusely." So much for Lewis's remark that she seemed to show no emotion on returning to her homeland.]* The meeting of those people was really affecting, particularly between Sacagawea and an Indian woman who had been taken prisoner at the same time with her, and who had afterwards escaped from the Minitaris and rejoined her nation. At noon the canoes arrived, and we had the satisfaction once more to find ourselves all together, with a flattering prospect of being able to obtain as many horses shortly as would enable us to prosecute our voyage by land, should that by water be deemed inadvisable.

We now formed our camp just below the junction of the forks on the larboard side in a level smooth bottom covered with a fine turf of greensward. Here we unloaded our canoes and arranged our baggage on shore, formed a canopy of one of our large sails and planted some willow brush in the ground to form a shade for the Indians to sit under while we spoke to them, which we thought it best to do this evening. Accordingly about four p.m. we called them together and through the medium of Labiche, Charbonneau and Sacagawea [*a translation train; Labiche translated the captains' English into French, Charbonneau then translated it into Hidatsa, and Sacagawea translated it from Hidatsa into Shoshone*] we communicated to them fully the objects which had brought us into this distant part of the country, in which we took care to make them a conspicuous object of our own good wishes and the care of our government. We made them sensible of their dependence on the will of our government for every species of merchandise as well as for their defense and comfort, and apprised them of the strength of our government and its friendly dispositions toward them. We also gave them as a reason why we wished to penetrate the country as far as the ocean to the west of them was to examine and find out a more direct way to bring merchandise to them. That as no trade could be carried on with them before our return to our homes, it was mutually advantageous to them as well as to ourselves that they should render us such aids as they had it in their power to furnish in order to hasten our voyage and of course our return home. That such were their horses to transport our baggage, without which we could not subsist, and that a pilot to conduct us through the mountains was also necessary if we could not descend the river by water. But that we did not ask either their horses or their services without giving a satisfactory compensation in return. That at present we wished them to collect as many horses as were necessary to transport our baggage to their village on the Columbia where we would then trade with them at our leisure for such horses as they could spare us.

They appeared well pleased with what had been said. The chief thanked us for friendship towards himself and his nation and declared his wish to serve us in every respect; that he was sorry to find that it must yet be some time before they could be furnished with firearms but said they could live as they had done heretofore until we brought them as we had promised. He said they had not horses enough with them at present to remove our baggage to their village over the mountain, but that he would return tomorrow and encourage his people to come over with their horses and that he would bring his own and assist us. This was complying with all we wished at present. We next inquired who were chiefs among them. Cameahwait pointed out two others who he said were chiefs. We gave him a medal of the small size with the likeness of Mr. Jefferson, the President of the United States, in relief on one side and clasped hands with a pipe and tomahawk on the other. To the other chiefs we gave each a small medal which was struck in the Presidency of George Washington. We also gave small medals of the last description to two young men who the first chief informed us were good young men and much respected among them. We gave the first chief a uniform coat shirt, a pair of scarlet leggings, a carrot of tobacco and some small articles. To each of the others we gave a shirt, leggings, handkerchief, a knife, some tobacco and a few small articles. We also distributed a good quantity of paint, moccasin awls, knives, beads, looking glasses etc., among the other Indians and gave them a plentiful meal of lyed corn [*corn that had been hulled in a bath of boiling lye*], which was the first they had ever eaten in their lives. They were much pleased with it.

Every article about us seemed to excite astonishment in their minds. The appearance of the men, their arms, the canoes, our manner of working them, the black man, York, and the sagacity of my dog were equally objects of admiration. I also shot my air gun, which was so perfectly incomprehensible that they immediately denominated it the great medicine. The idea which the Indians mean to convey by this appellation is something that emanates from or acts immediately by the influence or power of the Great Spirit, or that in which the power of god is manifest by its incomprehensible power of action.

Our hunters killed four deer and an antelope this evening, of which we also gave the Indians a good proportion. The ceremony of our council and smoking the pipe was in conformity to the custom of this nation, performed barefoot. On those occasions points of etiquette are quite as much attended to by the Indians as among civilized nations. To keep Indians in a good humor you must not fatigue them with too much business at one time. Therefore after the council we gave them to eat and amused them a while by showing them such articles as we thought would be entertaining to them, and then renewed our inquiries with respect to the country. The information we derived was only a repetition of what they had given me before and in which they appeared to be so candid that I could not avoid yielding confidence to what they had said.

Capt. Clark and myself now concerted measures for our future operations, and it was mutually agreed that he should set out tomorrow morning with eleven men furnished with axes and other necessary tools for making canoes, their arms, accoutrements and as much of their baggage as they could carry. Also to take the Indians, Charbonneau and the Indian woman with him. That on his arrival at the Shoshone camp he was to leave Charbonneau and the Indian woman to hasten the return of the Indians with their horses to this place, and to proceed himself with the eleven men down the Columbia in order to examine the river, and if he found it navigable and could obtain timber to set about making canoes immediately. In the meantime I was to bring on the party and baggage to the Shoshone camp, calculating that by the time I should reach that place he would have sufficiently informed himself with respect to the state of the river as to determine us whether to prosecute our journey from thence by land or water. In the former case we should want all the horses which we could purchase, and in the latter only to hire the Indians to transport our baggage to the place at which we made the canoes. In order to inform me as early as possible of the state of the river he was to send back one of the men with the necessary information as soon as he should satisfy himself on this subject. This plan being settled, we gave orders accordingly and the men prepared for an early march. The nights are very cold and the sun excessively hot in the day. We have no fuel here but a few dry willow brush, and from the appearance of the country I am confident we shall not find game here to subsist us many days. These are additional reasons why I conceived it necessary to get under way as soon as possible. This morning Capt. Clark had delayed until seven a.m. before he set out, just about which time Drouillard arrived with the Indian. He left the canoes to come on after him and immediately set out and joined me, as has been before mentioned. The spirits of the men were now much elated at the prospect of getting horses.

SUMMARY

AUGUST 18 TO SEPTEMBER 3, 1805

———◦◦◦◦———

Clark did set out the next morning as planned with 11 men to reconnoiter the Lemhi and the Salmon as a possible route to the Columbia; he took two of the three horses that Lewis had bartered for that morning to carry baggage and left at around ten o'clock with most of the Indians accompanying him. Lewis stayed behind to repack the supplies for the packhorses which were to return with more Indians so that the entire party with its supplies could travel to the Shoshone camp on the Lemhi where Lewis had first made contact. Two days later Clark reached the Shoshone camp, where he stayed for a few hours before he and his men set out down the Lemhi. The Shoshone supplied him with an old man, whom Lewis and Clark called Old Toby, as a guide. This same Indian became their guide across the Lolo Trail when they crossed the Bitterroot Mountains in September.

    Clark's investigation of the Lemhi and Salmon River route was in a sense unnecessary, as Cameahwait had already told Lewis that the route was impassable, both by water and land, but it's easy to understand why the captains thought it had to be considered. The Minitari had told them that the portage of the Great Falls of the Missouri, which delayed them two weeks, was the work of half a day, and none of the Minitari had said a word about the Marias River. Indian geographical knowledge was not entirely to be relied upon. Yet it was the only source of information they had, and they knew they would have to trust it at some point. In the meantime they would check it out for themselves.

The main object was to get to the mouth of the Columbia as soon as possible, before winter set in, and the men already needed two blankets, sometimes more, to keep them warm at night. During the next week ice would begin to form on water left in open vessels overnight. If the Salmon were navigable, it would almost certainly be the shortest, best route. On the 21st of August Clark reached the juncture of the Lemhi with the Salmon, which he named Lewis's River; the next day he found the going beginning to get rough, although the Indian horses, he noted, handled the terrain surprisingly well. He frightened a small Indian encampment; none of them knew a white man was in their country. They were eating what the country afforded, which was salmon and chokecherries, and not much else. On the way Clark noticed a bird, a nutcracker, which now bears his name.

On the 23rd the going got still rougher, rough enough to baffle even the horses; "the rocks," Clark wrote, "were so sharp, large and unsettled and the hillsides steep that the horses could with the greatest risk and difficulty get on." After a few miles they came to a place where the river was so narrow and the rocks so precipitous that the horses could not pass, so he left some men with the horses and, taking three men with him, continued on foot some 12 more miles. They stopped where a creek entered the river. "The river from the place I left my party to this creek is almost one continued rapid, five very considerable rapids. The passage of either with canoes is entirely impossible, as the water is confined between huge rocks and the current beating from one against another for some distance below." And this, the old Indian told him, was only the beginning. Clark goes on: "Those rapids which I had seen, he said, were small and trifling in comparison to the rocks and rapids below, at no great distance, and the hills or mountains were not like those I had seen but like the side of a tree straight up." The old Indian took him up to a ridge and then to a spur, from which they could see some 20 miles farther down, to point out the difficulty of the landscape. It was at this point that Clark turned back.

On the way back he formulated alternatives to present to Lewis for moving west. The first would be to obtain as many horses as possible and proceed by land, hiring the old man as a guide. The second was to divide the party in two, sending half down "this difficult river" and the other half on horseback by land. The third would be to divide the party in half, as before, and send one half over the mountains on horseback and the other back to the cached supplies on the Missouri and then up the Medicine River. Clark favored the first plan. So did Lewis, when he heard of it. Nobody wanted to divide the party in two, the Salmon River really was impassable, and it was simply too late in the season to send men back to the Great Falls and then up the Medicine River, crossing the Continental Divide by another route. The September snows would almost certainly shut the route down.

Lewis, indeed, had already decided that they should go by land, on horseback, should the Salmon prove impassable; he had said as much when he first heard about a land route from Cameahwait on the first day he met him, August 14. It was the route the Nez Perce took when they came east to hunt buffalo. "I felt perfectly satisfied," he had written, "that if the Indians could pass these mountains with their women and children, that we could also pass them." They would move north up the valley of the Lemhi past its juncture with the Salmon, then cross the mountains to the valley of the Bitterroot, and proceed north until they came to the trail, which Old Toby knew, across the Bitterroots to the country of the Nez Perce. They had little idea of how difficult that trail, famous now as the Lolo Trail, would be.

While Clark was exploring down the Salmon, Lewis was having the men make packsaddles, repack the supplies, build a cache for material they would not need, sink the canoes, and prepare for the long haul over the mountains. He had time to write and he wrote extensively, filling his notebook with detailed descriptions of Shoshone customs, dress, hunting equipment—writing what is easily the richest ethnographic account in the journals. It has not met with universal approval. James P. Ronda, the leading authority on the encounters between the expedition and its Indian hosts, believes that Lewis never got beyond his prejudices, judging the Shoshone according to white standards of behavior, seeing Shoshone men and women "not as adults but as mercurial and ignorant children." But it seems more than a little unfair to expect Lewis to have transcended the attitudes of his time, and he wrote vividly about the things he saw.

Furthermore he liked the Shoshone. He found them to be "frank, communicative, fair in dealing, generous with the little they possess, extremely honest, and by no means beggarly. Each individual is his own sovereign master and acts from the dictates of his own mind." He noted their marriage customs, the father sometimes disposing of his daughters even before they had reached puberty, but not delivering them until they had; thus was Sacagawea married off to a man twice her age before the Minitari had stolen her (the husband did not want her back, seeing that she had had a child by Charbonneau). This is reminiscent of customs prevailing among European aristocrats well into the 18th century.

On the matter of dress, Lewis was particularly interested in a garment called a tippet, a kind of scarf or short robe that the Shoshone made out of the skins of ermine. Cameahwait gave him his. Lewis called these tippets "the most elegant piece of Indian dress I ever saw." He was acutely observant about all their clothing: leggings made of antelope skin; robes of buffalo, beaver, marmots, or wolves, as well as deer and bighorn sheep; shirts decorated with porcupine quills; thread made of the sinews "taken from the back and loins of the deer, elk, buffalo." He described them at length, how they were made, how they fit, in which cases the hair was taken off the skins, in which cases left on. Some of the warriors, he noted, wore necklaces made of the claws of grizzly bears. "It is esteemed by them an act of equal celebrity the killing of one of these bears or an enemy, and with the means they have of killing this animal it must really be a serious undertaking."

He goes on to talk about the metal the Shoshone possessed and where it came from, their bows and arrows, the cutting implements made of elk horn. The Shoshone shields fascinated him, and he describes the ceremony with which they were made, always out of buffalo hide. It is worth quoting:

An entire skin of a bull buffalo two years old is first provided. A feast is next prepared and all the warriors, old men and jugglers [these would be medicine men or shamans] invited to partake. A hole is sunk in the ground about the same in diameter as the intended shield and about 18 inches deep. A passel of stones are now made red hot and thrown into the hole. Water is next thrown in and the hot stones cause it to emit a very strong, hot steam. Over this they spread the green skin, which must not have been suffered to dry after it has been taken off the beast. The flesh side is laid next to the ground and as many of the workmen as can reach it take hold on its edges and extend it in every direction. As the skin becomes heated, the hair separates and is taken off with the fingers, and the skin continues to contract until the whole is drawn within the compass designed for the shield. It is then taken off and laid on a parchment hide, where they pound it with their heels when barefoot. This operation of pounding continues for several days or as long as the feast lasts, when it is delivered to the proprietor and declared by the jugglers and old men to be a sufficient defense against the arrows of their enemies, or even bullets if the feast has been a satisfactory one. Many of them believe implicitly that a ball cannot penetrate their shields, in consequence of certain supernatural powers with which they have been inspired by their jugglers.

Lewis seems to have written these ethnographic descriptions while he was waiting for the Shoshone to come from their camp and take him, his men, and their supplies back to the Lemhi. His birthday came and went during this time; it inspired him to reflect that he had "as yet done but little, very little indeed, to further the happiness of the human race, or to advance the information of the succeeding generation. I viewed with regret the many hours I have spent in indolence, and now sorely feel the want of that information which those hours would have given me had they been judiciously expended. But since they are past and cannot be recalled, I dashed from me the gloomy thought, and resolved in the future to redouble my exertions and at least endeavor to promote those two primary objects of human existence, by giving them the aid of that portion of talents which nature and fortune have bestowed on me; or in future to live for mankind, as I have heretofore lived for myself."

One minor incident livened up the time spent waiting. On the 22nd, Drouillard was out hunting when he came upon a camp of Indians consisting of a young man, an old man, a boy, and three women. He rode up, dismounted from his horse to let it graze, and talked to them in the sign language at which he was so adept. After a little while the women abruptly saddled up, so he decided to go back to the hunt himself and walked off to get his horse, carelessly leaving his rifle behind. The young Indian grabbed it and all of them fled toward the mountains at top speed. Drouillard got his horse and went after them. The chase went on for ten miles, at which point the women's horses began to tire and he was able to come up to them. The young man slowed, too, and rode in circles around the women, as if to protect them. Drouillard waited for his opportunity, rode up next to the young man when he was off guard, and seized the gun. They wrestled for it; the Frenchman was stronger and took it away, but not before the young man opened the pan and dashed the primer out, so Drouillard could not shoot him without reloading. Then he rode off. Drouillard rode back the way he came and plundered their camp, bringing back skins, chokecherry cakes, and three kinds of roots. It was typical of Lewis that he would then describe the roots, which he did. One of them was the root now called Lewisia rediviva Pursh, *better known as bitterroot, which grew in the mountains named after it. Lewis found that he could not stand the taste of it.*

On the 24th the party finally set out from the forks of what is now called the Beaverhead, where they had met Clark, and proceeded on toward the Shoshone camp on the Lemhi. Lewis now had nine horses and a mule, but trading for horses was no longer so easy; the Shoshone knew they had a captive audience in desperate need of horses, and they traded some of their worst horses for goods far in excess of what he had paid for the first three. He comments on the way the Shoshone ride and has something to say about the many names they acquire during their lives, each name recording some notable event in which an Indian has distinguished himself. "Among the Shoshones," Lewis observes, "as well as all the Indians of America, bravery is esteemed the primary virtue, nor can anyone become eminent among them who has not at some period of his life given proofs of his possessing this virtue. With them there can be no preferment without some warlike achievement." He doubted now that the various tribes could be brought to a general peace, given the importance of warfare to their way of life.

If bravery was a virtue, so was honesty; if an Indian gave his word, he was supposed to keep it. Lewis had occasion to confront Cameahwait on this matter when he learned through Charbonneau that the chief was planning to take his people east to the plains to hunt buffalo before he had discharged his promise to Lewis that he would help him get started over the mountains. It was only a matter of a day or two, but these were crucial days. For both of them. Cameahwait was deeply concerned about getting to the buffalo; his people were slowly starving. The Indians to the north, a Salish-speaking people known to the Shoshone as Tushepah, to Lewis and Clark as the Flatheads, were coming down to join the Shoshone on the trip to the plains, and time was running short. Cameahwait admitted his breach of faith, and told Lewis the reason for it. That day Lewis gave the women and children a deer one of his hunters had killed, and went without supper himself. The next day, August 26, Lewis noted in passing that "one of the women who had been assisting in the transportation of the baggage halted at a little run about a mile behind us, and sent on the two pack horses which she had been conducting by one of her female friends. I inquired of Cameahwait the cause of her detention, and was informed by him in an unconcerned manner that she had halted to bring forth a child and would soon overtake us. In about an hour the woman arrived with her newborn babe and passed us on her way to the camp, apparently as well as she ever was." Lewis called it a "gift of nature" that Indian women seemed to have so little trouble in the act of childbirth.

In the end Cameahwait did wait until Lewis and Clark had traded for all the horses they needed and were on their way before he took his people to the buffalo country. On the 29th Lewis and Clark were reunited and bargained for more horses. The price was really high now; Clark had to trade his pistol, 100 balls, powder and a knife for a horse, evidently not a good one. On the 30th they brought the complement of horses to a total of 29, and left the Shoshone camp; the Shoshone left this day as well. Lewis had now stopped making journal entries, except sporadically, beginning once again one of his long silences; he did not pick up again until the first of January, 1806. Old Toby was serving as their guide, and four of his sons came along as well, but only for a day.

They were passing through very rough country. Clark describes them moving through "thickets in which we were obliged to cut a road, over rocky hillsides where our horses were in perpetual danger of slipping to their certain destruction, up and down steep hills where several horses fell, some turned over, and others slipped down steep hillsides, one horse crippled and two gave out." The next day was the same. They had little to eat, Clark said; he killed five pheasants, the hunters four more; with "a little corn it afforded us a kind of supper." Their last thermometer broke, no doubt when one of the horses fell, which they frequently did. "This day," Clark wrote, "we passed over immense hills and some of the worst road that ever horses passed." They had not yet reached the Lolo Trail. We rejoin them on the fourth of September, as they descend into the valley of the Bitterroot River and meet with a party of Flathead Indians on their way to join the Shoshone.

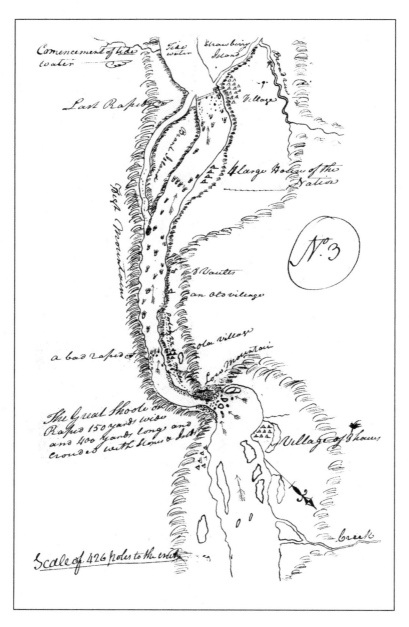

Great rapids (cascades) of the Columbia River drawn by Clark,
Oct. 30–Nov. 2, 1805

SEPTEMBER 4 TO SEPTEMBER 25, 1805

—◦◦◦◦—

September 4, 1805, Wednesday [Clark]

A very cold morning, everything wet and frosted. We detained until eight o'clock to thaw the covering for the baggage, etc. Ground covered with snow. We ascended a mountain and took a dividing ridge, which we kept for several miles, and fell on the head of a creek which appeared to run the course we wished to go. I was in front and saw several of the argali or ibex [*bighorn sheep*]; we descended the mountain by a very steep descent, taking advantage of the points and best places to the creek, where our hunters killed a deer, which we made use of, and pursued our course down the creek to the forks about five miles, where we met a part of the Flathead nation of 33 lodges, about 80 men, 400 total, and at least 500 horses. Those people received us friendly, threw white robes over our shoulders and smoked in the pipes of peace. We encamped with them and found them friendly, but nothing but berries to eat, a part of which they gave us. Those Indians are well dressed with skin shirts and robes. They are stout and light complexioned, more so than common for Indians. The chiefs harangued until late at night, smoked our pipe and appeared satisfied. I was the first white man who ever was on the waters of this river [*the Bitterroot*].

September 5, 1805, Thursday [Clark]

A cloudy morning. We assembled the chiefs and warriors and spoke to them (with much difficulty, as what we said had to pass through several languages before it got into theirs, which is a gurgling kind of language spoken much through the throat). We informed them who we were, where we came from, where bound, and for what purpose, etc., and requested to purchase and exchange a few horses with them. In the course of the day I purchased 11 horses and exchanged 7, for which we gave a few articles of merchandise. Those people possess elegant horses. We made 4 chiefs whom we gave medals and a few small articles with tobacco. The women brought us a few berries and roots to eat and the principal chief a dressed badger, an otter and two goat and antelope skins.

Those people wear their hair as follows: the men queued with otter skin on each side, falling over the shoulders forward, the women loose, promiscuously over their shoulders and face. They wear long shirts which come to the ankles and tied with a belt about their waist with a robe over. They have but few ornaments and what they do wear are similar to the Snake Indians [*i.e., the Shoshone*]. They call themselves Eoote-lash-Schute and consist of 450 lodges in all, divided into several bands on the heads of the Columbia River and the Missouri, some low down the Columbia River.

September 6, 1805, Friday [Clark]
Some little rain, purchased two fine horses and took a vocabulary of the language, lightened our loads and packed up. The rain continued until 12 o'clock. We set out at two o'clock; at the same time all the Indians set out on their way to meet the Snake Indians at the three forks of the Missouri. Crossed a small river from the right we call [*a blank here; Thwaites says it was the main river, i.e, the Bitterroot; Moulton the east fork of the Bitterroot*]. Soon after setting out, also a small creek from the north, all three forks coming together below our camp, at which place the mountains close on each side of the river. We proceeded on N. 30° W. Crossed a mountain and struck the river several miles down, at which place the Indians had encamped two days before. We proceeded on down the river, which is 30 yards wide, shallow and stony, crossing it several times, and encamped in a small bottom on the right side. Rained this evening, nothing to eat but berries, our flour out and but little corn. The hunters killed two pheasants only. All our horses purchased of the Flatheads (oote lash Shutes) we secured well for fear of their leaving us, and watched them all night for fear of their leaving us or the Indians pursuing and stealing them.

September 7, 1805, Saturday [Clark]
A cloudy and rainy day, the greater part of the day dark and drizzly. We proceeded on down the river through a valley, passed several small runs on the right and three creeks on the left. The valley from one to two miles wide, the snow topped mountains to our left, open hilly country on the right. Saw two horses left by the Indians. Those horses were as wild as elk. One of our hunters came up this morning without his horse; in the course of the night the horse broke loose and cleared out. We did not make camp until dark, for the want of a good place. One of our hunters did not join us this evening. He having killed an elk packed his horses and could not overtake us.

September 8, 1805, Sunday [Clark]
A cloudy morning. Set out early and proceeded on through an open valley for 23 miles. Passed four creeks on the right, some runs on the left. The bottoms as also the hills stony bad land. Some pine on the creeks and mountains, and partially on the hills to the right-hand side. Two of our hunters came up with us at 12 o'clock with an elk and buck. The wind from the N.W. and cold. The foot of the snow mountains approach the river on the left side. Some snow on the mountain to the right also. Proceeded on down the valley, which is poor stony land, and encamped on the right side of the river. A hard rain all evening; we are all cold and wet. On this part of the river on the head of Clark's River [*the name they gave the Bitterroot*] I observe great quantities of a peculiar sort of prickly pear growing in clusters, oval and about the size of a pigeon's egg, with strong thorns which are so bearded as to draw the pear from the cluster after penetrating our feet. Drouillard killed a deer. I killed a prairie fowl. We found two mares and a colt. The mares were lame. We ventured to let our late purchase of horses loose tonight.

September 9, 1805, Monday [Lewis]
Set out at seven a.m. this morning and proceeded down the Flathead River leaving it on our left. The country in the valley of this river is generally a prairie and from five to six miles wide. The growth is almost altogether pine, principally of the longleaf kind [*ponderosa pine*], with some spruce and a kind of fir resembling the scotch fir. Near the watercourses we find a small proportion of the narrow-leafed cottonwood; some redwood, honeysuckle, and rosebushes form the scant proportion of underbrush to be

seen. At 12 we halted on a small branch which falls into the river on the E. side, where we breakfasted on a scant proportion of meat which we had reserved from the hunt of yesterday, added to three geese which one of our hunters killed this morning. Two of our hunters have arrived; one of them brought with him a redheaded woodpecker of the large kind common to the United States. This is the first of the kind I have seen since I left the Illinois. Just as we were setting out Drouillard arrived with two deer.

We continued our route down the valley about four miles and crossed the river; it is here a handsome stream about 100 yards wide and affords a considerable quantity of very clear water. The banks are low and its bed entirely gravel. The stream appears navigable, but from the circumstance of there being no salmon in it I believe there must be a considerable fall in it below. Our guide could not inform us where this river discharged itself into the Columbia River. He informed us that it continues its course along the mountains to the N. as far as he knew it and that not very distant from where we then were it formed a junction with a stream nearly as large as itself which took its rise in the mountains near the Missouri to the east of us and passed through an extensive valley, generally open prairie, which forms an excellent pass to the Missouri. The point of the Missouri where this Indian pass intersects it is about 30 miles above the *gates of the Rocky Mountains*, or the place where the Missouri first widens into an extensive plain after entering the Rocky Mountains. The guide informed us that a man might pass to the Missouri from hence by that route in four days. [*Lewis would take that route on the way back east the following spring.*]

We continued our route down the W. side of the river about five miles further and encamped on a large creek which falls in on the west. As our guide informed us that we should leave the river at this place and the weather appearing settled and fair, I determined to halt the next day, rest our horses, and take some celestial observations. We called this creek *Travelers Rest*. It is about 20 yards wide, a fine bold clear-running stream. The land through which we passed is but indifferent, a cold white gravelly soil. We estimate our journey of this day at 19 miles.

September 10, 1804, Tuesday [Lewis]
The morning being fair I sent out all the hunters and directed two of them to proceed down the river as far as its junction with the eastern fork, which heads near the Missouri, and return this evening. This fork of the river we

determined to name the Valley Plain River. I think it most probable that this river continues its course along the Rocky Mountains northward as far or perhaps beyond the sources of the Medicine River and then turning to the west falls into the Tacoutche-Tesse. The Minitaris informed us that there was a large river west of, and at no great distance from, the sources of Medicine River, which passed along the Rocky Mountains from S. to N.

This evening one of our hunters returned accompanied by three men of the Flathead Nation whom he had met in his excursion up *Travelers Rest Creek*. On first meeting him the Indians were alarmed and prepared for battle with their bows and arrows, but he soon relieved their fears by laying down his gun and advancing towards them. The Indians were mounted on very fine horses of which the Flatheads have a great abundance; that is, each man in the nation possesses from 20 to a hundred head. Our guide could not speak the language of these people but soon engaged them in conversation by signs or gesticulation, the common language of all the aborigines of North America. It is one understood by all of them and appears to be sufficiently copious to convey with a degree of certainty the outlines of what they wish to communicate. In this manner we learned from these people that two men which they supposed to be of the Snake Nation had stolen 23 horses from them and that they were in pursuit of the thieves. They told us they were in great haste. We gave them some boiled venison, of which they ate sparingly. The sun was now set; two of them departed after receiving a few small articles which we gave them, and the third remained, having agreed to continue with us as a guide, and to introduce us to his relations, whom he informed us were numerous and resided in the plain below the mountains on the Columbia River, from whence he said the water was good and capable of being navigated to the sea; that some of his relations were at the sea last fall and saw an old white man who resided there by himself and who had given them some handkerchiefs such as he saw in our possession. He said it would require five sleeps. [*He means to reach his relatives. The Flathead were lighter in color than other Indians, and Sergeant Ordway, in his journal, notes that there was talk among expedition members that the Flatheads, because of the color of their skin, were the "Welsh" Indians, descendants of the legendary Welsh Prince Madoc, who had supposedly sailed to America with his followers in the 12th century and disappeared into the interior. The Mandan at one time were also rumored to be these same Welsh Indians. The myth of Welsh Indians survived well into the 20th century.*]

September 11, 1805, Wednesday [Clark]

A fair morning, wind from the N.W. We set out at three o'clock and proceeded on up the *Travelers' Rest Creek*, accompanied by the *Flathead* or Tushapaw Indian. About seven miles below this creek a large fork comes in from the right and heads up against the waters of the Missouri below the three forks. This river has extensive valleys of open level land and passes in its whole course through a valley. They call it Valley Plain River. Our guide tells us a fine large road passes up this river to the Missouri.

The loss of two of our horses detained us until three o'clock p.m. Our *Flathead* Indian being restless thought proper to leave us and proceed on alone. Sent out the hunters to hunt in advance as usual. (We have selected 4 of the best hunters to go in advance to hunt for the party. This arrangement has been made long since.) We proceeded on up the creek on the right side through a narrow valley and good road for seven miles and encamped at some old Indian lodges. Nothing killed this evening. Hills on the right high and rugged, the mountains on the left high and covered with snow. The day very warm. [*The expedition is starting up the Lolo Trail.*]

September 12, 1805, Thursday [Clark]

A white frost. Set out at seven o'clock and proceeded on up the creek, passed a fork on the right on which I saw near an old Indian encampment a sweat house covered with earth. At two miles ascended a high hill and proceeded through a hilly and thickly timbered country for nine miles on the right of the creek, passing several branches from the right of fine clear water, and struck at a fork, at which place the road forks, one passing up each fork. The timber is short- and longleaf pine, spruce pine, and fir. The road through this hilly country is very bad, passing over hills and through steep hollows, over fallen timber, etc. Continued on and passed some most intolerable road on the sides of the steep stony mountains, which might be avoided by keeping up the creek, which is thickly covered with undergrowth and fallen timber, etc. Crossed a mountain 8 miles without water and encamped on a hillside on the creek after descending a long steep mountain. Some of our party did not get up until 10 o'clock p.m. I made camp at 8. On this road and particularly on this creek the Indians have peeled a number of pine for the underbark, which they eat at certain seasons of the year. I am told in the spring they make use of this bark. Our hunters killed only one pheasant this afternoon. Party and horses much fatigued.

September 13, 1805, Friday [Clark]

A cloudy morning. Capt. Lewis and one of our guides lost their horses; Capt. Lewis and four men detained to hunt the horses. I proceeded on with the party up the creek. At two miles passed several springs which I observed the deer, elk, etc., had made roads to, and below one of the Indians had made a hole to bathe. I tasted this water and found it hot and not bad tasting. On further examination I found this water nearly boiling hot at the places it spouted from the rocks (which were a hard coarse grit, and of great size; the rocks on the side of the mountain were of the same texture). I put my finger in the water, at first could not bear it in a second. [*These springs are now known as Lolo Hot Springs.*]

As several roads led from these springs in different directions, my guide took a wrong road and took us out of our route 3 miles through an intolerable route. After falling into the right road I proceeded on through a tolerable route for about four or five miles and halted to let our horses graze, as well as wait for Capt. Lewis who has not yet come up. The pine country, fallen timber, etc., continues. This creek is very much dammed up with the beaver, but we can see none. Dispatched two men back to hunt Capt. Lewis's horse after he came up, and we proceeded over a mountain to the head of the creek, which we left to our left and at six miles from the place I nooned it, we fell on a small creek from the left which passed through open glades, some of which were half a mile wide. We proceeded down this creek about two miles to where the mountains closed on either side, crossing the creek several times, and encamped.

One deer and some pheasants killed this morning. I shot four pheasants of the common kind except the tail was black. The road over the last mountain was thick, steep and stony as usual. After passing the head of Traveler's Rest Creek, the road was very fine, level, open and firm. Some mountains in view to the S.E. and S.W. covered with snow.

September 14, 1805, Saturday [Clark]

A cloudy day. In the valleys it rained and hailed, on the top of the mountains some snow fell. We set out early and crossed a high mountain on the right of the creek for six miles to the forks of the Glade Creek. The right-hand fork which falls in is about the size of the other. We crossed to the left side at the forks, and crossed a very high, steep mountain for nine miles to a large fork from the left S.E. which appears to head in the snow-topped mountains southerly and we crossed Glade Creek above its mouth, at a place the Tushepaw or Flathead Indians have made two weirs across to catch salmon, and have but latterly left the place. I could see no fish, and the grass entirely eaten out by the horses, we proceeded on two miles and encamped opposite a small island at the mouth of a branch on the right side of the river, which is at this place 80 yards wide, swift and stony. Here we were compelled to kill a colt for our men and selves to eat for the want of meat and we named the south fork Colt-killed Creek, and this river we call *Flathead* River. The mountains which we passed today much worse than yesterday, the last excessively bad and thickly strewn with fallen timber and pine, spruce, fir, hackmatak and tamerack, steep and stony. Our men and horses much fatigued. The rain . . .

September 15, 1805, Sunday [Clark]
We set out early, the morning cloudy, and proceeded on down the right side of the river over steep points, rocky and bushy as usual, for four miles to an old Indian fishing place. Here the road leaves the river to the left and ascends a *mountain*, winding in every direction to get up the steep ascents and to pass the immense quantity of fallen timber, which had fallen from different causes, i.e., fire and wind, and has deprived the greater part of the southerly sides of this mountain of its green timber. Four miles up the mountain I found a spring and halted for the rear to come up and to let our horses rest and feed. In about two hours the rear of the party came up much fatigued, and horses more so. Several horses slipped and rolled down steep hills, which hurt them very much. The one which carried my desk and small trunk turned over and rolled down a mountain for 40 yards and lodged against a tree, broke the desk. The horse escaped and appeared but little hurt. Some others very much hurt. From this point I observed a range of high mountains covered with snow from S.E. to S.W. with their tops bald or void of timber.

After two hours delay we proceeded on up the mountain, steep and rugged as usual, more timber near the top. When we arrived at the top as we conceived we could find no water and concluded to camp and make use of the snow we found on the top to cook the remnants of our colt and make our supper. Evening very cold and cloudy. Two of our horses gave out, poor and too much hurt to proceed on and left in the rear. Nothing killed today except two pheasants.

From this mountain I could observe high rugged mountains in every direction as far as I could see. With the greatest exertion we could only make

12 miles up this mountain and encamped on the top of the mountain near a bank of old snow about three feet deep lying on the northern side of the mountain and in small banks on the top and level parts of the mountain. We melted the snow to drink and cook our horse flesh to eat.

September 16, 1805, Monday [Clark]
Began to snow about three hours before day and continued all day. The snow in the morning four inches deep on the old snow, and by night we found it from six to eight inches deep. I walked in front to keep the road and found great difficulty in keeping it, as in many places the snow had entirely filled up the track and obliged me to hunt several minutes for the track. At 12 o'clock we halted on the top of the mountain to warm and dry ourselves a little as well as to let our horses rest and graze a little on some long grass which I observed on the south. Knobs, steep hillsides and fallen timber continue today, and a thickly timbered country of eight different kinds of pine, which are so covered with snow that in passing through them we are continually covered with snow. I have been wet and as cold in every part as I ever was in my life. Indeed I was at one time fearful my feet would freeze in the thin moccasins which I wore. After a short delay in the middle of the day I took one man and proceeded on as fast as I could about six miles to a small branch passing to the right, halted and built fires for the party against their arrival, which was at dusk, very cold and much fatigued. We encamped at this branch in a thickly timbered bottom which was scarcely large enough for us to lie level, men all wet, cold and hungry. Killed a second colt which we all supped heartily on and thought it fine meat.

I saw four blacktail deer today before we set out which came up the mountain, and what is singular, snapped seven times at a large buck [*he means the gun failed to fire*]. It is singular as my gun has a steel frizzen and never snapped seven times before. In examining her found the flint loose. To describe the road of this day would be a repetition of yesterday except the snow, which made it much worse to proceed, as we had in many places to direct ourselves by the appearance of the rubbings of the packs against the trees, which have limbs quite low and bending downward. [*Clark is referring to the packs of the Indians who had recently moved over this trail.*]

September 17, 1805, Tuesday [Clark]
Cloudy morning. Our horses much scattered, which detained us until one o'clock p.m., at which time we set out. The falling snow and snow falling from

the trees kept us wet all the afternoon. Passed over several high rugged knobs and several drains and springs passing to the right, and passing on the ridge dividing the waters of two small rivers. Road excessively bad. Snow on the knobs, no snow in the valleys. Killed a few pheasants, which was not sufficient for our supper, which compelled us to kill something. A colt being the most useless part of our stock, he fell a prey to our appetites. The after part of the day fair. We made only 10 miles today. Two horses fell and hurt themselves very much. We encamped on the top of a high knob of the mountain at a run passing to the left. We proceeded on as yesterday, and with difficulty found the road.

September 18, 1805, Wednesday [Lewis]
Capt. Clark set out this morning to go ahead with six hunters. There being no game in these mountains, we concluded it would be better for one of us to take the hunters and hurry on to the level country ahead and there hunt and provide some provision while the other remained with and brought on the party. The latter of these was my part; accordingly I directed the horses to be gotten up early, being determined to force my march as much as the abilities of our horses would permit. The negligence of one of the party, Willard, who had a spare horse and not attending to him and bringing him up last evening was the cause of our detention this morning until half after eight a.m., when we set out. I sent Willard back to search for his horse and proceeded on with the party. At four in the evening he overtook us without the horse. We marched 18 miles this day and encamped on the side of a steep mountain. We suffered for water this day, passing one rivulet only; we were fortunate in finding water in a steep ravine about half a mile from our camp. This morning we finished the remainder of our last colt. We dined and supped on a scant proportion of portable soup, a few canisters of which, a little bear's oil and about 20 pounds of candles form our stock of provision, the only recourses being our guns and packhorses. The first is but a poor dependence in our present situation, where there is nothing upon earth except ourselves and a few small pheasants, small gray squirrels, and a blue bird of the vulture kind about the size of a turtle dove or jay bird. Our route lay along the ridge of a high mountain, course S. 20° W., 18 miles. Used the snow for cooking.

Clark, moving ahead, made 32 miles and camped on a creek he named Hungry Creek, as they had nothing at all to eat.

September 19, 1805, Thursday [Lewis]

Set out this morning a little after sunrise and continued our route about the same course of yesterday, or S. 20° W., for six miles, when the ridge terminated and we to our inexpressible joy discovered a large tract of prairie country lying to the S.W. and widening as it appeared to extend to the West. Through that plain, the Indian informed us, the Columbia River, in which we were in search, ran. This plain appeared to be about 60 miles distant, but our guide assured us that we should reach its borders tomorrow. The appearance of this country, our only hope for subsistence, greatly revived the spirits of the party, already reduced and much weakened for the want of food. The country is thickly covered with a very heavy growth of pine, of which I have enumerated eight distinct species. After leaving the ridge we ascended and descended several steep mountains in the distance of six miles further, when we struck a creek about 15 yards wide. Our course being S. 35° W. we continued our route 6 miles along the side of this creek upwards, passing two of its branches which flowed in from the N., first at the place we struck the creek and the other three miles further.

The road was excessively dangerous along this creek, being a narrow rocky path generally on the side of a steep precipice, from which in many places if either man or horse were precipitated they would inevitably be dashed in pieces. Frazer's horse fell from this road in the evening, and rolled with his load near a hundred yards into the creek. We all expected that the horse was killed but to our astonishment, when the load was taken off him, he arose to his feet and appeared to be but little injured. In 20 minutes he proceeded with his load. This was the most wonderful escape I ever witnessed. The hill down which he rolled was almost perpendicular and broken by large, irregular and broken rocks. The course of this is creek upward due W. We encamped on the starboard side of it in a little ravine, having traveled 18 miles over a very bad road. We took a small quantity of portable soup and retired to rest much fatigued. Several of the men are unwell of the dysentery. Breakings out, or irruptions of the skin, have also been common with us for some time.

Clark, up ahead, proceeded up Hungry Creek for six miles to a glade, where the men found a horse and begged to kill it for food. Clark gave permission and while one part of them was skinning and preparing the horse, the others went hunting and found not a single animal track of any kind. After satisfying their own hunger the party hung up the bulk of the horse for Lewis and the rest to find.

September 20, 1805, Friday [Clark]

I set out early and proceeded on through a country as rugged as usual, passed over a low mountain into the forks of a large creek, which I kept down two miles, and ascended a steep mountain, leaving the creek to our left hand. Passed the head of several drains on a dividing ridge, and at 12 miles descended the mountain to a level pine country. Proceeded on through a beautiful country for three miles to a small plain in which I found many Indian lodges. At the distance of one mile from the lodges I met three Indian boys; when they saw me they ran and *hid* themselves in the grass. I dismounted, gave my gun and horse to one of the men, searched in the grass and found two of the boys, gave them small pieces of ribbon and sent them forward to the village. Soon after a man came out to meet me with great caution and conducted us to a large spacious lodge, which he told me by signs was the lodge of his great chief, who had set out three days previous with all the warriors of the nation to war in a southwest direction and would return in 15 or 18 days. The few men that were left in the village and great numbers of women gathered around me with much apparent sign of fear, and appeared pleased. They gave us a small piece of buffalo meat, some dried salmon, berries and roots in different states, some round and much like an onion, which they call quamash. Of this they make bread and soup. The bread or cake is called Pas-she-co sweet. They also gave us the bread made of this root, all of which we ate heartily. I gave them a few small articles as presents, and proceeded on with a chief to his village two miles in the same plain, where we were treated kindly in their way and continued with them all night.

Those two villages consist of about 30 double lodges, but few men, a number of women and children. They call themselves *Cho pun-nish* or *Pierced Noses*; their dialect appears very different from the Flatheads, although originally the same people. They are darker than the Flatheads I have seen. Their dress is similar, with more beads—white and blue principally—brass and copper in different forms, shells, and wear their hair in the same way. They are large portly men, small women and handsome featured. Immense quantities of the quamash or *Pas-shi-co* root gathered and in piles about the plain. Those roots grow much like an onion in marshy places. The seeds are in triangular shells on the stalk. They sweat them in the following manner: dig a large hole three feet deep, cover the bottom with split wood, on the top of which they lay small stones of about three or four inches thick, a second layer of split wood, and set the whole on fire, which heats the stones. After the fire is extinguished they lay grass and mud mixed on the stones. On that dry grass, which supports the Pas-shi-co root, a thin coat of the same grass is laid on top, a small fire is kept when necessary in the center of the kiln, etc.

I find myself very unwell all the evening from eating the fish and roots too freely. Sent out hunters. They killed nothing. Saw some signs of deer.

Lewis, meanwhile, found the remainder of the horse Clark had left for them and they dined on it. One of the packhorses went missing; Lewis sent LePage, who was in charge of it, back for it, but he returned without it, so he sent two men back this time. The horse was important; it was carrying not only trade goods but all of Lewis's winter clothing. Lewis took note of several new birds, including the Steller's jay and three new species of pheasant or grouse. The Pierced Nose people are, of course, the Nez Perce. The roots Clark was eating were camas roots, a staple of Indian diets in the Northwest. Lewis was two days behind Clark.

September 21, 1805, Saturday [Clark]
A fine morning. Sent out all the hunters in different directions to hunt deer. I myself delayed with the chief to prevent suspicion and to collect by signs as much information as possible about the river and country in advance. The chief drew me a kind of chart of the river, and informed me that a greater chief than himself was fishing at the river half a day's march from his village, called the Twisted Hair, and that the river forked a little below his camp and at a long distance below; and below two large forks, one from the left and the other from the right, the river passed through the mountains, at which place was a great fall of the water passing through the rocks. At those falls white people lived, from whom they procured the white beads and brass, etc., which the women wore.

A chief of another band visited me today and smoked a pipe. I gave my handkerchief and a silver cord with a little tobacco to those chiefs. The hunters all returned without anything. I purchased as much provisions as I could with what few things I chanced to have in my pockets, such as salmon, bread, roots and berries, and sent one man, R. Fields, with an Indian to meet Capt. Lewis, and at four o'clock p.m. set out to the river. Met a man at dark on his way from the river to the village whom I hired and gave the neck handkerchief of one of the men to pilot me to the camp of the Twisted Hair. We did not arrive at the camp of the Twisted Hair but opposite until half past 11 o'clock p.m. Found at this camp five squaws and three children. My guide called to the chief, who was encamped with two others on a small island in the river. He soon joined me. I found him a cheerful man with apparent sincerity. I gave him a medal etc., and smoked until one o'clock a.m. and went to sleep. The country from the mountains to the river hills is a level, rich, beautiful pine country badly watered, thinly timbered and covered with grass. The weather very warm after descending into the low country. The river hills are very high and steep, small bottoms to this little river, which is Flathead [*it is now called the Clearwater*] and is 160 yards wide and shoaly. This river is the one we killed the first colt on near a fishing weir.

I am very sick today and puke, which relieves me.

Lewis was having trouble collecting his horses in the morning; the road was still full of fallen timber, slowing them down, and they were all weak from hunger. The next day, Sunday, September 22, he became irritated when one of the men again neglected to hobble his horses overnight and they could not get started until after eleven. Then Reuben Fields, whom Clark had sent to meet them with some food, came up and they stopped to eat. At five that afternoon they arrived at the Nez Perce encampment, and in his last entry until November 29 Clark writes, "The pleasure I now felt in having triumphed over the Rocky Mountains and descending once more to a level and fertile country where there was every rational hope of finding a comfortable subsistence for myself and party can be more readily conceived than expressed, nor was the flattering prospect of the final success of the expedition less pleasing."

September 22, 1805, Sunday [Clark]
A very warm day. The hunter Shields killed three deer this morning. I left them on the island and set out with the chief and his son on a young horse for the village, at which place I expected to meet Capt. Lewis. This young horse in fright threw himself and me three times on the side of a steep hill and hurt my hip much. Caught a colt which we found on the road and I rode it for several miles until we saw the chief's horses. He caught one and we arrived at his village at sunset, and himself and myself walked up to the second village where I found Capt. Lewis and the party encamped, much fatigued, and hungry, much rejoiced to find something to eat, of which they appeared to partake plentifully. I cautioned them of the consequences of eating too much, etc.

The plains appeared covered with spectators viewing the white men and the articles which we had. Our party weakened and much reduced in flesh as well as strength. The horse I left hung up they received at a time they were in great want, and the supply I sent by R. Fields proved timely and gave great encouragement to the party with Capt. Lewis. He lost three horses, one of which belonged to our guide. Those Indians stole out of R. F.'s [*Reuben Fields's*] shot pouch his knife, wipers, compass and steel, which we could not procure from them. We attempted to have some talk with those people but could not for the want of an interpreter through which we could speak. We were compelled to converse altogether by signs.

I got the Twisted Hair to draw the river from his camp down, which he did with great cheerfulness on a white elk skin, from the first fork, which is a few miles below, to the large fork on which the *Shoshone* or Snake Indians fish, south two sleeps. To a large river which falls in on the N.W. side and into which the *Clark's River* empties itself is five sleeps. From the mouth of that river to the *falls* is five sleeps. At the falls he places establishments of white people and informs us that great numbers of Indians reside on all those forks as well as the main river; one other Indian gave me a like account of the country. Some few drops of rain this evening. I procured maps of the country and river with the situation of Indian towns from several men of note separately, which varied but little.

September 23, 1805, Monday [Clark]
We assembled the principal men as well as the chiefs and by signs informed them where we came from, where bound, our wish to inculcate peace and good understanding between all the red people, etc., which appeared to satisfy them much. We then gave two other medals to other chiefs of bands, a flag to the *Twisted Hair,* left a flag and handkerchief to the grand chief, gave a shirt to the *Twisted Hair* and a knife and handkerchief with a small piece of tobacco to each. Finding that those people gave no provisions today we determined to purchase with our small articles of merchandise; accordingly we purchased all we could, such as roots dried, in bread, and in their raw state, berries of red haws and *fish* and in the evening set out and proceeded on to the second village two miles distant, where we also purchased a few articles, all amounting to as much as our weak horses could carry to the river. Capt. Lewis and two men very sick this evening, my hip very painful; the men trade a few old tin canisters for dressed elk skin to make themselves shirts. At dark a hard wind from the S.W. accompanied with rain which lasted half an hour. The *Twisted Hair* invited Capt. Lewis and myself to his lodge,

which was nothing more than pine bushes and bark, and gave us some broiled dried *salmon* to eat. Great numbers about us all night. At this village the women were busily employed in gathering and drying the *Pas-she-co* root, of which they had great quantities dug in piles.

September 24, 1805, Tuesday [Clark]
A fine morning. Collected our horses, sent J. Colter back to hunt the horses lost in the mountains and bring up some shot left behind, and at 10 o'clock we all set out for the river and proceeded on by the same route I had previously traveled, and at sunset we arrived at the island on which I found the *Twisted Hair* and formed a camp on a large island a little below. Capt. Lewis was scarcely able to ride on a gentle horse which was furnished by the chief. Several men so unwell that they were compelled to lie on the side of the road for some time, others obliged to be put on horses. I gave Rush's pills to the sick this evening. Several Indians follow us.

September 25, 1805, Wednesday [Clark]
A very hot day. Most of the party complaining and two of our hunters left here on the 22nd very sick. They had killed only two bucks in my absence. I set out early with the chief and two young men to hunt some trees calculated to build canoes, as we had previously determined to proceed on by water. I was furnished with a horse and we proceeded on down the river. Crossed a creek at one mile from the right, very rocky, which I call Rock Dam Creek, and passed down on the N. side of the river to a fork from the north which is about the same size and affords about the same quantity of water with the other fork. We halted about an hour; one of the young men took his gig and killed six fine salmon. Two of them were roasted and we ate. Two canoes came up loaded with the furniture and provisions of two families. Those canoes are long, steady and without much rake. I crossed the south fork and proceeded up on the south side, the most of the way through a narrow pine bottom in which I saw fine timber for canoes. One of the Indian canoes with two men with poles set out from the forks at the same time I did and arrived at our camp on the island within 15 minutes of the same time I did, notwithstanding three rapids which they had to draw the canoe through in the distance. When I arrived at camp found Capt. Lewis very sick, several men also very sick. I gave some salts and tartar emetic; we determined to go to where the best timber was and there form a camp.

SUMMARY

SEPTEMBER 26 TO OCTOBER 20, 1805

It was almost always Clark's method to give laxatives to men who were suffering from digestive tract problems, which only made matters worse. It's a wonder the men recovered. The problem was almost certainly the abrupt change in diet, from horsemeat to salmon and quamash roots (today known as camas). Bacteria on the dried salmon may also have been a source of their problems. They all did eventually recover—even Lewis, who was quite ill—but for days all Clark mentions is how sick the men are. On October 1 some of them tell him that eating the dried salmon is like taking a dose of salts. On the second they killed a horse to feed those men who were well enough to work on the new canoes that would take them to the Pacific. "We have nothing to eat but roots, which give the men violent pains in their bowels," writes Clark, "after eating much of them." The area held no game. The hunters went out every day but found nothing.

On September 26 they moved to the junction of the Clearwater with the North Fork of the Clearwater, in what is now northern Idaho, and began to build dugouts: four large ones and a smaller one to scout ahead on the difficult rapids. Their tools were not adequate, and they used the Indian method of burning out the insides of the logs. They were making the canoes out of ponderosa pine logs. Those who could work got meat whenever it was available, to help them keep up their strength. Colter, who had been sent back for stray horses, came back with a deer. Indians were constantly around, watching them, perhaps offering advice. On the fifth of October they collected all their 38 horses and branded them, leaving them with the Nez Perce, who promised to take care of them until the expedition's return in the spring. The next day they cached their saddles, along with some ammunition and powder. The diet was no better than before. Clark writes on the fifth that he and Captain Lewis had eaten a "supper of roots boiled, which swelled us in such a manner that we were scarcely able to breathe for several hours."

On October 7 they set out down the river the Nez Perce called, below the forks where they had camped, the Kooskooskee. They passed 10 rapids that day and 15 the next, and so it would go until they came to tidewater. The party met rapids after rapids, first on the Clearwater and then the Snake, with the Indians who lined the rivers watching them and often helping pilot them through. On the eighth, after making 16 miles, one of the canoes hit a rock in one of the rapids and sank. One man was a little hurt but everything was wet. The Indians, Clark comments, "appeared disposed to give us every assistance in their power during our distress." The next day, while they lay over to dry the contents of the canoe and make repairs, their Shoshone guide, Old Toby, and his son slipped away without taking any pay. The captains thought they should send a man after them and bring them back to get paid, but one of the Nez Perce chiefs with them advised against it. "His nation," he said, "would take his things from him before he passed their camps."

They left again on the 10th. They were buying dogs of the Indians now, pre-ferring the flesh of dogs to the dried flesh of salmon. Clark complained because he would not eat dog flesh. They reached the Snake River on the 10th, believing it was the Salmon River, which Clark had reconnoitered in the mountains a few weeks before. They were in the Columbian Plain now, a vast treeless basin in the rain shadow of the Cascades in eastern Washington. Here there was no game, no wood, only rapids and Indians. Clark does not write as fully about tribal customs and dress as Lewis, but he, too, is observant. He describes the dress of the Nez Perce and is interested in a sweat lodge they discover, a hole dug out of the bank of the river some six or eight feet deep. The Indians enter by this hole and take in rocks heated in a fire, then throw water on the rocks until the steam reaches the desired temperature. Nicholas Biddle, in his edition of the journals, describes a steam bath of this sort as something the Indians never take alone. It is, he says, "so essentially a social amusement that to decline going in to bathe when invited by a friend is one of the highest indignities which can be offered to him." On the 12th they came to a very bad rapid two miles long with many twists and turns; on the 13th they ran it without incident. They were in a hurry. "We should make more portages," Clark remarked, "if the season was not so far advanced and time precious with us." On the 14th one of the canoes turned broadside to the water on a rock and sank. They lost a number of articles. The next day they dried what was left as well as they could, then set out again. Lewis went out for a walk on the plains; there was nothing to be seen. Clark described the countryside as "wavering"; it was not level, that is, but undulating, and barren, and there was no driftwood. That night for the first time they took wood from an Indian house site that had been abandoned for the season in order to cook their food.

They were entering the territory of tribes now called the Yakima and Palouse and another called the Wanapam, all of whom lived as the Nez Perce did on salmon and roots and occasional game. On the 16th 200 men gathered around them, singing and dancing; they went through the usual ceremonies, giving the chiefs medals, shirts, handkerchiefs, speaking to them in sign language of their friendly intentions. This was the day the expedition reached the Columbia River. It must have been a moving moment, but Clark does not mention it.

On the 17th he took the small canoe and went up the Columbia some eight or nine miles, noting the large quantities of dead salmon in the river and along the banks. Not knowing the life cycle of salmon, he had no explanation for the phenomenon. Clark's entry for this day is full of information about the local Indians. These were true flatheads; they used a board to flatten the heads of their infants as they were growing, forming a straight line from the nose to the crown of the head. This was thought a mark of beauty. He describes their dress, notes that the men and women share the work a bit more fairly than in most tribes, and says they respect old people. "I observed an old woman in one of the lodges which I entered," he says; "she was entirely blind as I was informed by signs, had lived more than 100 winters. She occupied the best position in the house and when she spoke great attention was paid to what she said."

The expedition left on the 18th after buying 40 dogs from the Indians. They passed more rapids, saw Mount Hood in the distance, and passed more Indian lodges and more Indians drying salmon for the winter. On the 19th Clark, walking ahead of the boats on one of them, saw what he took to be Mount St. Helens but it was in fact Mount Adams. Later, in the small canoe, Clark and three of the men landed and approached some Indian lodges. He found the people terrified at his presence. Instead he gave them whatever was in his pockets, smoked with them, and took their hands, trying to convince them of his friendly intentions.

Sacagawea was a help, for "no woman," as Clark notes, "accompanies a war party." One of the two chiefs accompanying Lewis and Clark explained who the strangers were. That evening, Cruzatte "played on the violin," writes Clark, "which pleased and astonished those wretches, who are badly clad." It is clear that he pities them.

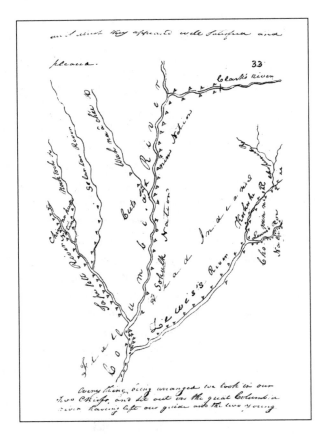

Confluence of Snake and Columbia Rivers drawn by Clark, circa October 1805

OCTOBER 21 TO NOVEMBER 7, 1805

October 21, 1805, Monday [Clark]

A very cool morning, wind from the S.W. We set out very early and proceeded on. Last night we could not collect more dry willows, the only fuel, than was barely sufficient to cook supper, and not a sufficiency to cook breakfast this morning. Passed a small island at five and a half miles, a large one eight miles in the middle of the river, some rapid water at the head and eight lodges of natives opposite its lower point on the starboard side. We came to at those lodges, bought some wood and breakfast. Those people received us with great kindness, and examined us with much attention, their employment, custom, dress and appearance similar to those above. They speak the same language. Here we saw two scarlet and a blue cloth blanket, also a sailor's jacket [*evidence of white men's presence on the Pacific coast*]. The dress of the men of this tribe only a short robe of deer or goat skin, and that of the women is a short piece of dressed skin which falls from the neck so as to cover the front of the body as low as the waist, a short robe, which is of one deer or antelope skin, and a flap around their waist and drawn tight between their legs. Their ornaments are but few.

We got from those people a few pounded roots, fish and *acorns* of the white oak. Those acorns they make use of as food raw and roasted and inform us they procure them of the natives who live near the falls below, which place they all describe by the term *Timm*. At two miles lower passed a rapid, large rocks stringing into the river of large size. Opposite to this rapid on the starboard shore are situated *two* lodges of the natives drying fish. Here we halted a few minutes to examine the rapid before we entered it, which was our constant custom, and at all that were very dangerous put out all who could not swim to walk around. After passing this rapid we proceeded on, passed another rapid at five miles lower down. Above this rapid *five* lodges of Indians fishing. Above this rapid many large rocks on each side at some distance from shore. At one mile passed an island close to the starboard side, below which are *two* lodges of natives. A little below is a bad rapid crowded with huge rocks scattered in every direction, which renders the passage very difficult. A little above this rapid on the larboard side immense piles of rocks appear, as if slipped from the cliffs under which they lay. Passed a great number of rocks in every direction scattered in the river. Five lodges a little below on the starboard side, and one lodge on an island near the starboard shore, opposite to which is a very bad rapid, through which we found much difficulty in passing. The river is crowded with rocks in every direction.

After passing this difficult rapid to the mouth of a small river on the larboard side, 40 yards wide, it discharges but little water at this time and appears to take its source in the open plains to the S.E. From this place I perceived some few small pines on the tops of the high hills and bushes in the hollows. Immediately above and below this little river commences a rapid which is crowded with large rocks in every direction, the passage both crooked and difficult. We halted at a lodge to examine those numerous islands of rock which appeared to extend many miles below. Great numbers of Indians came in canoes to view us at this place. After passing this rapid, which we accomplished without loss, winding through between the huge rocks for about two miles. Immediately below the last rapids there are four lodges of Indians on the starboard side. Proceeded on about two miles lower and landed and encamped near *five* lodges of natives drying fish. Those are the relations of those at the *great falls*; they are poor and have but little wood, which they bring up the river from the falls as they say. We purchased a little wood to cook our dog meat and fish. Those people did not receive us at first with the same cordiality of those above. They appear to be the same nation, speak the same language with a little corruption of many words. They dress and fish in the same way; all of them have *pierced noses* and the men when dressed wear a long tapered piece of shell or bead put through the nose. This part of the river is furnished with fine springs, which either rise high up the sides of the hills or on the bottom near the river, and run into the river. The hills are high and rugged, a few scattering trees to be seen on them, either small pine or scrubby white oak.

The probable reason of the Indians residing on the starboard side of this as well as the waters of Lewis's River [*the Snake River*] is their fear of the *Snake Indians* who reside, as the natives say, on a great river to the south and are at war with those tribes. One of the old chiefs who accompany us pointed out a place on the larboard side where they had a great battle, not many years ago, in which many were killed on both sides.

One of our party, J. Collins, presented us with some very good *beer* made of the *Pa-shi-co-quar-mash* bread, which bread is the remains of what was laid in as stores of provisions at the first Flathead or Cho-pun-nish nation at the head of the Kooskooskee River, which by being frequently wet, molded and soured. We made 33 miles today.

October 22, 1805, Tuesday [Clark]
A fine morning, calm and fair. We set out at nine o'clock, passed a very bad rapid at the head of an island close under the starboard side. Above this rapid on the starboard side are six lodges of natives drying fish. At nine miles passed a bad rapid at the head of a large island of high and uneven rocks jutting over the water. A small island in a starboard bend opposite the upper point, on which I counted 20 parcels of dried and pounded fish. On the main starboard shore opposite to this island, *five* lodges of Indians are situated. Several Indians in canoes killing fish with gigs. Opposite the center of this island of rocks, which is about four miles long, we discovered the entrance of a large river on the larboard side which appeared to come from the S.E.

We landed at some distance above the mouth of this river and Capt. Lewis and myself set out to view it [*the Deschutes River in Oregon*] above its mouth, as our route was intercepted by a deep narrow channel which runs out of this river into the Columbia a little below the place we landed, leaving a high, dry, rich island of about 400 yards wide and 800 yards long. Here we separated; I proceeded on to the river and struck it at the foot of a very considerable rapid. Here I beheld an immense body of water compressed in a narrow channel of about 200 yards in width, foaming over rocks, many of which presented their tops above the water, when at this place Capt. Lewis joined me, having delayed on the way to examine a root of which the natives had been digging great quantities in the bottoms of this river. At about two miles above, this river appears to be confined between two high hills, below which it is divided by numbers of large rocks and small islands covered with a low growth of timber, and has a rapid as far as the narrows. Three small islands in the mouth of this river. This river having no Indian name that we could find out, except "the river on which the Snake Indians live," we think it best to leave the naming of it until our return.

We proceeded on past the mouth of this river, at which place it appears to discharge one quarter as much water as runs down the Columbia. At *two* miles below this river passed eight lodges on the lower point of the rock island aforesaid. At those lodges we saw large logs of wood which must have been rafted down the *To war-ne hi ooks* River [*according to Moulton, this would be the river Clark had just described, the present-day Deschutes, given this name after they had returned this way*]. Below this island on the main starboard shore are 16 lodges of natives; here we landed a few minutes to smoke. About half a mile lower passed six more lodges on the same side and six miles below the upper mouth of *Towarnehiooks* River the commencement of the pitch of the great falls; opposite on the starboard side are 17 lodges of the natives.

We landed and walked down, accompanied by an old man, to view the falls and the best route to make a portage, which we soon discovered was much nearest on the starboard side, and the distance 1,200 yards—one third of the way on a rock, about 200 yards over a loose sand collected in a hollow blown by the winds from the bottoms below, which was disagreeable to pass, as it was steep and loose.

At the lower part of those rapids we arrived at five large lodges of natives drying and preparing fish for market. They gave us filberts and berries to eat. We returned, dropped down to the head of the rapids, and took every article except the canoes across the portage, where I had formed a camp on an eligible situation for the protection of our stores from theft, which we were more fearful of than their arrows. We dispatched two men to examine the river on the opposite side, who reported that the canoes could be taken down a narrow channel on the opposite side after a short portage at the head of the falls, at which place the Indians take over their canoes. Indians assisted us over the portage with our heavy articles on their horses. The waters are divided into several narrow channels which pass through a hard black rock forming islands of rocks at this stage of the water.

On those islands of rocks as well as at and about their lodges I observe great numbers of stacks of pounded salmon neatly preserved in the following manner, i.e., after it is sufficiently dried it is pounded between two stones fine and put into a species of basket neatly made of grass and rushes of better than two feet long and one foot diameter, which basket is lined with the skin of salmon stretched and dried for the purpose. In these it is pressed down as hard as possible. When full they secure the open part with the fish skins, across which they fasten through the loops of the basket that part very securely, and then on a dry situation they set those baskets, the corded part up. Their common custom is to set seven as close as they can stand and five on top of them, and secure them with mats, which are wrapped around them and made fast with cords and covered also with mats. Those 12 baskets of from 90 to 100 pounds each form a stack. Thus preserved those fish may be kept sound and sweet several years, as those people inform me. Great quantities as they inform us are sold to the white people who visit the mouth of this river, as well as to the natives below.

On one of those islands I saw several tombs but did not visit them. The principal chiefs of the bands residing about this place are out hunting in the mountains to the S.W. No Indians reside on the S.W. side of this river for fear of the Snake Indians, who are at war with the tribes on this river. They represent the Snake Indians as being very numerous and residing in a great number of villages on Towarnehiooks River, which falls in six miles above on the larboard side and reaches a great ways and is large a little above its mouth, at which part it is not intercepted with rapids. They inform us that one considerable rapid and many small ones are in that river, and that the Snake live on salmon, and they go to war to their first villages in 12 days. The course, they pointed out, is S.E. or to the S. of S.E. We are visited by great numbers of Indians today to view us. We purchased a dog for supper, some fish, and with difficulty procured as much wood as cooked supper, which we also purchased. We made 19 miles today.

October 23, 1805, Wednesday [Clark]
A fine morning. I with the great part of the men crossed in the canoes to the opposite side above the falls and hauled them across the portage of 457 yards, which is on the larboard side and certainly the best side to pass the canoes. I then descended through a narrow channel of about 150 yards wide forming a kind of half circle in its course of a mile to a pitch of eight feet in which the channel is divided by two large rocks. At this place we were obliged to let the canoes down by strong ropes of elk skin which we had for the purpose.

One canoe in passing this place got loose by the cords breaking and was caught by the Indians below. I accomplished this necessary business and landed safe with all the canoes at our camp below the falls by three o'clock p.m. nearly covered with fleas, which were so thick amongst the straw and fish skins at the upper part of the portage, at which place the natives had been camped not long since, that every man of the party was obliged to strip naked during the time of taking over the canoes that they might have an opportunity of brushing the fleas off their legs and bodies.

Great numbers of *sea otters* in the river below the falls. I shot one in the narrow channel today which I could not get. [*These were not sea otters, which are not found except in salt water, but probably harbor seals.*] Great numbers of Indians visit us both from above and below. One of the old chiefs who had accompanied us from the head of the river informed us that he heard the Indians say that the nation below intended to kill us. We examined all the arms, complete the ammunition to 100 rounds. The natives leave us earlier this evening than usual, which gives a shadow of confirmation to the information of our old chief. As we are at all times and places on our guard, we are under no greater apprehension than is common.

We purchased eight small fat dogs for the party to eat. The natives not being fond of selling their good fish compels us to make use of dog meat for food, the flesh of which the most of the party have become fond of from the habit of using it for some time past.

I observed on the beach near the Indian lodges two beautiful canoes of different shape and size to what we had seen above, wide in the middle and tapering to each end. On the bow curious figures were cut in the wood. Capt. Lewis went up to the lodges to see those canoes and exchanged our smallest canoe for one of them by giving a hatchet and a few trinkets to the owner, who informed us that he purchased it of a white man below for a horse. These canoes are neater made than any I have ever seen and calculated to ride the waves and carry immense burdens. They are dug thin and are supported by cross pieces of about 1 inch in diameter, tied with strong bark through holes in the sides. Our two old chiefs appeared very uneasy this evening.

October 24, 1805, Thursday [Clark]
The morning fair after a beautiful night. The natives approached us this morning with great caution. Our two old chiefs expressed a desire to return to their band from this place, saying "that they could be of no further service to

us, as their nation extended no further down the river than those falls, and as the nation below had expressed hostile intentions against us, would certainly kill them, particularly as they had been at war with each other." We requested them to stay with us *two* nights longer, and we would see the nation below and make a peace between them. They replied they "were anxious to return and see our horses." We insisted on their staying with us two nights longer, to which they agreed. Our views were to detain those chiefs with us until we should pass the next falls, which we were told were very bad, and at no great distance below, that they might inform us of any designs of the natives, and if possible to bring about a peace between them and the tribes below.

The first pitch of these falls is 20 feet perpendicular, then passing through a narrow channel for one mile to a rapid of about 18 feet fall, below which the water had no perceptible fall but is very rapid. It may be proper here to remark that from some obstruction below, the cause of which we have not yet learned, the water in high floods rises below these falls nearly to a level with the water above the falls, the marks of which can be plainly traced around the falls. At that stage of the water the salmon must pass up which abound in such great numbers above. [*The expedition, it should be noted, has reached the upper portion of the Dalles, famous, before the construction of the Dalles Dam, which inundated the area, for its difficulty.*] Below those falls are salmon, trout, and great numbers of the heads of a species of trout smaller than the salmon. Those fish they catch out of the salmon season, and are at this time in the act of burying those which they had dried for winter food. The mode of burying those fish is in holes of various sizes, lined with straw, on which they lay fish skins in which they enclose the fish, which are laid very close, and then covered with earth of about 12 or 15 inches thick. Capt. Lewis and three men crossed the river to the opposite side to view the falls, which he had not yet taken a full view of.

At nine o'clock a.m. I set out with the party and proceeded on down a rapid stream of about 400 yards wide. At two and a half miles the river widened into a large basin to the starboard side on which there are five lodges of Indians. Here a tremendous black rock presented itself, high and steep, appearing to choke up the river, nor could I see where the water passed further than the current was drawn with great velocity to the larboard side of this rock, at which place I heard a great roaring [*Clark seems to be saying that he could only see the current move downstream on the left side of this large rock or cliff, and he could not see how far this narrow passage ran*]. I landed at the lodges and the natives went with me to the top of this rock, which makes from the starboard side, from the top of which I could see the difficulties we had to pass for several miles below. At this place the water of this great river is compressed into a channel between two rocks not exceeding 45 yards wide and continues for a quarter of a mile, when it again widens to 200 yards and continues this width for about two miles, when it is again intercepted by rocks. This obstruction in the river accounts for the water in high floods rising to such a height at the last falls. The whole of the current of this great river must at all stages pass through this narrow channel of 45 yards wide.

As the portage of our canoes over this high rock would be impossible with our strength, and the only danger in passing through those narrows was the whorls and swells arising from the compression of the water, and which I thought (as also our principal waterman, Pierre Cruzatte) by good steering we could pass down safe, I determined to pass through this place, notwithstanding the horrid appearance of this agitated gut swelling, boiling and whirling in every direction—which from the top of the rock did not appear as bad as when I was in it. However, we passed safe to the astonishment of all the Indians of the last lodges who viewed us from the top of the rock.

Passed one lodge below this rock and halted on the starboard side to view a very bad place, the current divided by two islands of rocks, the lower of them large and in the middle of the river. This place being very bad I sent by land all the men who could not swim and such articles as were most valuable to us, such as papers, guns and ammunition, and proceeded down with the canoes two at a time to a village of 20 wood houses in a deep bend to the starboard side, below which a rugged black rock rose about 20 feet higher than the common high floods of the river, with several dry channels, which appeared to choke the river up quite across. This I took to be the second falls or the place the natives above call *timm*.

The natives of this village received me very kindly. One of them invited me into his house, which I found to be large and commodious, and the first wooden houses in which Indians have lived since we left those in the vicinity of the Illinois. They are scattered promiscuously on an elevated situation near a mound of about 30 feet above the common level, which mound has some remains of houses and has every appearance of being artificial. Those houses are about the same shape, size and form, 20 feet wide and 30 feet long, with one door raised 18 inches above ground. The doors are 29 and a half inches high and 14 wide, forming a half circle above. Those houses were sunk into the earth six feet; the roofs of them were supported by a ridgepole resting on three strong pieces of split timber, through one of which the door was cut. That and the walls, the tops of which were just above ground, supported a certain number of spars, which are covered with the bark of the white cedar, or *arbor vitae*, and the whole attached and secured by the fibers of the cedar. The eaves at or near the earth, the gable ends and side walls are secured with split boards, which are supported on the inner side with strong pieces of timber under the eaves. To keep those pieces erect and the earth from without pressing in on the boards, they are supported by strong posts at the corners, to which those poles were attached to give additional strength. Small openings were left above the ground, for the purpose, as I conjectured, of discharging their arrows at a besieging enemy. Light is admitted through an opening at the top, which also serves for the smoke to pass through. One half of those houses are appropriated for the storing away of dried and pounded fish, which is the principal food. The other part next the door is the part occupied by the natives, who have beds raised on either side, with a fireplace in the center of this space. Each house appeared to be occupied by about three families. That part which is appropriated for fish was crowded with that article, and a few baskets of berries. [*The kind of cedar house Clark is describing here is a Chinook house; they had passed out of the area controlled by Columbia Plateau Indians into the world of the Northwest Coast tribes.*]

I dispatched a sufficient number of the good swimmers back for the two canoes above the last rapid and with two men walked down three miles to examine the river over a bed of rocks, which the water at very high floods passes over. On those rocks I saw several large scaffolds on which the Indians dry fish. As this is out of season, the poles on which they dry those fish are tied up very securely in large bundles and put upon the scaffolds. I counted 107 stacks of dried pounded fish in different places on those rocks, which must have contained 10,000 pounds of neat fish.

The evening being late, I could not examine the river to my satisfaction. The channel is narrow and compressed for about two miles, when it widens into a deep basin to the starboard side, and again contracts into a narrow channel divided by a rock. I returned through a rocky open country infested with polecats to the village, where I met with Capt. Lewis, the two old chiefs who accompanied us, and the party and canoes who had all arrived safe, the canoes having taken in some water at the last rapids. Here we formed a camp near the village. The principal chief from the nation below with several of his men visited us, and afforded a favorable opportunity of bringing about a peace and good understanding between this chief and his people and the two chiefs who accompanied us, which we have the satisfaction to say we have accomplished. We have every reason to believe that those two bands or nations are and will be on the most friendly terms with each other. Gave this great chief a medal and some other articles, with which he was much pleased. Pierre Cruzatte played on the *violin* and the men danced, which delighted the natives, who show every civility toward us. We smoked with those people until late at night, when every one retired to rest.

October 25, 1805, Friday [Clark]
A cool morning. Capt. Lewis and myself walked down to see the place the Indians pointed out as the worst place in passing through the gut, which we found difficult of passing without great danger, but as the portage was impracticable with our large canoes, we concluded to make a portage of our most valuable articles and run the canoes through. Accordingly, on our return we divided the party, some to take over the canoes and others to take our stores across a portage of a mile to a place on the channel below this bad whorl and suck. With some others I had fixed on the channel with ropes to throw out to any who should unfortunately meet with difficulty in passing through. Great numbers of Indians viewing us from the high rocks under which we had to pass. The three first canoes passed through very well, the fourth nearly filled with water, the last passed through by taking in a little water. Thus safely below what I conceived to be the worst part of this channel, I felt myself extremely gratified and pleased. We loaded the canoes and set out and had not proceeded more than two miles before the unfortunate canoe which filled crossing the bad place above ran against a rock and was in great danger of being lost. This channel is through a hard, rough black rock, from 50 to 100 yards wide, swelling and boiling in a most tremendous manner, several places on which the Indians inform me they take the salmon as fast as they wish. We passed through a deep basin to the starboard side of one mile, below which the river narrows and is divided by a rock. The current we found quite gentle. Here we met with our two old chiefs, who had been to a village below to smoke a friendly pipe, and at this place they met the chief and party from the village above on his return from hunting, all of whom were then crossing over their horses. We landed to smoke a pipe with this chief, whom we found

to be a bold, pleasing looking man of about 50 years of age dressed in a war jacket, a cap, leggings and moccasins. He gave us some meat, of which he had but little, and informed us he in his route met with a war party of Snake Indians from the great river of the S.E. which falls in a few miles above and had a fight. We gave this chef a medal, and had a parting smoke with our two faithful friends, the chiefs who accompanied us from the head of the river, who had purchased a horse each with two robes and intended to return on horse back. We proceeded on down, the water fine, rocks in every direction for a few miles, when the river widens and becomes a beautiful gentle stream of about half a mile wide. Great numbers of the sea otter [*again, these are seals*] about those narrows and both below and above. We came to under a high point of rocks on the larboard side below a creek of 20 yards wide and much water, as it was necessary to make some celestial observations. We formed our camp on the top of a high point of rocks, which forms a kind of fortification in the point between the river and the creek, with a boat guard. This situation we conceive well calculated for defense, and convenient to hunt under the feet of the mountains to the west and S.W. where timber of different kinds grows, and appears to be handsome coverts for the deer. Sent out hunters to examine for game. George Drouillard killed a small deer and saw much sign. I killed a goose in the creek, which was very fat. One of the guard saw a drum fish today, as he conceived. Our situation well calculated to defend ourselves from any designs of the natives, should they be inclined to attack us.

For the next two days the expedition lay over to dry out the supplies and repair the canoes, and to hunt; the hunters brought in five deer on the 26th. They continued to meet with the chiefs of the various villages they were passing, and the men continued to be plagued with fleas. The expedition was lying at the eastern edge of Chinook territory, and the captains noticed how different the languages were from the Indians immediately upstream.

October 28, 1805, Monday [Clark]
A cool windy morning. We loaded our canoes and set out at nine o'clock a.m. As we were about to set out three canoes from above and two from below came to view us. In one of those canoes I observed an Indian with round hat, jacket and wore his hair queued. We proceeded on, river enclosed on each side in high cliffs of about 90 feet of loose dark-colored rocks. At four miles we landed at a village of eight houses on the starboard side under

some rugged rocks. Those people call themselves *Chil-luckit-te-quaw*, live in houses similar to those described, speak a somewhat different language with many words the same and understand those in their neighborhood. Capt. Lewis took a vocabulary of this language.

I entered one of the houses in which I saw a British musket, a cutlass, and several brass tea kettles, of which they appeared very fond. Saw them boiling fish in baskets with stones [*these tribes were capable of weaving baskets that held water*]. I also saw figures of animals and men cut and painted on boards in one side of the house which they appeared to prize, but for what purpose I will not venture to say. Here we purchased five small dogs, some dried berries, and white bread made of roots. The wind rose and we were obliged to lie by all day at one mile below on the larboard side. We had not been long on shore before a canoe came up with a man, woman and two children, who had a few roots to sell. Soon after many others joined them from above. The wind which is the cause of our delay does not retard the motions of those people at all, as their canoes are calculated to ride the highest waves; they are built of white cedar or pine, very light, wide in the middle and tapered at each end, with aprons, and heads of animals carved on the bow, which is generally raised. Those people make great use of canoes, both for transportation and fishing; they also use bowls and baskets made of grass and splits to hold water and boil their fish and meat. Many of the natives of the last village came down, sat and smoked with us. Wind blew hard, accompanied with rain all evening. Our situation not a very good one for an encampment, but such as it is we are obliged to put up with, the harbor is a safe one. We encamped on the sand, wet and disagreeable. One deer killed this evening, and another wounded near our camp.

October 29, 1805, Tuesday [Clark]
A cloudy morning, wind from the west but not hard. We set out at daylight and proceeded on about *five* miles. Came to on the starboard side at a village of seven houses built in the same form and materials of those above. Here we found the chief we had seen at the long narrows named [*blank*]. We entered his lodge and he gave us to eat pounded fish, bread made of roots, filberts, and the berries of Saccacommis [*bearberry*]. We gave to each woman of the lodge a brace of ribbon, of which they were much pleased. Each of those houses may be calculated to contain eight men and 30 souls. They are hospitable and good humored, speak the same language as the inhabitants

of the last village. We call this the friendly village. I observed in the lodge of the chief sundry articles which must have been procured from the white people, such as a scarlet and blue cloth, sword, jacket and hat. I also observed two wide split boards with images on them cut and painted in imitation of a man. I pointed to this image and asked a man to what use he put them. He said something; the only word I understood was "good," and then stepped to the image and took out his bow and quiver to show me, and some other of his war implements, from behind it.

The chief then directed his wife to hand him his medicine bag, which he opened, and showed us 14 fingers, which he said were the fingers of his enemies which he had taken in war, and pointed to S.E. from which direction I concluded they were Snake Indians. This is the first instance I ever knew of the Indians taking any other trophy of their exploits off the dead bodies of their enemies except the scalp. The chief painted those fingers with several other articles which were in his bag red and securely put them back, having first made a short harangue, which I suppose was bragging of what he had done in war. We purchased 12 dogs and 4 sacks of fish, and some few acid berries.

After breakfast we proceeded on. The mountains are high on each side [*they were passing through the Cascades*], containing a scattering of pine, white oak and undergrowth, hillsides steep and rocky. At four miles lower we observed a small river falling in with great rapidity on the starboard side, below which is a village of 11 houses. Here we landed to smoke a pipe with the natives and examine the mouth of the river, which I found to be 60 yards wide, rapid and deep. The inhabitants of the village are friendly and cheerful. Those people inform us also as those at the last village that this little river is long and full of falls, no salmon pass up it, it runs from the N.N.E. *Ten* nations live on this river and its waters, on berries and what game they can kill with their bows and arrows.

We purchased four dogs and set out and proceeded on. The country on each side begins to be thicker timbered with pine and low white oak, very rocky and broken. Passed three large rocks in the river. The middle rock is large, long, and has several square vaults on it. We call this rocky island the sepulcher. The last river we passed we shall call the *Cataract* River from the number of falls which the Indians say is on it.

Passed two lodges of Indians a short distance below the Sepulcher Island on the starboard side, river wide; at four miles passed two houses on the starboard side, six miles lower passed four houses above the mouth of a small river 40 yards wide on the larboard side. A thick timbered bottom above and back of those houses. Those are the first houses which we have seen on the south side of the Columbia River, for fear of the approach of their common enemies, the Snake Indians. Passed 14 houses on the starboard side scattered on the bank. From the mouth of this little river, which we shall call Labiche River, the *falls mountain* [*Mount Hood*] is south and the top is covered with snow. One mile below we pass the mouth of a large rapid stream on the starboard side opposite to a large sandbar. In this creek the Indians above take their fish; here we saw several canoes, which induced us to call this Canoe Creek. It is 28 yards wide. About four miles lower and below the sandbar is a beautiful cascade falling over a rock of about 100 feet. A short distance lower passed four Indian houses on the larboard side in a timbered bottom, a few miles further on we came to at three houses on starboard side, back of which is a pond in which I saw great numbers of small swan. Capt. Lewis and I went into the houses of those people, who appeared somewhat surprised at first. Their houses are built on the same construction of those above, they speak the same language and dress in the same way, robes of the skins of wolves, deer, elk, wild cat, or lourcirvia [*lynx*] and fox. Also saw a mountain sheepskin, the wool of which is long, thick, and coarse, with long coarse hair on the top of the neck and back, something resembling the bristles of a goat. The skin was of white hair. Those animals, these people inform me by signs, live in the mountains among the rocks; their horns are small and straight. Otter skins are highly prized among those people, as well as those on the river above. They queue their hair, which is divided on each shoulder, and also wear small strips about their necks with the tail hanging down in front.

Those people gave us high-bush cranberries, bread made of roots, and roots; we purchased three dogs for the party to eat. We smoked with the men, all much pleased with the violin. Here the mountains are high on each side. Those to the larboard side have some snow on them at this time, more timber than above and of greater variety.

October 30, 1805, Wednesday [Clark]
A cool morning, a moderate rain all last night. After eating a partial breakfast of venison we set out. Passed several places where the rocks projected into the river and have the appearance of having separated from the mountains and fallen promiscuously into the river. Small niches are formed in the banks

below those projecting rocks, which is common in this part of the river. Saw 4 cascades caused by small streams falling from the mountains on the larboard side. A remarkable circumstance in this part of the river is, the stumps of pine trees are in many places at some distance in the river, and give every appearance of the river being dammed up below from some cause which I am not at this time acquainted with. The current of the river is also very gentle, not exceeding one and a half miles per hour and about three-quarters of a mile in width. Some rain. We landed above the mouth of a small river on the starboard side and dined. J. Shields killed a buck and Labiche three ducks. Here the river widens to about one mile, large sandbar in the middle. A great rock both in and out of the water, large stones or rocks are also promiscuously scattered about in the river.

This day we saw some few of the large buzzard [*California condor*]. Capt. Lewis shot at one. Those buzzards are much larger than any other of their species or the largest eagle, white under part of their wings. The bottoms above the mouth of this little river are rich, covered with grass and fern and are about three-quarters of a mile wide and rise gradually. Below the river the country rises with steep ascent. We call this little river New Timbered River from a species of ash that grows on its banks that is very large and different from any we had before seen, and a timber resembling the beech in bark and growth but different in its leaf, which is smaller and the tree smaller.

Passed many large rocks in the river and a large creek on the starboard side, in the mouth of which is an island; passed on the right of three islands near the starboard side, and landed on an island close under the starboard side at the head of the great chute, and a little below a village of eight large houses on a deep bend on the starboard side, and opposite two small islands immediately in the head of the chute, which islands are covered with pine. Many large rocks also in the head of the chute. Ponds back of the houses, and country low for a short distance. [*They had reached the Cascades of the Columbia, beyond which they would enter tidewater.*]

The day proved cloudy, dark, and disagreeable with some rain all day which kept us wet. The country a high mountain on each side thickly covered with timber, such as spruce, pine, cedar, oak, cotton, etc. I took two men and walked down three miles to examine the chute and river below, proceeded along an old Indian path, passed an old village at 1 mile on an elevated situation. This village contained very large houses built in a different form from any I had seen, and lately abandoned, and most of the boards put into a pond of water near the village, as I conceived to drown the fleas, which were immensely numerous about the houses. I found by examination that we must make a portage of the greater proportion of our stores two and a half miles, and the canoes we could haul over the rocks. I returned at dark. Capt. Lewis and five men had just returned from the village. Capt. Lewis informed me that he found the natives kind; they gave him berries, nuts and fish to eat; but he could get nothing from them in the way of information. The greater part of the inhabitants of this village were absent down the river some distance collecting roots. Capt. Lewis saw one gun and several articles which must have been procured from the white people. A wet disagreeable evening. The only wood we could get to burn on this little island on which we have encamped is the newly discovered *ash*, which makes a tolerable fire. We made 15 miles today.

October 31, 1805, Thursday [Clark]
A cloudy rainy disagreeable morning. I proceeded down the river to view with more attention the rapids we had to pass on the river below. The two men with me, Joseph Fields and Pierre Cruzatte, proceeded down to examine the rapids. The great chute which commenced at the island on which we encamped continued with great rapidity and force through a narrow channel, much compressed and interspersed with large rocks for half a mile. At a mile lower is a very considerable rapid, at which place the waves are remarkably high. We proceeded on in an old Indian path two and a half miles by land through a thick wood and hillside to the river where the Indians make a portage. From this place I dispatched Pierre Cruzatte, our principal water-man, back to follow the river and examine the practicability of the canoes passing, as the rapids appeared to continue down below as far as I could see.

I with Joseph Fields proceeded on. At a half mile below the end of the portage we passed a house where there had been an old town for ages past. As this house was old, decayed, and a place of fleas I did not enter it. About half a mile below this house in a very thick part of the woods are eight vaults which appeared closely covered and highly decorated with ornaments. Those vaults are all nearly the same size and form 8 feet square, five feet high, sloped a little so as to convey off the rain, made of pine or cedar boards closely connected and securely covered with wide boards, with a door left in the east side which is partially stopped with wide boards curiously engraved. In several of those vaults the dead bodies were wrapped up very securely in skins tied around with cords of grass and bark, laid on a mat, all east and west. Some of those vaults had as many as four bodies lying on the side of each other. The other vaults contain bones only. Some contained bones to the depth of four feet. On the tops and on poles attached to those vaults hung brass kettles and frying pans pierced through their bottoms, baskets, bowls of wood, seashells, skins, bits of cloth, hair, bags of trinkets and small pieces of bone, etc., and independent of the curious engravings and paintings on the boards which formed the vaults I observed several wooden images, cut in the figures of men and set up on the sides of the vaults all around. Some of those were so old and worn by time that they were nearly out of shape. I also observed the remains of vaults rotted entirely into the ground and covered with moss. This must be the burying place for many ages for the inhabitants of those rapids; the vaults are of the most lasting timber, pine and cedar.

I cannot say certainly that those natives worship those wooden idols as I have every reason to believe they do not, as they are set up in the most conspicuous parts of their houses and treated more like ornaments than objects of adoration.

At two miles lower and five below our camp I passed a village of four large houses abandoned by the natives with their doors barred up. I looked into those houses and observed as much property as is usual in the houses of those people, which induced me to conclude that they were at no great distance, either hunting or collecting roots to add to their winter subsistence. From a short distance below the vaults the mountain, which is but low on the starboard side, leaves the river and a level stony open bottom succeeds on the said starboard side for a great distance down. The mountains high and rugged on the larboard side. This open bottom is about two miles. A short distance below this village is a bad stony rapid and it appears to be the last in view. I observed at this lower rapid the remains of a large and ancient village which I could plainly trace by the sinks in which they had formed their houses, as also those in which they had buried their fish.

From this rapid to the lower end of the portage the river is crowded with rocks of various sizes, between which the water passes with great velocity, creating in many places large waves. An island which is situated near the larboard side occupies about half the distance, the lower point of which is at this rapid. Immediately below this rapid the high water passes through a narrow channel through the starboard bottom, forming an island of three miles long and one wide. I walked through this island, which I found to be very rich land and had every appearance of having been at some distant period cultivated. At this time it is covered with grass, interspersed with strawberry vines. I observed several places on this island where the natives had dug for roots and from its lower point I observed five Indians in a canoe below the upper point of an island near the middle of the river covered with tall timber, which induced me to believe that a village was at no great distance below. I could not see any rapids below in the extent of my view, which was for a long distance down the river, which from the last rapids widened and had every appearance of being affected by the tide.

I determined to return to camp 10 miles distant. A remarkable high detached rock stands in a bottom on the starboard side near the lower point of this island on the starboard side about 800 feet high and 400 paces around. We call it the Beacon Rock. A brook falls into the narrow channel that forms the Strawberry Island, which at this time has no running water but has every appearance of discharging immense torrents. Jo. Fields shot a sandhill crane. I returned by the same route on an Indian path, passing up on the N.W. side of the river to our camp at the great chute. Found several Indians from the village; I smoked with them. Soon after my return two canoes loaded with fish and bear grass for the trade below came down from the village at the mouth of the Cataract River. They unloaded and turned their canoes upside down on the beach and camped under a shelving rock below our camp.

One of the men shot a goose above this great chute, which was floating into the chute when an Indian observed it, plunged into the water and swam to the goose and brought it on shore, at the head of the suck. As this Indian richly earned the goose I suffered him to keep it, which he about half picked and spitted it up with the guts in it to roast.

This great chute or falls is about half a mile with the water of this great river compressed within the space of 150 paces, in which there are great numbers of both large and small rocks, water passing with great velocity, foaming and boiling in a most horrible manner, with a fall of about 20 feet. Below it widens to about 200 paces and the current is gentle for a short distance. A short distance above are three small rocky islands, and at the head of those falls, three small rocky islands are situated crosswise the river. Several rocks above in the river and four large rocks in the head of the chute. Those obstructions together with the high stones which are continually breaking loose from the mountain on the starboard side and rolling down into the chute, added to those which break loose from those islands above and lodge in the chute, must be the cause of the river's damming up to such a distance above, where it shows such evident marks of the common current of the river being much lower than at the present day.

[At the end of his field notes, which Thwaites regularly calls his first draft, for this day, Clark has this sentence: "Those Indians cut off the hands of those they kill and preserve the fingers." He does not elaborate on this remark.]

November 1, 1805, Friday [Clark]

A very cool morning, wind hard from the N.E. The Indians who arrived last evening took their canoes on their shoulders and carried them below the great chute. We set about taking our small canoe and all the baggage by land 940 yards of bad, slippery and rocky way. The Indians we discovered took their loading the whole length of the portage, two and a half miles, to avoid a second chute which appears very bad to pass. Great numbers of sea otters [once again, seals]; they are so cautious that I with difficulty got a shot at one today, which I must have killed, but could not get him as he sank.

We got all our baggage over the portage of 940 yards, after which we got the four large canoes over by slipping them over the rocks on poles placed across from one rock to another, and at some places along partial streams of the river. In passing those canoes over the rocks three of them received injuries, which obliged us to delay to have them repaired.

Several Indian canoes arrived at the head of the portage; some of the men, accompanied by those of the village, came down to smoke with us. They appear to speak the same language with a little different accent.

I visited the Indian village, found that the construction of the houses was similar to those above described, with this difference only, that they are larger, say from 35 to 50 feet by 30 feet, raised about five feet above the earth, and nearly as much below. The doors in the same form and size, cut in the wide post which supports one end of the ridge pole, and which is carved and painted with different figures and hieroglyphics. Those people gave me to eat nuts, berries and a little dried fish, and sold me a hat of their own taste without a brim, and baskets in which they hold their water. Their beds are raised about four and a half feet, under which they store away their dried fish. Between the part on which they lie and the back wall they store away their roots, berries, nuts, and valuable articles on mats, which are spread also around the fireplace, which is sunk about one foot lower than the bottom floor of the house.

This fireplace is about eight feet long and six feet wide, secured with a frame. Those houses are calculated for four, five, and six families, each family having a nice painted ladder to ascend up to their beds. I saw in those houses several wooden *images* all cut in imitation of men, but differently fashioned and placed in the most conspicuous parts of the houses, probably as an ornament.

I cannot learn certainly as to the traffic those Indians carry on below, if white people or the Indians who trade with the whites are either settled or visit the mouth of this river. I believe mostly with the latter, as their knowledge of the white people appears to be very imperfect, and the articles which they appear to trade mostly, i.e., pounded fish, bear grass, and roots, cannot be an object of commerce with foreign merchants. However they get in return for those articles blue and white beads, copper teakettles, brass arm bands, some scarlet and blue robes and a few articles of old clothes. They prefer beads to anything and will part with the last mouthful or articles of clothing they have for a few of those beads. Those beads they traffic with Indians still higher up this river for robes, skins, cha-pel-el bread, bear grass, etc., who in their turn traffic with those under the Rocky Mountains for bear grass, quamash roots and robes, etc.

The natives of the waters of the Columbia appear healthy. Some have tumors on different parts of their bodies, and sore and weak eyes are common. Many have lost their sight entirely, great numbers with one eye out and frequently the other very weak. This misfortune I must again ascribe to the water. They have bad teeth, which is not common with Indians. Many have worn their teeth down and some quite into their gums. This I cannot satisfactorily account for. I ascribe it in some measure to their method of eating their food, roots particularly, which they make use of as they are taken out of the earth, frequently nearly covered with sand. I have not seen any of their long roots offered for sale clear of sand. They are rather below the common size, high cheeks, women small and homely, and have swelled legs and thighs, and their knees are remarkably large, which I ascribe to the method in which they sit on their hams. They go nearly naked, wearing only a piece of leather tied about their breast, which falls down nearly as low as the waist, a small robe about three feet square and a piece of leather tied about their breech. They have all flat heads in this quarter. They are dirty in the extreme, both in their person and cookery, wear their hair loose hanging in every direction. They ask high prices for what they sell and say that the white people below give great prices for everything.

The noses are all pierced and when they are dressed they have a long tapered piece of white shell or wampum put through the nose. Those shells are about two inches in length. I observed in many of the villages which I have passed the heads of the female children in the press for the purpose of compressing their heads in their infancy into a certain form, between two boards.

November 2, 1805, Saturday [Clark]
Examined the rapid below us more particularly. The danger appearing too great to hazard our canoes loaded, dispatched all the men who could not swim with loads to the end of the portage below. I also walked to the end of the portage with the carriers, where I delayed until every article was brought over and canoes arrived safe. Here we breakfasted and took a meridian altitude. About the time we were setting out seven squaws came over loaded with dried fish and bear grass neatly bundled up. Soon after four Indian men came down over the rapid in a large canoe. Passed a rapid at two miles and one at four miles opposite the lower point of a high island on the larboard side, and a little below four houses on the starboard bank. A small creek on the larboard side opposite Strawberry Island, which heads below the last rapid; opposite the lower point of this island passed three islands covered with tall timber opposite the Beacon Rock. Those islands are nearest the starboard side. Immediately below on the starboard side passed a village of *nine* houses, which is situated between two small creeks, and are of the same construction as those above. Here the river widens to near a mile, and the bottoms are more extensive and thickly timbered, as also the high mountains on each side, with pine, spruce pine, cottonwood, a species of ash, and alder.

At 17 miles passed a rock near the middle of the river about 100 feet high and 80 feet in diameter. Proceeded on down a smooth gentle stream of about two miles wide, in which the tide has its effect as high as the Beacon Rock or the last rapids at Strawberry Island. Saw great numbers of waterfowl of different kinds, such as swan, geese, white and gray brants, ducks of various kinds, gulls, and plover. Labiche killed 14 brants, Joseph Fields three and Collins one. We encamped under a high projecting rock on the larboard side. Here the mountains leave the river on each side, which from the great chute to this place is high and rugged, thickly covered with timber, principally of the pine species. The bottoms below appear extensive and thickly covered with wood. River here about two and a half miles wide. Seven Indians in a canoe on their way down to trade with the natives below encamp with us. Those we left at the portage passed us this evening and proceeded on down. The ebb tide rose here about 9 inches, the flood tide must rise here much higher. We made 29 miles today from the great chute.

November 3, 1805, Sunday [Clark]
The fog so thick this morning that we could not see a man 50 steps off. This fog detained us until 10 o'clock, at which time we set out, accompanied by our Indian friends who are from a village near the great falls. Previous to our setting out Collins killed a large buck, and Labiche killed three geese flying. I walked on the sand beach larboard side, opposite the canoes as they passed along. The undergrowth, rushes, vines in the bottoms too thick to pass through. At three miles I arrived at the entrance of a river which appeared to scatter over a sandbar, the bottom of which I could see quite across and did not appear to be four inches deep in any part. I attempted to wade this stream and to my astonishment found the bottom a quicksand, and impassable. I called to the canoes to put to shore; I got into the canoe and landed below the mouth, and Capt. Lewis and myself walked up this river about one and a half miles to examine this river, which we found to be a very considerable stream discharging its waters through two channels, which form an island of about three miles in length on the river and one and a half miles wide composed of coarse sand, which is thrown out of this quicksand river, compressing the waters of the Columbia and throwing the whole current of its waters against its northern banks within a channel of half of a mile wide. Several small islands 1 mile up this river. This stream has much the appearance of the *River Platte*, rolling its quicksands into the bottoms with great velocity, after which it is divided into two channels by a large sandbar before mentioned. The narrowest part of this river is 120 yards. On the opposite side of the Columbia a large creek falls in; above this creek on the same side is a small prairie. Extensive low country on each side thickly timbered.

The Quick Sand River appears to pass through the low country at the foot of the high range of mountains in a southerly direction. The large creeks which fall into the Columbia on the starboard side rise in the same range of mountains to the N.N.E. and pass through some ridgy land. A mountain which we suppose to be Mt. Hood is S. 85° E. about 47 miles distant from the mouth of Quick

Sand River. This mountain is covered with snow and in the range of mountains which we have passed through and is of a conical form, but rugged.

After taking dinner at the mouth of this river we proceeded on. Passed the head of an island near the larboard side, back of which on the same side and near the head a large creek falls in, and nearly opposite and three miles below the upper mouth of Quick Sand River is the lower mouth. This island is three and a half miles long, has rocks at the upper point, some timber on the borders of this island, in the middle open and pondy. Some rugged rocks in the middle of the stream opposite this island.

Proceeded on to center of a large island in the middle of the river which we call Diamond Island from its appearance. Here we met 15 Indian men in two canoes from below. They informed us they saw three vessels below. We landed on the north side of this Diamond Island and encamped. Capt. Lewis walked out with his gun on the island, sent out hunters and fowlers.

Below Quick Sand River the country is low, rich, and thickly timbered on each side of the river, the islands open and some ponds. River wide and immense numbers of fowls flying in every direction, such as swan, geese, brants, cranes, storks, white gulls, cormorants and plovers. Also great numbers of sea otters in the river. A canoe arrived from the village below the last rapid with a man, his wife and three children, and a woman who had been taken prisoner from the Snake Indians on Clark's River. I sent the interpreter's wife, who is a *Shoshone* or Snake Indian of the Missouri, to speak to this squaw; they could not understand each other sufficiently to converse. This family and the Indians we met from below continued with us. Capt. Lewis borrowed a small canoe of those Indians and four men took her across to a small lake in the island. Capt. Lewis and three men set out after night in this canoe in search of the swans, brants, ducks, etc., which appeared in great numbers in the lake. He killed a swan and several ducks, which made our number of fowls this evening three swan, eight brant and five ducks, on which we made a sumptuous supper. We gave the Indian who lent the canoe a brant, and some meat to the others. One of those Indians, the man from the village near the lower rapids, has a gun with a brass barrel and cock, which he prizes highly. The mountain we saw from near the forks proves to be Mount *Hood.*

November 4, 1805, Monday [Clark]
A cloudy cool morning, wind from the west. We set out at half past eight o'clock. One man, Shannon, set out early to walk on the island to kill

something. He joined us at the lower point with a buck. This island is six miles long and near three miles wide, thinly timbered. Tide rose last night 18 inches perpendicular at camp. Near the lower point of this Diamond Island is the head of a large island separated from a small one by a narrow channel, and both situated nearest the larboard side. Those islands as also the bottoms are thickly covered with pine. River wide, country low on both sides. On the main larboard shore a short distance below the last island we landed at a village of 25 *houses:* 24 of those houses were thatched with straw and covered with bark, the other house is built of boards in the form of those above, except that it is above ground and about 50 feet in length and covered with broad split boards. This village contains about 200 men of the *Skil-loot* nation. I counted 52 canoes on the bank in front of this village, many of them very large and raised in bow. We recognized the man who overtook us last night. He invited us to a lodge in which he had some part and gave us a roundish root about the size of a small Irish potato, which they roasted in the embers until they became soft. This root they call *Wap-pa-to*, the bulb of which the *Chinese* cultivate in great quantities, called the Sa-git-ti folia or common arrowhead. It has an agreeable taste and answers very well in place of bread. We purchased about four bushels of this root and divided it to our party.

At seven miles below this village passed the upper point of a large island nearest the larboard side, a small prairie in which there is a pond opposite on the starboard. Here I landed and walked on shore about three miles, a fine open prairie for about one mile, back of which the country rises gradually and woodland commences, such as white oak, pine of different kinds, wild crabs with the taste and flavor of the common crab and several species of under-growth with which I am not acquainted. A few cottonwood trees and the ash of this country grow scattered on the riverbank. Saw some elk and deer sign and joined Capt. Lewis at a place he had landed with the party for dinner. Soon after several canoes of Indians from the village above came down dressed for the purpose as I supposed of paying us a friendly visit. They had scarlet and blue blankets, sailor's jackets, overalls, shirts and hats independent of their usual dress. The most of them had either war axes, spears, or bows sprung with quivers of arrows, muskets or pistols, and tin flasks to hold their powder. Those fellows we found assuming and disagreeable; however, we smoked with them and treated them with every attention and friendship.

During the time we were at dinner those fellows stole my pipe tomahawk which they were smoking with. I immediately searched every man and the canoes, but could find nothing of my tomahawk. While searching for the tomahawk one of those scoundrels stole a greatcoat of one of our interpreters, which was found stuffed under the root of a tree near the place they sat. We became much displeased with those fellows, which they discovered and moved off on their return home to their village, except two canoes which had passed on down.

We proceeded on, met a large and a small canoe from below, with 12 men; the large canoe was ornamented with *images* carved in wood, the figures of a bear in front and a man in stern, painted and fixed very neatly on the bow and stern of the canoe, rising to near the height of a man. Two Indians very finely dressed and with hats on were in this canoe. Passed the lower point of an island which is *nine* miles in length, having passed two islands on the starboard side of this large island, three small islands at its lower point. The Indians make signs that a village is situated back of those islands on the larboard side and I believe that a channel is still on the larboard side as a canoe passed in between the small islands; they made signs that way, probably to traffic with some of the natives living on another channel. At three miles lower, and 12 leagues below Quick Sand River, passed a village of four large houses on the larboard side, near which we had a full view of *Mt. St. Helens*, which is perhaps the highest pinnacle in America from its base. It bears N. 25° E. about 90 miles. This is the mountain I saw from the Mussel Shell rapid on the 19th of October last covered with snow. It rises something in the form of a sugar loaf. About a mile lower passed a single house on the larboard side, and one on the starboard side. Passed a village on each side and camped near a house on the starboard side. We proceeded on until one hour after dark with a view to get clear of the natives, who were constantly about us and troublesome. Finding that we could not get shut of those people for one night, we landed and encamped on the starboard side. Soon after two canoes came to us loaded with Indians. We purchased a few roots of them.

This evening we saw vines much resembling the raspberry, which is very thick in the bottoms. A range of high hills at about five miles on the larboard side, which runs S.E. and N.W., covered with tall timber. The bottoms below in this range of hills and the river are rich and level. Saw white geese with a part of their wings black. The river here is one and a half miles wide, and current gentle. Opposite to our camp on a small sandy island the brant and geese make such a noise that it will be impossible for me to sleep. We *made 29 miles* today.

November 5, 1805, Tuesday [Clark]

Rained all the after part of last night. Rain continues this morning. I slept but very little last night for the noise kept during the whole of the night by the swans, geese, white and gray brant, ducks, etc., on a small sand island close under the larboard side. They were immensely numerous and their noise horrid.

We set out early. Here the river is not more than three-quarters of a mile in width. Passed a small prairie on the starboard side. Passed two houses about half a mile from each other on the larboard side. A canoe came from the upper house with three men in it merely to view us. Passed an island covered with tall trees and green briars separated from the starboard shore by a narrow channel at nine miles. On the channel, which passes on the starboard side of this island, a short distance above its lower point is situated a large village, the front of which occupies nearly one quarter of a mile fronting the channel, and closely connected; I counted 14 houses in front. Here the river widens to about one and a half miles. Seven canoes of Indians came out from this large village to view and trade with us. They appeared orderly and well disposed; they accompanied us a few miles and returned back. About one and a half miles below this village on the larboard side behind a rocky sharp point we passed a channel one quarter of a mile wide, which I take to be the one the Indian canoe entered yesterday from the lower point of *Image Canoe* Island so named. Some low cliffs of rocks below this channel, a large island close under the starboard side opposite, and two small islands below. Here we met two canoes from below.

Below those islands a range of high hills form the starboard bank of the river, the shore bold and rocky, covered with a thick growth of pine [*they have entered the coast range*]. An extensive low island, separated from the larboard side by a narrow channel; on this island we stopped to dine. I walked out, found it open and covered with grass interspersed with small ponds in which was a great number of fowl. The remains of an old village on the lower part of this island. I saw several deer. Our hunters killed on this island a swan, four white, six gray brant and two ducks; all of them were divided. Below the lower point of this island a range of high hills which runs S.E. forms the larboard bank of the river. The shores bold and rocky and hills covered with pine. The high hills leave the river on the starboard side, a high bottom between the hill and river. We met four canoes of Indians from below in where there were 26 Indians. One of those canoes is large and ornamented with *images* on the bow and stern. That in the bow the likeness of a bear, and in the stern the picture of a man.

We landed on the larboard side and camped a little below the mouth of a creek on the starboard side, a little below the mouth of which is an old village, which is now abandoned. Here the river is about one and a half miles wide, and deep. The high hills which run in a N.W. and S.E. direction form both banks of the river, the shore bold and rocky, the hills rise gradually and are covered with a thick growth of pine. The valley which is from above the mouth of Quick Sand River to this place may be computed at 60 miles wide on a direct line, and extends a great distance to the right and left, rich, thickly covered with tall timber, with a few small prairies bordering on the river and on the islands. Some few standing ponds and several small streams of running water on either side of the river. This is certainly a fertile and a handsome valley, at this time crowded with Indians. The day proved cloudy with rain the greater part of it; we are all wet, cold and disagreeable. I saw but little appearance of frost in this valley, which we call *Wap-pa-to* from that root or plant growing spontaneously in this valley only. In my walk of today I saw 17 striped snakes. I killed a grouse which was very fat, and larger than common. This is the first night we have been entirely clear of Indians since our arrival on the waters of the Columbia River. We made 32 miles today by estimation.

November 6, 1805, Wednesday [Clark]

A cool wet rainy morning. We set out early, at four miles pass two lodges of Indians in a small bottom on the larboard side. I believe those Indians to be travelers. Opposite is the head of a long narrow island close under the starboard side. Back of this island two creeks fall in about six miles apart and appear to head in the high hilly country to the N.E. [*At this point the text becomes very difficult to understand, but the gist of it is that they also passed the mouth of the Cowlitz River, which heads at Mount Rainier.*] Opposite this long island are two others, one small and about the middle of the river, the other larger and nearly opposite its lower point, and opposite a high cliff of black rocks on the larboard side at 14 miles. Here the Indians of the two lodges we passed today came in their canoes with sundry articles to sell. We purchased of them *Wap-pa-to* roots, *salmon trout*, and I purchased two beaver skins for which I gave five small fishhooks. Here the hills leave the river on the larboard side. A beautiful open and extensive bottom in which there is an old village, one also on the starboard side a little above, both of which are abandoned by all their inhabitants except two small dogs nearly starved, and an unreasonable portion of fleas.

The hills and mountains are covered with several kinds of pine, *arbor vitae* or white cedar, *red laurel*, alder and several species of undergrowth. The bottoms have common rushes, nettles, and grass. The slashy parts have bull rushes and flags. Some willow on the water's edge. Passed an island 3 miles long and one mile wide close under the starboard side below which the starboard hills are very [*high?*] from the riverbank and continued high and rugged on that side all day.

We overtook two canoes of Indians going down to trade. One of the Indians spoke a few words of English and said that the principal man who traded with them was Mr. Haley, and that he had a woman in his canoe whom Mr. Haley was fond of. He showed us a bow of iron and several other things which he said Mr. Haley gave him. We came to dine on the long narrow island. Found the woods so thick with undergrowth that the hunters could not get any distance into the island. The red wood and green briars interwoven, and mixed with pine, alder, a species of beech, ash. We killed nothing today. The Indians leave us in the evening, river about one mile wide, hills high and steep on the starboard. No place for several miles sufficiently large and level for our camp. We at length landed at a place which by moving the stones we made sufficiently large for the party to lie level on the smaller stones clear of the tide.

Cloudy with rain all day. We are all wet and disagreeable, had large fires made on the stone and dried our bedding and killed the fleas, which collected in our blankets at every old village we encamped near. I had like to have forgotten a very remarkable knob rising from the edge of the water to about 80 feet high, and about 200 paces around at its base and situated above and nearly opposite to the two lodges we passed today. It is some distance from the high land and in a low part of the island.

November 7, 1805, Thursday [Clark]
A cloudy foggy morning, some rain. We set out early, proceeded under the starboard shore under high rugged hills with steep ascents, the shore bold and rocky, the fog so thick we could not see across the river. Two canoes of Indians met and returned with us to their village, which is situated on the starboard side behind a cluster of marshy islands on a narrow channel

of the river, through which we passed to the *village* of four houses. They gave us to eat some fish and sold us fish, *Wap pa to* roots, three *dogs* and two otter skins, for which we gave fishhooks principally, of which they were very fond.

Those people call themselves *War-ci-a-cum* and speak a language different from the natives above with whom they trade for the *Wapato* roots, of which they make great use as food. Their houses differently built, raised entirely above ground, eaves about five feet from the ground, supported and covered in the same way of those above, doors about the same size but in the side of the house in one corner. One fireplace and that near the opposite end, around which they have their beds raised about four feet from the floor, which is of earth; under their beds they store away baskets of dried fish, berries and *wappato*; over the fire they hang the flesh as they take them and which they do not make immediate use of. Their canoes are of the same form as those above. The dress of the men differs very little from those above. The women altogether different; their robes are smaller, only covering their shoulders and falling down to near the hip, and sometimes when it is cold a piece of fur curiously plaited and connected so as to meet around the body from the arms to the hips.

Clark here corrects his text, quoting from what Lewis has to say about this matter some five months later, as follows:

The garment which occupies the waist and thence as low as the knee before and mid-leg behind cannot properly be called a petticoat in the common acceptance of the word. It is a tissue formed of white cedar bark bruised or broken into small strands, which are interwoven in their center by means of several cords of the same materials, which serves as well for a girdle as to hold in places the strands of bark which form the tissue, and which strands, confined in the middle, hang with their ends pendulous from the waist, the whole being of sufficient thickness when the female stands erect to conceal those parts usually covered from familiar view. But when she stoops or places herself in any other attitude this battery of Venus is not altogether impervious to the penetrating eye of the Amorite. This tissue is sometimes formed of little strings of the silk grass twisted and knotted at their ends.

Those Indians are all low and ill-shaped, all flat heads.

After delaying at this village one hour and a half we set out, piloted by an Indian dressed in a sailor's dress to the main channel of the river. The tide being in, we should have found much difficulty in passing into the main channel from behind those islands without a pilot. A large marshy island near the middle of the river, near which several canoes came alongside with skins, roots, fish to sell, and had a temporary residence on this island. Here we saw great numbers of waterfowl about those marshy islands. Here the high mountainous country approaches the river on the larboard side, a high mountain to the S.W. about 20 miles; the high mountainous country continues on the starboard side about 14 miles below the last village. At 18 miles of this day we landed at a village of the same nation. This village is at the foot of the high hills on the starboard side back of two small islands. It contains seven indifferent houses built in the same form as those above. Here we purchased a dog, some fish, *wappato* roots and I purchased two beaver skins for the purpose of making me a *robe*, as the robe I have is rotten and good for nothing. Opposite to this village the high mountainous country leaves the river on the larboard side, below which the river widens into a kind of bay and is crowded with low islands subject to being covered by the tides.

We proceeded on about 12 miles below the village under a high mountainous country on the starboard side, shore bold and rocky, and encamped under a high hill on the starboard side opposite to a rock situated half a mile from the shore, about 50 feet high and 20 feet in diameter. We with difficulty found a place clear of the tide and sufficiently large to lie on and the only place we could get was on round stones on which we lay our mats. Rain continued moderately all day and two Indians accompanied us from the last village, they were detected in stealing a knife, and returned. Our small canoe which got separated in the fog this morning joined us this evening from a large island situated nearest the larboard side below the high hills on that side, the river being too wide to see either the form, shape or size of the islands on the larboard side.

Great joy in camp, we are in *view* of the *ocean*, this great Pacific Ocean which we have been so long anxious to see. The roaring or noise made by the waves breaking on the rocky shores (as I suppose) may be heard distinctly.

We made 34 miles today as computed.

SUMMARY

NOVEMBER 8, 1805 TO APRIL 12, 1806

—◦◦◦—

It was not the ocean they were looking at, but the Columbia River estuary. The day was rainy and foggy, the estuary was four or five miles wide, they could not see the Oregon side of the river or Point Adams at the mouth of the river in the distance, through the fog. But they were close enough. They had reached their goal. They had crossed North America—and they were about to find out what a Pacific Northwest Coast winter was like. They were already becoming familiar with the rain. Now they faced oceanlike waves and swells. The next day, November 8th, they paddled cautiously into Grays Bay and found themselves forced ashore by the waves onto a small beach backed up to steep cliffs, the beach itself jammed with the huge driftwood logs that are common to beaches all along the Northwest Coast. Some of these logs were 200 feet long and 4 to 7 feet thick.

The next day it rained all day. The wind blew and the waves tossed the logs around, threatening the canoes, which were full of water, and when the tide came in, there was no place for the men to go but no way they could leave. "Our camp," remarks Clark, "was entirely underwater during the height of the tide, every man as wet as water could make them all the last night and today all day." Not until the next day did the storm abate enough that they could move around a point to a somewhat larger cove just below Point Ellice, still in the estuary but closer to the actual mouth of the Columbia.

The cove was somewhat larger, but not large enough. They were there for five days, and their stay was miserable. The men tried to find places to lie down among the driftwood logs, in crevices and on wherever they could find that was flat. Stones fell on them from the cliffs above. Waves once again broke on their little area. The underbrush and the fallen logs in the woods behind them were so thick that the area was impassable; the hunters could not get through. They had nothing to eat but the pounded fish they had bought from the Indians upriver. It rained constantly. On the 12th Clark wrote,

> It would be distressing to a feeling person to see our situation at this time, all wet and cold with our bedding, etc., also wet, in a cove scarcely large enough to contain us, our baggage in a small hollow about half a mile from us, and canoes at the mercy of the waves and driftwood . . . Our party has been wet for eight days… their robes and leather clothes are rotten from being continually wet, and they are not in a situation to get others, and we are not in a situation to restore them.

On the 14th he noted that it had been raining for 10 days without more than a two-hour letup.

On the 15th it cleared up long enough for them to pack up quickly and paddle around yet another point to a sandy beach. This one faced the ocean, which they could now see. Point Adams was some 8 miles off to the southwest, Cape Disappointment 14 miles to the west, and in between lay open sea. "This I could plainly see," Clark writes, "would be the extent of our journey by water, as the waves were too high at any state for our canoes to proceed further down." He added up the distance: 4,162 miles from the mouth of the Missouri.

They stayed on this "beautiful sand beach" for 10 days, using it as a base to explore the area. First Lewis, then Clark took small parties of the corps on foot to Cape Disappointment and then for a short distance up the Long Beach peninsula. The captains carved their names on trees, Clark on a "small pine, the day of the month and year, etc." The men, Clark said, "appear much satisfied with their trip, beholding with astonishment the high waves dashing against the rocks and this immense ocean." He described the country they walked through, noticing the fallen nurse logs in the rain forest serving as sources of nourishment for new trees: "pine of three or four feet through growing on the bodies of large trees which had fallen down."

Cape Disappointment, Point Adams, and the major mountains like Mount St. Helens, Mount Rainier, Mount Adams, and Mount Hood, had been named years before by ships' captains, but the captains still found features they could name. Clark named a point he could see from Long Beach about 20 miles away to the north Point Lewis. Seeing a high point at some distance on the south side of the Columbia, he left a blank in the notebook, to fill in the name later. It is now called Tillamook Head.

But the weather remained insupportable. It rained all the time and when the wind blew their position was exposed; it was a sand beach but it was still covered with driftwood logs, which to this day sometimes roll over on and kill campers foolish enough to lie beside them, thinking that they might provide a kind of shelter, unaware of the tide line.

They did not like the Indians who lived nearby, either. They were Chinook and they pilfered. A group of them stole Shannon's rifle when he was out hunting and alone; only the timely arrival of Lewis with a contingent of men saved the day. They were caught stealing knives or anything else they could get their hands on. They also demanded high prices in trade, so high that in many cases the captains could not afford the price. They were fondest of blue beads, preferring them to all other items. On the 20th Clark was trying to trade for sea otter skins, "more beautiful than any fur I had ever seen." He finally got them in trade for Sacagawea's belt, which was made of blue beads. The next day Clark gave her a blue coat to make up for the loss of her belt.

Chinook women were coming to trade their sexual favors as well; "the young women sport openly with our men," said Clark, "and appear to receive the approbation of their friends and relations for so doing." Some of the men contracted venereal disease from these women; the captains were still treating their symptoms the following February. But Lewis and Clark did not stand in the way of sexual relations. "We divided some ribbon between the men of our party," Clark reports, "to bestow on their favorite lasses." In March, however, when the same women reappeared for the same purpose, the captains asked the men to pledge that they would not have sexual relations with them again. They did not want men in poor health making the trip back across the West.

Sexual favors or not, they could not stay where they were. The Chinooks were thieves, the beach was exposed, and there was no game, no elk in particular, in the hills behind them. On the 22nd a high tide and storm waves came at their camp again. "The wind, which was from the S.S.E., blew with such violence that we were almost overwhelmed with water blown from the river. This storm did not cease at day but blew with nearly equal violence throughout the whole day accompanied with rain. O! how horrible is the day. Waves breaking with great violence against the shore throwing the water into our camp. All wet and confined to our shelters." The shelters were rotting in this weather. The captains had to find a place to spend the winter where they could build a fort and feed themselves reasonably well and protect themselves and their canoes from the storms, and it wasn't where they were.

So they discussed their options: They could go back upriver to a drier place, or they could cross the river and examine the south side, where the Clatsop reported there were elk. In a way it was a foregone conclusion that they would stay near the mouth of the Columbia. They were hoping for one thing, that a ship would appear that could take back copies of the journals they had written to date, thereby increasing the chances of these records surviving, and from which they could acquire trade goods to use on their return trip. They were almost out—Clark had said at the beginning that they didn't bring enough— and they would need trade goods to acquire horses and food. They also needed a place to make salt from seawater, and they needed a warm situation; so much of their clothing had rotted that they would have suffered mightily from the cold upriver.

Despite all these reasons, however, on November 24 they did something highly unusual for a military unit of any kind. They voted whether to search out a situation on the Oregon side of the river, or go back upriver to someplace like the falls. Not only did they vote, they included everyone in the vote— Clark's black slave, York, and Sacagawea, too, who is listed as "Janey" in Clark's voting tally. She, it turned out, was in favor of finding a place where there were plenty of wappato roots, of which she was very fond. Almost everyone else voted that they should cross the Columbia and examine the southern side. On the 25th they packed up and made their way back upriver to a place where it was safe to risk crossing the river and did just that.

By the 27th they had reached present-day Tongue Point, where the weather forced them to camp. Once again they were pinned down, and everyone and everything was soaked through. "We are all wet, bedding and stores, having nothing to keep ourselves or stores dry, our lodge nearly worn out, and the pieces of sails and tents so full of holes and rotten that they will not keep anything dry." They were once again reduced to eating pounded fish, and not much of that. The weather held them there for days. Clark took the opportunity to carve his name on a tree once again, this time a large pine tree: "William Clark December 3rd, 1805. By Land from the U. States in 1804 and 1805." Lewis, meanwhile, set out with a few men in the small Indian canoe they had traded for to find a site to spend the winter. He didn't come back for more than a week, and Clark became increasingly anxious for his safety. But on December 5 he did return, and with good news. He had found a place up a small stream (now the Lewis and Clark River) behind the coastal headlands that ran south from Point Adams. It was elevated enough to protect them from the tide, it was sheltered behind the hills from the ocean, and there were enough elk to live on in the area. On December 7 they left Tongue Point and in less than a day arrived at the site that would become Fort Clatsop.

Lewis immediately set to work with the bulk of the men to build the fort while Clark slogged over the hills and through and around swamps with a few others to the coast to find a place where they could set up a saltworks. They would make salt, as it happened, until the middle of February, when they felt they had enough to take them back to their cache on the Missouri, where they had left more. By Christmas they were in the fort, in their log cabins, and could celebrate after a fashion, even though it continued to rain more or less constantly. In the time they would spend on the Pacific coast it would rain every day but 12, and Clark at one point remarks that he cannot see why it is called the Pacific Ocean, since he has yet to see it calm.

On Christmas Day the men awoke the captains with a volley from their firearms, a shout and a song, and they exchanged presents. Clark received from Lewis some fleece-lined hosiery, a vest, and other articles of clothing; Private Whitehouse gave him a pair of moccasins, and Sacagawea some two dozen weasels' tails. "We would have spent this day, the nativity of Christ, in feasting," he notes, "had we anything either to raise our spirits or gratify our appetites. Our dinner consisted of poor elk, so much spoiled that we eat it through mere necessity, some spoiled pounded fish and a few roots." Elk was reasonably plentiful, but it was hard in the warm weather to get it back to camp and smoke it before it spoiled. The rain forest that surrounded them was extremely difficult to navigate. Thick undergrowth and fallen timber littered the forest floor. Fleas afflicted them in the fort, and they could not get rid of them, try as they might.

On the first of January, 1806, the men fired off another volley of small arms, and Lewis remarks,

> This was the only mark of respect which we had it in our power to pay this celebrated day. Our repast of this day, though better than that of Christmas, consisted principally in the anticipation of the 1st day of January 1807, when in the bosom of our friends we hope to participate in the mirth and hilarity of the day, and when with the zest given by the recollection of the present, we shall completely, both mentally and corporally, enjoy the repast which the hand of civilization has prepared for us.

Lewis was ready to go home.

Lewis returned to making regular journal entries on the first of January, and from that day until they left Fort Clatsop in March, Clark merely copied Lewis's entries, with almost no variation. There was little to report. Early in January news of a whale washing up on what is now Cannon Beach in Oregon reached the camp. Clark set out with a few men—and Sacagawea—over difficult terrain to bring back some whale blubber. Sacagawea insisted on going. She told Clark "that she had traveled a long way with us to see the great waters, and now that that monstrous fish was also to be seen, she thought it very hard that she could not be permitted to see either (she had never yet been to the ocean)." This and the moment when she recognized Cameahwait, the Shoshone chief, to be her brother are virtually the only times in the two years she was with Lewis and Clark that we hear Sacagawea's voice. Unfortunately, by the time they got there the Indians had reduced the whale to a skeleton (105 feet long, says Clark; if true, that would have made it a blue whale, the largest of whales), and he had to barter hard for a mere 300 pounds of blubber from the local tribe. But, he says, "small as this stock is I prize it highly, and thank Providence for directing the whale to us; and think Him much more kind to us than He was to Jonah, having sent this monster to be swallowed by us instead of swallowing of us as Jonah's did."

But on most days Lewis writes only that nothing happened, "no occurrence worthy of relation took place today," and then fills in the space with extensive natural history notes and observations on Indian customs and dress. This material, to be sure, is often fascinating. Through much of January Lewis systematically went through different aspects of the local Indian culture:

canoe burial, in which the dead are laid wrapped in skins inside canoes that are raised off the surface of the earth on poles; their methods of taking fish; their houses and how they were built; the canoes themselves and the skill with which they managed them, which never failed to impress the captains. Lewis writes,

> Some of the large canoes, are upwards of 50 feet long and will carry from 8 to 10 thousand pounds or from 20 to 30 persons and some of them, particularly on the seacoast, are waxed, painted, and ornamented with curious images at bow and stern. Those images sometimes rise to the height of five feet. The pedestals on which these images are fixed are sometimes cut out of the solid stick with the canoe, and the imagery is formed of separate small pieces of timber firmly united with tenons and mortices without the assistance of a single spike of any kind.

Both Lewis and Clark were impressed by the images, but because of language difficulties they could never discover what they were for, whether they were objects of worship or served some other function.

If not writing about Indians, Lewis was writing about plants and animals. He went through and identified every species of tree he could find, every shrub, every bird, every quadruped. He wrote the first scientific descriptions of the mountain beaver, the eulachon (which is a small fish, often called a candlefish), sea otters, the Sitka spruce, the Columbian black-tailed deer, the California condor, various shellfish, the Oregon crabapple. Just before Christmas Joseph Fields had presented each captain with a writing board and Lewis used it well; his curiosity penetrated to small details, and he was thorough, precise, and a born naturalist. This was unknown territory full of unknown species, fertile ground for such a person.

But mostly it was a boring time. The men went out hunting for elk, deer, bear, shorebirds, and whatever they could find to eat. It rained all the time. Sometimes the hunts were successful, sometimes not. Indians came by from time to time to trade, but less as the winter passed because the expedition had nothing left to trade with, and no ship had come. Lewis remarks on March 16 that "two handkerchiefs would now contain all the small articles of merchandise which we possess. The balance of the stock consists of six blue robes, one scarlet ditto, one uniform artillerist's coat and hat, five robes made of our large flag, and a few old clothes trimmed with ribbon. On this stock we have wholly to depend for the purchase of horses and such portion of our subsistence from the Indians as it will be in our power to obtain." They were trying to trade for an Indian canoe, but there was nothing to trade with.

In the end they stole one. Lewis justified the theft as retaliation for six elk his hunters had killed that the Indians had taken before they could send a party out to bring them back to the fort. It strikes an odd note in the expedition's history. To that point the captains had maintained a level of trust between Indians and whites that can only be described as exemplary. Now they were not only stealing a canoe, but Lewis was expatiating on Indian treachery.

One night in February one of the local chiefs came for his first visit, and Lewis, although he found him friendly, remarks on how they never trust the Indians and will not let them spend the night in the fort under any circumstances, "for notwithstanding their apparent friendly disposition, their great avarice and hope of plunder might induce them to be treacherous . . . We well know that the treachery of the aborigines of America and the too great confidence of our countrymen in their sincerity and friendship has caused the destruction of many hundreds of us." In light of the later history of Indian and white relations, this takes a decidedly one-sided view.

In mitigation, Lewis may have had in mind something that happened on the beach when Clark was out trading for whale blubber. One of the men, McNeal, had wandered off to the lodging of some nearby Indians, and an Indian had invited him to go to another lodge for some fish, locking arms with him in a sign of friendship. He had taken McNeal into that lodge, given him a piece of fish, and then invited him to another. At that point the Indian woman in the lodge had grabbed McNeal's blanket and made signs to him not to go and sent another woman to raise the alarm. Clark immediately sent Sergeant Pryor to the lodges, and the Indian who had invited McNeal to the lodge disappeared. He was, said the woman, going to cut McNeal's throat for his blanket and clothes.

But incidents of any kind were rare. On March 3 Lewis writes, "No movement of the party today worthy of notice. Everything moves on in the old way and we are counting the days which separate us from the first of April and which bind us to Fort Clatsop." April 1 was the day they had planned to leave. Then they reconsidered. With the weather so constantly bad, they might not be able to leave on that day; that in turn might slow them down getting to the Rockies in good time to cross them when the snows had melted. Perhaps they should leave before. They started packing up in the middle of March. The men had made themselves plenty of elkskin clothes and no fewer than 358 pairs of moccasins.

They left a notice that they had been there and a list of their names with the Indians for them to give to whatever ship came into the Columbia Estuary to trade; the list actually made it back to the East Coast on an American trading ship, but by that time Lewis and Clark had returned to St. Louis. On March 20 Lewis summed up a bit: "Although we have not fared sumptuously this winter and spring at Fort Clatsop, we have lived quite as comfortably as we had any reason to expect we should, and have accomplished every object which induced our remaining at this place except that of meeting with the traders who visit the entrance of this river. Our salt will be very sufficient to last us to the Missouri, where we have a stock in store." He does not mention the rain. A storm was on that very day holding up their departure. It didn't let up enough for them to leave until March 23.

For the rest of March they moved slowly back up the Columbia, fighting the weather, and trading with the Indians on the way for dogs and other sources of food. On the 28th, on an island the Indians called Deer Island, Joseph Fields shot a large buck and left it to continue hunting; by the time he got back to the carcass he found that the vultures had dragged it some 30 yards, skinned it, and broken the backbone. Those were California condors and this gives some indication of their strength.

While camped at the mouth of the Sandy River, which runs off Mount Hood, they found out from one of the Indians who were constantly coming and going that they had missed, once again, the mouth of the Willamette, which drains much of western Oregon, because it was concealed behind some islands, so Clark went back with a few men to explore it briefly. They gave the river its Indian name, Multnomah.

They were worried about feeding themselves as they went upriver. Indians coming down the Columbia reported that game was scarce on the Columbia Plateau, and the salmon had yet to begin their spring runs. "This information gave us much uneasiness with respect to our future means of subsistence," writes Lewis. "Above the falls on through the plains from thence to the Chopunnish [their name for the Nez Perce] there are no deer, antelope or elk on which we can depend for subsistence; their horses are very poor, most probably, at this season, and if they have no fish their dogs must be in the same situation." They had no choice but to pass through this country and they had to get back to their horses, which the Nez Perce were holding for them, before that tribe left for the Great Plains to hunt buffalo, which they intended to do, they had told the captains, "as soon as the season would permit"— probably the beginning of May.

On April 2 they decided that the best solution was to stay where they were for a week and hunt elk, drying the meat to use as provisions until they could reach the Nez Perce and their horses. They would then "exchange our pirogues for canoes with the natives on our way to the great falls of the Columbia or purchase such canoes from them for elkskins and merchandise as would answer our purposes. These canoes we intend exchanging with the natives of the plains for horses as we proceed until we obtain as many as will enable us to travel altogether by land." Then they would send a small party ahead to collect their horses from the Nez Perce.

For a week, then, they camped, hunting elk, deer, and whatever else would answer, while Indians came downriver from the Columbia Plateau looking to feed their families, and other Indians came upriver to trade with the expedition. Some of them were simply curious; they wanted to see the white men before they left. Others had theft in mind, and it drove the captains to distraction. On April 9 an Indian who had been seen stealing a spoon the day before "crept upon his belly with his hands and feet," says Clark, "with a view as I suppose to take some of our baggage which was in several different parcels on the bank." The sentinel saw him, came at him with his gun "in a position as if going to shoot," and the Indian ran off.

Clark clearly means the incident to seem comical; but farther upriver Indians stole Lewis's dog and tried to take another dog from John Shields that he had just bought. Shields had to draw his knife to defend himself. Lewis got his dog back, too, but he was getting seriously angry. He sent three men after his dog with orders to shoot if there was any trouble at all from the two Indians who stole it, and he informed the remaining Indians "by signs that if they made any further attempts to steal our property or insulted our men we should put them to instant death." The chief of these people tried to make amends. "I hope that the friendly interposition of this chief may prevent our being compelled to use some violence with these people," Lewis writes. "Our men seem well disposed to kill a few of them."

By the 12th of April they had passed the rapids of the Cascades and were approaching the worse rapids of the Dalles. Beyond that were the Great Falls of the Columbia, where the Columbia Plateau country begins and where they *hoped to trade for horses. We rejoin them there, where they continued to have trouble with the Indians. The problem now was less theft than the prices the Indians were asking for horses. They had already lost one pirogue and one Indian canoe to the rapids. They needed horses badly. The Indians must have sensed that fact, and they behaved accordingly.*

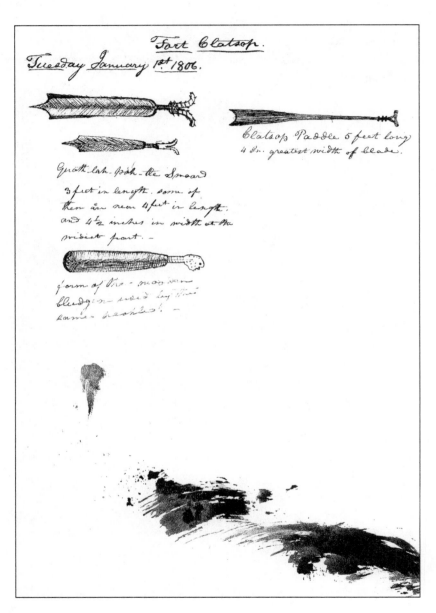

Two swords, a bludgeon, and a paddle, January 1, 1806

April 13, 1806, Sunday [Lewis]

The loss of one of our pirogues rendered it necessary to distribute her crew and cargo among the two remaining pirogues and two canoes, which being done we loaded and set out at eight a.m. We passed the village immediately above the rapids where only one house at present remains entire, the other eight having been taken down and removed to the opposite side of the river. We found the additional lading which we had been compelled to put on board rendered our vessels extremely inconvenient to manage and in short rather unsafe in the event of high winds. I therefore left Capt. Clark with the two pirogues to proceed up the river on the N. side, and with the two canoes and some additional hands passed over the river above the rapids to the Y-eh-huh village in order to purchase one or more canoes. I found the village consisting of 11 houses crowded with inhabitants; it appeared to me that they could have mustered about 60 fighting men then present. They appeared very friendly disposed, and I soon obtained two small canoes from them for which I gave two robes and four elkskins. I also purchased four paddles and three dogs from them with deerskins. The dog now constitutes a considerable part of our subsistence and with most of the party has become a favorite food. Certain I am that it is a healthy strong diet, and from habit it has become by no means disagreeable to me. I prefer it to lean venison or elk, and it is very far superior to the horse in any state. After remaining about two hours at this village I departed and continued my route with the four canoes along the S. side of the river, the wind being too high to pass over to the entrance of Cruzatte's river [*present-day Wind River; they had named it Cruzatte's River in the fall on the way west*], where I expected to have overtaken Capt. Clark. Not seeing the pirogues on the opposite side I ascended the river until one o'clock, or about five miles above the entrance of Cruzatte's river. Being convinced that the pirogues were behind I halted and directed the men to dress the dogs and cook one of them for dinner. A little before we completed our meal Capt. Clark arrived with the pirogues and landed opposite to us.

After dinner I passed the river to the pirogues and found that Capt. Clark had halted for the evening and was himself hunting with three of the party. The men informed me that they had seen nothing of the hunters whom we had sent on the 11th to the entrance of Cruzatte's River. I directed Sgt. Ordway to take the two small canoes for his mess and the lading which he had formerly carried in the pirogue we lost yesterday, and to have them dried this evening and payed with rosin. Capt. Clark returned in about an hour and being convinced that the hunters were yet behind, we dispatched Sgt. Pryor in search of them with two men and an empty canoe to bring the meat they may have killed. John Shields returned a little after six p.m. with two deer which he had killed. These were also of the blacktailed fallow deer; there appears to be no other species of deer in these mountains. Capt. Clark informed me that the wind had detained him several hours a little above Cruzatte's River, that while detained there he sent out some men to hunt. One of them wounded two deer but got neither of them. The wind having lulled in the evening and not seeing anything of Drouillard and the Fieldses, he had proceeded on to this place where he intended waiting for me, and as he did not see my canoes when he landed had taken a hunt with some of the men as before mentioned.

Clark was still copying Lewis's entries almost verbatim.

April 14, 1805, Monday [Lewis]
This morning at seven o'clock we were joined by Sgt. Pryor and the three hunters. They brought with them four deer which Drouillard had killed yesterday. We took breakfast and departed. At nine a.m. the wind arose and continued hard all day, but not so violent as to prevent our proceeding. We kept close along the N. shore all day. The river from the rapids as high as the commencement of the narrows [*at the Dalles*] is from one half to three

quarters of a mile in width, and possesses scarcely any current. The bed is principally rock except at the entrance of Labiche's river [*now Hood River*], which heads in Mount Hood and like the Quick Sand River [*i.e., the Sandy, which they had just passed*] brings down from thence vast bodies of sand. The mountains through which the river passes nearly to the sepulcher rock are high, broken, rocky, partially covered with fir, white cedar, and in many places exhibit very romantic scenes. Some handsome cascades are seen on either hand tumbling from the stupendous rocks of the mountains into the river. Near the border of the river I observed today the long-leafed pine [*the ponderosa pine*]. This pine increases in quantity as you ascend the river and about the sepulcher rock where the lower country commences it supersedes the fir altogether. Throughout the whole course of this river from the rapids as high as the Chilluckkittequaws, we find the trunks of many large pine trees standing erect as they grew at present in 30 feet of water. They are much doated [*decayed*] and none of them vegetating; at the lowest tide of the river many of these trees are in ten feet of water. Certain it is that those large pine trees never grew in that position, nor can I account for this phenomenon except it be that the passage of the river through the narrow pass at the rapids has been obstructed by the rocks which have fallen from the hills into that channel within the last 20 years. The appearance of the hills at that place justify that opinion. They appear constantly to be falling in, and the apparent state of the decayed trees would seem to fix the era of their decline about the time mentioned.

At one p.m. we arrived at a large village situated in a narrow bottom on the N. side a little above the entrance of Canoe Creek. Their houses are rather detached and extend for several miles. They are about 20 in number. These people call themselves We-ock-sock, Wil-la-cum. They differ but little in appearance, dress, etc., from those of the rapids. Their men have some leggings and moccasins among them. These are in the style of the Chopunnish. They have some good horses of which we saw ten or a dozen. These are the first horses we have met with since we left this neighborhood last fall. The country below this place will not permit the use of this valuable animal except in the Columbian valley and there the present inhabitants have no use for them, as they reside immediately on the river and the country is too thickly timbered to admit them to run the game with horses if they had them. We halted at this village and dined. Purchased five dogs, some roots, shappalell [*a root commonly known as cous*], filberts and dried berries of the inhabitants.

Here I observed several habitations entirely under ground; they were sunk about eight feet deep and covered with strong timber and several feet of earth in a conic form. These habitations were evacuated at present. They are about 16 feet in diameter, nearly circular, and are entered through a hole at the top which appears to answer the double purpose of a chimney and a door. From this entrance you descend to the floor by a ladder. The present habitations of these people were on the surface of the ground and do not differ from those of the tribes of the rapids. Their language is the same with that of the Chilluckkittequaws. These people appeared very friendly. Some of them informed us that they had lately returned from a war excursion against the Snake Indians who inhabit the upper part of the Multnomah River to the S.E. of them. They call them *To-wan-nah-hi-ooks*. They had been fortunate in their expedition and had taken from their enemies most of the horses which we saw in their possession.

After dinner we pursued our voyage; Capt. Clark walked on shore with Charbonneau. I ascended the river about six miles, at which place the river washed the base of high cliffs on the larboard side. Here we halted a few minutes and were joined by Capt. Clark and Charbonneau and proceeded on to the entrance of a small run on the N. side a little below a large village on the same side opposite the sepulcher rock [*this rock was the small island the captains noted coming down the Columbia in the fall where there were a number of Indian burials*]. This village can raise about a hundred fighting men; they call themselves Smack-shops. They do not differ in any respect from the village below. Many of them visited our camp this evening and remained with us until we went to bed. They then left us and retired to their quarters.

April 15, 1806, Tuesday [Lewis]
We delayed this morning until after breakfast in order to purchase some horses of the Indians. Accordingly we exposed some articles in exchange for horses. The natives were unwilling to barter; we therefore put up our merchandise and at eight a.m. we set out. We halted a few minutes at the sepulcher rock and examined the deposits of the dead at that place. These were constructed in the same manner of those already described below the rapids. Some of them were more than half filled with dead bodies. There were 13 sepulchers on this rock, which stands near the center of the river and has a surface of about two acres above high water mark. From hence we returned

to the northern shore and continued up it about four miles to another village of the same nation with whom we remained last night. Here we halted and informed the natives of our wish to purchase horses. They produced us several for sale but would not take the articles which we had in exchange for them. They wanted an instrument which the Northwest traders call an eye-dag [*Biddle identifies this as a kind of war ax*] which we had not. We procured two dogs of them and departed. A little below the entrance of Cataract River we halted at another village of the same people, at which we were equally unsuccessful in the purchase of horses. We also halted at the two villages of the Chilluckkittequaws a few miles above with no better success.

At three in the evening we arrived at the entrance of Quinnette Creek, which we ascended a short distance and encamped at the place we have called Rockfort Camp. Here we were visited by some of the people from the villages at the great narrows and falls. We informed them of our wish to purchase horses and agreed to meet them on the opposite or north side of the river tomorrow for the purpose of bartering with them. Most of them returned to their villages this evening; three only remained with us all night. These people are much better clad than any of the nations below. Their men have generally leggings, moccasins, and large robes. Many of them wear shirts of the same form as those of the Chopunnish and Shoshones, highly ornamented with the quills of the porcupine, as are also their moccasins and leggings. They conceal the parts of generation with the skin of a fox or some other small animal drawn underneath a girdle and hanging loosely in front of them like a narrow apron. The dress of their women differs very little from those about the rapids. Both men and women cut their hair in the forehead which comes down as low as the eyebrows. They have long earlocks cut square at the end. The other part of their hair is dressed in the same manner as those of the rapids. After we landed and formed our camp this evening Drouillard and some others took a hunt and killed a deer of the long-tailed kind. It was a buck and the young horns had shot forth about two inches.

The next day Lewis remained in camp while Clark went across the river to trade for horses; Lewis spent the time collecting esculent plants in the neighborhood. He noted that "our present station is the last point at which there is a single stick of timber on the river for a great distance and is the commencement of the open plains which extend nearly to the base of the Rocky Mts." The entry for this day is Clark's:

April 16, 1806, Wednesday [Clark]
About eight o'clock this morning I passed the river with the two interpreters and nine men in order to trade with the natives for their horses, for which purpose I took with me a good part of our stock of merchandise. Capt. Lewis sent out the hunters and set several men at work making packsaddles. Twelve horses will be sufficient to transport our baggage and some pounded fish with our dried elk, which we intend taking with us as a reserved store for the plains and Rocky Mountains. I formed a camp on the N. side and sent Drouillard and Goodrich to the Skillute village, and Charbonneau and Frazer down to the Chilluckkittequaws villages with directions to inform the natives that I had crossed the river for the purpose of purchasing horses, and if they had horses to sell us to bring them to my camp.

Great numbers of Indians came from both villages and delayed the greater part of the day without trading a single horse. Drouillard returned with the principal chief of the Skillutes, who was lame and could not walk. After his arrival some horses were offered for sale, but they asked nearly half the merchandise I had with me for one horse. This price I could not think of giving. The chief informed me if I would go to his town with him, his people would sell me horses. I therefore concluded to accompany him to his village seven miles distant. We set out and arrived at the village at sunset. After some ceremony I entered the house of the chief. I then informed him that I would trade with them for their horses in the morning, for which I would give for each horse the articles which I had offered yesterday. The chief set before me a large platter of onions which had been sweated. I gave a part of those onions to all my party and we all ate of them. In this state the root is very sweet and the tops tender. The natives requested the party to dance, which they very readily consented, and Pierre Cruzatte played on the violin and the men danced several dances and retired to rest in the houses of the first and second chief.

This village is moved about 300 yards below the spot it stood last fall at the time we passed down. They were all above ground and built in the same form of those below already described. We observed many stacks of fish remaining untouched on either side of the river. The inhabitants of this village wear the robe of deer, elk, goat, etc., and most of the men wear leggings and moccasins and shirts highly ornamented with porcupine quills and beads. The women wear the truss most commonly, though some of them have long shirts. All of those articles they procure from other nations who visit them for the purpose of exchanging those articles for their pounded fish, of which they prepare great quantities. This is the great mart of all this country. Ten different tribes who reside on the Yakima and Cataract Rivers visit those people for the purpose of purchasing their fish, and the Indians on the Columbia and Lewis's Rivers [*the Snake River*] quite to the Chopunnish nation visit them for the purpose of trading horses, buffalo robes, for beads, and such articles as they have not. The Skillutes procure the most of their cloth, knives, axes and beads from the Indians from the north of them who trade with white people who come into the inlets to the north at no great distance from the Yakima. Their horses, of which I saw great numbers, they procure from the Indians who reside on the banks of the Columbia above, and what few they take from the To war ne hi ooks or Snake Indians. I smoked with all the principal men of this nation in the house of their great chief and lay myself down on a mat to sleep but was prevented by the mice and vermin with which this house abounded and which were very troublesome to me.

April 17, 1806, Thursday [Lewis]
This morning early I sent out the hunters and set several additional hands about the packsaddles. I find that the sturgeon is not taken by any of the natives above the Columbian valley. The inhabitants of the rapids at this time take a few of the white salmon trout and considerable quantities of a small indifferent mullet on which they principally subsist. I have seen none except dried fish of the last season in the possession of the people above that place; they subsist on roots principally, with some dried and pounded fish. The salmon not having made their appearance proves a serious inconvenience to us. But few of the natives visited my camp today and those only remained a few hours. Even at this place, which is merely on the border of the plains of Columbia, the climate seems to have changed; the air feels drier and more pure. The earth is dry and seems as if there had been no rain for a week or ten days. The plain is covered with a rich verdure of grass and herbs from four to nine inches high and exhibits a beautiful scene, particularly pleasing after having been so long imprisoned in mountains and those almost impenetrably thick forests of the seacoast. Joseph Fields brought me today three eggs of the parti-colored corvus; they are about the size and shape of those of the pigeon. They are bluish white, much freckled with dark reddish brown irregular spots; in short it is rather a mixture of those colors in which the reddish brown predominates, particularly towards the larger end.

This evening Willard and Cruzatte returned from Capt. Clark and brought me a note in which Capt. Clark informed me that he had still been unsuccessful, having not obtained a single horse as yet from the natives, and the state of our stores is so low that I begin to fear we shall not be enabled to obtain as many horses at this place as will convey our baggage; and unless we do obtain a sufficient number for that purpose we shall not hasten our progress, as a part of our baggage must still be conveyed by water. Capt. Clark informed me that he should proceed as far as the Eneshur villages today and would return tomorrow and join me at the Skillute village, to which place I mean to proceed with the party tomorrow. I dispatched Shannon with a note to Capt. Clark in which I requested him to double the price we have heretofore offered for horses and if possible obtain as many as five. By this means we shall be enabled to proceed immediately with our small canoes and those horses to the villages in the neighborhood of the Musselshell Rapid, where horses are more abundant and cheaper. With the remainder of our merchandise in addition to the canoes we can no doubt obtain as many horses there as will answer our purposes. Delay in the villages at the narrows and falls will be expensive to us, inasmuch as we will be compelled to purchase both fuel and food of the Indians, and might the better enable them to execute any hostile design, should they meditate any against us.

All the hunters returned in the evening. Shields had killed one deer, which he brought with him. The packsaddles were completed this evening. I had some elkskins put in the water today to make harnesses for the pack horses but shall not cut them until I know the number we can obtain.

Lewis then describes a species of hyacinth he had discovered. Clark, meanwhile, was able to purchase two horses, just as he was packing up to leave, and then another from another Indian who came up at the end. With this encouragement, he decided to stay at this village one more day. Charbonneau, meanwhile, managed to purchase a "very fine mare, for which he gave ermine, elks' teeth, a belt and some other articles of no great value." The next day, the 18th, Lewis reached the first rapids of the Dalles in the canoes, now much more formidable than they had been the previous fall; he then walked up and joined Clark. The entry for the day is Clark's:

April 18, 1806, Friday [Clark]
Early this morning I was awoken by an Indian man of the Chopunnish Nation who informed me that he lived in the neighborhood of our horses. This man

delivered me a bag of powder and ball which he had picked up this morning at the place the goods were exposed yesterday. I had a fire made of some poles purchased of the natives at a short distance from the houses and the articles exposed as yesterday. Collected the four horses purchased yesterday and sent Frazer and Charbonneau with them to the basin where I expected they would meet Capt. Lewis and commence the portage of the baggage on those horses. About 10 a.m. the Indians came down from the Eneshur villages and I expected would take the articles which they had laid by yesterday. But to my astonishment not one would make the exchange today. Two other parcels of goods were laid by and the horses promised at two p.m. I paid but little attention to this bargain; however, I suffered the bundles to lie.

I dressed the sores of the principal chief, gave some small things to his children, and promised the chief some medicine to cure his sores. His wife, who I found to be a sulky bitch, was somewhat afflicted with pains in her back. This I thought a good opportunity to get her on my side, giving her something for her back. I rubbed a little camphor on her temples and back, and applied warm flannel to her back, which she thought had nearly restored her to her former feelings. This I thought a favorable time to trade with the chief, who had more horses than all the nation besides. I accordingly made him an offer, which he accepted and sold me two horses.

Great numbers of Indians from different directions visited me at this place today. None of them appeared willing to part with their horses, but told me that several were coming from the plains this evening. Among other nations who visit this place for the purpose of trade is the *Skad-datt's*. Those people bartered the Skillutes to play at a singular kind of game. In the course of the day the Skillutes won all their beads, skins, arrows, etc. This game was composed of nine men on a side. They set down opposite to each other at the distance of about 10 feet. In front of each party a long pole was placed, on which they struck with a small stick to the time of their songs. After the bets were made up, which was nearly half an hour after they set down, two round bones were produced about the size of a man's little finger, or something smaller, and two and a quarter inches in length, which they held in their hands, changing it from one hand to the other with great dexterity. Two men on the same side performed this part, and when they had the bone in the hand they wished, they looked at their adversaries, swinging arms around their shoulders for their adversary to guess, which they performed by the motion of the hand either to the right or left. If the opposite party guessed the hand of both of the men who had the bones, the bones were given to them. If neither the bones were retained and nothing counted. If they guessed one and not the other, one bone was delivered up and the party possessing the other bone counted one, and one for every time the adversary misguessed until they guessed the hand in which the bone was in. In this game each party has five sticks, and one side wins all the sticks, once, twice, or thrice, as the game may be set.

I observed another game which those people also play; it is played by two persons with four sticks about the size of a man's finger and about seven inches in length. Two of those sticks are black and the other two white and something larger than the black ones. Those sticks they place in different positions which they perform under a kind of trencher made of bark, round and about 14 inches in diameter. This is a very intricate game and I cannot sufficiently understand it to describe it. The man who is in possession of the sticks places them in different positions, and the opposite party tells the position of the black sticks by a motion of either or both of his hands. This game is counted in the same way as the one before mentioned. All their games are accompanied with songs and time.

At three p.m. Sgt. Ordway and three men arrived from Capt. Lewis. They brought with them several elkskins, two of my coats, and four robes of the party to add to the stores I had with me for the purchase of horses. Sgt. Ordway informed me that Capt. Lewis had arrived with all the canoes into the basin two miles below and wished some dogs to eat. I had three dogs purchased and sent down. At five p.m. Capt. Lewis came up. He informed me that he had come up the river to the basin with much difficulty and danger, having made one portage. As I had not slept but very little for the two nights past on account of mice and vermin, with which those Indian houses abounded, and having no blanket with me, and the means of keeping a fire sufficient to keep me warm outdoors was too expensive, I determined to proceed with Capt. Lewis down to camp at the basin. I left the articles of merchandise etc. with Drouillard, Werner, Shannon and Goodrich until the morning. At the basin we cut up two of our canoes for firewood, very much to the chagrin of the natives, notwithstanding they would give us nothing for them. In my absence several Indians visited Capt. Lewis at his camp; among others was the great chief of the Chilluckkitquaws, who continued with him until he left Rockfort Camp. Capt. Lewis had 12 pack-saddles completed and strings prepared of the elkskins for lashing the loads.

He also kept out all the hunters who killed just deer enough for the party with him to subsist on. The chief who had visited Capt. Lewis promised him that he would bring some horses to the basin and trade with him, but he was not as good as his word. Capt. Lewis gave a large kettle for a horse that was offered to him at the basin this evening.

April 19, 1806, Saturday [Lewis]
This morning early we had our small canoes drawn out and employed all hands in transporting our baggage on their backs, and by means of the four pack horses, over the portage. This labor we had accomplished by three p.m. and established our camp a little above the present Skillute village, which has been removed a few hundred yards lower down the river than when we passed them last fall, and like others below have the floors of their summer dwellings on the surface of the earth instead of those cellars in which they resided when we passed them. There was great joy with the natives last night in consequence of the arrival of the salmon; one of those fish was caught; this was the harbinger of good news to them. They informed us that these fish would arrive in great quantities in the course of about five days. This fish was dressed and being divided into small pieces was given to each child in the village. This custom is founded in a superstitious opinion that it will hasten the arrival of the salmon.

With much difficulty we obtained four other horses from the Indians today; we were obliged to dispense with two of our kettles in order to acquire those. We have now only one small kettle to a mess of eight men. In the evening Capt. Clark set out with four men to the Eneshur villages at the grand falls in order to make a further attempt to procure horses. These people are very faithless in their contracts. They frequently receive the merchandise in exchange for their horses and after some hours insist on some additional article being given them or revoke the exchange. They have pilfered several small articles from us this evening.

I directed the horses to be hobbled and suffered to graze at a little distance from our camp under the immediate eye of the men who had them in charge. One of the men, Willard, was negligent in his attention to his horse and suffered it to ramble off; it was not to be found when I ordered the others to be brought up and confined to the pickets. This, in addition to the other difficulties under which I labored, was truly provoking. I reprimanded him more severely for this piece of negligence than had been usual with me. I had the remaining horses well secured by pickets; they were extremely restless and it required the attention of the whole guard through the night to retain them, notwithstanding they were hobbled and picketed. They frequently threw themselves by the ropes by which they were confined. All except one were stone horses, for the people in this neighborhood do not understand the art of gelding them, and this is a season at which they are most vicious. Many of the natives remained about our camp all night.

April 20, 1806, Sunday [Lewis]
Some frost this morning. The Eneshur and Skillutes are much better clad than they were last fall. Their men have generally leggings, moccasins, and large robes; many of them wear shirts of the same form with those of the Shoshone, Chopunnish, highly ornamented with porcupine quills. The dress of their women differs very little from those of the great rapids and above. Their children frequently wear robes of the large gray squirrel skins. Those of the men and women are principally deerskins, some wolf, elk, bighorn and buffalo; the latter they procure from the nations who sometimes visit the Missouri. Indeed a considerable proportion of their wearing apparel is purchased from their neighbors to the N.W. in exchange for pounded fish, copper and beads. At present the principal village of the Eneshur is below the falls on the N. side of the river. One other village is above the falls on the S. side and another a few miles above on the N. side. The first consists of 19, the second of 11, and the third of five lodges. Their houses, like those of the Skillutes, have their floors on the surface of the ground, but are formed of sticks and covered with mats and straw. They are large and contain usually several families each. For fuel they use straw, small willows and the southern wood [*i.e., sagebrush*]. They use the silk grass in manufacturing their fishing nets and bags, the bear grass and cedar bark are employed in forming a variety of articles. They are poor, dirty, proud, haughty, inhospitable, parsimonious, and faithless in every respect. Nothing but our numbers, I believe, prevents their attempting to murder us at this moment.

This morning I was informed that the natives had pilfered six tomahawks and a knife from the party in the course of the last night. I spoke to the chief on this subject. He appeared angry with his people and addressed them but the property was not restored. One horse which I had purchased and paid for yesterday and which could not be found when I ordered the horses into close confinement yesterday I was now informed had been gambled away by the rascal who had sold it to me and had been taken away by a man of another nation. I therefore took the goods back from this fellow. I purchased a gun from the chief for which I gave him two elkskins. In the course of the day I obtained two other indifferent horses for which I gave an extravagant price. I found that I should get no more horses and therefore resolved to proceed tomorrow morning with those which I had and to convey the baggage in two small canoes that the horses could not carry. For this purpose I had a load made up for seven horses; the eighth Bratton was compelled to ride as he was yet unable to walk [*Bratton had been suffering from incapacitating back pain for well over a month*]. I bartered my elkskins, old irons and two canoes for beads. One of the canoes for which they would give us but little I had cut up for fuel. These people have yet a large quantity of dried fish on hand yet they will not let us have any but for an exorbitant price. We purchased two dogs and some shappellel from them. I had the horses grazed until evening and then picketed and hobbled within the limits of our camp. I ordered the Indians from our camp this evening and informed them that if I caught them attempting to purloin any article from us I would beat them severely. They went off in rather a bad humor and I directed the party to examine their arms and be on their guard. They stole two spoons from us in the course of the day.

Clark, meanwhile, was having an equally frustrating day at the Eneshur village upriver. He was offering "a blue robe, a calico shirt, a silk handkerchief, five parcels of paint, a knife, a wampum moon, eight yards of ribbon, several pieces of brass, a moccasin awl, and six braces of yellow beads" for a horse, which was twice what they had paid for horses to the Flathead and Shoshones. He also offered "my large blue blanket, my coat, sword and plume, none of which seemed to entice those people to sell their horses." He acquired not a single horse during the course of the day. At the end of the day he gave up, packed away the merchandise, and camped; then he returned to the lodges to smoke. When he and his men slept that night they slept with their merchandise "under our heads and guns, etc., in our arms, as we always have in similar situations."

April 21, 1806, Monday [Lewis]
Notwithstanding all the precautions I had taken with respect to the horses, one of them had broken his cord of five strands of elk skin and had gone

off spanseled [*i.e., hobbled*]. I sent several men in search of the horse with orders to return at 10 a.m. with or without the horse, being determined to remain no longer with these villains. They stole another tomahawk from us this morning. I searched many of them but could not find it. I ordered all the spare poles, paddles, and the balance of our canoe put on the fire, as the morning was cold, and also so that not a particle should be left for the benefit of the Indians. I detected a fellow in stealing an iron socket of a canoe pole and gave him several severe blows and made the men kick him out of camp. I now informed the Indians that I would shoot the first of them that attempted to steal an article from us, that we were not afraid to fight them, that I had it in my power at that moment to kill them all and set fire to their houses, but it was not my wish to treat them with severity provided they would let my property alone. That I would take their horses if I could find out the persons who had stolen the tomahawks, but that I had rather lose the property altogether than take the horse of an innocent person. The chiefs were present, hung their heads and said nothing.

At nine a.m. Windsor returned with the lost horse; the others who were in search of the horse soon after returned also. The Indian who promised to accompany me as far as the Chopunnish country produced me two horses, one of which he politely gave me the liberty of packing. We took breakfast and departed a few minutes after 10 o'clock, having nine horses loaded and one which Bratton rode, not being able as yet to march. The two canoes I had dispatched early this morning. At one p.m. I arrived at the Eneshur village, where I found Capt. Clark and party; he had not purchased a single horse. He informed me that these people were quite as unfriendly as their neighbors the Skillutes, and that he had subsisted since he left me on a couple of platters of pounded roots and fish, which an old man had the politeness to offer him. His party fared much better on dogs, which he purchased from those people.

The man resided here from whom I had purchased the horse which ran off from me yesterday. I had given him a large kettle and a knife in exchange for that horse, which I informed him should be taken from him unless he produced me the lost horse or one of equal value in his stead. The latter he preferred and produced me a very good horse, which I very cheerfully received. We soon made the portage with our canoes and baggage and halted about half a mile above the village where we grazed our horses and took dinner on some dogs which we purchased of these people. After dinner we proceeded on about four miles to a village of nine mat lodges of the Eneshur a little below the entrance of Clark's River [*this is now named the Deschutes River*] and encamped. One of the canoes joined us, the other, not observing us halt, continued on. We obtained two dogs and a small quantity of fuel of these people, for which we were obliged to give a higher price than usual. Our guide continued with us; he appears to be an honest, sincere fellow. He tells us that the Indians a little above will treat us with much more hospitality than those we are now with. We purchased another horse this evening but his back is in such a horrid state that we can put but little on him. We obtained him for a trifle, at least for articles which might be procured in the United States for 10 shillings in Virginia currency. We took the precaution of picketing and spanseling our horses this evening near our camp.

The party had now reached the great falls of the Columbia, or Celilo Falls, and portaged it.

April 22, 1806, Tuesday [Lewis]
Last night two of our horses broke loose from the pickets and straggled off some little distance. The men who had charge of them fortunately recovered them early. At seven a.m. we set out, having previously sent on our small canoe with Colter and Potts. We had not arrived at the top of a hill over which the road leads opposite the village before Charbonneau's horse threw his load, and taking fright at the saddle and robe which still adhered, ran at full speed down the hill. Near the village he disengaged himself from the saddle and robe. An Indian hid the robe in his lodge. I sent our guide and one man who was with me in the rear to assist Charbonneau in retaking his horse, which having done they returned to the village on the track of the horse in search of the lost articles. They found the saddle but could see nothing of the robe. The Indians denied having seen it. They then continued on the track of the horse to the place from whence he had set out, with the same success. Being now confident that the Indians had taken it, I sent the Indian woman on to request Capt. Clark to halt the party and send back some of the men to my assistance, being determined either to make the Indians deliver the robe or burn their houses. They have vexed me in such a manner by such repeated acts of villainy that I am quite disposed to treat them with every severity; their defenseless state pleads forgiveness so far as respects their lives.

With this resolution I returned to their village, which I had just reached as Labiche met me with the robe, which he informed me he found in an Indian lodge hidden behind their baggage. I now returned and joined Capt. Clark, who was waiting my arrival with the party. The Indian woman had not reached Capt. Clark until about the time I arrived and he returned from a position on the top of a hill not far from where he had halted the party. From the top of this eminence Capt. Clark had an extensive view of the country. He observed the range of mountains in which Mount Hood stands to continue nearly south as far as the eye could reach. He also observed the snow-clad top of Mount Jefferson, which bore S.10°W. Mount Hood from the same point bore S.30°W. The tops of the range of western mountains are covered with snow. Capt. Clark also discovered some timbered country in a southern direction from him at no great distance. Clark's river, which mouths immediately opposite this point of view, forks at the distance of 18 or 20 miles from hence. The right hand fork takes its rise in Mount Hood, and the main branch continues its course to the S.E.

We now made the following regulations as to our future order of march, that Capt. Clark and myself should divide the men who were disencumbered by horses and march alternately each day the one in front and the other in rear. Having divided the party agreeably to this arrangement, we proceeded on through an open plain country about eight miles to a village of six houses of the Eneshur Nation. Here we observed our two canoes passing up on the opposite side; the wind being too high for them to pass the river, they continued on. We halted at a small run just above the village, where we dined on some dogs which we purchased of the inhabitants, and suffered our horses to graze about three hours. There is no timber in this country; we are obliged to purchase our fuel of the natives, who bring it from a great distance. While we halted for dinner we purchased a horse. After dinner we proceeded on up the river about four miles to a village of seven mat lodges of the last mentioned nation. Here our Chopunnish guide informed us that the next village was at a considerable distance and that we could not reach it tonight. The people at this place offered to sell us wood and dogs, and we therefore thought it better to remain all night. A man belonging to the next village above proposed exchanging a horse for one of our canoes. Just at this moment one of our canoes was passing. We hailed them and ordered them to come over, but the wind continued so high that they could not join us until after sunset and the Indian who wished to exchange his horse for the canoe had gone on. Charbonneau purchased a horse this evening. We obtained four dogs and as much wood as answered our purposes on moderate terms. We can only afford ourselves one fire, and are obliged to lie without shelter. The nights are cold and days warm. Colter and Potts had passed on with their canoe.

Clark adds that Charbonneau obtained the horse for a shirt, a tomahawk, a plume, and something he calls a "red rapper," possibly a cloak of some kind, taking "rapper" to mean "wrapper." The men found the horses difficult, "particularly the stud, which compose 10/13 of our number of horses." The next entry is Clark's:

April 23, 1806, Wednesday [Clark]
At daylight this morning we were informed that the two horses of our interpreter Charbonneau were missing. On inquiry we were informed that he had neglected to tie up his horses as directed last evening. We immediately dispatched him, R. Fields and Labiche in search of the horses. One of them was found at no great distance. The other was not found. R. Fields returned without finding the horse, set out with Sgt. Gass in the small canoe at about eight a.m. At 10 Charbonneau and Labiche returned, also unsuccessful. They had gone on the back trail nearly to the last village and took a circle around on the hills. As our situation was such that we could not detain for a horse, which would prevent our making a timely stage, which is a great object with us in these open plains, we concluded to give up the horse and proceed on to the next village, which we were informed was at some distance and would take us the greater part of the day.

At 11 a.m. we packed up and set out and proceeded up on the N. side of the Columbia on a high narrow bottom and rocky for 12 miles to the *Wah-how-pum* village near the rock rapid of 12 temporary mat lodges. Those people appeared pleased to see us. They sold us four dogs, some shapalell, and wood for our small articles, such as awls, pieces of tin and brass. We passed several lodges on the bank of the river where they were fixed waiting for the salmon. I overtook a Chopunnish man whom I had seen at the long narrows [*the Dalles*] and who had found a bag of our powder and brought it to me at that place. This man had his family and about 13 head of horses that appeared young and unbroken. His spouse, as also that of the other, gave me a cake of shapalell and proceeded on with me to the Wah-how-pum village and formed his camp near us. We caused all the old and brave men to set around and smoke with us. We caused the fiddle to be played and some of the men danced. After them the natives danced. They dance differently from any Indians I have seen. They dance with their shoulders together and pass from side to side, different parties passing each other, from two to seven, and four parties dancing at the same time and concluding the dance by passing promiscuously through and between each other. After which we sent off the Indians and retired to bed. Those people speak a language very similar to the Chopunnish and with a very inconsiderable difference. Their dress and appearance is more like those of the great falls of the Columbia.

We had all our horses side-hobbled and let out to feed. At this village a large creek falls in on the N. side which I had not observed as I descended the river. The river is by no means as rapid as it was at the time we descended. The natives promised to give us a horse for one of our canoes, and offer to sell us another for a scarlet robe, which we have not at present. Charbonneau made a bargain with one of the Indian men going with us for a horse, for which he gave his shirt and two of the leather suits of his wife. The sand through which we walked today is so light that it renders the march very fatiguing. Made 12 miles by land.

SUMMARY

APRIL 24 TO JUNE 25, 1806

———⟨∘∘∘⟩———

The captains continued to acquire horses, and on better terms, as they contin-ued east. On the 24th they traded for three more and hired three from the Chopunnish (or Nez Perce) man who with his family was traveling with them, and the day after that they acquired two more. The captains called these last two "nags" and rode them. They found the Indians upriver friendlier than those they had just dealt with. On April 27 they reached a Walla Walla village and acquired an "elegant white horse" from the local chief, who took Clark's sword, some ammunition, and some small articles in exchange. They discov-ered here that they could cut their trip 80 miles short by leaving the Columbia and marching cross-country. On the 29th they did just that, crossing the Columbia and setting out from its south bank toward the Clearwater, where they had left their previous stock of horses with the Nez Perce in the fall. By the 30th of April they had 23 horses. "Most of them," says Lewis, "[are] excellent young horses, but much the greater portion of them have sore backs. These Indians are cruel horse-masters; they ride hard, and their saddles are so ill-constructed that they cannot avoid wounding the backs of their horses. But regardless of this they ride them when the backs of these poor animals are in a horrid condition."

Yet the captains were finding reasons to approve of Indian behavior, too. On the evening of May 1, Lewis tells us, "three young men arrived from the Walla Walla village bringing with them a steel trap belonging to one of our party which had been negligently left behind. This is an act of integrity rarely witnessed among Indians. During our stay with them they several times found the knives of the men which had been carelessly lost by them and returned them. I think we can justly affirm to the honor of these people that they are the most hospitable, honest, and sincere people that we have met with in our voyage." On May 7, as they were coming within sight of the spurs of the Bitterroot range, "perfectly covered with snow," a Nez Perce they met produced two canisters of powder his dog had dug up from one of the caches the expedition had left behind the previous fall. "As he had kept them safe and had honesty enough to return them to us, we gave him a fire steel by way of compensation," Lewis reports. He was similarly impressed a few days later when he offered to exchange with the Nez Perce a "good horse in rather low order for a young horse in tolerable order," with a view to using the latter as food. They had used up their dried elk on the Columbia Plateau and were subsisting mostly on dog. The chief would not hear of it. "He told us that his young men had a great abundance of young horses and if we wished to eat them we should be furnished with as many as we wanted. Accordingly they soon produced us two fat young horses, one of which we killed." Lewis commented that "this is a much greater act of hospitality than we have witnessed from any nation or tribe since we have passed the Rocky Mountains." The fact that they were eating dog drew down the contempt of one young Nez Perce warrior, who, says Lewis, "threw a poor half-starved puppy nearly into my plate by way of derision for our eating dogs and laughed very heartily at his own impertinence. I was so provoked at this insolence that I caught the puppy and threw it with great violence at him and struck him in the breast and face, seized my tomahawk and showed him by signs that if he repeated his insolence I would tomahawk him." Despite the kindnesses of the Nez Perce, Lewis was clearly in no mood to take any disrespect from his Indian hosts. Two years in the wilderness, dealing constantly with people he regarded as savages, was beginning to tell on his nerves.

By May 4 they had reached the junction of the Clearwater and the Snake Rivers, where they had made canoes the previous September, and were moving back the way they had come to the foot of the Bitterroot Mountains, which were still snowed in, the snow ten feet deep in some places. The Nez Perce did not think the snows would melt sufficiently for them to get through for at least a month. They would have to find a campsite, settle in and wait. They chose a site on the Clearwater under the mountains that they called Camp Chopunnish; they would be there from May 14 until the 9th of June. The delay was frustrating; they were all ready to go home. On May 17, at the end of his entry for the day,

Lewis notes, "I am pleased at finding the river rise so rapidly. It no doubt is attributable to the melting snows of the mountains—that icy barrier which separates me from my friends and country, from all which makes life estimable. Patience, patience." Clark, who was still mostly copying Lewis's entries each day, echoes the sentiment in his own entry, and adds that he frequently consults "the natives on the subject of passing this tremendous barrier which now presents itself to our view for a great extent; they all appear to agree as to the time those mountains may be passed, which is about the middle of June."

In the meantime they would have to make do. They soon fell into a feast or famine situation. Some days the hunters came back with ample supplies of game, other days they could find nothing. The salmon had not yet returned, an event both the Indians and the men of the expedition were hoping and waiting for. When game was not to be found, they slaughtered a horse for food; the Nez Perce were generous with horses. By the time the expedition was ready to leave, the men had accumulated 65 of them, a few of them outright gifts from the Indians, the rest the sum of those they had purchased on their way up from the mouth of the Columbia and the horses they had left behind in the fall in the care of Twisted Hair, one of the Nez Perce chiefs.

One reason the Indians were generous was because Clark was generous in return with his medical treatment. When they first reached the Nez Perce in early May, Clark traded medical care for food. He had established a reputation among the Indians for his skills the previous fall. Finding a man with a tumor on his thigh who could not walk, he cleansed and dressed the wound and left him some soap to wash the sore. He soon got well and "this man assigned the restoration of his leg to me," says Clark. He had treated another man with liniment for a sore leg and knee; this man also thought Clark was a miracle worker. Clark knew better, but he did what he could nevertheless and Indians came to him by the score. The most common disorder was eye trouble, for which Clark administered "eye water," a solution of, among other things, lead acetate and zinc sulphate. It seemed to work, or at least to help. "We take care," he remarks in his entry for May 5, "to give them no article which can possibly injure them, and in many cases can administer and give such medicine and surgical aid as will effectually restore in simple cases." Clark understood well the first principle of medical care: Do no harm.

He did take on serious cases. Bratton was one; his back pain had incapacitated him for months, making him unable to work or even to walk. At Camp Choppunish John Shields suggested that they try to sweat the disorder out of him, as he had seen done elsewhere, so they built a sweat lodge to that purpose, digging a large hole in the ground, building a fire in it, then putting out the fire and covering the hole with a tent of willow poles and blankets. "The patient, being stripped naked," writes Lewis, "was seated under this awning in the hole and the blankets well secured on every side. The patient was furnished with a vessel of water which he sprinkles on the bottom and sides of the hole and by that means creates as much steam or vapor as he could possibly bear. In this situation he was kept about 20 minutes, after which he was taken out and suddenly plunged in cold water twice, and was then immediately returned to the sweat hole, where he was continued three quarters of an hour longer, then taken out, covered up in several blankets, and suffered to cool gradually. During the time of his being in the sweat hole, he drank copious draughts of a strong tea of horse mint." Bratton felt better almost at once and was soon well. A few days later they tried the same treatment on an old Indian chief of high standing among the Nez Perce whose limbs were paralyzed but who was otherwise apparently quite well. After repeated treatments the chief also improved. Clark treated Sacagawea's child, who developed an infection in his neck accompanied by high fever, with poultices. He too improved, and eventually threw off the infection. It's no wonder that the Nez Perce regarded Clark as a powerful medicine man.

While Clark served as a doctor, Lewis did what he always did—took notes on natural history. He puzzled for a while over how many species of bear they had encountered, given the color variation they were seeing. There were plenty of grizzlies in the area, as well as a variation on the black bear known as the cinnamon bear, and Lewis correctly deduced that the color variations were just that, variations of one species, the grizzly, Ursus arctos horribilis. Lewis was truly a gifted naturalist. "It is not common," he writes, "to find two bear here of this species precisely of the same color, and if we were to attempt to distinguish them by their colors and to denominate each color a distinct species we should soon find at least twenty . . . The most striking differences between this species of bear and the common black bear are that the former are larger, have longer talons and tusks, prey more on other animals, do not lie so long nor so closely in winter quarters, and will not climb a tree though ever so hardly pressed." He found the grizzlies to the west of the Rockies less fierce than those on the Missouri, a fact he attributed to the scarcity of game; the western bears were used to getting their food out of the ground. He was observant on the climate as well, noticing that "the air on the top of the river hills or high plain forms a distinct *climate; the air is much colder, and vegetation is not as forward by at least 15 or perhaps 20 days. The rains which fall in the river bottoms are snows on the plain. At the distance of 15 miles from the river and on the eastern border of this plain, the Rocky Mountains commence and present us with winter at its utmost extreme. The snow is yet many feet deep even near the base of these mountains. Here we have summer, spring and winter within the short space of 15 or 20 miles."*

The Nez Perce, it is worth noting, had come to the same conclusion with respect to the bears. There were two species, the black bear and the grizzly; the latter came in any number of colors. He took the time to write about the Nez Perce themselves, finding them to be "stout well formed active men." ["Stout" does not mean "fat" in this context; it means the Nez Perce are strong and brave, "stout-hearted."] They were, he noted, "cheerful but not gay;" they liked to gamble, they were expert marksmen and good horsemen, well-clothed, and not as addicted to "baubles" as they had found other Indians to be, with one exception. They loved blue beads. "This article," says Lewis, "among all the nations of this country may be justly compared to gold or silver among civilized nations." He also found of interest the Nez Perce method of gelding their horses, which he saw, as the wounds healed, was a much better method than the one in use in Virginia.

But there was not much to do, really, but wait. The captains divided up the remaining trade goods among the men and told them to go off and trade with the Indians individually for breads made out of camas and coues, and the roots themselves, to sustain them during the trip across the Bitterroots, where they did not expect to find any game. "Each man's stock in trade," Lewis explains, "amounts to no more than one awl, one knitting pin, a half ounce of vermilion, two needles, a few skeins of thread and about a yard of ribbon, a slender stock indeed with which to lay in a store of provision for that dreary wilderness. We would make the men collect these roots themselves but there are several species of hemlock which are so much like the coues that it is difficult to discriminate them from the coues and we are afraid that they might poison themselves." This was a real danger; an herbaceous hemlock growing in the area was indeed quite poisonous. The time dragged on. By the 29th of May Lewis was writing once again, "No movement of the party today worthy of notice." They staged foot races with the Indians and games to keep the men fit. Those not out hunting had little to keep them busy. Lewis described the insects of the region, and the birds. By May 26 they had exhausted their supply of meat; on the 27th they butchered a horse. That day the hunters came in with five deer; the next day they killed eight. But by June 9 they had eaten the last of their meat again and were living on roots. The expedition numbered some 30 people. Meat was the principal item on their diet. They needed a lot of it.

The next day they broke down the camp and moved up to Weippe Prairie, where they had first found food after struggling down the Lolo Trail the previous September. They hoped to find game there, and to begin the crossing of the Bitterroots after a few more days. The key to success was finding grass for the horses on the trail; if the snow had not melted enough to open up patches of ground where grass was sprouting, they would have to wait still longer. They did not know what faced them. They moved still higher into the mountains. On the 14th of June, having spent three or four days trying to stock up on meat, Lewis summed up the situation:

> From hence to Traveler's Rest we shall make a forced march. At that place we shall probably remain one or two days to rest ourselves and horses and procure some meat. We have now been detained near five weeks in consequence of the snows, a serious loss of time at this delightful season for traveling. I am still apprehensive that the snow and the want of food for our horses will prove a serious embarrassment to us, as at least four days journey of our route in these mountains lies over heights and along a ledge of mountains never entirely destitute of snow. Everybody seems anxious to be in motion, convinced that we have not now any time to delay if the calculation is to reach the United States this season. This I am determined to accomplish if within the compass of human power.

Clark added his own note to this: "Even now I shudder with the expectation of great difficulties in passing those mountains, from the depth of snow and the want of grass sufficient to subsist our horses."

They set out on the 15th and turned back two days later, stopped by the snow. "The party were a good deal dejected," writes Lewis, "though not as much as I had apprehended they would have been. This is the first time since we have been on this long tour that we have ever been compelled to retreat or make a retrograde march. It rained on us most of this evening." The problem was not the snow itself but the fact that it concealed the trail; they did not know where they were going. The snow was deep, 12 to 15 feet deep in places, but it was also firm enough to support the horses. "If we proceeded," as Lewis went on to explain, "and should get bewildered in these mountains, the certainty was that we should lose all our horses and consequently our baggage, instruments, perhaps our papers, and thus imminently risk the loss of the discoveries which we had already made, if we should be so fortunate as to escape with life. The snow bore our horses very well and the traveling was therefore infinitely better than the obstruction of rocks and fallen timber which we met with in our passage over last fall, when the snow lay on this part of the ridge in detached spots only. Under these circumstances we conceived it madness in this stage of the expedition to proceed without a guide . . ." The captains immediately sent Drouillard and Shannon back to recruit guides from the Nez Perce.

Meanwhile they left some of their baggage behind, to pick up when they returned, and retreated to Weippe Prairie and waited some more. Not until June 23 did Drouillard and Shannon return with three Nez Perce men, men known to them, who agreed to guide them over the mountains and all the way to the Great Falls of the Missouri for two guns. On the 24th they turned around and started to make their way uphill again, into the mountains. We return to them for the next few days while they repeat their journey of the previous fall over the Lolo Trail.

ending. 1 2 3 represents the rim of the que
we de wattier ascending as they, recede
6.7.8 are the round holes through which
serted.—
canoe   me
ntile we B   c reached
te grand   rappids.
it is common to all the nation but
the Killamucks and others of the coast
st canoes. B is the bow and comb. c, the

Canoe with carved images, February 1, 1806

———————————◁◦◦◦▷———————————

June 26, 1806, Thursday [Lewis]
This morning we collected our horses and set out after an early breakfast or at six a.m. We passed by the same route we had traveled on the 17th to our deposit on the top of the snowy mountain to the N.E. of Hungry Creek. Here we necessarily halted about two hours to arrange our baggage and prepare our loads. We cooked and made a hasty meal of boiled venison and mush of coues. The snow has subsided near four feet since the 17. We now measured it accurately and found from a mark which we had made on a tree when we were last here on the 17th that it was then 10 feet 10 inches, which appeared to be about the common depth, though it is deeper still in some places. It is now generally about seven feet. On our way up this mountain about the border of the snowy region we killed two of the small black pheasant and a female of the large speckled pheasant. The former have 16 feathers in their tail and the latter 20, while the common pheasant have only 18. The Indians informed us that neither of these species drummed. They appear to be very silent birds, for I never heard either of them make a noise in any situation.

The Indians hastened to be off and informed us that it was a considerable distance to the place which they wished to reach this evening where there was grass for our horses. Accordingly we set out with our guides, who led us over and along the steep sides of tremendous mountains entirely covered with snow, except about the roots of the trees where the snow had sometimes melted and exposed a few square feet of earth. We ascended and descended several lofty and steep heights, but keeping on the dividing ridge between the Chopunnish and Kooskooske Rivers we passed no stream of water [*this would be the North Fork of the Clearwater and the Lochsa Rivers*]. Late in the evening, much to the satisfaction of ourselves and the comfort of our horses, we arrived at the desired spot and encamped on the steep side of a mountain convenient to a good spring. There we found an abundance of fine grass for our horses. This situation was the side of an untimbered mountain with a fair southern aspect where the snow from appearance had been dissolved about 10 days. The grass was young and tender, of course, and had much the appearance of the greensward. There is a great abundance of a species of bear grass which grows on every part of these mountains. Its growth is luxuriant and continues green all winter, but the horses will not eat it. Soon after we had encamped we were overtaken by a Chopunnish man who had pursued us with a view to accompany me to the falls of the Missouri. We were now informed that the two young men whom we met on the 21st and detained several days are going on a party of pleasure merely to the Oote-lash-shoots or as they call them Shalees, a band of the Tush-she-pah nation who reside on Clark's River in the neighborhood of Traveler's Rest. One of our guides lost two of his horses, which he returned in search of. He found them and rejoined us a little before dark.

June 27, 1806, Friday [Lewis]
We collected our horses early and set out. The road still continued on the heights of the same dividing ridge on which we had traveled yesterday for nine miles or to our encampment of the 17th of September last. About one mile short of this encampment on an elevated point we halted by the request of the Indians a few minutes and smoked the pipe. On this eminence the natives have raised a conic mound of stones of six or eight feet high and on its summit erected a pine pole of 15 feet long. From hence, they informed us, that when passing over with their families some of the men were usually sent on foot by the fishery at the entrance of Colt Creek in order to take fish and again meet the main party at the Quawmash glade on the head of the Kooskooske River. From this place we had an extensive view of these stupendous mountains, principally covered with snow like that on which we stood. We were entirely surrounded by those mountains, from which to one

unacquainted with them it would have seemed impossible ever to have escaped. In short, without the assistance of our guides I doubt much whether we who had once passed them could find our way to Traveler's Rest in their present situation, for the marked trees on which we had placed considerable reliance are much fewer and more difficult to find than we had apprehended. These fellows are most admirable pilots; we find the road wherever the snow has disappeared, though it be only for a few hundred paces.

After smoking the pipe and contemplating this scene sufficient to have dampened the spirits of any except such hardy travelers as we have become, we continued our march and at the distance of three miles descended a steep mountain and passed two small branches of the Chopunnish River just above their forks and again ascended the ridge on which we passed several miles and at a distance of seven miles arrived at our encampment of the 16th of September, near which we passed three small branches of the Chopunnish River and again ascended to the dividing ridge, on which we continued nine miles, when the ridge became lower and we arrived at a situation very similar to our encampment of the last evening, though the ridge was somewhat higher and the snow had not been so long dissolved. Of course there was but little grass.

Here we encamped for the night, having traveled 28 miles over these mountains without relieving the horses from their packs or their having any food. The Indians inform us that there is an abundance of the mountain sheep or what they call the white buffalo. We saw three black-tailed or mule deer this evening but were unable to get a shot at them. We also saw several tracks of those animals in the snow. The Indians inform us that there is great abundance of elk in the valley about the fishery on the Kooskooske River. Our meat being exhausted, we issued a pint of bear's oil to a mess, which with their boiled roots made an agreeable dish. Potts's leg, which has been much swollen and inflamed for several days, is much better this evening and gives him but little pain. We applied the pounded roots and leaves of the wild ginger, from which he found great relief. Near our encampment we saw a great number of the yellow lily with reflected petals in bloom. This plant was just as forward here at this time as it was in the plains on the 10th of May.

June 28, 1806, Saturday [Lewis]
This morning we collected our horses and set out as usual after an early breakfast. Several of our horses had straggled to a considerable distance in

search of food but we were fortunate enough to find them in good time. They look extremely gaunt this morning; however, the Indians informed us that at noon we would arrive at a place where there was good food for them. We continued our route along the dividing ridge, passing one very deep hollow, and at the distance of six miles passed our encampment of the 15th of September last. One and a half miles further we passed the road which leads by the fishery falling in on the right immediately on the dividing ridge. About 11 o'clock we arrived at an untimbered side of a mountain with a southern aspect just above the fishery. Here we found an abundance of grass for our horses as the Indians had informed us. As our horses were very hungry and much fatigued and from information that there was no other place where we could obtain grass for them within the reach of this evening's travel, we determined to remain at this place all night, having come 13 miles only. The water was distant from our encampment; we therefore melted snow and used the water. The whole of the route of this day was over deep snows. We find the traveling on the snow not worse than without it, as the easy passage it gives us over rocks and fallen timber fully compensate for the inconvenience of slipping. Certain it is that we travel considerably faster on the snow than without it. The snow sinks from two to three inches with a horse, is coarse and firm, and seems to be formed of the larger and more dense particles of the snow. The surface of the snow is rather harder in the morning than after the sun shines on it a few hours, but it is not in that situation so dense as to prevent the horse from obtaining good foothold.

We killed a small black pheasant. This bird is generally found in the snowy region of the mountains and feeds on the leaves of the pine and fir. There is a species of small whortleberry common to the heights of the mountains, and a species of grass with a broad succulent leaf which looks not unlike a flag. Of the latter the horses are very fond, but as yet it is generally under the snow or merely making its appearance, as it is confined to the upper parts of the highest mountains.

June 29, 1806, Sunday [Lewis]
We collected our horses early this morning and set out, having previously dispatched Drouillard and R. Fields to the warm springs to hunt. We pursued the heights of the ridge on which we have been passing for several days. It terminated at the distance of five miles from our encampment and we descended to and passed the main branch of the Kooskooske one and a half

miles above the entrance of Quawmash Creek, which falls in on the N.E. side. When we descended from this ridge we bid adieu to the snow. Near the river we found a deer which the hunters had killed and left us. This was a fortunate supply, as all our oil was now exhausted and we were reduced to our roots alone without salt [*they had run out of the salt they produced on the Pacific coast the previous winter*]. The Kooskooske at this place is about 30 yards wide and runs with great velocity. The bed, as all the mountains streams, is composed of smooth stones.

Beyond the river we ascended a very steep acclivity of a mountain about two miles and arrived at its summit, where we found the old road which we had passed as we went out coming in on our right. The road was now much plainer and more beaten, which we were informed happened from the circumstance of the Ootslashshoots visiting the fishery frequently from the valley of Clark's River, though there was no appearance of their having been here this spring. At noon we arrived at the Quawmash flats on the creek of the same name and halted to graze our horses and dine, having traveled 12 miles. We passed our encampment of the 13th of September at 10 miles where we halted. There is a pretty little plain of about 50 acres plentifully stocked with quawmash and from appearances this forms one of the principal stages or encampments of the Indians who pass the mountains on this road. We found after we had halted that one of our packhorses with his load and one of my riding horses were left behind. We dispatched J. Fields and Colter in search of the lost horses.

After dinner we continued our march seven miles further to the warm springs [*Lolo Hot Springs*], where we arrived early in the evening and sent out several hunters, who as well as R. Fields and Drouillard returned unsuccessful. Late in the evening Colter and J. Fields joined us with the lost horses and brought with them a deer which they had killed. This furnished us with supper. These warm springs are situated at the base of a hill of no considerable height on the N. side and near the bank of Traveler's Rest Creek, which at that place is about 10 yards wide. These springs issue from the bottoms and through the interstices of a gray freestone rock; the rock rises in irregular massy cliffs in a circular range around the springs on their lower side. Immediately above the springs on the creek there is a handsome little quawmash plain of about 10 acres. The principal spring is about the temperature of the warmest baths used at the hot springs in Virginia. In this bath, which had been prepared by the Indians by stopping the run with stone and gravel, I bathed and remained in 19 minutes. It was with difficulty I could remain this long and it caused a profuse sweat. Two other bold springs adjacent to this are much warmer, their heat being so great as to make the hand of a person smart extremely when immersed. I think the temperature of these springs about the same as the hottest of the hot springs in Virginia. Both the men and Indians amused themselves with the use of a bath this evening. I observed that the Indians after remaining in the hot bath as long as they could bear it ran and plunged themselves into the creek, the water of which is now as cold as ice can make it. After remaining here a few minutes they returned again to the warm bath, repeating this transition several times but always ending with the warm bath.

I killed a small black pheasant near the quawmash grounds this evening which is the first I have seen below the snowy region. I also saw some young pheasants which were about the size of chickens of three days old. Saw the track of two barefoot Indians who were supposed to be distressed refugees who had fled from the Minnitaris.

June 30, 1806, Monday [Lewis]
We dispatched Drouillard and J. Fields early this morning to hunt on the road and endeavor to obtain some meat for us. Just as we had prepared to set out at an early hour a deer came in to lick at these springs and one of our hunters killed it. This secured us our dinners and we proceeded down the creek, sometimes in the bottoms and at other times on the top or along the steep sides of the ridge to the N. of the creek. At one mile from the springs we passed a stout branch of the creek on the north side and at noon, having traveled 13 miles, we arrived at the entrance of a second northern branch of the creek where we had nooned it on the 12th of September last. Here we halted, dined and grazed our horses. While here Shields took a small turn and killed a deer. At this place a road turns off to the right which the Indians informed us leads to Clark's River some distance below, where there is a fine extensive valley in which the Shalees or Ootslashshoots sometimes reside. In descending the creek this morning on the steep side of a high hill my horse slipped with both his hind feet out of the road and fell. I also fell off backwards and slid near 40 feet down the hill before I could stop myself, such was the steepness of the declivity. The horse was near falling on me in the first instance but fortunately recovered and we both escaped unhurt.

I saw a small gray squirrel today much like those of the Pacific coast only that the belly of this was white. I also met with the plant in bloom which is sometimes called the Lady's Slipper or Moccasin Flower. It is in shape and appearance like ours, only that the corolla is white, marked with small veins of pale red longitudinally on the inner side. After dinner we resumed our march. Soon after setting out Shields killed another deer and in the course of the evening we picked up three others which Drouillard had killed along the road, making a total of six today. Deer are very abundant in the neighborhood of Traveler's Rest of both species, also some bighorn and elk. A little before sunset we arrived at our old encampment on the south side of the creek a little above its entrance into Clark's River. Here we encamped with a view to remain two days in order to rest ourselves and horses and make our final arrangements for separation. We came 19 miles after dinner, the road being much better than it has been since we entered the mountains. We found no appearance of the Ootslashshoots having been here lately. The Indians express much concern for them and apprehend that the Minnitaris of Fort de Prairie have destroyed them in the course of the last winter and spring, and mention the tracks of the bare-foot Indians which we saw yesterday as an evidence of their being much distressed. Our horses have stood the journey surprisingly well. Most of them are yet in fine order and only want a few days rest to restore them perfectly.

July 1, 1806, Tuesday [Lewis]
This morning early we sent out all our hunters. Set Shields at work to repair some of our guns, which were out of order. Capt. Clark and myself concerted the following plan, viz.: from this place I determined to go with a small party by the most direct route to the falls of the Missouri, there to leave Thompson, McNeal, and Goodrich to prepare carriages and gear for the purpose of transporting the canoes and baggage over the portage, and myself and six volunteers to ascend Marias River with a view to explore the country and ascertain whether any branch of that river lies as far north as latitude 50 and again return and join the party who are to descend the Missouri at the entrance of Maria's River. I now called for the volunteers to accompany me on this route. Many turned out, from whom I selected Drouillard, the two Fieldses, Werner, Frazer, and Sgt. Gass.

The other part of the men are to proceed with Capt. Clark to the head of Jefferson's River, where we deposited sundry articles and left our canoes. From hence Sgt. Ordway with a party of nine men are to descend the river with the canoes. Capt. Clark with the remaining ten, including Charbonneau and York, will proceed to the Yellowstone River at its nearest approach to the three forks of the Missouri; here he will build a canoe and descend the Yellowstone River with Charbonneau, the Indian woman, his servant York and five others to the Missouri, where should he arrive first he will wait my arrival. Sgt. Pryor with two other men are to proceed with the horses by land to the Mandan and thence to the British posts on the Assiniboine with a letter to Mr. Heney, whom we wish to engage to prevail on the Sioux chiefs to join us on the Missouri and accompany us to the seat of the general government.

These arrangements being made, the party were informed of our design and prepared themselves accordingly. Our hunters killed 13 deer in the course of this day, of which seven were fine bucks; the deer are large and in fine order. The Indians inform us that there are a great number of white buffalo or mountain sheep on the snowy heights of the mountains west of this river; they state that they inhabit the most rocky and inaccessible parts, and run but badly, that they kill them with great ease with their arrows when they can find them. The Indian warrior who overtook us on the 26th [*of June*] made me a present of an excellent horse, which he said he gave for the good counsel we had given himself and nation and also to assure us of his attachment to the white men and his desire to be at peace with the Minnitaris of Fort de Prairie.

We had our venison fleeced and exposed in the sun on poles to dry. The dove, the black woodpecker, the lark woodpecker, the logcock, the prairie lark, sandhill crane, prairie hen with the short and pointed tail, the robin, a species of brown plover, a few curloos, small black birds, ravens, hawks, and a variety of sparrows, as well as the bee martin and the several species of the corvus genus, are found in this valley.

Windsor burst his gun near the muzzle a few days since. This Shields cut off and I then exchanged it with the chief for the one we had given him for conducting us over the mountains. He was much pleased with the exchange and shot his gun several times. He shoots very well for an inexperienced person.

Lewis then launches into a detailed description of the "barking squirrel" or prairie dog. Clark adds on this date that Lewis took only 17 horses with him, and intended to take only eight up the Marias River. The Indians who had guided them so safely and quickly over the Bitterroots expressed a desire to leave and return to their nation; Clark says they asked them only to accompany Lewis two more nights to help him on his way to the falls of the Missouri, and they agreed to do so.

On July 3 the two captains split up and took their separate paths. Clark turned south with 20 men, plus Sacagawea and her child, and 50 horses, heading toward their cache at the forks of the Beaverhead and the pirogues they had left there. Sacagawea would prove invaluable in the next week or two. This was her territory. She knew all the best routes. After two days in the Bitterroot Valley they took a different pass over the ridge that divided the Bitterroot from the Lemhi watershed, using what is now called Gibson Pass instead of Lost Trail Pass, then headed, under Sacagawea's guidance, toward Big Hole Pass. On the Fourth of July the party stopped a little early to celebrate the occasion with a good dinner, then moved on. On the 7th they found nine horses missing overnight, and suspected Indian theft. Clark left a small party behind to look for them; they were their best horses. The next day they reached their cache at the Beaverhead. The cache was intact. One canoe was somewhat damaged, but generally the canoes were in good shape. "The most of the party with me being chewers of tobacco," Clark remarks, "became so impatient to be chewing it that they scarcely gave themselves time to take their saddles off their horses before they were off to the deposit." He gave each man who used tobacco "about two feet off a part of a roll." They had come 164 miles in five days. The party left behind to find the nine horses found them and brought them on. Indians had not stolen them. They had seen no Indians. Clark would not see any Indians until he reached the Missouri.

They spent the next day drying out the canoes, repairing them, and getting ready to depart the day after. Now this party would split up, too, although not immediately; on the 10th he sent some men down in canoes, the rest with the horses, but they kept company to the Forks of the Missouri. They were making good time. The water was higher than when they had come up the previous summer, the river wider. In one day, July 10, they traveled downriver the same distance it had taken them six days to come up in August 1805. The water was swift enough that it occasionally got them into difficulties. On the 12th Clark's canoe was driven by a puff of wind under a log projecting out from a bank and nearly overturned. They also suffered, as usual, from swarms of mosquitoes, from which most of the men had no protection whatever. But in general the trip was trouble free. They were moving quickly; they had all their horses; things were going as planned.

On the 13th they reached the Forks early in the day and that afternoon Sergeant Ordway left with six canoes and ten men down the Missouri to the Great Falls, where they were to meet Captain Lewis. They were there in six days. Two hours after Ordway left, Clark himself left on horseback for the Yellowstone. He had with him Sergeant Pryor, Shields, Hall, Shannon, Bratton, Labiche, Windsor, Gibson, and Charbonneau, along with his servant, York, and Sacagawea and her child, whom the men all called "Pomp." They also had 49 horses and a colt. They set out up the Gallatin River. "The Indian woman, who has been of great service to me as a pilot through this country," he remarks, "recommends a gap in the mountain more south which I shall cross." The gap in question was Bozeman Pass, where the Yellowstone leaves the Absaroka range and descends to the High Plains. The route she was taking them on is now the route followed by Interstate 90.

It took just two days to reach the Yellowstone, where Clark at once started to look for trees big enough to carve into canoes. He moved slowly downriver on horseback; the horses' hooves were sore and he could not make good time. Nor could he find suitable trees. On the 16th they killed their first buffalo, using the green skin to make "moccasins" for the horses. They were in country once more where game was abundant everywhere one looked. The trip was still largely without incident; Clark describes the country in his journal entries, but has little else to report. On the 18th of July Charbonneau's horse threw him when it stepped into a gopher hole; he was only bruised. They saw Indian smoke at a distance, but no Indians. Gibson fell while mounting his horse and punctured his thigh with a sharp stick. The wound made it painful for him to travel for a few days but it wasn't serious. Shields got chased by a couple of grizzlies out of a timber bottom where he was looking for wild ginger to use as a plaster for Gibson's wound. Swarms of grasshoppers were defoliating the plains.

On the 19th they stopped for five days in a grove of timber to cut down the biggest cottonwoods they could find and make two small canoes, which they planned to lash together for sturdiness. The canoes were 28 feet long and some 16 to 24 inches wide. They woke up on the morning of July 21 to find half the horses gone; the Crow, famous horse thieves, had struck. Because the surface of the ground was hard and stony, they couldn't find any tracks and therefore couldn't pursue them. Not until the 23rd did they discover Indian sign of any kind, but it was obvious they themselves were being tracked. By then the two canoes were ready to go, and Clark gave Sergeant Pryor his instructions: Take the remaining horses to the Mandan villages, find Mr. Heney, if necessary at his establishment on the Assiniboine River, and deliver the letter Lewis and Clark had drafted to him asking him to persuade the Sioux chiefs to go to Washington to meet the president, leaving whatever horses were not necessary for that trip at the Mandan villages until Lewis and Clark's arrival. The horses were proving difficult to manage. Pryor had two men with him and 24 horses. They were Indian horses, trained when they saw bison to run after them. That's exactly what happened; the loose horses took off after the bison as soon as they saw them, scattering the bison, and themselves, all over the plains. The only way to prevent this was for Pryor, riding ahead, to scare the bison out of their path and out of sight.

On the 24th the two parties separated. Clark, the current with him, was once again moving fast. That day he made 70 miles downriver. Clark once again mentions the abundance of game: "for me to mention or give an estimate of the different species of wild animals on this river, particularly buffalo, elk, antelopes and wolves, would be increditable. I shall therefore be silent on the subject further." The next day, the 25th, they reached a small rock mesa standing out beside the river and christened it Pompey's Tower, after Sacagawea's son. Clark carved his name on a rock on the top of it. Now called Pompey's Pillar, it's still there. So is Clark's name. The buffalo were in the rutting season and keeping the men up at night with their bellowing; to sleep they had to frighten them off. They were all short of clothing and killing deer mostly for the skins, to make what they needed. They were also making time: 62 miles on July 26, 80 miles the next day. Mosquitoes were driving them all crazy. On July 30 they hit some shoals, and had to let the two canoes down by hand. Day by day they raced down the Yellowstone—66 miles one day,

45 miles another, 86 miles the next. On August 1 they had to stop for an hour to let a huge herd of buffalo cross the river in front of them. One day a bear pursued them, swimming after them, attracted by the smell of meat in the canoes. The mosquitoes were so bad some nights no one could sleep. Clark's mosquito bier was worn out, had holes in it; even he was tormented by them. The deer were getting thin because they couldn't feed in the bottoms; the mosquitoes drove them out into the plains. Some days it rained and, without protection, they were miserably wet. They no longer had tents; their blankets had holes in them. When it rained at night they slept wet, if they could sleep at all.

At 8 a.m. on August 3 they reached the Missouri. Conditions were no better there; mosquitoes forced them downriver; they left a note for Lewis. When Clark went ashore to shoot a bighorn ram "the mosquitoes were so numerous that I could not keep them off my gun long enough to take sight and by that means missed."

On August 8 Pryor, Shannon, Hall, and Windsor showed up in two canoes made of buffalo skin. They had kept the horses for less than two days. "Sgt. Pryor informed me," writes Clark,

> that the second night after he parted with me on the Yellowstone he arrived about four p.m. on the banks of a large creek which contained no running water. He halted to let the horses graze, during which time a heavy shower of rain raised the creek so high that several horses which had straggled across the channel of this creek were obliged to swim back. Here he determined to continue all night, it being in good food for the horses. In the morning he could see no horses. In looking about their camp they discovered several tracks within 100 paces of their camp, which they pursued, found where they had caught and drove off all the horses. They pursued on five miles; the Indians there divided into two parties. They continued in pursuit of the largest party five miles further. Finding that there was not the smallest chance of overtaking them, they returned to their camp and packed up their baggage on their backs and steered a N.E. course to the River Yellowstone, which they struck at Pompey's Tower. There they killed a buffalo bull and made a canoe in the form and shape of the Mandans and Arikaras, made in the following manner: viz., two sticks of one

and a quarter inch diameter are tied together so as to form a round hoop of the size you wish the canoe, or as large as the skin will allow to cover. Two of those hoops are made, one for the top or brim and the other for the bottom the depth you wish the canoe. Then sticks of the same size are crossed at right angles and fastened with a thong to each hoop and also where each stick crosses each other. Then the skin when green is drawn tight over this frame and fastened with thongs to the brim of our outer hoop so as to form a perfect basin. One of those canoes will carry six or eight men and their loads.

Pryor built two canoes so they wouldn't lose everything if something happened to one. Both canoes made it down the Yellowstone without incident. "They passed through the worst parts of the rapids and shoals in the river without taking a drop of water." But there were no more horses.

Over the next few days they continued to move slowly down the Missouri, hunting as they went, mostly for skins. They needed skins not only for clothing but as trade goods. The Mandan were fond of deer and antelope skins, and skins were all they could hope to obtain to trade for Mandan corn. A change in the weather drove the mosquitoes off, at least for the time being. It had become imperative to camp in windy situations, for wind drove them off, too. On August 11 they met two Americans coming upriver to trap beaver on the Yellowstone. They couldn't give them much news of civilization. They had left St. Louis two years before, in 1804, and wintered with the Teton Sioux. The Mandan and Minitari, they said, were at war again with the Arikara. The captains' efforts to make peace between these tribes had come to nothing.

The next day, August 12, Lewis caught up. Clark was delaying on shore to wait for Shannon and Gibson; the former had left his tomahawk at the previous night's camp, and Clark sent the two men back to find it. At noon Lewis arrived with the rest of the party. He himself was wounded. "I found him lying in the pirogue," writes Clark;

he informed me that his wound was slight and would be well in 20 or 30 days. This information relieved me very much. I examined the wound and found it a very bad flesh wound. The ball had passed through the fleshy part of his left thigh below the hip bone and cut the cheek of the right buttock for three inches in length and the depth of the ball. Capt. Lewis informed me the accident happened the day before by one of the men, Pierre Cruzatte, mistaking him in the thick bushes to be an elk. Capt. Lewis with this Cruzatte and several other men were out in the bottom shooting of elk . . . Cruzatte, seeing Capt. Lewis passing through the bushes and taking him to be an elk from the color of his clothes, which were of leather and very nearly that of the elk, fired, and unfortunately the ball passed through the thigh as aforesaid. Capt. Lewis, thinking it Indians who had shot him, hobbled to the canoes as fast as possible and was followed by Cruzatte. The mistake was then discovered. This Cruzatte is nearsighted and has the use of but one eye. He is an attentive industrious man and one whom we both have placed the greatest confidence in during the whole route.

Clark cleaned and dressed the wound, and Lewis did recover without any trouble. But he wrote no more in his journal. Lewis's final entry in the journals is dated August 12.

Clark's exploration of the Yellowstone had been a failure in one sense. He had gone to meet Indians and give them the news, that this was now the territory of the United States and that the United States hoped to bring peace to the warring tribes, and trade. He had not seen one single Indian on the route, although Charbonneau had spotted one looking them over from a height above the river. But Clark had seen plenty of game and had noticed the possibilities for beaver and otter trapping, and the river might also make a good route toward New Mexico and trade with the Spanish there. On July 24 they had passed a river coming into the Yellowstone that they thought, from information they had picked up from their Indian sources at the Mandan villages, was the Bighorn River. When they reached the actual Bighorn two days later, they renamed the first tributary Clark's Fork of the Yellowstone. It was a good site, the captains later concluded, for a trading post, far enough south of Blackfoot and Minitari territory that Indians such as the Nez Perce and the Shoshone could feel safe coming there to trade. A year later Manuel Lisa built Fort Raymond at the confluence of the Yellowstone and the Bighorn, to trade with the Crow. They had lost all their horses, then, but Clark's party had opened up the Yellowstone and discovered it to be an easier route than the Missouri into the mountains.

We return now to Traveler's Rest and Lewis's journey to the Great Falls, following the route that had been recommended to the captains the previous August by the Shoshone, and from thence up the Marias River. Clark's trip had been without incident. Lewis's had incidents to spare, including one that the Blackfeet remembered for many years to come.

An American, having struck a bear but not killed him, escapes into a tree.
From the journals of Patrick Gass.

JULY 3 TO AUGUST 12, 1806

LEWIS ON THE MARIAS

—◦◦◦—

July 3, 1806, Thursday [Lewis]
All arrangements being now completed for carrying into effect the several schemes we had planned for execution on our return, we saddled our horses and set out. I took leave of my worthy friend and companion Capt. Clark and the party that accompanied him. I could not avoid feeling much concern on this occasion, although I hoped this separation was only momentary. I proceeded down Clark's River [*the Bitterroot*] seven miles with my party of nine men and five Indians [*the party included Sergeant Gass, Drouillard, the two Fields brothers, Frazer, McNeal, Goodrich, Werner, and Thompson*]. Here the Indians recommended our passing the river, which was rapid and 150 yards wide. Two miles above this place I passed the entrance of the east branch of Clark's River, which discharges itself by two channels. The water of this river is more turbid than the main stream and is from 90 to 120 yards wide. As we had no other means of passing the river, we busied ourselves collecting dry timber for the purpose of constructing rafts; timber being scarce, we found considerable difficulty in procuring as much as made three small rafts. We arrived at 11 a.m. and had our rafts completed by 3 p.m., when we dined and began to take over our baggage, which we effected in the course of three hours, the rafts being obliged to return several times. The Indians swam over their horses and drew over their baggage in little basins of deerskins which they constructed in a very few minutes for that purpose. We drove our horses

in after them and they followed to the opposite shore. I remained myself with two men who could scarcely swim until the last. By this time the raft, by passing so frequently, had fallen a considerable distance down the river to a rapid and difficult part of it crowded with several small islands and willow bars, which were now overflown. With these men I set out on the raft and was soon hurried down with the current a mile and a half before we made shore. On our approach to the shore the raft sunk and I was drawn off the raft by a bush and swam on shore. The two men remained on the raft and fortunately effected a landing at some little distance below. I wet the chronometer by this accident which I had placed in my fob, as I conceived for greater security.

I now joined the party and we proceeded with the Indians about three miles to a small creek and encamped at sunset. I sent out the hunters, who soon returned with three very fine deer, of which I gave the Indians half. These people now informed me that the road which they showed me at no great distance from our camp would lead us up the east branch of Clark's River and a river they call Cokahlarishkit or the *river of the road to buffalo* [*the Blackfoot River*] and thence to Medicine River and the Falls of the Missouri, where we wished to go. They alleged that as the road was a well-beaten track we could not now miss our way and as they were afraid of meeting with their enemies the Minitaris they could not think of continuing with us any longer; they wished now to proceed down Clark's River in search of their friends the Shalees [*the Flathead that Lewis and Clark had met the previous fall*]. They informed us that not far from the dividing ridge between the waters of this and the Missouri Rivers the roads forked. They recommended the left hand as the best route but said they would both lead us to the Falls of the Missouri.

I directed the hunters to turn out early in the morning and endeavor to kill some more meat for these people, whom I was unwilling to leave without giving them a good supply of provision after their having been so obliging as to conduct us through those tremendous mountains. The mosquitoes were so excessively troublesome this evening that we were obliged to kindle large fires for our horses. These insects tortured them in such manner until they placed themselves in the smoke of the fires that I really thought they would become frantic. About an hour after dark the air became so cold that the mosquitoes disappeared. We saw the fresh track of a horse this evening in the road near our camp, which the Indians supposed to be a Shalee spy. We killed a prairie hen with the short and pointed tail. She had a number of young which could just fly.

July 4, 1806, Friday [Lewis]
I arose early this morning and sent out Drouillard and the Fieldses to hunt. At six a.m. a man of the Pallote pellows [*a Nez Perce?*] arrived from the west side of the Rocky Mountains. He had pursued us a few days after our departure and overtook us at this place. He proved to be the same young man who had first attempted to pass the Rocky Mountains early in June last when we lay on the Kooskooske and was obliged to relinquish the enterprise in consequence of the depth and softness of the snow. I gave a shirt, a handkerchief, and a small quantity of ammunition to the Indians. At half after eleven the hunters returned from the chase unsuccessful. I now ordered the horses saddled, smoked a pipe with these friendly people, and at noon bid them adieu. They had cut the meat which I gave them last evening thin and exposed it in the sun to dry, informing me that they should leave it in this neighborhood until they returned as a store for their homeward journey. It is worthy of remark that these people were about to return by the same pass by which they had conducted us through the difficult part of the Rocky Mountains, although they were about to descend Clark's River several days journey in search of the Shalees, their relations, a circumstance which to my mind furnished sufficient evidence that there is not so near or so good a route to the plains of Columbia by land along that river as that which we came. The several war routes of the Minitaris which fall into this valley of Clark's River concenter at Traveler's Rest, beyond which point they have never yet dared to venture in pursuit of the nations beyond the mountains. All the nations also on the west side of the mountains with whom we are acquainted inhabiting the waters of Lewis's River [*the Snake*] and who visit the plains of the Missouri pass by this route.

These affectionate people, our guides, betrayed every emotion of unfeigned regret at separating from us. They said that they were confident that the Pahkees, the appellation they give the Minitaris, would cut us off. The first five miles of our route was through a part of the extensive plain in which we were encamped. We then entered the mountains with the east fork of Clark's River through a narrow confined pass on its N. side, continuing up that river five miles further to the entrance of the Cokahlahishkit River [*again, the Blackfoot*], which falls in on the N.E. side, is 60 yards wide, deep and rapid. The banks are bold, not very high, but never overflow. The east fork below its junction with this stream is 100 yards wide and above it about 90. The waters of both are turbid but the east branch much the most so; their beds are composed of sand and gravel; the east fork possesses a large portion of the former. Neither of those streams is navigable in consequence of the rapids and shoals which obstruct their currents. Thus far a plain or untimbered country bordered the river which near the junction of these streams spread into a handsome level plain of no great extent. The hills were covered with long-leafed pine and fir. I now continued my route up the N. side of the Cokahlahishkit River through a timbered country for eight miles and encamped in a handsome bottom on the river where there was an abundance of excellent grass for our horses. The evening was fine, air pleasant and no mosquitoes. A few miles before we encamped I killed a squirrel of the species common to the Rocky Mountains and a ground squirrel of a species which I had never before seen. I preserved the skins of both these animals.

At this point until July 9 Lewis's journal stops including narrative descriptions of the days' events. We know what happened only because of the notes that he wrote to accompany his course and mileage directions for the day. These notes largely consist of descriptions of the countryside they are passing through. Part of the way they were following the same route recently taken by what Lewis believed to be a Fort de Prairie Minitari war party; from the freshness of the sign they were close enough behind that they kept on their guard. On July 7 they crossed the Continental Divide at the pass now called Lewis and Clark Pass, which Clark, of course, never saw. Lewis found it to be "low and an easy ascent." They were now leaving the Rocky Mountains behind. On July 8 they began to see buffalo again and reached the Medicine River, which they intended to hunt down to the Falls. On July 10 a large grizzly bear chased Thompson and Sergeant Gass, who were on horseback; "they were afraid to fire on the bear lest their horses should throw them," Lewis says, "as they were unaccustomed to the gun." Lewis, too, was bothered by the bellowing of the buffalo bulls through the night. They reached the upper portage camp at the White Bear Islands on the Missouri the next day, July 11.

July 11, 1806, Friday [Lewis]
The morning was fair and the plains looked beautiful. The grass much improved by the late rain. The air was pleasant and a vast assemblage of little birds which crowd to the groves on the river sang most enchantingly. We set

out early. I sent the hunters down Medicine River to hunt elk and proceeded with the party across the plain to the White Bear Islands, which I found to be eight miles distant. My course S. 75° E. through a level, beautiful and extensive high plain covered with immense herds of buffalo. It is now the season at which the buffalo begin to copulate and the bulls keep a tremendous roaring; we could hear them for many miles and there are such numbers of them that there is one continual roar. Our horses had not been acquainted with the buffalo; they appeared much alarmed at their appearance and bellowing. When I arrived in sight of the White Bear Islands the Missouri bottoms on both sides of the river were crowded with buffalo. I sincerely believe that there were not less than ten thousand buffalo within a circle of two miles around that place. I met with the hunters at a little grove of timber opposite to the island where they had killed a cow and were waiting our arrival. They had met with no elk. I directed the hunters to kill some buffalo as well for the benefit of their skins to enable us to pass the river [*i.e., by making the Indian-style buffalo boats*] as for their meat for the men I meant to leave at this place.

We unloaded our horses and encamped opposite to the islands. Had the cow skinned and some willow sticks collected to make canoes of the hides. By 12 o'clock they killed 11 buffalo, most of them in fine order. The bulls are now generally much fatter than the cows and are fine beef. I sent out all hands with the horses to assist in butchering and bringing in the meat. By three in the evening we had brought in a large quantity of fine beef and as many hides as we wanted for canoes, shelters, and gear. I then set all hands to prepare two canoes. The one we made after the Mandan fashion with a single skin in the form of a basin and the other we constructed of two skins on a plan of our own. We were unable to complete our canoes this evening. The wind blew very hard. We continued our operations until dark and then retired to rest. I intend giving my horses a couple of days' rest at this place and deposit all my baggage which is not necessary to my voyage up Medicine River.

July 12, 1806, Saturday [Lewis]
We arose early and resumed our operations in completing our canoes, which we completed by ten a.m. About this time two of the men whom I had dispatched this morning in quest of the horses returned with seven of them only. The remaining ten of our best horses were absent and not to be found. I fear that they are stolen. I dispatched two men on horseback in search of

them. The wind blew so violently that I did not think it prudent to attempt passing the river. At noon Werner returned, having found three others of the horses near Fort Mountain. Sgt. Gass did not return until three p.m., not having found the horses. He had been about eight miles up Medicine River. I now dispatched Joseph Fields and Drouillard in quest of them. The former returned at dark unsuccessful and the latter continued absent all night. At five p.m. the wind abated and we transported our baggage and meat to the opposite shore in our canoes, which we found answered even beyond our expectations. We swam our horses over also and encamped at sunset. Mosquitoes extremely troublesome. I think the river is somewhat higher than when we were here last summer. The present season has been much more moist than the preceding one. The grass and weeds are much more luxuriant than they were when I left this place on the 13th of July 1805. Saw the brown thrush, pigeons, doves, etc.

The yellow currants beginning to ripen.

July 13, 1806, Sunday [Lewis]
Removed above to my old station opposite the upper point of the White Bear Island. Formed our camp and set Thompson, etc., at work to complete the gear for the horses. Had the cache opened, found my bearskins entirely destroyed by the water, the river having risen so high that the water had penetrated. All my specimens of plants also lost. The chart of the Missouri fortunately escaped. Opened my trunks and boxes and exposed the articles to dry. Found my papers damp and several articles damp. The stopper had come out of a phial of laudanum and the contents had run into the drawer and destroyed a great part of my medicine in such manner that it was past recovery. Waited very impatiently for the return of Drouillard. He did not arrive. Mosquitoes excessively troublesome, insomuch that without the protection of my mosquito bier I should have found it impossible to write a moment. The buffalo are leaving us fast and passing on to the S. East. Killed a buffalo picker, a beautiful bird [*a cowbird*].

July 14, 1806, Monday [Lewis]
Had the carriage wheels dug up, found them in good order. The iron frame of the boat had not suffered materially. Had the meat cut thinner and exposed to dry in the sun, and some roots of coues of which I have yet a small stock pounded into meal for my journey. I find the fat buffalo meat a

great improvement to the mush of these roots. The old cache being too damp to venture to deposit my trunks, etc., in, I sent them over to the large island and had them put on a high scaffold among some thick brush and covered with skins. I take this precaution lest some Indians may visit the men I leave here before the arrival of the main party and rob them. The hunters killed a couple of wolves. The buffalo have almost entirely disappeared. Saw the bee martin. The wolves are in great numbers howling around us and lolling about in the plains in view at the distance of two or three hundred yards. I counted 27 about the carcass of a buffalo which lies in the water at the upper point of the large island. These are generally of the large kind. Drouillard did not return this evening.

July 15, 1806, Tuesday [Lewis]
Dispatched McNeal early this morning to the lower part of the portage in order to learn whether the cache and white pirogue remained untouched or in what state they were. The men employed in drying the meat, dressing deerskins, and preparing for the reception of the canoes. At one p.m. Drouillard returned without the horses and reported that after a diligent search of two days he had discovered where the horses had passed Dearborn's River, at which place there were 15 lodges that had been abandoned about the time our horses were taken. He pursued the tracks of a number of horses from these lodges to the road which we had traveled over the mountains, which they struck about three miles south of our encampment of the 7th and had pursued this road westwardly. I have no doubt but they are a party of the Tushapahs who have been on a buffalo hunt. Drouillard informed me that their camp was in a small bottom on the river of about five acres, enclosed by the steep and rocky and lofty cliffs of the river and that so closely had they kept themselves and horses within this little spot that there was not a track to be seen of them within a quarter of a mile of that place. Every spire of grass was eaten up by their horses near their camp, which had the appearance of their having remained here some time. His horse being much fatigued with the ride he had given him, and finding that the Indians had at least two days the start of him, he thought it best to return.

His safe return has relieved me from great anxiety. I had already settled it in my mind that a white bear had killed him and should have set out tomorrow in search of him, and if I could not find him to continue my route to Marias River. I knew that if he met with a bear in the plains even he would attack him, and that if any accident should happen to separate him from his horse in that situation the chances in favor of his being killed would be as nine to 10. I felt so perfectly satisfied that he had returned in safety that I thought but little of the horses, although they were seven of the best I had. This loss, great as it is, is not entirely irreparable, or at least remaining, two of the best and two of the worst of which I leave to assist the party in taking the canoes and baggage over the portage and take the remaining six with me. These are but indifferent horses most of them, but I hope they may answer our purposes. I shall leave three of my intended party, Gass, Frazer, and Werner, and take the two Fieldses and Drouillard. By having two spare horses we can relieve those we ride. Having made this arrangement I gave orders for an early departure in the morning, indeed I should have set out instantly, but McNeal rode one of the horses which I intend to take and has not yet returned.

A little before dark McNeal returned with his musket broken off at the breech and informed me that on his arrival at Willow Run he had approached a white bear within ten feet without discovering him, the bear being in the thick brush; the horse took the alarm and turning short threw him immediately under the bear. This animal raised himself on his hinder feet for battle, and gave him time to recover from his fall, which he did in an instant and with his clubbed musket he struck the bear over the head and cut him with the guard of the gun and broke off the breech. The bear, stunned with the stroke, fell to the ground and began to scratch his head with his feet. This gave McNeal time to climb a willow tree which was near at hand and thus fortunately made his escape. The bear waited at the foot of the tree until late in the evening before he left him, when McNeal ventured down and caught his horse, which had by this time strayed off to the distance of two miles, and returned to camp. These bears are a most tremendous animal. It seems that the hand of providence has been most wonderfully in our favor with respect to them, or some of us would long since have fallen a sacrifice to their ferocity. There seems to be a certain fatality attached to the neighborhood of these falls, for there is always a chapter of accidents prepared for us during our residence at them.

The mosquitoes continue to infest us in such manner that we can scarcely exist. For my own part I am confined by them to my bier at least three-quarters of my time. My dog even howls with the torture he experiences from them. They are almost insupportable. They are so numerous that we frequently get them in our throats as we breathe.

July 16, 1806, Wednesday [Lewis]
I dispatched a man early this morning to drive up the horses as usual; he returned at eight a.m. with one of them only. Alarmed at this occurrence, I dispatched one of my best hands on horseback in search of them. He returned at ten a.m. with them and I immediately set out. Sent Drouillard and R. Fields with the horses to the lower side of Medicine River and proceeded myself with all our baggage and J. Fields down the Missouri to the mouth of Medicine River in our canoe of buffalo skins. We were compelled to swim the horses above the White Bear Island and again across Medicine River, as the Missouri is of great width below the mouth of that river. Having arrived safely below Medicine River, we immediately saddled our horses and proceeded down the river to the handsome fall of 47 feet, where I halted about two hours and took a hasty sketch of these falls. In the meantime we had some meat cooked and took dinner, after which we proceeded to the grand falls, where we arrived at sunset. On our way we saw two very large bears on the opposite side of the river. As we arrived in sight of the little wood below the falls we saw two other bears enter it. This being the only wood in the neighborhood we were compelled of course to contend with the bears for possession, and therefore left our horses in a place of security and entered the wood, which we searched in vain for the bears; they had fled.

Here we encamped and the evening having the appearance of rain made our beds and slept under a shelving rock. These falls have abated much of their grandeur since I first arrived at them in June 1805, the water being much lower at present than it was at that moment. However they are still a sublimely grand object. I determined to take a second drawing of it in the morning. We saw a few buffalo as we passed today. The immense herds which were about this place on our arrival have principally passed the river and directed their course downwards. We see a number of goats or antelope always in passing through the plains of the Missouri above the Mandans. At this season they are thinly scattered over the plains but seem universally distributed in every part; they appear very inquisitive usually to learn what we are as we pass, and frequently accompany us at no great distance for miles, frequently halting and giving a loud whistle through their nostrils. They are a very pretty animal and astonishingly fleet and active. We spent this evening free from the torture of the mosquitoes. There are a great number of geese which usually raise their young above these falls about the entrance of Medicine River. We saw them in large flocks of several hundred as we passed today. I saw both yesterday and today the cuckoo or as it is sometimes called the *rain crow*. This bird is not met with west of the Rocky Mountains nor within them.

July 17, 1806, Thursday [Lewis]

I arose early this morning and made a drawing of the falls, after which we took breakfast and departed. It being my design to strike Marias River about the place at which I left it on my return to its mouth in the beginning of June 1805, I steered my course through the wide and level plains, which have somewhat the appearance of an ocean, not a tree nor a shrub to be seen. The land is not fertile, at least far less so, than the plains of the Columbia or those lower down this river. It is a light-colored soil intermixed with a considerable proportion of coarse gravel without sand. When dry it cracks and appears thirsty and is very hard. In its wet state it is as soft and slippery as so much soft soap. The grass is naturally but short and at present has been rendered much more so by the grazing of the buffalo. The whole face of the country as far as the eye can reach looks like a well-shaved bowling green, in which immense and numerous herds of buffalo were seen feeding, attended by their scarcely less numerous shepherds, the wolves. We saw a number of goats as usual today, also the parti-colored plover with the brick red head and neck. This bird remains about the little ponds which are distributed over the face of these plains and here raise their young.

We killed a buffalo cow as we passed through the plains and took the hump and tongue which furnish ample rations for four men in one day. At five p.m. we arrived at Rose River, where I purposed remaining all night, as I could not reach Marias River this evening and unless I did there would be but little probability of our finding any wood and very probably no water either. On our arrival at the river we saw where a wounded and bleeding buffalo had just passed and concluded it was probable that the Indians had been running them and were near at hand. The Minitaris of Fort de Prairie and the Blackfoot Indians rove through this quarter of the country and as they are a vicious, lawless, and rather an abandoned set of wretches I wish to avoid an interview with them if possible. I have no doubt but they would steal our horses if they have it in their power and finding us weak should they happen to be numerous will most probably attempt to rob us of our arms and baggage. At all events I am determined to take every possible precaution to avoid them if possible.

I hurried over the river to a thick wood and turned out the horses to graze, sent Drouillard to pursue and kill the wounded buffalo in order to determine whether it had been wounded by the Indians or not, and proceeded myself to reconnoiter the adjacent country, having sent R. Fields for the same purpose by a different route. I ascended the river hills and by the help of my glass examined the plains but could make no discovery. In about an hour I returned to camp, where I met with the others, who had been as unsuccessful as myself. Drouillard could not find the wounded buffalo. J. Fields, whom I had left at camp, had already roasted some of the buffalo meat and we took dinner, after which I sent Drouillard and R. Fields to resume their researches for the Indians, and set myself down to record the transactions of the day. *Rose* River [*present-day Teton River*] is at this place fifty yards wide. The water, which is only about three feet deep, occupies about 35 yards and is very turbid, of a white color. The general course of this river is from east to west so far as I can discover its track through the plains; its bottoms are wide and well timbered with cottonwood, both the broad- and narrow-leafed species. The bed of this stream is small gravel and mud. Its banks are low but never overflow, the hills are about 100 or 150 feet high. It possesses bluffs of earth like the lower part of the Missouri; except the depth and velocity of its stream and it is the Missouri in miniature. From the size of Rose River at this place and its direction I have no doubt but it takes its source within the first range of the Rocky Mountains. The bush which bears the red berry is here in great plenty in the river bottoms.

The spies returned having killed two beaver and a deer. They reported that they saw no appearance of Indians.

July 18, 1806, Friday [Lewis]
We set out this morning a little before sunrise, ascended the river hills and continued our route as yesterday through the open plains. At about six miles we reached the top of an elevated plain which divides the waters of the Rose River from those of Marias River. From hence the North Mountains, the South Mountains, the Falls Mountain and the Tower Mountain [*respectively the Bear's Paw range, the Highwood Mountains, the Little or*

Big Belt range, and the Sweet Grass Hills] and those around and to the east of the latter were visible. Our course led us nearly parallel with a creek of Marias River which takes its rise in these high plains at the place we passed them. At noon we struck this creek about six miles from its junction with Marias River, where we found some cottonwood timber; here we halted to dine and graze our horses. The bed of this creek is about 25 yards wide at this place but is nearly dry at present, the water being confined to little pools in the deeper parts of its bed. From hence downwards there is a considerable quantity of timber in its bottom. We passed immense herds of buffalo on our way; in short, for about 12 miles it appeared as one herd only, the whole plains and valley of this creek being covered with them. Saw a number of wolves of both species, also antelope and some horses. After dinner we proceeded about five miles across the plain to Marias River, where we arrived at six p.m. We killed a couple of buffalo in the bottom of this river and encamped on its west side in a grove of cottonwood some miles above the entrance of the creek. Being now convinced that we were above the point to which I had formerly ascended this river and fearing that a fork of this stream might fall in on the north side between this place and the point to which I ascended it, I directed Drouillard, who was with me on my former excursion, and Joseph Fields to descend the river early in the morning to the place from whence I had returned, and examine whether any stream fell in or not. I keep a strict lookout every night. I take my tour of watch with the men.

July 19, 1806, Saturday [Lewis]
Drouillard and J. Fields set out early this morning in conformity to my instructions last evening. They returned at half after 12 o'clock and informed me that they had proceeded down the river to the place from which I had returned June last and that it was six miles distant. They passed the entrance of Buffalo Creek at two miles. The course of the river from hence downwards as far as they were is N. 80° E. They killed eight deer and two antelope on their way; most of the deer were large fat mule bucks. Having completed my observation of the sun's meridian altitude we set out, ascended the river hills, having passed the river and proceeded through the open plains up the N. side of the river 20 miles and encamped. At 15 miles we passed a large creek on the N. side a little above its entrance; there is but little running water in this creek at present. Its bed is about 30 yards wide and appears to come

from the Broken Mountains, so called from their ragged and irregular shape. There are three of them extending from east to west, almost unconnected; the center mountain terminates in a conic spire and is that which I have called the Tower Mountain. They are destitute of timber. From the entrance of this creek they bore N. 10° W. The river bottoms are usually about half a mile wide and possess a considerable quantity of timber, entirely cotton-wood. The underbrush is honeysuckle, rose bushes, the narrow-leafed willow, and the bush which bears the acid red berry called by the French *engagés grease de buff* [*buffaloberry*]. Just as we halted to encamp R. Fields killed a mule doe. The plains are beautiful and level but the soil is but thin. In many parts of the plains there are great quantities of prickly pears. Saw some herds of buffalo today but not in such quantities as yesterday, also antelope, wolves, geese, pigeons, doves, hawks, ravens, crows, larks, sparrows, etc. The curlew has disappeared.

July 20, 1806, Sunday [Lewis]
We set out at sunrise and proceeded through the open plain as yesterday up the North side of the river. The plains are more broken than they were yesterday and have become more inferior in point of soil. A great quantity of small gravel is everywhere distributed over the surface of the earth, which renders traveling extremely painful to our barefoot horses. The soil is generally a white or whitish blue clay; this where it has been trodden by the buffalo when wet has now become as firm as a brickbat and stands in innumerable little points quite as formidable to our horses' feet as the gravel. The mineral salts common to the plains of the Missouri have been more abundant today than usual. The bluffs of the river are about 200 feet high, steep, irregular, and formed of earth which readily dissolves with water, slips and precipitates itself into the river as before mentioned frequently of the bluffs of the Missouri below, which they resemble in every particular, differing essentially from those of the Missouri above the entrance of this river, they being composed of firm red or yellow clay, which does not yield readily to the rains, and a large quantity of rock. The soil of the river bottom is fertile and well timbered. I saw some trees today which would make small canoes. The timber is generally low. The underbrush the same as before mentioned.

We have seen fewer buffalo today than usual, though more elk, and not less wolves and antelope, also some mule deer. This species of deer seems most prevalent in this quarter. Saw some geese, ducks, and other birds common to the country. There is much appearance of beaver on this river, but not any of otter. From the apparent descent of the country to the north and above the Broken Mountains I am induced to believe that the south branch of the Saskatchewan receives a part of its water from the plain even to the borders of this river, and from the breaks visible in the plains in a northern direction think that a branch of that river descending from the Rocky Mountains passes at no great distance from Marias River and to the N.E. of the Broken Mountains.

The day has proved excessively warm and we lay by four hours during the heat of it. We traveled 28 miles and encamped as usual in the river bottom on its N. side. There is scarcely any water at present in the plains and what there is lies in small pools and is so strongly impregnated with the mineral salts that it is unfit for any purpose except the use of the buffalo. These animals appear to prefer this water to that of the river. The wild liquorice and sunflower are very abundant in the plains and river bottoms; the latter is now in full bloom. The silkgrass and sand rush are also common to the bottomlands. The mosquitoes have not been troublesome to us since we left the White Bear Islands.

July 21, 1806, Monday [Lewis]
We set out at sunrise and proceeded a short distance up the north side of the river. We found the ravines which made in on this side were so steep and numerous that we passed the river, in doing which the packhorse which carried my instruments missed the ford and wet the instruments. This accident detained us about half an hour. I took the instruments out, wiped them, and dried their cases. They sustained no material injury. We continued on the S. side of the river about three miles when we again passed over to the N. side and took our course through the plains at some distance from the river. We saw a large herd of elk this morning. The buffalo still become more scarce. At two p.m. we struck a northern branch of Marias River about 30 yards wide at the distance of about eight miles from its entrance. This stream is closely confined between cliffs of freestone rocks, the bottom narrow below us and above the rocks confine it on each side. Some little timber below but not any above. The water of this stream is nearly clear. From the appearance of this rock and the apparent height of the bed of the stream I am induced to believe that there are falls in these rivers somewhere about their junction. Being convinced that this stream came from the mountains I determined to pursue it, as it will lead me to the most northern

point to which the waters of Marias River extend, which I now fear will not be as far north as I wished and expected. After dinner we set out up the north branch, keeping on its S. side. We pursued it until dark and not finding any timber halted and made a fire of the dung of the buffalo. We lay on the south side in a narrow bottom under a cliff. Our provision is nearly out. We wounded a buffalo this evening but could not get him.

July 22, 1806, Tuesday [Lewis]
We set out very early this morning as usual and proceeded up the river. For the first seven miles of our travel this morning the country was broken, the land poor and intermixed with a greater quantity of gravel than usual. The ravines were steep and numerous and our horses' feet have become extremely sore in traveling over the gravel. We therefore traveled but slow. We met with a doe elk which we wounded but did not get her. The river is confined closely between cliffs of perpendicular rocks in most parts.

After the distance of seven miles the country became more level, less gravelly, and some bottoms to the river, but not a particle of timber nor underbrush of any description is to be seen. We continued up the river on its south side for 17 miles, when we halted to graze our horses and eat. There being no wood we were compelled to make our fire with the buffalo dung, which I found answered the purpose very well. We cooked and ate all the meat we had except a small piece of buffalo meat which was a little tainted. After dinner we passed the river and took our course through a level and beautiful plain on the N. side. The country has now become level, the river bottoms wide, and the adjoining plains but little elevated above them. The banks of the river are not usually more than from three to four feet yet it does not appear to overflow them. We found no timber until we had traveled 12 miles further, when we arrived at a clump of large cotton-wood trees in a beautiful and extensive bottom of the river about ten miles below the foot of the Rocky Mountains where this river enters them. As I could see from hence very distinctly where the river entered the mountains and the bearing of this point being S. of west, I thought it unnecessary to proceed further and therefore encamped, resolving to rest ourselves and horses a couple of days at this place and take the necessary observations.

This plain on which we are is very high. The Rocky Mountains to the S.W. of us appear but low from their base up yet are partially covered with snow nearly to their bases. There is no timber on those mountains within our view. They are very irregular and broken in their form and seem to be composed principally of clay with but little rock or stone. The river appears to possess at least double the volume of water which it had where we first arrived on it below. This no doubt proceeds from the evaporation caused by the sun and air and the absorbing of the earth in its passage through these open plains. The course of the mountains still continues from S.E. to N.W. The front range appears to terminate abruptly about 35 miles to the N.W. of us. I believe that the waters of the Saskatchewan approach the borders of this river very nearly. I now have lost all hope of the waters of this river ever extending to N. latitude 50°, though I still hope and think it more than probable that both *White Earth* River and Milk River extend as far north as latitude 50°. We have seen but few buffalo today, no deer, and very few antelope. Game of every description is extremely wild, which induces me to believe that the Indians are now, or have been lately in this neighborhood. We wounded a buffalo this evening but our horses were so much fatigued that we were unable to pursue it with success.

For the next three days they camped here on the Marias. If the river had curved farther north, beyond the 50th parallel, before turning west, it would have extended the boundary of the United States into what is now Canada; the Louisiana Purchase granted the United States all territory drained by the Missouri River and its tributaries. They conducted some minor reconnaissance of the area and fed themselves on pigeons, game otherwise being extremely scarce. It rained a good part of the time, and Lewis was unable to take sun sightings to determine latitude. The party sensed that there were Indians in the area; on the 25th Drouillard found recent native campsites on the south fork of the Marias, now called Two Medicine River. Lewis decided to give up and head for home the next day. "I now begin," he writes, "to be apprehensive that I shall not reach the United States within this season unless I make every exertion in my power, which I shall certainly not omit when once I leave this place, which I shall do with much reluctance without having obtained the necessary data to establish its longitude. As if the fates were against me my chronometer from some unknown cause stopped today. When I set her to going she went as usual."

July 26, 1806, Saturday [Lewis]
The morning was cloudy and continued to rain as usual, though the clouds seemed somewhat thinner. I therefore postponed setting out until nine a.m. in the hope that it would clear off, but finding the contrary result I had the

horses caught and we set out, bidding a last adieu to this place, which I now call Camp Disappointment. I took my route through the open plains S.E. five miles, passing a small creek at two miles from the mountains, where I changed my direction to S. 75° E. for 7 miles further and struck a principal branch of Marias River 65 yards wide, not very deep. I passed this stream to its south side and continued down it two miles on the last mentioned course, when another branch of nearly the same dignity formed a junction with it, coming from the S.W. This last is shallow and rapid, has the appearance of overflowing its banks frequently and discharging vast torrents of water at certain seasons of the year. The beds of both these streams are pebbly, particularly the S. branch. The water of the N. branch is very turbid while that of the S. branch is nearly clear, notwithstanding the late rains. I passed the S. branch just above its junction and continued down the river, which runs a little to the N. of E. one mile, and halted to dine, and graze our horses.

Here I found some Indian lodges which appeared to have been inhabited last winter in a large and fertile bottom well stocked with cottonwood timber. The rose, honeysuckle, and redberry bushes constitute the undergrowth, there being but little willow in this quarter. Both these rivers above their junction appeared to be well stocked with timber, or comparatively so with other parts of this country. Here it is that we find the three species of cotton-wood which I have remarked in my voyage assembled together. That species common to the Columbia I have never before seen on the waters of the Missouri, also the narrow- and broad-leafed species.

During our stay at this place R. Fields killed a buck, a part of the flesh of which we took with us. We saw a few antelope, some wolves, and two of the smallest species of fox of a reddish brown color with the extremity of the tail black. It is about the size of the common domestic cat and burrows in the plains. After dinner I continued my route down the river to the north of east about three miles when the hills putting in close on the S. side I determined to ascend them to the high plain, which I did accordingly, keeping the Fieldses with me. Drouillard passed the river and kept down the valley of the river. I had intended to descend this river with its course to its junction with the fork which I had ascended and from thence have taken across the country obliquely to Rose River and descend that stream to its confluence with Marias River. The country through which this portion of Marias River passes to the fork which I ascended appears much more broken than that above and between this and the mountains.

I had scarcely ascended the hills before I discovered to my left at the distance of a mile an assemblage of about 30 horses. I halted and used my spyglass, by the help of which I discovered several Indians on the top of an eminence just above them who appeared to be looking down towards the river, I presumed at Drouillard. About half the horses were saddled. This was a very unpleasant sight. However I resolved to make the best of our situation and to approach them in a friendly manner. I directed J. Fields to display the flag which I had brought for that purpose and advanced slowly towards them. About this time they discovered us and appeared to run about in a very confused manner as if much alarmed. Their attention had been previously so fixed on Drouillard that they did not discover us until we had begun to advance upon them. Some of them descended the hill on which they were and drove their horses within shot of its summit and again returned to the height as if to wait our arrival or to defend themselves. I calculated on their number being nearly or quite equal to that of their horses, that our running would invite pursuit, as it would convince them that we were their enemies, and our horses were so indifferent that we could not hope to make our escape by flight. Added to this Drouillard was separated from us and I feared that his not being apprised of the Indians in the event of our attempting to escape, he would most probably fall a sacrifice.

Under these considerations I still advanced towards them. When we had arrived within a quarter of a mile of them, one of them mounted his horse and rode full speed towards us, which when I discovered I halted and alighted from my horse. He came within a hundred paces, halted, looked at us and turned his horse about and returned as briskly to his party as he had advanced. While he halted near us I held out my hand and beckoned to him to approach, but he paid no attention to my overtures. On his return to his party they all descended the hill and mounted their horses and advanced towards us, leaving their horses behind them. We also advanced to meet them. I counted eight of them but still supposed that there were others concealed, as there were several other horses saddled. I told the two men with me that I apprehended that these were the Minitaris of Fort de Prairie and from their known character I expected that we were to have some difficulty with them, that if they thought themselves sufficiently strong I was convinced they would attempt to rob us, in which case be their numbers what they would I should resist to the last extremity, preferring death to that of being deprived of my papers, instruments, and gun, and desired that they would form the same resolution and be alert and on their guard.

When we arrived within a hundred yards of each other the Indians except one halted. I directed the two men with me to do the same and advanced singly to meet the Indian, with whom I shook hands and passed on to those in his rear, as he did also to the two men in my rear. We now all assembled and alighted from our horses. The Indians soon asked to smoke with us, but I told them that the man whom they had seen pass down the river had my pipe and we could not smoke until he joined us. I requested as they had seen which way he went that they would one of them go with one of my men in search of him. This they readily consented to and a young man set out with R. Fields in search of Drouillard. I now asked them by signs if they were the Minitaris of the north, which they answered in the affirmative [*they were in fact a Blackfeet war party; they may have misunderstood Lewis's question*]. I asked if there was any chief among them and they pointed out three. I did not believe them; however, I thought it best to please them and gave to one a medal, to a second a flag, and to the third a handkerchief, with which they appeared well satisfied. They appeared much agitated with our first interview, from which they had scarcely yet recovered. In fact I believe they were more alarmed at this accidental interview than we were.

From no more of them appearing, I now concluded they were only eight in number and became much better satisfied with our situation, as I was convinced that we could manage that number should they attempt any hostile measures. As it was growing late in the evening I proposed that we should remove to the nearest part of the river and encamp together. I told them that I was glad to see them and had a great deal to say to them. We mounted our horses and rode towards the river, which was at but a short distance. On our way we were joined by Drouillard, Fields, and the Indian. We descended a very steep bluff about 250 feet high to the river, where there was a small bottom of nearly half a mile in length and about 250 yards wide in the widest part. The river washed the bluffs both above and below us and through its course in this part is very deep. The bluffs are so steep that there are but few places where they could be ascended, and are broken in several places by deep niches which extend back from the river several hundred yards, their bluffs being so steep that it is impossible to ascend them.

In this bottom there stand three solitary trees [*James P. Ronda, in his book on the relations between Lewis and Clark and the Indians, tells us these trees are still there, but whether this is the actual spot in question remains uncertain*], near one of which the Indians formed a large semicircular camp of dressed buffalo skins and invited us to partake of their shelter, which Drouillard and myself accepted and the Fieldses lay near the fire in front of the shelter.

With the assistance of Drouillard I had much conversation with these people in the course of the evening. I learned from them that they were a part of a large band which lay encamped at present near the foot of the Rocky Mountains on the main branch of Marias River one half day's march from our present encampment; that there was a white man with their band; that there was another large band of their nation hunting buffalo near the Broken Mountains and were on their way to the mouth of Marias River, where they would probably be in the course of a few days. They also informed us that from hence to the establishment where they trade on the Saskatchewan River is only six days easy march, or such as they usually travel with their women and children, which may be estimated at about 150 miles; that from these traders they obtain arms, ammunition, spirituous liquor, blankets, etc., in exchange for wolf and some beaver skins. I told these people that I had come a great way from the east up the large river which runs towards the rising sun, that I had been to the great waters where the sun sets and had seen a great many nations, all of whom I had invited to come and trade with me on the rivers on this side of the mountains, that I had found most of them at war with their neighbors and had succeeded in restoring peace among them, that I was now on my way home and had left my party at the falls of the Missouri with orders to descend that river to the entrance of Marias River and there wait my arrival, and that I had come in search of them in order to prevail on them to be at peace with their neighbors, particularly those on the west side of the mountains, and to engage them to come and trade with me when the establishment is made at the entrance of this river—to all of which they readily gave their assent and declared it to be their wish to be at peace with the Tushepahs [*these would be the Indians better known as Flathead*], whom they said had killed a number of their relations lately, and pointed to several of those present who had cut their hair as an evidence of the truth of what they had asserted. I found them extremely fond of smoking and plied them with the pipe until late at night. I told them that if they intended to do as I wished them they would send some of their young men to their band with an invitation to their chiefs and warriors to bring the white man with them and come down and council with me at the entrance of Marias River, and that the balance of them would accompany me to that place, where I was anxious now to meet my men, as I had been absent from them some time and knew that they would be uneasy until they saw me. That if they would go with me I would give them ten horses and some tobacco. To this proposition they made no reply. I took the first watch tonight and set up until half after eleven. The Indians by this time were all asleep. I roused up R. Fields and lay down myself. I directed Fields to watch the movements of the Indians and if any of them left the camp to awake us all, as I apprehended they would attempt to steal our horses. This being done I fell into a profound sleep and did not wake until the noise of the men and Indians awoke me a little after light in the morning.

July 27, 1806, Sunday [Lewis]
This morning at daylight the Indians got up and crowded around the fire. J. Fields, who was on post, had carelessly laid his gun down behind him near where his brother was sleeping. One of the Indians, the fellow to whom I had given the medal last evening, slipped behind him and took his gun and that of his brother, unperceived by him. At the same instant two others advanced and seized the guns of Drouillard and myself. J. Fields, seeing this, turned about to look for his gun and saw the fellow just running off with her and his brother's. He called to his brother, who instantly jumped up and pursued the Indian with him, whom they overtook at the distance of 50 or 60 paces from the camp, seized their guns and wrested them from him, and R. Fields, as he seized his gun, stabbed the Indian to the heart with his knife. The fellow ran about 15 steps and fell dead. Of this I did not know until afterwards. Having recovered their guns, they ran back instantly to the camp. Drouillard, who was awake, saw the Indian take hold of his gun and instantly jumped up and seized her and wrested her from him, but the Indian still retained his pouch. His jumping up and crying, "Damn you, let go of my gun," awakened me. I jumped up and asked what was the matter, which I quickly learned when I saw Drouillard in a scuffle with the Indian for his gun. I reached to seize my gun but found her gone. I then drew a pistol from my holster and turning myself about saw the Indian making off with my gun. I ran at him with my pistol and bid him lay down my gun, which he was in the act of

doing when the Fieldses returned and drew up their guns to shoot him, which I forbid as he did not appear to be about to make any resistance or commit any offensive act. He dropped the gun and walked slowly off. I picked her up instantly. Drouillard having about this time recovered his gun and pouch asked me if he might not kill the fellow, which I also forbid as he did not appear to wish to kill us.

As soon as they found us all in possession of our arms they ran and endeavored to drive off all the horses. I now hollered to the men and told them to fire on them if they attempted to drive off our horses. They accordingly pursued the main party who were driving the horses up the river and I pursued the man who had taken my gun, who with another was driving off a part of the horses which were to the left of the camp. I pursued them so closely that they could not take twelve of their own horses but continued to drive one of mine with some others. At the distance of 300 paces they entered one of those steep niches in the bluff with the horses before them. Being nearly out of breath I could pursue no further. I called to them as I had done several times before that I would shoot them if they did not give me my horse and raised my gun. One of them jumped behind a rock and spoke to the other, who turned around and stopped at the distance of 30 steps from me and I shot him through the belly. He fell to his knees and on his right elbow, from which position he partly raised himself up and fired at me, and turning himself about crawled in behind a rock which was a few feet from him.

He overshot me; being bareheaded I felt the wind of his bullet very distinctly. Not having my shot pouch I could not reload my piece and as there were two of them behind good shelters from me I did not think it prudent to rush on them with my pistol, which had I discharged I had not the means of reloading until I reached camp. I therefore returned leisurely toward camp; on my way I met with Drouillard, who having heard the report of the guns had returned in search of me and left the Fieldses to pursue the Indians. I desired him to hasten to the camp with me and assist in catching as many of the Indian horses as were necessary and to call to the Fieldses if he could make them hear to come back, that we still had a sufficient number of horses. This he did but they were too far to hear him. We reached the camp and began to catch the horses and saddle them and put on the packs. The reason I had not my pouch with me was that I had not time to return about 50 yards to camp after getting my gun before I was obliged to pursue the Indians or suffer them to collect and drive off all the horses.

We had caught and saddled the horses and begun to arrange the packs when the Fieldses returned with four of our horses. We left one of our horses and took four of the best of those of the Indians. While the men were preparing the horses I put four shields and two bows and quivers of arrows, which they had left on the fire, with sundry other articles; they left all their baggage at our mercy. They had but two guns and one of them they left. The others were armed with bows and arrows and eye-dags. The gun we took with us. I also retook the flag but left the medal about the neck of the dead man that they might be informed who we were. We took some of their buffalo meat and set out, ascending the bluffs by the same route we had descended last evening, leaving the balance of nine of their horses which we did not want. The Fieldses told me that three of the Indians whom they pursued swam the river, one of them on my horse, and that two others ascended the hill and escaped from them with a part of their horses. Two I had pursued into the niche, one lay dead near the camp, and the eighth we could not account for but suppose that he ran off early in the contest. Having ascended the hill we took our course through a beautiful level plain a little to the S. of east. My design was to hasten to the entrance of Marias River as quickly as possible in the hope of meeting with the canoes and party at that place, having no doubt but that they would pursue us with a large party; and as there was a band near the Broken Mountains or probably between them and the mouth of that river, we might expect them to receive intelligence from us and arrive at that place nearly as soon as we could.

No time was therefore to be lost and we pushed our horses as hard as they would bear. At eight miles we passed a large branch, 40 yards wide, which I called Battle River. At three p.m. we arrived at Rose River about five miles above where we had passed it as we went out, having traveled by my estimate compared with our former distances and courses about 63 miles. Here we halted an hour and a half, took some refreshment, and suffered our horses to graze. The day proved warm but the late rains had supplied the little reservoirs in the plains with water and had put them in fine order for traveling. Our whole route so far was as level as a bowling green, with but little stone and few prickly pears. After dinner we pursued the bottoms of Rose River, but finding it inconvenient to pass the river so often we again ascended the hills on the S.W. side and took to the open plains. By dark we had traveled about 17 miles further. We now halted to rest ourselves and horses about two hours. We killed a buffalo cow and took a small quantity of the meat.

After refreshing ourselves we again set out by moonlight and traveled leisurely; heavy thunderclouds lowered around us on every quarter but that from which the moon gave us light. We continued to pass immense herds of buffalo all night, as we had done in the latter part of the day. We traveled until two o'clock in the morning, having come by my estimate after dark about 20 miles. We now turned out our horses and laid ourselves down to rest in the plain, very much fatigued, as may be readily conceived. My Indian horse carried me very well, in short much better than my own would have done, and leaves me with but little reason to complain of the robbery.

July 28, 1806, Monday [Lewis]
The morning proved fair. I slept soundly but fortunately awoke as day appeared. I awoke the men and directed the horses to be saddled. I was so sore from my ride yesterday that I could scarcely stand, and the men complained of being in a similar situation; however, I encouraged them by telling them that our own lives as well as those of our friends and fellow travelers depended on our exertions at this moment. They were alert soon. Prepared the horses and we again resumed our march. The men proposed to pass the Missouri at the grog spring where Rose River approaches it so nearly and pass down on the S.W. side. To this I objected as it would delay us almost all day to reach the point by this circuitous route and would give the enemy time to surprise and cut off the party at the point if they had arrived there. I told them that we owed much to the safety of our friends and that we must risk our lives on this occasion, that I should proceed immediately to the point and if the party had not arrived that I would raft the Missouri a small distance above, hide our baggage and march on foot up the river through the timber until I met the canoes or joined them at the falls. I now told them that it was my determination that if we were attacked in the plains on our way to the point that the bridles of the horses should be tied together and we would stand and defend them, or sell our lives as dear as we could.

We had proceeded about 12 miles on an east course when we found ourselves near the Missouri. We heard a report which we took to be that of a gun but were not certain. Still continuing down the N.E. bank of the Missouri about eight miles further, being then within five miles of the grog spring, we heard the report of several rifles very distinctly on the river to our right. We quickly repaired to this joyful sound and on arriving at the bank of the river had the unspeakable satisfaction to see our canoes coming down. We hurried down from the bluff on which we were and joined them, stripped our horses and gave them a final discharge, embarking without loss of time with our baggage.

I now learned that they had brought all things safe, having sustained no loss nor met with any accident of importance. Weiser had cut his leg badly with a knife and was unable in consequence to work. We descended the river opposite to our principal cache [*they had buried material at the juncture of the Marias and the Missouri the previous year*], which we proceeded to open, after reconnoitering the adjacent country. We found that the cache had caved in and most of the articles buried therein were injured. I sustained the loss of two very large bearskins, which I much regret. Most of the fur and baggage belonging to the men was injured. The gunpowder, corn, flour, pork, and salt had sustained but little injury. The parched meal was spoiled, or nearly so. Having no time to air these things, which they much wanted, we dropped down to the point to take in the several articles which had been buried at that place in several small caches. These we found in good order and recovered every article except three traps belonging to Drouillard, which could not be found.

Here as good fortune would have it Sgt. Gass and Willard who brought the horses from the falls joined us at one p.m. I had ordered them to bring down the horses to this place in order to assist them in collecting meat, which I had directed them to kill and dry here for our voyage, presuming that they would have arrived with the pirogue and canoes at this place several days before my return. Having now nothing to detain us, we passed over immediately to the island in the entrance of Marias River to launch the red pirogue, but found her so much decayed that it was impossible with the means we had to repair her and therefore merely took the nails and other ironwork about her which might be of service to us and left her. We now re-embarked on board the white pirogue and five small canoes and descended the river about 15 miles and encamped on the S.W. side near a few cottonwood trees, one of them being of the narrow-leafed species and was the first of that kind which we had remarked on our passage up the river. We encamped late but having little meat I sent out a couple of hunters who soon returned with a sufficient quantity of the flesh of a fat cow. There are immense quantities of buffalo and elk about the junction of the Missouri and Marias Rivers. During the time we halted at the entrance of Marias

River we experienced a very heavy shower of rain and hail, attended with violent thunder and lightning.

The expedition was back together now, with the exception of the party with Clark, who was at this date still on the Yellowstone. The party that Clark had left with the canoes at the Forks of the Missouri had brought the canoes down to the White Bear Islands, having arrived on July 19; they there joined the group of men under Sergeant Gass that Lewis had left at the Great Falls to portage canoes and material they had cached there around them. Gass and Willard had then brought the remaining horses to the mouth of the Marias.

The next day, July 29, Lewis sent out hunters in two small canoes to hunt, both for meat and for skins to use to shelter the men and their equipment from the rain; they had no shelter of any kind. They reached the Missouri Breaks that day, shooting bighorn sheep for specimen skins and skeletons. They continued to move downriver at the rate, Lewis estimated, of seven miles an hour. It was rainy all day, as it had been the day before. The evening of July 31 they took shelter in some abandoned Indian lodges; that and elkskins protected them from the rain. It continued to rain the next day. Lewis finally stopped for a bit to dry out his bighorn skins, which were in danger of rotting. On August 2, finally, it turned fair and Lewis had everything put out to dry.

Speed was of the essence now. Lewis directed that they not stop to cook during the day, but rather cook enough meat the night before to carry them through the next day. "By this means," writes Lewis, "we forward our journey at least 12 or 15 miles per day." The hunters were killing animals not for flesh but for their skins, presumably as articles of trade for the Mandan; the Fields brothers, sent out to hunt, killed 25 deer in two days. The hunters in their separate canoes were so busy that they often missed the party at night; some of them were gone for a week. Ordway and Willard got so wrapped up in hunting on the fourth that it was dark before they were on the river; the current then drew them in "among a passel of sawyers, under one of which the canoe was driven and threw Willard, who was steering, overboard. He caught the sawyer and held by it. Ordway with the canoe drifted down about half a mile among the sawyers under a falling bank, the canoe struck frequently but did not overset. He at length gained the shore and returned by land to learn the fate of Willard, whom he found was yet on the sawyer. It was impossible for him to take the canoe to his relief. Willard at length tied a couple of sticks together which had lodged against the sawyer on which he was and set himself adrift among the sawyers, which he fortunately escaped, and was taken up about a mile below by Ordway with the canoe . . . It was fortunate for Willard that he could swim tolerably well."

It was fortunate for them all that no one but Sergeant Floyd died. Close calls were endemic.

On August 5 they killed a bear that measured nine feet from nose to tail. On Thursday, August 7, they were 83 miles by Lewis's calculation from the Yellowstone and resolved to reach it that day. At four in the afternoon they did, only to find Clark gone. "I found a paper on a pole," Lewis reports, "at the point which merely contained my name in the handwriting of Capt. Clark. We also found the remnant of a note which had been attached to a piece of elk's horn in the camp. From this fragment I learned that game was scarce at the point and mosquitoes troublesome, which were the reasons given for his going on. I also learnt that he intended halting a few miles below, where he intended waiting my arrival."

But they did not find him, so on August 8 Lewis stopped to let the men dry things out again and make themselves some clothes; "the men with me have not had leisure since we left the west side of the Rocky Mountains to dress any skins or make themselves clothes and most of them are therefore extremely bare." They stayed there through the 9th and did not leave until late on the 10th.

August 11, 1806, Monday [Lewis]

We set out very early this morning, it being my wish to arrive at the burnt hills by noon in order to take the latitude of that place, as it is the most northern point of the Missouri. Informed the party of my design and requested that they would exert themselves to reach the place in time, as it would save us the delay of nearly one day. Being as anxious to get forward as I was, they plied their oars faithfully and we proceeded rapidly. I had instructed the small canoes that if they saw any game on the river to halt and kill it and follow on. However we saw but little game until about nine a.m., when we came up with a buffalo swimming the river, which I shot and killed. Leaving the small canoes to dress it and bring on the meat, I proceeded. We had gone but little way before I saw a very large grizzly bear and put to in order to kill it, but it took wind of us and ran off. The small canoes overtook us and informed us that the flesh of the buffalo was unfit for use and that they had therefore left it. Half after 11 a.m. we saw a large herd of elk on the N.E. shore and I directed the men in the small canoes to halt and kill some of them and continued on in the pirogue to the burnt hills. When I arrived here it was about 20 minutes after noon and of course the observation for the sun's meridian altitude was lost.

Just opposite to the burnt hills there happened to be a herd of elk on a thick willow bar and finding that my observation was lost for the present I determined to land and kill some of them. Accordingly we put to and I went out with Cruzatte only. We fired on the elk; I killed one and he wounded another. We reloaded our guns and took different routes through the thick willows in pursuit of the elk. I was in the act of firing on the elk a second time when a ball struck my left thigh about an inch below my hip joint. Missing the bone, it passed through the left thigh and cut the thickness of the bullet across the hinder part of the right thigh. The stroke was very severe. I instantly supposed that Cruzatte had shot me in mistake for an elk, as I was dressed in brown leather and he cannot see very well. Under this impression I called out to him, "Damn you, you have shot me," and looked toward the place from whence the ball had come. Seeing nothing, I called Cruzatte several times as loud as I could but received no answer. I was now persuaded that it was an Indian that had shot me, as the report of the gun did not appear to be more than 40 paces from me and Cruzatte appeared to be out of hearing of me.

In this situation, not knowing how many Indians there might be concealed in the bushes, I thought best to make good my retreat to the pirogue, calling out as I ran for the first hundred paces as loud as I could to Cruzatte to retreat, that there were Indians, hoping to alarm him in time to make his escape also. I still retained the charge in my gun, which I was about to discharge at the moment the ball struck me. When I arrived in sight of the pirogue I called the men to their arms, to which they flew in an instant. I told them that I was wounded but I hoped not mortally, by an Indian, I believed, and directed them to follow me, that I would return and give them battle and relieve Cruzatte if possible, who I feared had fallen into their hands. The men followed me as they were bid and I returned about a hundred paces, when my wounds became so painful and my thigh so stiff that I could scarcely get on. In short I was compelled to halt and ordered the men to proceed and if they found themselves overpowered by numbers to retreat in order, keeping up a fire.

I now got back to the pirogue as well as I could and prepared myself with a pistol, my rifle, and air gun, being determined as a retreat was impracticable to sell my life as dearly as possible. In this state of anxiety and suspense I remained about 20 minutes, when the party returned with Cruzatte and reported that there were no Indians nor the appearance of any. Cruzatte seemed much alarmed and declared if he had shot me it was not his intention, that he had shot an elk in the willows after he left or separated from me. I asked him whether he did not hear me when I called to him so frequently, which he absolutely denied. I do not believe that the fellow did it intentionally, but after finding that he had shot me was anxious to conceal his knowledge of having done so. The ball had lodged in my breeches which I knew to be the ball of the short rifles such as that he had, and there being no person out with me but him and no Indians that we could discover I have no doubt in my own mind of his having shot me.

With the assistance of Sgt. Gass I took off my clothes and dressed my wounds myself as well as I could, introducing tents of patent lint into the ball holes. The wounds bled considerably but I was happy to find that it had touched neither bone nor artery. I sent the men to dress the two elk which Cruzatte and myself had killed, which they did in a few minutes and brought the meat to the river. The small canoes came up shortly after with the flesh of one elk. My wounds being so situated that I could not without infinite pain make an observation [*a solar observation*], I determined to relinquish it and proceeded on. We came within eight miles of our encampment of the 15th of April 1805 and encamped on the N.E. side. As it was painful to me to be removed I slept on board the pirogue. The pain I experienced excited a high fever and I had a very uncomfortable night. At four p.m. we passed an encampment which had been evacuated this morning by Capt. Clark. Here I found a note from Capt. Clark informing me that he had left a letter for me at the entrance of the Yellowstone River, but that Sgt. Pryor, who had passed that place since he left it, had taken the letter, that Sgt. Pryor, having been robbed of all his horses, had descended the Yellowstone River in skin canoes and had overtaken him at this encampment. This, I fear, puts an end to our prospects of obtaining the Sioux chiefs to accompany us, as we have not now leisure to send and engage Mr. Heney on this service, or at least he would not have time to engage them to go as early as it is absolutely necessary we should descend the river.

August 12, 1806, Tuesday [Lewis]
Being anxious to overtake Capt. Clark, who, from the appearance of his camps, could be at no great distance before me, we set out early and proceeded with all possible expedition. At eight a.m. the bowman informed me that

there was a canoe and a camp he believed of white men on the N.E. shore. I directed the pirogue and canoes to come to at this place and found it to be the camp of two hunters from the Illinois by the name of Joseph Dickson and Forest Hancock. These men informed me that Capt. Clark had passed them about noon the day before. They also informed me that they had left the Illinois in the summer of 1804, since which time they had ascended the Missouri hunting and trapping beaver; that they had been robbed by the Indians and the former wounded last winter by the Tetons of the Burnt Woods; that they had hitherto been unsuccessful in their voyage, having as yet caught but little beaver, but were still determined to proceed. I gave them a short description of the Missouri, a list of distances to the most conspicuous streams and remarkable places on the river above, and pointed out to them the places where the beaver most abounded. I also gave them a file and a couple of pounds of powder with some lead. These were articles which they assured me they were in great want of. I remained with these men an hour and a half, when I took leave of them and proceeded. While I halted with these men Colter and Collins, who separated from us on the third of August, rejoined us. They were well, no accident having happened. They informed me that after proceeding the first day and not overtaking us, they had concluded that we were behind and had delayed several days in waiting for us and had thus been unable to join us until the present moment.

My wounds felt very stiff and sore this morning, but gave me no considerable pain. There was much less inflammation than I had reason to apprehend there would be. I had last evening applied a poultice of Peruvian barks [*cinchona, known to be useful against malarial fevers but used for other disorders at the time as well*]. At one p.m. I overtook Capt. Clark and party and had the pleasure of finding them all well. As writing in my present situation is extremely painful to me I shall desist until I recover and leave to my friend Capt. Clark the continuation of our journal.

However I must notice a singular cherry which is found on the Missouri in the bottomlands about the beaver bends and some little distance below the White Earth River. This production is not very abundant even in the small tract of country to which it seems to be confined. The stem is compound, erect, and subdivided or branching without any regular order; it rises to the height of eight or ten feet, seldom putting up more than one stem from the same root, not growing in copse as the choke cherry does. The bark is smooth and of a dark brown color. The leaf is petiolate, oval, acutely pointed at its apex, from one and a quarter to one and a half inches in length and from one half to three-quarters of an inch in width, finely or minutely serrate, pale green and free from pubescence. The fruit is a globular berry about the size of a buckshot of a fine scarlet red. Like the cherries cultivated in the United States, each is supported by a separate cylindric flexible branch peduncle, which issues from the extremities of the boughs. The peduncle of this cherry swells as it approaches the fruit, being largest at the point of insertion. The pulp of this fruit is of an agreeable acid flavor and is now ripe. The style and stigma are permanent. I have never seen it in bloom.

—◦◦◦—

When they left the camp where they were reunited on August 12, the captains were only two days from the Mandan villages. They pulled into the upper, Minitari village on August 14 and fired a salute; the Indians crowded around and were "extremely pleased to see us." They stayed in the area three days, and it was an intense three days. One of the Minitari chiefs had lost a son to the Blackfeet; he cried when he saw Lewis and Clark. The Mandan chief Black Cat's village was half its size. There had been a dispute; the other half of the village had removed to the other side of the river. The Mandan gave them corn, so much that they had to refuse some of it. There were departures. The two white trappers whom they had just met moving upriver had asked John Colter to join them, on favorable terms. He asked to go with them and the captains paid him off and let him go. Colter spent the next four years in the Rockies and the High Plains; he was one of the first mountain men. Charbonneau, too, was here let go, although he wanted to stay with them, offering to interpret for any chiefs who might go downriver with the expedition and on to Washington. Since none would go, however, his services "were no longer of use to the U. States and he was therefore discharged and paid up." Clark did offer to raise little Pomp, his son, as soon as he was weaned and evidently took him into his home when he was six and raised him. Pomp later became a mountain man and a scout.

The captains found Indian affairs no more peaceful this time around than when they first encountered the Mandan in 1804. The Minitari told Clark that the Arikara had stolen some of their horses; they had killed two Arikaras in reprisal. No sooner than Lewis and Clark had left in 1804, indeed, a Minitari war party had gone west into the Rockies and attacked the same Shoshone who had sheltered the expedition in the mountains. In this engagement the Minitari had lost two men. The Sioux, meanwhile, had killed eight Mandan. Clark once again preached peace; at the same time he gave the Minitari the swivel gun, which was of no use to the expedition without the keelboat to mount it on, and showed them how to fire it. It had been naïve of the captains to think they could talk the Indians into not fighting with each other. It remained so.

The Mandan chief known as Big White did finally decide to go with the expedition downriver to meet the president of the United States. None of the others wanted to run the Sioux gauntlet. Nothing had been heard of the Arikara chief who had left for Washington with the keelboat in the spring of 1805 (he had in fact died in Washington). Even if the expedition got past the Sioux going downriver, it was by no means clear that Minitari or Mandan chiefs, sworn enemies of the Sioux, could get back upriver safely, even with the protection Clark promised them. But Big White made the trip, and it is interesting to note that when he returned upriver in 1807 it was the Arikara who kept him from reaching his home.

They left the Mandan villages on the 17th, putting Big White and his wife and son and the interpreter Jusseaume and his family in two canoes that had been connected with poles for maximum stability. The weather continued to be miserable with rain and headwinds slowing their progress, but they made up to 80 miles some days nevertheless. On the night of the 19th of August Jusseaume let Clark use "a piece of a lodge" for shelter: "The squaws pitched or stretched it over some sticks. Under this piece of leather I slept dry; it is the only covering which I have had sufficient to keep off the rain since I left the Columbia." Big White told Clark a Mandan origin story:

He told me his nation first came out of the ground where they had a great village. A grape vine grew down through the earth to their village and they saw light. Some of their people ascended by the grape vine upon the earth and saw buffalo and every kind of animal, also grapes, plums, etc. They gathered some grapes and took them down the vine to the village, and they tasted and found them good, and determined to go up and live upon the earth, and great numbers climbed the vine and got upon earth men, women, and children. At length a large, big-bellied woman in climbing broke the vine and fell and all that were left in the village below have remained there ever since. The Mandans believe when they die that they return to this village.

On the 20th of August they made 81 miles, and the next day they reached the Arikara. A large encampment of Cheyenne were there, too; the Cheyenne were part of the plains trade, which Lewis and Clark never understood, in which the Arikara traded corn and horses with the Sioux and Cheyenne for furs and trade goods acquired from Canadian traders. The Cheyenne proved receptive to Clark and interested in trading with Americans. "Their country was full of beaver," the Cheyenne chiefs told Clark, "and they would then be encouraged to kill beaver, but now they had no use for them as they could get nothing for their skins and did not know well how to catch beaver. If the white people would come amongst them they would become acquainted and the white people would learn them how to take the beaver." This was a better reaction than Clark could have hoped for, given the Cheyenne chief's initial fear of Clark. When Clark had tried to give him a medal, the chief gave it back to him "and informed me that he knew that the white people were all medicine and that he was afraid of the medal or anything that white people gave to them." Clark had to explain to him what the medal signified before he would take it.

Otherwise, however, diplomacy with the Arikara did not turn out well. Big White sat in council with Clark and the Arikara and peace was once more promised, but an undertone of tension ran through the meeting. Big White spoke his piece in an animated and evidently unapologetic fashion, and at one point an Arikara chief named One Arm spoke to Big White "in a loud and threatening tone." The Arikara put the blame for all hostilities on the backs of the conveniently hostile Sioux. Or it was their headstrong young men. The Arikara and the Mandan did not ultimately form an alliance until 1845, by which time both tribes were much reduced in numbers and power. No Arikara chief went with Lewis and Clark to Washington. The death of the chief who had gone down the year before left the Arikara suspicious of Americans for years.

They still had the Teton Sioux to deal with. They made 40 miles on the 23rd of August, 43 miles the next day, then 48, then 60, then 45. On August 28 *they stopped for a day to hunt for animals they wanted specimens of, mule deer and antelope in particular, to take the skins and skeletons, but they could find none. The next day Clark walked up to a high point and gazed about and saw 20,000 buffalo. The day after that they had their encounter with the Teton Sioux, when some 80 or 90 men appeared on the banks of the Missouri, all armed, as they were passing down. Clark landed on a sandbar close enough to shore that he could talk with them. Three Sioux came over. When he found out they were Black Buffalo's men, Clark spoke without any pretense at being diplomatic. "I told those Indians that they had been deaf to our councils and ill treated us as we ascended this river two years past; that they had abused all the whites who had visited them since. I believed them to be bad people and should not suffer them to cross to the side on which the party lay, and directed them to return with their band to their camp; that if any of them came near our camp we should kill them certainly." A Sioux swam over who understood Pawnee; through Jusseaume, Clark told him to tell his people that "we viewed them as bad people and no more traders would be suffered to come to them, and whenever the white people wished to visit the nations above they would come sufficiently strong to whip any villainous party who dare to oppose them." He also let them know that he had given a cannon to the Minitari to defend themselves. The expedition camped on a sandbar that night in a defensive position. "Our encampment of this evening was a very disagreeable one, bleak, exposed to the winds, and the sand wet." But it was safe. They were still on their guard two days later when they ran into a small party of Yankton Sioux on the banks and thought they were Teton. Believing they were about to be attacked, Clark took up defensive positions on shore until they realized their error. That day, September 1, the party came to the same island they had camped on exactly two years before; "at this island," he remarks, "we brought two years together."*

They were starting now to see trees and other species indigenous to the lower Missouri. They saw the first black walnut trees on September 4; two days before they had seen the linden and the slippery elm. On the 3rd they met James Aird, an agent of the trading firm Dickson and Co., with two boats and several other men coming upriver; they were on their way to trade with the Sioux. He brought them the first news of civilization they had had for more than two years. "Our first enquiry," writes Clark, "was after the President of our country and then our friends and the state of the politics of our country and the state of Indian affairs." They found out that Gen. James Wilkinson was governor of the Louisiana Territory; Wilkinson was a frontier general who was secretly working for the Spaniards at the time. They heard about two Indians who had been hung in St. Louis for killing a white man, and that "Mr. Burr and Gen. Hamilton fought a duel; the latter was killed." They spent the night with Aird and the next morning he gave them tobacco and a barrel of flour; they gave him corn in return. That day the party stopped at Floyd's Bluff and visited Sergeant Floyd's grave, which natives had opened. They refilled it. The mosquitoes were driving them to distraction. On September 4 they made 36 miles, but 73 the next day. We rejoin them on September 6, all of them eager for the trip to be over.

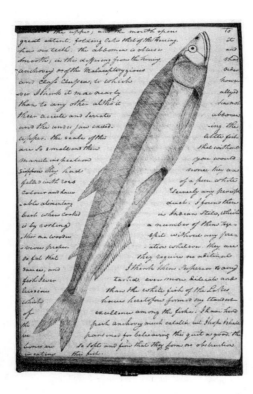

Eulachon (Thaleichthys pacificus) fish drawn by Lewis, *February 24, 1806*

SEPTEMBER 6 TO SEPTEMBER 26, 1806

THE FINAL DAYS

———————————————— ⋙◉◉◉⋘ ————————————————

September 6, 1806, Saturday [Clark]

The mosquitoes excessively troublesome. We set out early at the great cutoff [*they are now in Iowa*], saw a herd of elk. We landed and sent out several hunters to kill some of the elk. They returned without killing any, as the elk were wild and ran off much frightened. I sent the two small canoes on ahead with directions to hunt in two bottoms below, and after a delay of half an hour proceeded on, wind hard ahead. At the lower point seven of Pelican Island a little above the Petite Rivière de Sioux [*Little Sioux River*] we met a trading boat of Mr. Auguste Chouteau of St. Louis bound to the River Jacques to trade with the Yanktons. This boat was in the care of a Mr. Henry Delorn; he had exposed all his loading and sent out five of his hands to hunt. They soon arrived with an elk. We purchased a gallon of whiskey of this man and gave to each man of the party a dram, which is the first spirituous liquor which had been tasted by any of them since the 4th of July 1805. Several of the party exchanged leather for linen shirts and beaver for coarse hats. Those men could inform us nothing more than that all the troops had moved from the Illinois and that Gen. Wilkinson was preparing to leave St. Louis. We advised this trader to treat the Tetons with as much contempt as possible and stated to him where he would be benefited by such treatment and at one p.m. set out. Those men gave us two shots from a swivel they had on the bow of their boat, which we returned in our turn.

Proceeded on about three miles and came up with two of the hunters; they had not killed anything. At five miles we overtook the canoe of the other hunters with Shannon in it floating down. The two Fields being in the woods behind, we came to on a sandbar on the N.E. side and delayed all the after part of the day for the two Fields, sent out three men to hunt in the bottom up the river and observe if they saw any sign of the hunters. The evening proved cloudy and the wind blew hard. Two pelicans were killed today. We came 30 miles only today. The two Fieldses did not join us. I think they are below. The chief and the squaws and children are weary of their journey. Children cry.

September 7, 1806, Sunday [Clark]
As we were doubtful that the two Fields were behind I directed Sgt. Ordway with four men to continue until meridian and if those men did not arrive by that hour to proceed on. If we met with them at any short distance a gun should be fired, which would be a signal for him to proceed on. We had proceeded on about eight miles by water and the distance through not more than one mile when we saw the fire of those two men. I directed a gun be fired as a signal for Sgt. Ordway to proceed on, and took the boys on board. They had killed nothing and informed me they had been somewhat alarmed at our delay, that the distance across from the Little Sioux River was about one and a half miles only, the bottoms thick and grass very high. We proceeded on with a stiff breeze ahead. (*Note,* the evaporation on this portion of the Missouri has been noticed as we ascended this river, and it now appears to be greater than it was at that time. I am obliged to replenish my inkstand every day with fresh ink, at least 9/10 of which must evaporate.)

We proceeded on to a bottom on the S.W. side a little above the Soldier River and came to and sent out all the hunters. They killed three elk which were at no great distance. We sent out the men and had the flesh brought in. Cooked and dined. Sgt. Ordway came up and after taking a sumptuous dinner we all set out at four p.m., wind ahead as usual. At dusk we came to on the lower part of a sandbar on the S.W. side, found the mosquitoes excessively tormenting not withstanding a stiff breeze from the S.E. [*They were camping regularly on sandbars in an attempt to escape the mosquitoes.*] A little after dark the wind increased, the mosquitoes dispersed. Our camp of this night is about two miles below our encampment of the 4th of August

1804 ascending. We came 44 miles today only. [*It had taken them, in other words, more than four months to reach this point in 1804. They would cover the same distance going downriver now in under three weeks.*]

September 8, 1806, Monday [Clark]
Set out very early this morning, passed an old trading house on the S.W. side a few miles above the Council Bluffs. At 11 a.m. we came to at the bluffs and Capt. Lewis and myself walked up on the bluffs and around to examine the country and situation more particularly. The situation appeared to us equally as eligible as when we passed up for an establishment, the hill high and commanding with a high rich bottom of great extent below. We proceeded on very well. All being anxious to get to the River Platte today they plied their oars very well, and we arrived at our old encampment at White Catfish Camp 12 miles above the River Platte, at which place we lay from the 22nd to the 26th of July 1804. Here we encamped, having made 78 miles today. The Missouri at this place does not appear to contain more water than it did 1,000 miles above this. The evaporation must be immense. In the last 1,000 miles this river receives the water of 20 rivers and many creeks. Several of the rivers are large and the size of this river or the quantity of water does not appear to increase any.

September 9, 1806, Tuesday [Clark]
Set out early, at eight a.m. passed the entrance of the great River Platte, which is at this time low, the water nearly clear, the current turbulent as usual. The sandbars which choked up the Missouri and confined the river to a narrow, snaggy channel are wasted away and nothing remains but a few small remains of the bar, which is covered with driftwood. Below the River Platte the current of the Missouri becomes evidently more rapid than above and the snags much more numerous and bad to pass. Late in the evening we arrived at the Bald-Pated Prairie and encamped immediately opposite our encampment of the 16th and 17th of July 1804, having made 73 miles only today. The river bottoms are extensive, rich, and covered with tall large timber, and the hollows of the ravines may be said to be covered with timber such as oak, ash, elm, and some walnut and hickory. Our party appears extremely anxious to get on, and every day appears to produce new anxieties in them to get to their country and friends. My worthy friend Capt. Lewis has entirely recovered, his wounds

are healed up and he can walk and even run nearly as well as ever he could. The parts are yet tender.

The mosquitoes are yet troublesome, though not so much so as they were above the River Platte. The climate is every day perceptibly warmer and air more sultry than I have experienced for a long time. The nights are now so warm that I sleep comfortably under a thin blanket. A few days past two were not more than sufficient.

September 10, 1806, Wednesday [Clark]
We set out very early this morning and proceeded on very well with wind moderately ahead. We met a Mr. Alexander Lafrost and three Frenchmen from St. Louis in a small pirogue on his way to the River Platte to trade with the Pawnee Loup or Wolf Indians. This man was extremely friendly to us, he offered us anything he had. We accepted of a bottle of whiskey only, which we gave to our party. Mr. Lafrost informed us that Gen. Wilkinson and all the troops had descended the Mississippi and Mr. Pike and young Mr. Wilkinson had set out on an expedition up the Arkansas River or in that direction. After a delay of half an hour we proceeded on about three miles and met a large pirogue and seven men from St. Louis bound to the Omahas for the purpose of trade. This pirogue was in charge of a Mr. La Croix. We made some few inquiries of this man and again proceeded on through a very bad part of the river crowded with snags and sawyers and encamped on a sandbar about four miles above the Grand Nemaha. We find the river in this timbered country narrow and with more moving sands and a much greater quantity of sawyers or snags than above. Great caution and much attention is required to steer clear of all those difficulties in this low state of the water. We made 65 miles today. We saw deer, raccoons and turkeys on the shores today. One of the men killed a raccoon, which the Indians very much admired.

September 11, 1806, Thursday [Clark]
A heavy cloud and wind from the N.W. detained us until after sunrise, at which time we set out and proceeded on very well, passed the Nemaha, which was low and did not appear as wide as when we passed up. Wolf River scarcely runs at all. At three p.m. we halted a little above the Nodaway River on the S. side of the Missouri to kill some meat, that which we killed a few days past being all spoiled. Sent out six hunters, they killed and brought in two deer

only. We proceeded on a few miles below the Nodaway Island and encamped on a small island near the N.E. side, having come 40 miles only today, river rapid and in many places crowded with snags. I observe on the shores much deer sign.

The mosquitoes are no longer troublesome on the river. From what cause they are numerous above and not so on this part of the river I cannot account. Wolves were howling in different directions this evening after we had encamped, and the barking of the little prairie wolves resembled those of our common small dogs, so that three quarters of the party believed them to be the dogs of some boat ascending, which was yet below us. The barking of those little wolves I have frequently taken notice of on this as also the other side of the Rocky Mountains, and their bark so much resembles or sounds to me like our common small cur dogs that I have frequently mistaken them for that species of dog.

The paw paws nearly ripe.

September 12, 1806, Friday [Clark]
A thick fog a little before day which blew off at daylight. A heavy dew this morning. We set out at sunrise, the usual hour, and proceeded on very well about seven miles, met two pirogues from St. Louis. One contained the property of Mr. Chouteau bound to the Pawnees on the River Platte, the other going up trapping as high as the Omahas. Here we met one of the Frenchmen who had accompanied us as high as the Mandans. He informed us that Mr. McClellan was a few miles below. The wind blew ahead soon after we passed those pirogues. We saw a man on shore who informed us that he was one of Mr. McClellan's party and that he was a short distance below. We took this man on board and proceeded on and met Mr. McClellan at the St. Michael Prairie. We came to here; we found Mr. Joseph Gravelines, the Arikara interpreter whom we had sent down with an Arikara chief in the spring of 1805, and old Mr. Dorion, the Sioux interpreter. We examined the instructions of those interpreters and found that Gravelines was ordered to the Arikaras with a speech from the President of the United States to that nation and some presents which had been given the Arikara chief who had visited the United States and unfortunately died at the city of Washington. He was instructed to teach the Arikaras agriculture and make every enquiry after Capt. Lewis, myself and the party. Mr. Dorion was instructed to accompany Gravelines and through his influence pass him with his presents by the Teton bands of

Sioux, and to prevail on some of the principal chiefs of those bands, not exceeding six, to visit the seat of the government next spring. He was also instructed to make every inquiry after us. We made some small addition to his instructions by extending the number of chiefs to 10 or 12 or 13 from each band, including the Yanktons. Mr. McClellan received us very politely and gave us all the news and occurrences which had taken place in the Illinois within his knowledge. The evening proving to be wet and cloudy we concluded to continue all night. We dispatched the two canoes ahead to hunt with five hunters in them.

September 13, 1806, Saturday [Clark]
Rose early. Mr. McClellan gave each man a dram and a little after sunrise we set out. The wind hard ahead from the S.E. At eight a.m. we landed at the camp of the five hunters whom we had sent ahead; they had killed nothing. The wind being too high for us to proceed in safety through the immensity of snags which was immediately below, we concluded to lie by and sent on the small canoes a short distance to hunt and kill some meat. We sent out two men in the bottom; they soon returned with one turkey and informed us that the rushes were so high and thick that it was impossible to kill any deer. I felt myself very unwell and directed a little chocolate which Mr. McClellan gave us prepared, of which I drank about a pint and found great relief. At 11 a.m. we proceeded on about one mile and came up with the hunters, who had killed four deer. Here we delayed until five p.m. when the hunters all joined us and we again proceeded on down a few miles and encamped on the N.E. side of the Missouri, having descended 18 miles only today. The day disagreeably warm. One man, George Shannon, left his horn and pouch with his powder, ball, and knife and did not think of it until night. I walked in the bottom in the thick rushes and the growth of timber common to the Illinois, such as cottonwood, sycamore, ash, mulberry, elm of different species, walnut, hickory, hornbeam, paw paw, arrow wood, willow, prickly ash, and grape vines, peas of three species. Birds most common the buzzard, crow, the hoot owl, and hawks.

September 14, 1806, Sunday [Clark]
Set out early and proceeded on very well. This being the part of the Missouri the Kansas nation resort to at this season of the year for the purpose of robbing the pirogues passing up to other nations above, we have every reason

to expect to meet with them, and agreeably to their common custom of examining everything in the pirogues and taking what they want out of them, it is probable they may wish to take those liberties with us, which we are determined not to allow of and for the smallest insult we shall fire on them.

At two p.m., a little below the lower of the old Kansas villages, we met three large boats bound to the Yanktons and Omahas, the property of Mr. La Croix, Mr. Aitken and Mr. Chouteau, all from St. Louis. Those young men received us with great friendship and pressed on us some whiskey for our men, biscuit, pork and onions, and part of their stores. We continued near two hours with those boats, making every inquiry into the state of our friends and country. Those men were much afraid of meeting with the Kansas. We saw 37 deer on the banks and in the river today, five of which we killed. Those dear were meager. We proceeded on to an island near the middle of the river below our encampment of the 1st of July 1804 and encamped, having descended only 53 miles today. Our party received a dram and sang songs until 11 o'clock at night in the greatest harmony.

September 15, 1805, Monday [Clark]
We set out early with a stiff breeze ahead. Saw several deer swimming the river soon after we set out. At 11 a.m. passed the entrance of the Kansas River, which was very low; about a mile below we landed and Capt. Lewis and myself ascended a hill which appeared to have a commanding situation for a fort. The shore is bold and rocky immediately at the foot of the hill. From the top of the hill you have a perfect command of the river. This hill fronts the Kansas and has a view of the Missouri a short distance above that river. We landed one time only to let the men gather paw paws or the custard apple with which this country abounds, and the men are very fond of. We discovered a buck elk on a small island and sent the two Fields and Shannon in pursuit of it. They soon came up with and killed the elk. He was large and in fine order; we had his flesh secured and divided.

As the winds were unfavorable the greater part of the day we only descended 49 miles and encamped a short distance above Hay Cabin Creek. We are not tormented by the mosquitoes in this lower portion of the river as we were above the River Platte and as high up as the Yellowstone and for a few miles up that river, and above its entrance into the Missouri. We passed some of the most charming bottomlands today and the uplands by no means bad, all well timbered. The weather disagreeably warm and if it was not for the constant winds which blow from the S. and S.E. we should be almost suffocated. Coming out of a northern country, open and cool, between the latitude of 46° and 49° north, in which we had been for nearly two years, rapidly descending into a woody country in a warmer climate between the latitudes 38° and 39° north, is probably the cause of our experiencing the heat much more sensibly than those who have continued within the parallel of latitude.

September 16, 1806, Tuesday [Clark]
We set out early this morning and proceeded on tolerably well. The day proved excessively warm and disagreeable, so much so that the men rowed but little. At ten a.m. we met a large trading pirogue bound for the Pawnees. We continued but a short time with them. At 11 a.m. we met young Mr. Robidoux with a large boat of six oars and two canoes. The license of this young man was to trade with the Pawnees, Omahas, and Otoes, rather an extraordinary license for so young a man and without the seal of the territory annexed. As Gen. Wilkinson's signature was not to this instrument we were somewhat doubtful of it. Mr. Brown's signature we were not acquainted with without the Territorial Seal. We made some inquiries of this young man and cautioned him against pursuing the steps of his brother in attempting to degrade the American character in the eyes of the Indians. We proceeded on to an island a little above our encampment of the 16th and 17th of June 1804, having come 52 miles only today.

September 17, 1806, Wednesday [Clark]
We set out as usual early, passed the island of the little Osage village, which is considered by the navigator of this river to be the worst place in it. At this place the water of the Missouri is confined between an island and the S.E. main shore and passes through a narrow channel for more than two miles which is crowded with snags in many places quite across, obliging the navigator to pick his passage between those snags as he can, in many places the current passing with great velocity against the banks, which causes them to fall in. At 11 a.m. we met a Captain McClellan, late a Capt. of Artillery of the United States Army, ascending in a large boat. This gentleman, an acquaintance of my friend Capt. Lewis, was somewhat astonished to see us return and appeared rejoiced to meet us. We found him a man of information and from whom we received a partial account of the

political state of our country. We were making enquiries and exchanging answers until near midnight. This gentleman informed us that we had been long since given out by the people of United States generally and almost forgotten. The President of the U. States had yet hopes of us. We received some civilities of Capt. McClellan; he gave us some biscuit, chocolate, sugar and whiskey, for which our party were in want and for which we made a return of a barrel of corn and much obliged to him.

Capt. McClellan informed us that he was on rather a speculative expedition to the confines of New Spain, with the view to introduce a trade with those people. His plan is to proceed up this river to the entrance of the River Platte, there to form an establishment from which to trade partially with the Pawnees and Otoes, and to form an acquaintance with the Pawnees and prevail on some of their principal chiefs to accompany him to Santa Fe, where he will appear in a style calculated to attract the Spanish government in that quarter; and through the influence of a handsome present he expects to be permitted to exchange his merchandise for silver and gold, of which those people abound. He has a kind of introductory speech from Gov. Wilkinson to the Pawnees and Otoes and a quantity of presents of his own, which he purposes distributing to the Pawnees and Eliatans, with a view to gain their protection in the execution of his plans. If the Spanish government favors his plans, he purposes taking his merchandise on mules and horses, which can easily be procured of the Pawnees, to some point convenient to the Spanish settlements within the Louisiana Territory, to which place the inhabitants of New Mexico may meet him for the purpose of trade. Capt. McClellan's plan I think a very good one if strictly pursued.

We sent five hunters ahead with directions to halt below Grand River and hunt until we arrived, which would be in the morning. This day proved warm. We descended only 30 miles today and encamped four miles above Grand River on the S.E. side.

September 18, 1806, Thursday [Clark]
We rose early. Capt. McClellan wrote a letter and we took our leave and proceeded on. Passed the Grand River at seven a.m. A short distance below we came up with our hunters; they had killed nothing. At ten o'clock we came to and gathered paw paws to eat. We have nothing but a few biscuits to eat and are partly compelled to eat paw paws, which we find in great quantities on the shores. The weather we found excessively hot as usual. The lands fine,

particularly the bottoms. A charming oak bottom on the S.E. side of the Missouri above the two Chariton rivers. We find the current of this part of the Missouri much more gentle than it was as we ascended. The water is now low and where it is much confined it is rapid. We saw very little appearance of deer. Saw one bear at a distance and three turkeys only today. Our party entirely out of provisions, subsisting on paw paws. We divide the biscuit, which amounted to nearly one biscuit per man; this in addition to the paw paws is to last us down to the settlements, which is 150 miles. The party appears perfectly contented and tell us that they can live very well on the paw paws. We made 52 miles today only. One of our party, J. Potts, complains very much of one of his eyes, which is burnt by the sun from exposing his face without a cover from the sun. Shannon also complains of his face and eyes. Encamped on an island nearly opposite to the entrance of Lamine River.

September 19, 1806, Friday [Clark]
Set out this morning a little after day and proceeded on very well. The men ply their oars and we descended with great velocity, only came to once for the purpose of gathering paw paws. Our anxiety as also the wish of the party to proceed on as expeditiously as possible to the Illinois induce us to continue on without halting to hunt. We calculate on arriving at the first settlements on tomorrow evening which is 140 miles, and the object of our party is to divide the distance into two days, this day to the Osage River and tomorrow to the Chariton, a small French village [*the name of the village was actually La Charette*]. We arrived at the entrance of Osage River at dark and encamped on the spot we had encamped on the 1st and 2nd of June 1804, having come 72 miles. A very singular disorder is taking place amongst our party, that of the sore eyes. Three of the party have their eyes inflamed and swollen in such a manner as to render them extremely painful, particularly when exposed to the light. The eyeball is much inflamed and the lid appears burnt with the sun. The cause of this complaint of the eye I can't account for. From its sudden appearance I am willing to believe it may be owing to the reflection of the sun on the water.

September 20, 1806, Saturday [Clark]
As three of the party were unable to row from the state of their eyes, we found it necessary to leave one of our craft and divide the men into the other canoes. We left the two canoes lashed together which I had made high up the River

Yellowstone; those canoes we set adrift and a little after daylight we set out and proceeded on very well. The Osage River very low and discharges but a small quantity of water at this time for so large a river. At meridian we passed the entrance of the Gasconade River, below which we met a pirogue with five Frenchmen bound to the Osage grand village. The party being extremely anxious to get down ply their oars very well. We saw some cows on the bank, which was a joyful sight to the party and caused a shout to be raised for joy. At ... p.m. we came in sight of the little French village called Chariton [*La Charette*]. The men raised a shout and sprung upon their oars and we soon landed opposite to the village. Our party requested to be permitted to fire off their guns, which was allowed, and they discharged three rounds with a hearty cheer, which was returned from five trading boats which lay opposite the village.

We landed and were very politely received by two young Scotchmen from Canada, one in the employ of Mr. Aird, a Mr. [*blank*], and the other Mr. Reed, two other boats the property of Mr. Lacombe and Mr. [*blank*]; all of those boats were bound to the Osage and Otoes. Those two young Scotch gentlemen furnished us with beef, flour and some pork for our men, and gave us a very agreeable supper. As it was like to rain we accepted of a bed in one of their tents. We purchased of a citizen two gallons of whiskey for our party, for which we were obliged to give eight dollars in cash, an imposition on the part of the citizen. Every person both French and American seems to express great pleasure at our return and acknowledged themselves much astonished in seeing us return. They informed us that we were supposed to have been lost long since, and were entirely given out by every person.

Those boats are from Canada in the bateau form and wide in proportion to their length. Their length about 30 feet and the width eight feet and pointed bow and stern, flat bottom and rowing six oars only, the Schenectady form. Those bottoms are prepared for the navigation of this river; I believe them to be the best calculated for the navigation of this river of any which I have seen. They are wide and flat, not subject to the dangers of the rolling sands, which larger boats are on this river. The American inhabitants express great disgust for the government of this territory. From what I can learn it arises from a disappointment of getting all the Spanish grants confirmed. Came 68 miles today.

It took some six years to sort out the titles that had been granted, in many cases without adequate documentation and with no formal surveys, before the United States took over the Louisiana Territory. Thwaites points out that the commission named to settle the matter met for the first time the very day Clark wrote this entry. The whole subject was controversial. Moulton points out that both Lewis and Clark would subsequently have to deal with it as territorial officials.

September 21, 1806, Sunday [Clark]
Rose early this morning, collected our men. Several of them had accepted of the invitation of the citizens and visited their families. At half after seven a.m. we set out. Passed 12 canoes of Kickapoos ascending on a hunting expedition. Saw several persons, also stock of different kinds, on the bank, which revived the party very much. At three p.m. we met two large boats ascending. At four p.m. we arrived in sight of St. Charles. The party rejoiced at the sight of this hospitable village, plied their oars with great dexterity, and we soon arrived opposite the town. This day being Sunday we observed a number of gentlemen and ladies walking on the bank. We saluted the village by three rounds from our blunderbusses and the small arms of the party and landed near the lower part of the town. We were met by great numbers of inhabitants; we found them excessively polite. We received invitations from several of those gentlemen, a Mr. Proulx, Tabeau, Duquette, Tice, Dejonah, and Querie and several who were pressing on us to go to their houses. We could only visit Mr. Proulx and Mr. Duquette in the course of the evening. Mr. Querie undertook to supply our party with provisions. The inhabitants of this village appear much delighted at our return and seem to vie with each other in their politeness to us all. We came only 48 miles today. The banks of the river thinly settled.

September 22, 1806, Monday [Clark]
This morning being very wet and the rain still continuing hard, and our party being all sheltered in the houses of those hospitable people, we did not think proper to proceed on until after the rain was over, and continued at the house of Mr. Proulx. I took this opportunity of writing to my friends in Kentucky. At ten a.m. it ceased raining and we collected our party and set out and proceeded on down to the cantonment at Coldwater Creek about three miles up the Missouri on its southern banks. At this place we found Col. Hunt and a Lt. Peters and one company of artillerists. We were kindly received by the gentlemen of this place. Mrs. Wilkinson, the lady of the Gov. and Gen., we were sorry to find in delicate health.

We were honored with a salute of gun and a hearty welcome. At this place there is a public store kept in which I am informed the U.S. have $60,000 worth of Indian goods.

September 23, 1806, Tuesday [Clark]
We rose early, took the chief to the public store and furnished him with some clothes. Took an early breakfast with Col. Hunt and set out, descended to the Mississippi and down that river to St. Louis, at which place we arrived about 12 o'clock. We suffered the party to fire off their pieces as a salute to the town. We were met by all the village and received a hearty welcome from its inhabitants. Here I found my old acquaintance Maj. W. Christy, who had settled in this town in a public line as a tavern keeper. He furnished us with storerooms for our baggage and we accepted of the invitation of Mr. Pierre Chouteau and took a room in his house. We paid a friendly visit to Mr. August Chouteau and some of our old friends this evening. As the post had departed from St. Louis, Capt. Lewis wrote a note to Mr. Hay in Cahokia to detain the post at that place until 12 tomorrow, which was rather later than his usual time of leaving it.

September 24, 1806, Wednesday [Clark]
I slept but little last night. However we rose early and commenced writing our letters. Capt. Lewis wrote one to the President and I wrote Gov. Harrison and my friends in Kentucky and sent off George Drouillard with those letters to Cahokia and delivered them to Mr. Hay. We dined with Mr. Chouteau today, and after dinner went to a store and purchased some clothes, which we gave to a tailor and directed to be made. Capt. Lewis in opening his trunk found all his papers wet, and some seeds spoiled.

September 25, 1806, Thursday [Clark]
Had all of our skins sunned and stored away in a storeroom of Mr. Caddy Chouteau. Paid some visits of form to the gentlemen of St. Louis. In the evening a dinner and ball.

September 26, 1806, Friday [Clark]
A fine morning. We commenced writing.

APPENDIX

LIST OF SUPPLIES

ARTICLES WANTED BY CAPT. LEWIS.

MATHEMATICAL INSTRUMENTS

1 Hadley's Quadrant

1 Mariner's Compas & 2 pole chain

1 Sett of plotting instruments

3 Thermometers

1 Cheap portable Microscope

1 Pocket Compass

1 brass Scale one foot in length

6 Magnetic needles in small straight silver or brass cases opening on the side with hinges.

1 Instrument for measuring made of tape with feet & inches mark'd on it

2 Hydrometers

1 Theodolite

1 Sett of planespheres

2 Artificial Horizons

1 Patent log

6 papers of Ink powder

4 Metal Pens brass or silver

1 Set of Small Slates & pencils

2 Creyons

Sealing wax one bundle
1 Miller's edition of Lineus in 2 Vol:
Books
Maps
Charts
Blank Vocabularies
Writing paper
1 Pair large brass money scales with two setts of weights

ARMS & ACCOUTREMENTS
15 Rifles
15 Powder Horns & pouches complete
15 Pairs of Bullet Moulds
15 d°. Of Wipers or Gun worms
15 Ball Screws
24 Pipe Tomahawks
24 large knives
    Extra parts of Locks & tools for repairing arms
15 Gun Slings
500 best Flints

AMMUNITION
200 lbs. Best rifle powder
400 lbs. Lead

CLOTHING
15 3 pt. Blankets
15 Match Coats with Hoods & belts
15 Woolen Overalls
15 Rifle Frocks of waterproof Cloth if possible
30 Pairs of Socks or half Stockings
20 Fatigue Frocks or hunting shirts
30 Shirts of Strong linnen
30 yds. Common flannel.

CAMP EQUIPAGE
6 Copper kettles (1 of 5 Gallons, 1 of 3, 2 of 2, & 2 of 1)

35 falling Axes.

4 Drawing Knives, short & strong

2 Augers of the patent kind

1 Small permanent Vice

1 Hand Vice

36 Gimblets assorted

24 Files d°.

12 Chisels d°.

10 Nails d°.

2 Steel plate hand saws

2 Vials of Phosforus

1 d°. Of Phosforus made of allum & sugar

4 Groce fishing Hooks assorted

12 Bunches of Drum Line

2 Foot Adzes

12 Bunches of Small cord

2 Pick Axes

3 Coils of rope

2 Spades

12 Bunches Small fishing line assorted

1 lb. Turkey or Oil Stone

1 Iron Mill for Grinding Corn

20 yds. Oil linnen for wrapping & securing Articles

10 yds d°. d°. Of thicker quality for covering and lining boxes. &c

40 yds D°. D°. To form two half faced Tents or Shelters

4 Tin blowing Trumpets

2 hand or spiral spring Steelyards

20 yds Strong Oznaburgs

24 Iron Spoons

24 Pint Tin Cups (without handles)

30 Steels for striking or making fire

100 Flints for d°. d°. d°.

2 Frows

6 Saddlers large Needles

6 D°. Large Awls

Muscatoe Curtains

2 patent chamber lamps & wicks

15 Oil Cloth Bags for securing provision
1 Sea Grass Hammock

Provisions and Means of Subsistence
150 lbs. Portable Soup.
3 bushels of Allum or Rock Salt
   Spicies assorted
6 Kegs of 5 Gallons each making 30 Gallons of rectified spirits such as is used
   for the Indian trade
6 Kegs bound with iron Hoops

Indian Presents
5 lbs. White Wampum
5 lbs. White Glass Beads mostly small
20 lbs. Red D°. D°. Assorted
5 lbs. Yellow or Orange D°. D°. Assorted
30 Calico Shirts
12 Pieces of East India muslin Hanckerchiefs striped or check'd with
   brilliant Colours.
12 Red Silk Hanckerchiefs
144 Small cheap looking Glasses
100 Burning Glasses
4 Vials of Phosforus
288 Steels for striking fire
144 Small cheap Scizors
20 Pair large D°.
12 Groces Needles Assorted N°. 1 to 8 Common points
12 Groces D°. Assorted with points for sewing leather
288 Common brass thimbles—part W. office
10 lbs. Sewing Thread assorted
24 Hanks Sewing Silk
8 lbs. Red Lead
2 lbs. Vermillion—at War Office
288 Knives Small such as are generally used for the Indian trade, with fix'd
   blades & handles inlaid with brass
36 Large knives
36 Pipe Tomahawks—at H. Ferry

12 lbs. Brass wire Assorted

12 lbs. Iron d°. d°. generally large

6 Belts of narrow Ribbons colours assorted

50 lbs. Spun Tobacco.

20 Small falling axes to be obtained in Tennessee

40 fish Giggs such as the Indians use with a single barbed point—
     at Harper's ferry

3 Groce fishing Hooks assorted

3 Groce Mockerson awls assorted

50 lbs. Powder secured in a Keg covered with oil Cloth

24 Belts of Worsted feiret or Gartering Colours brilliant and Assorted

15 Sheets of Copper Cut into strips of an inch in width & a foot long

20 Sheets of Tin

12 lbs. Strips of Sheet iron 1 In. wide 1 foot long

1 Pc. Red Cloth second quality

1 Nest of 8 or 9 small copper kettles

100 Block-tin rings cheap kind ornamented with Colour'd Glass or
       Mock-Stone

2 Groces of brass Curtain Rings & sufficently large for the Finger

1 Groce Cast Iron Combs

18 Cheap brass Combs

24 Blankets.

12 Arm Bands Silver at War Office

12 Wrist d°. d°. D°.

36 Ear Trinkets D°. Part d°.

6 Groces Drops of D°. Part D°.

4 doz Rings for Fingers of d°.

4 Groces Broaches of d°.

12 Small Medals d°.

MEANS OF TRANSPORTATION

1 Keeled Boat light strong at least 60 feet in length her burthen equal
    to 8 Tons

1 Iron frame of Canoe 40 feet long

1 Large Wooden Canoe

12 Spikes for Setting-Poles

4 Boat Hooks & points Complete

2 Chains & Pad-Locks for confining the Boat & Canoes &c.

MEDICINE

15 lbs. Best powder's Bark

10 lbs. Epsom or Glauber Salts

4 oz. Calomel

12 oz. Opium

1/2 oz. Tarter emetic

8 oz. Borax

4 oz. Powder'd Ipecacuana

8 oz. Powder Jalap

8 oz. Powdered Rhubarb

6 Best lancets

2 oz. White Vitriol

4 oz. Lacteaum Saturni

4 Pewter Penis syringes

1 Flour of Sulphur

3 Clyster pipes

4 oz. Turlingtons Balsam

2 lbs. Yellow Bascilicum

2 Sticks of Symple Diachylon

1 lb. Blistering Ointments

2 lbs. Nitre

2 lbs. Coperas

MATERIALS FOR MAKING UP THE VARIOUS ARTICLES INTO PORTABLE PACKS

30 Sheep skins taken off the Animal as perfectly whole as possible, without being split on the belly as usual and dress'd only with lime to free them from the wool; or otherwise about the same quantity of Oil Cloth bags well painted

Raw hide for pack strings

Dress'd letter for Hoppus-Straps

Other packing

D°.= ditto
&c. = etcetera
Oznaburgs = strong cloth
Worsted feiret [ferret] = woven wool tape, used for embellishment and trade
Hoppus = might possibly refer to an Indian term for knapsack

INDEX

---

hunting 150, 151
lodges 149
name 129
raiding parties 135, 242
refugees 392
relations with Ahwahharway
146
relations with Arikara 130,
399, 435–436
relations with Assiniboine
135
relations with Blackfeet 435
relations with Lewis's Indian
guides 404
relations with Mandan 130,
140–141, 146
relations with Nez Perce 139
relations with Shoshone 130,
271, 436
relations with Sioux 126–127,
140, 436
sub-tribes 146
villages 129
war routes 405
weapons 436, 438
Minitaris of Fort de Prairie
and Corps 420–421
Indian guides' desire for
peace with 394
Lewis's opinion of 412–413
relations with Ootslashshoot
393
relations with Shoshone 279
war parties 273, 406
Miry Creek, N. Dak. 149
Mississippi River and Valley, U.S.
maps 52, 100
source 30
Missouri Breaks, Mont. 194–198,
428
Missouri Indians 68–69, 76, 79, 82,
87
Missouri plover 174
Missouri River and Valley, U.S.
Big Bend 98
birds 446
bottoms 249–250
confluence with Marias River,
Mont. 426, 427
confluence with Mississippi
River 52
confluence with Yellowstone
River 167–168, 169–170
course changes 81, 83,
170–171

current 150, 194, 450
depth 235
description 157, 247
freezing 142
navigability 150, 261, 448
sketch **144**
source 21, 267–268
Three Forks, Mont. 394
vegetation 168, 446
volume 443
water level 58, 65
width 63, 83, 98, 110, 114,
115, 169
Moccasin flowers 393
Monbrun Tavern (cave), Mo. 62
Monongahela River, Pa.-Va. 46
Montgomery, Samuel 45
Moreau Creek, Mo. 63
Moreau River, S. Dak. 114
Mosquitoes
avoidance efforts 442
Great Falls portage 238
Iowa 81, 82, 441
Lewis's trip on Marias 404,
408, 410–411
Missouri River 398, 445
Montana 234
near Boyers Creek, Mo. 78, 79
Nebraska 83, 84
North Dakota 149–150
precautions against 72, 246
and weather conditions 399
White Catfish Camp, Iowa 75
Yellowstone River trip 396,
397–398
Moulton, Gary E.
clarification of place-names
300, 322
Clark's Fourth of July entry
72–73
Clark's mileage 283
Cruzatte's encounter with
grizzly 124
as editor of journals 18, 24–25
on grizzly bear 172
Lewis's entry on Missouri
River sand 73
Lewis's reports for Jefferson
142–143
Louisiana Territory land
grants 452
species identification 111
Teton Sioux offer of women
105
weather diary 227

Mounds 75, 76
Mountain lions 250
Mountain sheep 389, 394
Mouse River, N. Dak. 149, 159
Mulberry trees 77
Mule deer 96, 165, 191, 389, 438
Multnomah (Willamette) River,
Oreg. 357, 364
Muskingum River, Ohio 45
Muskrats 258
Mussels 85, 225
Musselshell Rapid, Columbia River
368

N
New Mexico 449
New Timbered River, Wash. 333
Newman, John 13, 119, 120, 134
Nez Perce Indians
alternate names for 357
clothing 310
Columbian Plateau 320–321
compared to Flatheads 310
and Corps 17, 315–316, 380,
381, 385
diet 310–311, 317
encampment 311–312
geographic knowledge 276,
277–278
horses 315–316, 358, 379,
380, 381, 383
illness 381, 382
Pallote pellows 405
physical description 310, 383
relations with Minitari 139
relations with Shoshone 321
sweat lodges 316
trails 293
Nightingale Creek, Mo. 63
Nightingales 63, 64
No Timber Creek, S. Dak. 109
Nodaway Island 445
Nodaway River, Iowa-Mo. 76,
444–445
North Fork, Clearwater River,
Idaho 315, 388
North West Company 127, 133,
138, 177, 271
Northern lights 135
Northwest Coast Indians
burial customs 334–335, 355
canoes 344–345, 355
clothing 338, 347
and Corps 326–329, 342–343,
347–348

ILLUSTRATIONS CREDITS

Cover: Lewis and Clark Expedition (oil on canvas), Burnham, Thomas Mickell (1818–1866)/David David Gallery, Philadelphia, PA, USA/Bridgeman Images.

Pages 34, 52: William Clark Field Notes. Yale Collection of Western Americana, Beinecke Rare Book and Manuscript Library.

Pages 74, 100, 298, 318, 360, 386, 440: American Philosophical Society.

Page 144: Lewis and Clark Expedition Maps and Receipt. Yale Collection of Western Americana, Beinecke Rare Book and Manuscript Library.

Pages 200, 244, 402: From *A Journal of the Voyages and Travels of a Corps of Discovery, 1810,* Patrick Gass. Beinecke Rare Book and Manuscript Library, Yale University.

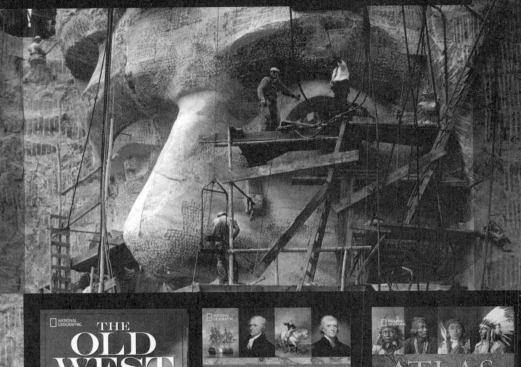
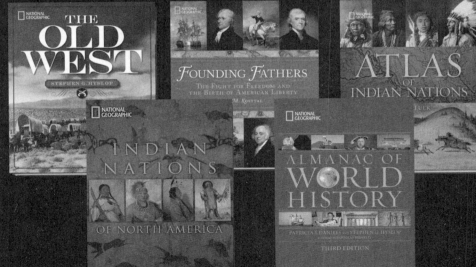